Suicide V

Suicide Warfare

Culture, the Military, and the Individual as a Weapon

ROSEMARIE SKAINE

Praeger Security International

 PRAEGER

AN IMPRINT OF ABC-CLIO, LLC
Santa Barbara, California • Denver, Colorado • Oxford, England

Library of Congress Cataloging-in-Publication Data

Skaine, Rosemarie.
    Suicide warfare : culture, the military, and the individual as a weapon / Rosemarie Skaine.
        p. cm.
    Includes bibliographical references and index.
    ISBN 978-0-313-39864-3 (hbk. : alk. paper) — ISBN 978-0-313-39865-0 (ebook)   1. Suicide—Political aspects.   2. Suicide bombings.   3. Kamikaze airplanes.   I. Title.
    HV6545.S477   2013
    355.4′22—dc23   2012035383

ISBN: 978-0-313-39864-3
EISBN: 978-0-313-39865-0

17 16 15 14 13   1 2 3 4 5

This book is also available on the World Wide Web as an eBook.
Visit www.abc-clio.com for details.

Praeger
An Imprint of ABC-CLIO, LLC

ABC-CLIO, LLC
130 Cremona Drive, P.O. Box 1911
Santa Barbara, California 93116-1911

This book is printed on acid-free paper ∞

Manufactured in the United States of America

Contents

Tables and Maps

MAPS

Preface

On May 1, 2011, American Special Forces Navy SEALs raided Osama bin Laden's compound in Abbottabad, Pakistan, in the dead of night. They found him and killed him. Nearly a decade after the 9/11 suicide attacks on the United States had claimed over 3,000 lives, the United States had achieved its most significant response to al Qaeda's 9/11 attack.[1]

Suicide attacks in modern warfare have become more frequent and significant. In an increasing number of conflicts, suicide is or has been part of the strategy of one of the combatants in the conflict. Suicide warfare occurs in conflicts within a single country, in regional conflicts, and in conflicts that span across the globe. The damage caused by suicide attacks is sobering. When I conducted a global search on the *Chicago Project on Security and Terrorism (CPOST)*, from 1981 to 2011, I found 2,236 suicide attacks that caused 29,472 deaths and wounded 72,255. The deaths matched the population of the city of LaGrange, Georgia, 29,588, and of Winsford, England, 30,007.[2] The tragedy is that the casualty numbers are much higher today.

This book examines suicide in war from the perspective of culture, the military, and the individual as a weapon. Understanding these elements and how they interrelate within a conflict explains why some groups embrace suicide warfare and others refuse to.

Suicide happens in every society, in every culture. Each society comes to terms with suicide in its own way. Some societies reject suicide in all circumstances. Some reject it in most situations, but justify it in others. When suicide is justified, it is frequently associated with sacrificing for the society's greater good.

In the United States, suicide is unacceptable in nearly all cases. Some accept assisted suicide in cases of the terminally ill, but the majority does not. The U.S. military does not use suicide attackers, but does recognize that sending soldiers on dangerous missions may result in their giving their lives sacrificially and honor them for doing so. The group that sent the young men to pilot the planes that carried out the attacks on the World Trade Center in New York City and the Pentagon outside Washington, D.C., and that crashed in Pennsylvania on September 11, 2001, had a different view: they glorified sacrifice through suicide.

This book has two parts and a concluding chapter. Part I presents the theoretical analysis of suicide warfare. Part II consists of case studies of conflicts in which suicide warfare was a part. Chapter 11 presents my conclusions about suicide in warfare.

PART I: CHAPTERS 1–5

Chapter 1, "Defining Suicide Warfare," addresses suicide warfare as understood in the context of the interaction of society, the military, and the individual in which it occurs. The participants are presented in the context of the power of the society in which they live, of the group of which they are a member, and of the society as part of the larger global community. Durkheim's theory and conflict theory offer a theoretical base for suicide warfare. Durkheim's theory of collective consciousness enables us to see that "each social group really has a collective inclination for the act, quite its own, and the source of all individual inclination, rather than the result."[3] Modern conflict theory enables us to see the common characteristics of the core of how groups struggle for power as they are constrained by resources.[4] Through the examination of the myriad of definitions of terrorism and related components, I found it amazing that no agreement exists on the definition of these acts when in reality no one disputes what they are. The critical connection between suicide and society significantly underscores the need to understand belief systems of cultures and groups that have employed suicide as a weapon and cultures that must respond to its use. Identifying sacred values in different cultures and understanding how they compete for people's affection are at the center of suicide warfare.

Chapter 2, "Suicide Warfare in Modern Conflicts," examines suicide as a defense and as an offense. Missions and attacks are distinguished as are methods such as assassinations and targeted killings. Other types of terrorism bear a relationship to suicide attacking, including bioterrorism with a suicide attacker employing a biological weapons attack. Court testimony documents suicide bombs as weapons of mass destruction. Suicide attacks that succeed and those attacks that fail are examined. The importance of the realization of the relationship of group goals as well as the individual purpose and societal context helps ensure attack success. Most importantly, the relationship demonstrates that the acts of suicide bombers are not random or mindless, but a tactic of war that reflects the goals of the organization. The Department of Defense concludes that the objectives of suicide bombing and the emerging profile of the suicide bomber are that there is no one profile. An insight into the scope of these attacks is presented.

Steps in the operational cycle for suicide bombing attacks are examined. The process has many variations and includes phases that begin with the identification and recruitment of bombers; proceed with their indoctrination, training, target selection, purchase of needed parts, making of devices, final preparation, and movement to the target; and end with the detonation of the device, escape, and exploitation. The chapter concludes with an examination of the insurgencies in Afghanistan and Iraq and their relationship to state military presence in these countries.

Chapter 3, "Suicide Warfare and Policies of War," traces U.S. foreign policy and gives special attention to U.S. policies in 2012. International law is discussed including prisoners of war, torture law, detention, and prosecution. Suicide and society are examined in terms of the justification for using suicide warfare. This examination requires understanding both Western and non-Western belief systems. Part of this understanding is based in the just war theory in Western societies and in Sharia law in Muslim societies. Traditional rules and principles of warfare center on traditional ethical principles for war and address the decision to go to war (*jus ad bellum*) and the conduct of the war (*jus in bello*). An analysis of the differences in traditional and irregular warfare is presented. A noted scholar reports that the literature is basically silent on nonviolent alternatives to war.

Chapter 4, "Strategies of Suicide Warfare," discusses strategies specifically related to suicide warfare. Demonstrating surprise and terror as a key tactic, strategies of various groups are examined, such as the global jihad, the Iraq and Afghanistan insurgencies, and the Taliban. Organizations that employ women as suicide attackers are explored. Other explorations include aspects of counterterrorism, financing terror, and the metamorphic traditional rules of war to asymmetric warfare and modular defense.

Chapter 5, "Effects of Suicide Warfare," analyzes what was accomplished in instances where suicide attack was used. The 9/11 attacks are examples of effecting immense change and provoked the United States into two wars, Afghanistan and Iraq. Government expanded through the creation of the Department of Homeland Security. Failed suicide attacks also accomplish goals. Timely media attention is part of the attack's effectiveness. The issue of prisoners of war is renewed through the treatment of them at Abu Ghraib and Guantanamo prisons. The effects of suicide warfare in Muslim countries are examined. Effects common to all people conclude the chapter.

PART II: CHAPTERS 6–10

Chapter 6, "Japan's Kamikaze Pilots," examines the first extensive use of suicide as a weapon in World War II when Japan employed kamikaze pilots against the U.S. Navy. The kamikazes first appeared during the Battle of Leyte Gulf on October 25, 1944. They had no choice in mission; they died whether or not they supported an emperor-centered ideology. The kamikazes were secular but state directed, yet among the pilots, some were devout Christians and on their final flight carried the Bible or sang hymns on the last night before flight. The Japanese aestheticized its military actions through choosing the cherry blossom as the central symbol of the Japanese soul. In spite of the courageous spirit of the Japanese, they could not defeat U.S. forces.

Chapter 7, "Hezbollah and Palestinian Conflicts with Israel," addresses the long history of conflict between the Palestinians and Israel and the more recent conflict between Hezbollah and Israel. Hezbollah was formed during the civil war in Lebanon, 1975–1990, that involved Israel. One weapon used was the suicide attacker. Hezbollah's suicide campaign began in 1983. Well-known attacks include the American Embassy in Beirut, 1983; the U.S. Marine Corp Barracks in Beirut, Lebanon, 1983; and Jewish targets in Argentina, 1992, 1994. In 2000, Israeli defense withdrew from Lebanon. Israel invaded Lebanon again in 2006 and was forced to withdraw by Hezbollah.

In the Palestinian–Israeli conflict, Hamas, al-Aqsa Martyrs' Brigades and Palestinian Islamic Jihad used suicide attackers, particularly in the second intifada, 2000. The Palestinians did not use suicide attacks in the first intifada.

Chapter 8, "Sri Lanka and the Tamil Tigers," details the Tamil Tigers' (Liberation Tigers of Tamil Eelam's) struggle for an independent homeland within Sri Lanka. The Tigers began using suicide warfare in 1987. They were successful in assassinating two heads of state: a prime minister in 1991 and a president in 1993. Since its first suicide attack, they conducted the longest running campaign. They invented the suicide belt and involved women more in suicide attacks.

Chapter 9, "Chechen Separatists," highlights the most well-known incident when the separatists launched an attack in the Moscow theater center or Dubrovka House of Culture seizure in 2002. They also had four attacks in 2004: a subway bomb, a suicide bomb killing Moscow-backed Chechen president, the downing of passenger planes, and an attack on Beslan school. Eighteen of the organization's women's arm, the Black Widows, worked with 32 men in the Beslan's School Number One attack. The Beslan attack marked for the first time in the history of female suicide warfare that such a team was established, signaling a shift from an individual action to a group missions.

Chapter 10, "Al Qaeda," concludes that the killing of Osama bin Laden altered the trajectory of al Qaeda. Questions remain as to what effect bin Laden's death will have on al Qaeda's campaign of terror. Since his death, drone attacks have taken the lives of top al Qaeda leaders. The *Letters from Abbottabad* provide insight into Osama bin Laden's thinking shortly before he was killed. Most relevant is bin Laden's concern about the killing of members of the Muslim societies. This concern demonstrates the interrelationship of culture, the military, and the individual as a weapon.

CONCLUSION

"Suicide as a Weapon in War," affirms that the interaction of culture, the military, and the individual as a weapon determines the ultimate success or failure of the use of suicide warfare. In today's world, there is clear evidence that it will continue to be used in modern conflicts.

Acknowledgments

My deepest appreciation extends to my editor, Maxine Taylor, Military History, for her expertise, guidance, and encouragement that assisted to achieve the best possible result. Special appreciation is extended to Sasikala Rajesh, Project Manager, and her staff for the production of this book.

I thank the following individuals for their interviews: Marie Breen-Smyth, chair of international politics, codirector of Centre for International Intervention, and director of research at the School of Politics, University of Surrey, Guildford, U.K.; Max L. Gross, former senior research fellow on the Islam in Southeast Asia project at the Center for Strategic Intelligence Research, Joint Military Intelligence College, Washington D.C., and former dean, School of Intelligence Studies, Joint Military Intelligence College; Richard Jackson, professor of international politics at Aberystwyth University, U.K., and author of several articles and books on terrorism studies—most helpful were his books *Conflict Resolution in the 21st Century: Principles, Methods, and Approaches* and *Critical Terrorism Studies: A New Research Agenda*; and Rear Admiral D.M. Williams, Jr., USN (Retd.), former commander, Naval Investigative Service (NIS) Command.

I am appreciative to Karunya Jayasena, terrorism analyst at California State University, Northridge, for her literature review and to Jordan Derhammer, Cedar Falls, Iowa, for technical support.

Finally, I am grateful to my husband, James C. Skaine, for the support and assistance, to family members, Richard L. and Nancy L. Craft Kuehner and William V. and Carolyn E. Guenther Kuehner, and to my friend, Wanda Pape. I am appreciative to my writing colleague Captain J. Michael Brower, U.S. Army (Retd.), for his enthusiasm and support. For his lasting gift of inspiration, I thank Cass Paley, friend and mentor.

PART I

Theoretical Analysis of Suicide Warfare

Theoretical analysis of suicide warfare starts with an analysis of the phenomena of suicide. Chapter 1 provides the definitional framework and theoretical foundation for suicide warfare through Emile Durkheim's collective inclination, Lewis Coser's conflict theory, and various approaches to conflict resolution. These bases explain the relationship among culture, the military, and the individual as a weapon. The individual in this sense means the suicide attacker. In understanding the relationship among these three elements, the people in a society need to understand what is happening in the world and what is happening in themselves in relation to their biography and history within society. Sociologist C. Wright Mills calls this understanding "the sociological imagination."[1] The sociological imagination is important because all players need to understand their own experience and gauge their own fate by locating themselves within a particular period of history. They can know their chances in this particular life situation by becoming aware of those of all individuals in their circumstances. Peter Berger believed that we are located in society in space and time.[2] Berger's premise makes history important. Leaders have said that we are in a different kind of war, but Abdel Bari Atwan notes Zaki Badaw's point that Samson's destruction of the Philistines' temple is probably the first reference to a martyrdom attack. In the biblical story, Samson killed himself while killing the Philistines.[3]

PEACEFUL RESOLUTION

During the process of understanding the relationships among culture, military, and individual, engaging in conflict resolution can benefit all three. The need to demonize terrorists perpetuated counterterrorism rather than dialogue with terrorists to bring conflict resolution and peace (see Chapter 3). In *Conflict Resolution in the 21st Century: Principles, Methods, and Approaches*, Richard Jackson and Jacob Bercovitch provide a context for terrorism and an application to suicide warfare. There is a means for solution through conflict resolution and peace studies. In my interview with Richard Jackson, he explained,

[T]he root problem is political conflict which is sometimes expressed through terrorism or which some groups in a particular conflict will try and contend through a range of violent strategies, including terrorism. Terrorism is not a special or unique form of conflict in and of itself; it is just one of the strategies or tactics that groups or nations in conflict sometimes employ to achieve their goals. Therefore, everything we know about the causes and peaceful resolution of conflict applies equally to conflicts where terrorism is sometimes used.

I would go further and argue that terrorism is far from the worst strategy used in contemporary conflict; genocide, ethnic cleansing and war crimes have killed, injured and displaced infinitely more people than terrorism ever has, and slaughtering hundreds of thousands of people using clubs and machetes seems far worse to me than planting a bomb somewhere (although they are clearly both horrific). The point is that the UN and western countries have supported conflict resolution and reconciliation processes involving genocide in Cambodia, Rwanda, Bosnia, and elsewhere; why is all the knowledge we have about the causes of those conflicts and the necessary steps for reconciliation and peace-building not applied in contemporary conflicts involving terrorism? Why does the US and the EU support negotiations and constructive dialogue with Serbian groups in Bosnia or among the Rwandan factions, but it won't consider dialogue with Hamas, Hezbollah or al Qaeda?

[C]onflict resolution and peace studies have a great many possible answers to how we might understand and end the use of terrorism and resolve the political conflicts in which it currently occurs, but political interests and a dominant public discourse of terrorism in which terrorists are seen as being inherently "evil" and beyond all redemption prevents this knowledge from being known and applied. The evidence suggests that Western governments simply don't want to negotiate with certain groups and are concerned to protect certain interests; this necessarily entails promoting a discourse which demonizes and excludes these groups from political processes.[4]

MILITARY FORCE RESOLUTION

In the place of meaningful dialogue for peaceful resolution, the use of military force to combat terrorism has been steady, as seen in the wars in Afghanistan and Iraq and targeted killings of al Qaeda leadership. In the U.S. military, these protracted wars have caused the all-volunteer military and the society it serves to evaluate their relationship. The issues that were evaluated at the Strategic Studies Institute Conference in 2011 included the role of the military and the potential divergence of military professional values from those of the society from which it derives.[5] According to Lieutenant General John E. "Jack" Sterling, Jr., some examples of this divergence that signal stress are friction between civilian and military leaders with the most difficult task being translating strategic policy objectives into action on the ground as noted by Bob Woodward, kill teams in brigade that include the soldiers who killed four Afghans or premeditated murder of noncombatants, and the rising suicide rates.[6]

Military misuse of power has caused American society to doubt, Sterling stated. The U.S. Army is aware. Since the founding of the army, it has had a special relationship with the American people. The relationship began with concern about the necessity of a standing army. Professionalism began in World War I, but it has increased in importance since it became the single dominant military power. The nation relies on the military to achieve strategic goals. American people give it enormous responsibility through equipment, destructive weapons, sons and daughters, permission to use lethal force and action in their name, and punishment to personnel who disobey in the *Uniform Code of Military Justice*—up to and including death. Sterling asks, "Why does the American public place trust and confidence to use lethal force in their best interests?"[7] The key is trust. Although the profession continues to demonstrate it is worthy of that trust, some events have caused some in American society to begin to question that trust.

To address this problem, Sterling references a white paper by Don Synder, "What We Believe the Profession Is." Answers to three questions are necessary:

1. What does it mean for the army to be a profession of arms?
2. What does it mean to be a professional soldier?
3. After nine years of war, how are we as individual professionals and as a profession meeting those aspirations?[8]

Military supremacy comes with a price. Problems arise with the individual in relationship to the military. If left unchecked, the harm spills over into larger societies. Brigadier General Rhonda Cornum, Medical Corps, U.S. Army, said at the 2009 WREI Conference that the nation is asking a lot from the young men and women in the military. Not only must they "be prepared for 'full spectrum' warfare (from peacekeeping through high intensity conflict), but must engage in offense, defense, and 'nation building,' simultaneously. Our soldiers, often led by junior leaders in small groups, must continue to show trust, respect and compassion towards members of local populations, even when their loyalties and actions are suspect."[9]

The military is a profession only if it displays those attributes the American public expects in order to maintain an ethic that demonstrates proper and ethical action, said Sterling. The army has been granted autonomy and discretion by the public as long as it possesses attributes their client, society, expects. Profession of arms is an ancient and revered sacred trust to defend the Constitution and the American people. It is a unique profession because it is a lethal profession: prepared to kill and die when needed in service to public. The military has a monopoly on the use of force. This monopoly places incredible responsibility on the army to develop character, integrity, and a sense of belonging to something greater than themselves that make the soldiers able to handle the profession of arms as opposed to an occupation. Kill teams failed because character, integrity, and the sense of belonging to a greater power were not developed in that case.

MILITARY AND SOCIETAL CHALLENGES IN OTHER COUNTRIES

Countries other than the United States may face similar challenges in its relationship of the military and the individual to society: cases in point include Pakistan, Lebanon, and Kenya. Pakistan has an imbalance of power between its civilian and military branches that needs to be corrected so that it can effectively govern, according to Aqil Shah. The interrelationship among society, the military, and the individual is in Shah's statement, "Militant extremism can be fought effectively only through serious governance reforms that ensure the rule of law and accountability. This will require a strong democracy, a viable economy, and well-balanced civil-military relations."[10]

In the country of Lebanon, for example, the state has an intricate relationship with Hezbollah as well as foreign powers. Hezbollah is both a societal organization and a quasi-state entity. It comprises the largest party block in the democratically elected parliament and is the state's largest nonstate provider of health care and social services. Bryan R. Early wrote, "The nature of Hezbollah's relationship with the Lebanese state and its position with the country's larger society suggests that U.S. attempts to dislodge and disarm the organization could very well suffer the same fate as Israel's did, and, furthermore, could potentially lead to the organization's empowerment."[11]

The 1998 bombings of the U.S. embassies in Kenya and Tanzania caused world attention to focus on East Africa over the threat of global jihadist terrorism. As a result, an ongoing need for civil society to contribute to policy discussions and public debates was evident in Kenya, according to Jeremy Lind and Jude Howell. Pressure to achieve political and military objectives of the War on Terror was met with muted response in civil society. Young Muslims felt the War on Terror had sidelined their interests. It is civil society that can contribute to the shifting of political landscape.[12]

In 2011, the Heritage Foundation found that from 1969 to 2009, approximately 5,600 people lost their lives and more than 16,300 were injured as a result of international terrorism directed at the United States.[13] Suicide attacks in the countries produce a great loss of human life, much destruction, and ongoing threat of violence. The individual, the military, and their societies are affected. Although most who were killed on 9/11 were non-Muslims, Muslims have borne the brunt of the attacks because most of the responses have occurred in predominantly Muslim countries.[14] Direct war casualties were about 225,000 dead and about 365,000 wounded in the Iraq and Afghan wars as of June 2011. The great majority of the casualties were civilians in these countries.[15]

Part I discusses suicide warfare's theoretical foundations, suicide, and suicide as it relates to war, policy, strategy, and effects. The interrelationship of culture, military, and individual demonstrate that it does not happen in a vacuum.

CHAPTER 1

Defining Suicide Warfare

Suicide warfare is a strategy increasingly used in armed conflicts in the world. To understand why it is used and why its use is expanding, it is essential to define the basic terms and explore the interrelationships among them. The terms are suicide, warfare, suicide warfare, terrorism, and suicide terrorism. The connection between suicide and society significantly underscores the need to understand the belief systems of cultures and groups that have employed suicide as a weapon and the cultures that must respond to its use. Identifying sacred values in different cultures and understanding how they compete for people's affection is at the center of suicide warfare. These insights can be seen from the Western point of view and from cultures other than the West that justify the use of suicide warfare. Cultural points of view are evident in the international attempts to define terrorism, especially in military conflict.

SUICIDE, WARFARE, SUICIDE WARFARE, TERRORISM, AND SUICIDE TERRORISM

Suicide

Suicide is the taking of one's own life. The act of suicide differs from person to person, from one time to another, from one circumstance to another, and motivations vary.[1] Aspects of suicide behavior may differ in number, method, and reasons from culture to culture. Lee A. Headley's early study concluded that Asia's suicide profile is the opposite of the Western profile. Countries with the highest number of suicides among youth find the number decreases with age.[2]

Emile Durkheim's Suicide Typology

Nineteenth-century social theorist Emile Durkheim's typology of suicide is at times cited for understanding suicide and suicide terrorism. Ronald M. Holmes and Stephen T. Holmes have added to Durkheim's typology, but they believe no typology is better than Durkheim's. To Durkheim's typology of egoistic, altruistic, anomic, and fatalistic, they add dutiful, existential, revengeful, and political or ideological.[3] In Durkheim's four categories of suicide, egoistic results from lack of integration of a person into society. Egoistic suicide occurs less in ordered institutions such as Catholicism than in less regulated ones like Protestantism, in families with more density or structure, and in more integrated societies and where individuals participate actively in social life. Egoism in these instances is constrained, and the will to live is strengthened. Suicide rate, then, varies with the degree of integration of social groups.[4]

To account for suicide in social groups where there is a greater degree of integration, Durkheim identified altruistic suicide. A person may take his or her own life for reasons of religious sacrifice or political allegiance. This type of suicide takes place in the military, where obedience is predominant. In Durkheim's third type, anomic suicide, society regulates needs and satisfaction. Common beliefs and practices learned make the individual the personification of the collective consciousness. The fourth type, fatalistic suicide, Durkheim notes only minimally. It is the opposite of the other types in that it derives from excessive regulation to the point of oppression.[5]

The motives of individuals apt to commit suicide are interrelated with the social conditions wherein it occurs. So it is for suicide bombers. In *Female Suicide Bombers,* I concluded that the inclination to engage in suicide bombing is most easily understood in Durkheim's collective inclination. Social facts are realities to suicide bombers. Durkheim stated, "the individual inclination to suicide is explicable scientifically only by relation to the collective inclination, and this collective inclination is itself a determined reflection of the structure of the society in which the individuals lives."[6] Based on Durkheim's theory, I concluded,

An individual's views are more than a sum of those views. The views are an existence in itself; what Durkheim calls the collective conscience, the totality of beliefs and practices, of folkways and mores. And from this collective conscience, each individual conscience draws its moral sustenance. When a society is in crisis, the adjustment of an individual to common beliefs is upset and anomic or breakdown or absence of social norms and values appears and is manifested through suicide. Life-histories of some suicide bombers and attempted suicides interrelate with sociological variables.[7]

That said, how does this definition of suicide affect warfare? Durkheim believed "each social group really has a collective inclination for the act, quite its own, and the source of all individual inclination, rather than the result."[8] What are the sociological variables that are part of the collective consciousness? At this point, it is helpful to introduce the role of conflict theory and suicide warfare.

Suicide Warfare and Conflict Theory

Based on an earlier work of Randall Collins, scholars Jörg Rössel and Randall Collins concluded that an increase in explanatory results of conflict theory increases the need for a micro-foundation of meso- and macro-sociological principles. Micro-conflict theory integrates many theories of sociology: Marx, Weber, and Durkheim, among them. This modern theory combines empirical research to make isolated areas of study important in their relation to the whole.[9] The authors maintain that conflict theory enables us to see the common characteristics of the core of how groups struggle for power while constrained by resources.[10] This concept is key to the lack of sophisticated weaponry as one of the reasons for suicide warfare.

John Carpenter lists several causes of war: conflict over land and other natural resources, values and ideologies, racial and ethnic hostilities, defense against hostile attacks, revolution, and nationalism. The conflicts occur over values and ideologies such as democracy versus fascism as in World War II, capitalism versus communism during the Cold War, and differing religious beliefs have led to some of the worst wars in history.[11]

For these causes of war to escalate into terrorism accompanied by behaviors such as suicide bombing, there often exists an element of extreme ideological clashes in religious and/or secular beliefs. Certain circumstances also present are a failed or weak state that is unable to control terrorist operations; rapid modernization, when, for example, a country's sudden wealth leads to rapid social change; extreme ideologies—religious or secular; a history of political violence, civil wars, and revolutions; repression by a foreign occupation (i.e., invaders to the inhabitants); large-scale racial or ethnic discrimination; and the presence of a charismatic leader.[12]

Warfare

Definitions of basic types of warfare highlight the difference between irregular and traditional and between conventional and unconventional. The *Air Force Doctrine* provides the following definitions:

- Traditional warfare—A confrontation between nation-states or coalitions/alliances of nation-states (Joint Publication [JP] 1, Doctrine for the Armed Forces of the United States). This confrontation typically involves force-on-force military operations in which adversaries employ a variety of conventional military capabilities against each other in the air, land, maritime, space, and cyberspace domains. The objective may be to convince or coerce key military or political decision-makers, defeat an adversary's armed forces, destroy an adversary's war-making capacity, or seize or retain territory in order to force a change in an adversary's government or policies.

- Irregular warfare (IW)—A violent struggle among state and nonstate actors for legitimacy and influence over the relevant populations.

- Conventional warfare—A broad spectrum of military operations conducted against an adversary by traditional military or other government security forces that do not include chemical, biological, radiological, or nuclear weapons.

- Unconventional warfare—A broad spectrum of military and paramilitary operations, normally of long duration, predominantly conducted through, with, or by indigenous or surrogate forces who are organized, trained, equipped, supported, and directed in varying degrees by an external source. It includes, but is not limited to, guerrilla warfare, subversion, sabotage, intelligence activities, and unconventional assisted recovery (JP 1-02, Department of Defense Dictionary of Military and Associated Terms).[13]

Types of warfare in the United States have some similarities to types in Islam. Carrying out IW presents some differences. The doctrine of the U.S. Air Force on IW stated that, because of the United States' overwhelming dominance in recent conventional wars, most adversaries are not likely to choose to fight the United States in a traditional, conventional manner. As a result, relatively weaker powers, including nonstate entities, have found the option of IW attractive and more necessary. IW opponents have their own asymmetric (close operations taking place throughout the entire area of military operations)[14] capabilities including suicide bombers, improvised explosive devices, and the cover of civilian populations.

John Kelsay refers to two types of jihad or forms of warfare in Islam: regular and irregular.[15] The classic definitions of Islamic warfare fail to explain the popularity of the jihadist vision, according to Youssef H. Aboul-Enein and Sherifa Zuhur.[16] Their research adheres to the strict rules of warfare and definitions that involve regular jihad. This type is designed to expand Muslim territory and involves two or more nations at war. Irregular jihad includes uprisings, revolutions, or internal rebellions and expands the definitions of the Islamic rules of war. Each type demonstrates differing ideas of leadership. The authors believed the two types are not considered equally valid.

Suicide Warfare

Suicide warfare involves an individual or individuals being equipped with explosives or chemicals that when detonated will kill the individual(s) and destroy or damage the targeted civilians or military or political personnel. It is most often used by the nonstate combatants in a conflict, but a state military's use of the individual as a weapon, though less frequent, has occurred. The suicide attacks of the Japan's kamikaze pilots on American warships during World War II are the best-known instances of a state employing it, but the Russians, Germans, and British employed suicide attacks during World War II to a lesser degree.[17] Al Qaeda's attacks on the United States on 9/11 targeted civilians and military personnel and would have targeted political persons if Flight 93 had not crashed before reaching its target.

Terrorism

Terrorism was first an action without a label, Joseph S. Tuman maintains. In early cultures such as the first century AD, Jewish group, the Zealots-Sicarii (who defended Judea, now Israel), used violent actions for political, ideological, religious, and economic reasons. Other groups such as the Ismailis-Nizari or Assassins (1090–1275 AD) coordinated their murders in crowded places generally on religious holidays to gain public attention.[18]

How then did the early unlabeled violent actions become labeled as terrorism? Tuman places the change at the time of the Jacobins, a revolutionary group during the French Revolution, who used the term "terror" to describe themselves and to justify their actions. Their leader, Maximillian Robespierre, later helped bring in a period wherein terror was the policy of the new French Republic. The terror policy sought to eliminate any resistance to the revolution and centralize the absolute power of the new government. From September 5, 1793, to July 27, 1794, estimates are that terror was responsible for between 200,000 and 300,000 deaths, usually by guillotine execution. The people executed were largely private citizens who did not work against the revolutionaries, but who had benefitted from the system that oppressed the lower classes. According to Tuman, for the next two centuries, terrorism was used to describe violence in conflict over power and control around the world.[19]

From this context, scholars questioned why the use of the word "terrorism" "referenced intimidation practiced by individuals against innocent victims, designed to coerce governments and nation-states, but did not seem to cover the multitude of examples of terror practiced by government on other people."[20] From this question, a belief surfaced that distinguished terrorism from below or from those outside the dominant group who focused their attention on those above. Terrorism from above applies to the state or is sponsored by the state indirectly and practiced by surrogates who employ coercive intimidation. Tuman believed these distinctions allow the addition of other types of terrorism such as individual or group dissent, criminal enterprise, and state-sponsored or direct state terrorism.

Efforts to define terrorism have produced multiple definitions. The U.S. Department of State says there is no single definition of terrorism that has achieved universal acceptance, but in their *Global Patterns of Terrorism 2001* report (renamed in 2004, *Country Reports*), the department selected the definition of terrorism found in Title 22 of the U.S. Code, Section 2656f(d). This definition has been in effect since 1983. Title 22 defines terrorism as "premeditated, politically motivated violence perpetrated against non-combatant . . . targets by subnational groups or clandestine agents, usually intended to influence an audience." Boaz Ganor notes that the research of Alex P. Schmid and Albert J. Jongman produced 109 definitions.[21] Ganor stresses the need to produce an agreed-upon definition of terrorism. Without a common definition, devising or enforcing international agreements against terrorism is impossible. Without agreement, responsibility cannot be imposed on countries supporting terrorism, nor can efforts be made to combat terrorist organizations and their allies. Ganor writes that agreeing upon a definition is critical to developing an effective international strategy.

The definition Ganor proposed is, "terrorism is the intentional use of, or threat to use violence against civilians or against civilian targets, in order to attain political aims."[22] This definition is based on three important points. First, the activity must be violent or contain the threat of violence. Second, the aim is political in nature. Third, the targets are civilians. Defining terrorism and guerrilla activity is difficult because of the fine line separating the two concepts. The difference between individual terrorism and urban guerrilla warfare centers on the identity of the intended target. He explains, "An attack against military personnel, or against a leading decision-maker who formulates policy (including counter-terrorist policy), could be considered, according to the proposed definition, an 'urban guerrilla' activity. However, if the target is a civilian not acting in a decision-making capacity, but merely someone who is at most a political or social symbol (a well known singer, a journalist, a past leader, a judge, the head of a community or ethnic group, etc.), this will be an act of 'individual terrorism' according to the proposed definition."[23]

While scholars Jaideep Saikia and Ekaterina Stepanova parallel Ganor's definition, they believe terrorist and guerrilla tactics are sometimes used by a single armed group or movement. The use of each tactic has different implications in international humanitarian law. For example, in armed conflict, attacks against civilians are not allowed, but attacks on government forces are. They believe the core message of terrorism "is directed at someone far more important (usually the state) than their innocent, unarmed victims—elements that the terrorists cannot normally effectively challenge by using conventional military tactics."[24] Terrorism then is politically motivated, actual, or threatened violence conducted in an asymmetrical manner to exert pressure on the opponent.

According to Gus Martin, guerrilla warfare and terrorism are not synonymous. Guerrilla warfare involves a larger group of armed individuals who function as a military unit, attack enemy military forces, and seize and hold territory and at the same time, having some type of sovereignty or control over a specified geographical area and its people. In Martin's review of formal definitions, common features included use of illegal force, subnational actors, unconventional methods, political motives, and attacks against civilians and passive military targets with the purpose of affecting an audience. He points out that state terrorism occurs in fewer cases. It has been responsible for more deaths and suffering than terrorism by small bands of terrorists.[25]

H.H.A. Cooper, the president of Nuevevidas International, Inc., a Texas consulting company specializing in safety and survival issues, offers a definition of terrorism as "the intentional generation of massive fear by human beings for the purpose of securing or maintaining control over other human beings."[26] Acknowledging the frustration of defining terrorism he posed the question, "How can terrorism be defined when the process of defining is wholly frustrated by the presence of irreconcilable antagonisms?"[27] He suggested that we focus, for instance, on examples of ethnic cleansing in the former Yugoslavia or East Timor. People who experienced the horrors may not be able to capture the terror in one or two sentences, but the unpleasant incidents are forever fixed in their psyches. These incidences may not provide an answer, but they do offer a focal point for a controversial debate on definitions. Cooper maintains defining terrorism is futile because, "As with obscenity, we know terrorism well enough when we see it. For the minds and bodies affected by it, this suffices."[28]

In general, the chief characteristics of terrorism, according to Cindy C. Combs and Martin Slann, could include the following:

- Purposeful attacks on random selected targets.
- Desire to intimidate governments and entire populations.
- The goal to gain publicity for a particular cause.
- Some forms are not politically motivated.
- It is dynamic, in that it takes different forms and the forms themselves change: for example, the relatively new onset of cyberterrorism.
- It is a permanent feature in the present and in the foreseeable future.[29]

Official Definitions of Terrorism

Terrorism has been defined by agencies and organizations throughout the world. Some also reference suicide terrorism. Terms that appear often are unlawful, violence, civilian, intimidation, domestic, international, and politically motivated.

In the sources I reviewed, it appears internationally, as within the United States, that a universal definition of terrorism is yet to be formulated, but some common characteristics have been identified. George P.

Fletcher, Cardozo Professor of Jurisprudence at the Columbia University School of Law, states that the concept of terrorism fulfills many functions. A better way to think of terrorism is as a higher and more dangerous crime that incorporates some of the characteristics of warfare. Eight major factors bear on terrorism: violence, intention, nature of the victims, connection of the offender to the state, justice and motive of their cause, level of organization, element of theater, and the absence of guilt. All factors do not appear in every terrorism incident. Fletcher maintains, "The way to think about terrorism is, therefore, to become aware of all the relevant factors but not to expect that they will all be fulfilled in any particular case."[30] He adds that although the concept of terrorism is relatively new, the one label, "terrorism," stands out as a linguistic landmark. The reason that it is a landmark is that a sharing of the same word among different languages exists. In spite of the difficulty of definition, political leaders and the public believe in the notion of terrorism.

Suicide Terrorism

The U.S. Department of the Army defines suicide terrorism as "the readiness to sacrifice one's life in the process of destroying or attempting to destroy a target to advance a political goal."[31] The U.S. Army handbook offers three definitions of suicide terrorism. The common element of suicide terrorism within these definitions is that the terrorist attack will only succeed if the attacker kills himself or herself. The army makes a distinction: "This is different from what is often described as suicidal terrorism. This is a high-risk operation where the terrorist may not kill himself in conducting the attack but his chance of survival is very slim. However, the success of the mission does not depend on the terrorist actually killing himself."[32]

Terrorists versus Freedom Fighters

The difficulty of defining terrorist is exemplified by the following: In 2002, Leila Khaled, a former hijacker and central committee member of the Popular Front for the Liberation of Palestine, addressed students at the School for Oriental and African Studies, London, "There are no suicide bombers. They are freedom fighters."[33] Neville Nagler, director general, Board of Deputies of British Jews, believed, "Leila Khaled, as a known and self-confessed terrorist who has never changed her views, is an affront to all decent-minded citizens."[34] Nagler wrote a letter to the home secretary saying Khaled should have never been allowed in the country and requested that she be expelled. The definition of terrorist depends on perception.

President George W. Bush's commentary that Ayat al-Akhras' attack is symbolic of the severity of the conflict between the Israelis and the

Palestinians: "When an 18-year-old Palestinian girl is induced to blow herself up and in the process kills a 17-year-old Israeli girl, the future itself is dying."[35] My reaction in *Female Suicide Bombers* was, and is now, that such an acknowledgment is a recognition that human life is taken on both sides of war. We must ask, how do the United States and its allies, when engaged in conflicts, look upon the concept of freedom fighter versus terrorist? What are their military strategic responses? Rear Admiral (RADM) D.M. Williams, Jr., U.S. Navy (Retd.), former commander, Naval Investigative Service (NIS), provided one answer. These ideological concepts may hinder agreement. Accomplishing the elimination of terrorism through locating terrorists has little chance of success without the adoption of policy.[36] This lack of consensus confirms the need for conformity in the definitions, especially in military conflict.

Freedom Fighters, Nationalists, and Armed Conflict

Contrary to the opinion of many, Antonio Cassese, professor of international law at the University of Florence, Italy, stated that the international community has developed a definition of terrorism in time of peace at the level of customary law. The disagreement is over whether the definition may also be applied in time of armed conflict. The legal classification of the use of terror during armed conflict causes the most problems at the political level. Cassese believed the classification has become the political albatross for final agreement on a treaty definition of terrorism.[37]

In dispute is whether freedom fighters' acts in national liberation wars are exempt from the definition. Should their attacks on civilians be defined as lawful? Cassese suggested the world community is trending in three ways: exempt freedom fighters as terrorists; exclude attacks against civilians in armed conflict from international rules and thus assign regulation to international humanitarian law; and combine the application of international norms on terrorism and international humanitarian law to actions in armed conflict, and classifying as terrorist rather than as war crimes, attacks on civilians in the conflicts with a view to spreading fear.[38]

Marco Sassòli, a professor of international law at the University of Geneva, Switzerland, and associate professor at the University of Québec at Montréal, Canada, agreed that the most controversial aspect of international antiterrorism law is the definition of terrorism. He added, "All involved try to include as many of their enemies' activities as possible into the term and to exclude their own behavior and that of their friends."[39] This idea is relevant not only to the definition of terrorism. For example, according to RADM Williams, the U.S. military is only allowed to attack military objectives, that is, the military does not attack civilians.[40] Yet, recent reports in Afghanistan and Iraq, for example, indicate the coalition forces have taken the lives of civilians in attacks.[41] The deaths are labeled collateral damage. The Department of Defense defines collateral damage as "Unintentional or incidental injury or damage to persons or objects that would not be lawful military targets in the circumstances ruling at the time. Such damage is not unlawful so long as it is not excessive in light of the overall military advantage anticipated from the attack."[42]

Three controversies must be resolved before terrorism can be defined, Sassòli stated. First, it is not useful to address terrorism and the fight against terrorism as war. Two exceptions exist: terrorist acts committed in an armed conflict and defined by the usual rules of international humanitarian law and peacetime terrorist acts, by analogy defined as acts forbidden in wartime. Second, it is controversial whether state behavior should be included or excluded from the definition of terrorism. Third, it is controversial as to whether the term should only cover acts prohibited by international humanitarian law, especially in military conflict because it implies contradictions between international humanitarian law and antiterrorism law. Critical is Sassòli's comment to the issue of those conflicts based in causes of nationalism: "However those controversies are solved, the solution should not refer to the legitimacy of the cause for which someone is fighting, but to the methods they are applying. Furthermore, the two sides of a genuine armed conflict should not be treated differently by international anti-terrorism law."[43] Lastly, acts in armed conflicts should not be criminalized as terrorist if international humanitarian law does not prohibit that act, because that type of definition would weaken the incentives to obey the law.

Organized Terror and State-Sponsored Terrorism

Organized Terror

Mette Eilstrup-Sangiovanni and Calvert Jones found a growing body of literature shows that the major conflict "in world politics is no longer between states but between states and terrorist networks such as al Qaeda, drug smuggling networks such as those in Colombia and Mexico, nuclear smuggling networks in places such as North Korea and Pakistan, and insurgent networks such as those in Iraq."[44] The main advantage of networks is organization. The authors believe that although networks have other possible advantages, such as flexibility, scalability, and resilience, some issues such as distance collaboration, programs involving collective action, learning, training, and security are best undertaken by more centralized hierarchical structures of the states.

Another growing trend is the link between terrorism and organized crime, according to Thomas M. Sanderson. Because the global war on terrorism has restricted the flow of financial support to terror groups, transnational terrorist organizations have moved deeper into organized criminal activity.[45] Ron Chepesiuk acknowledged the trend, describing it as dangerous. The reasons terrorist organizations collaborate with organized crime include access to failed states, drug-trafficking routes, kidnapping, human and contraband smuggling, counterfeiting money and CDs, fraud (credit card, cell phone cloning, and identity theft) and extortion, and armed robbery. All of these activities are profitable. Chepesiuk proposed that this trend calls for "the need for a new paradigm in strategic thinking."[46] Factors to address the issue include a focus on the financial links between the two groups, knowledge of the Internet, and intelligence communities better investigating the crossover points between the groups.

State-Sponsored Terrorism

Daniel Byman offered a chilling perspective of state-sponsored terrorism: "For all the talk of 'nonstate actors' or 'networked organizations,' states remain at the core of the war on terror. . . . States are often more anxious to support terrorism not to cause trouble for others but to keep it out of their own backyards."[47] Pakistan and Saudi Arabia and countries like them adopted an approach of passivity while terrorists recruit, raise money, and construct their organizations on their territory.

Yemen presents another way that states try to address terrorism, wrote Byman. Yemen is a U.S. ally, but gives suspected militants a choice. They can stay and be arrested if they target citizens, or they can leave and go to another country. Key in Byman's analysis is the shift in power relationships from state proxies to government partners. Governments may not control their own intelligence, or terrorists may have captured part or all of the state machinery. An example of this shift is the Hezbollah–Iran relationship, which began with Iran providing Hezbollah with military training, financial support, weapons, and ideological guidance. Hezbollah in return pledged its allegiance to Iran. This relationship has shifted from proxy to partner because Hezbollah has its own financial support and training means, successfully captured part of the Lebanese state, and sponsors other terrorist organizations such as Hamas, Palestinian Islamic Jihad, and other groups opposed to Israel.[48] These examples serve to illustrate a critical issue in state-sponsored terrorism. How do countries like the United States combat terrorism in Pakistan, Saudi Arabia, and Lebanon if, on the one hand, some of these countries agree to be an ally in the fight against terror, and, on the other hand, put themselves in the service of terror?[49]

Henry A. Giroux, writing in 2006, examined the role of the United States and state-sponsored terrorism. War and warriors were synonymous with models of national greatness. He believed, "Sovereignty is reduced to waging a war on terrorism that mimics the very terror it claims to be fighting."[50] Noting the work of Giorgio Agamben, Giroux stated that the organization of state violence is centered around the forces of security and terrorism that reinforce one another and that increasingly "form a single deadly system, in which they justify and legitimate each other's actions."[51] Giroux defined fundamentalism as only one way of organizing reality, and it has affected the United States in the form of finance capital and the elevation of the market to a universal level that generates other fundamentalisms, "religious and secular, either in alliance with them or in opposition. These forces are at the heart of globalization."[52]

The continued debate between the West and the Islamic extremists about who is terrorizing whom remains one of the most notable controversies since 9/11, according to Adam Lankford.[53] Al Qaeda has fueled a number of accusations. On May 1, 2010, Faisal Shahzad attempted to blow up an SUV in Times Square. At a plea hearing, Shahzad claimed, "I am part of the answer to the U.S. terrorizing the Muslim nations and the Muslim people."[54] Further, he said that, as a Muslim soldier, he was avenging the war in Afghanistan and American interventions in Pakistan, Iraq, Yemen, and Somalia.

Along with many examples of accusations of the United States committing acts of terror, critics point to such historical events as the Boston Tea Party, President Harry Truman's decision to drop nuclear bombs on Hiroshima and Nagasaki in 1945, President Dwight D. Eisenhower's decision to allow CIA operatives to infiltrate Iran and overthrow the prime minister in 1953, President Ronald Reagan's decision to bomb Libya in 1986, and President George W. Bush's decision to invade Iraq in 2003. Lankford maintained that, in order to win the War on Terror, the United States needs to take the charges seriously and decide whether or not there is any truth to them.[55]

Paul R. Pillar maintained a reduction in state-sponsored terrorism has occurred. The decrease reflects governments' analysis of costs and benefit. This trend is evidenced in countries such as Libya, Syria, North Korea, Sudan, and Cuba. Iran has cut back on its assassinations of exiled dissidents in the interests improving relations with Western Europe, where many of the killings took place. Increased interdependence recognized as globalization is the chief reason for the reduction of state-sponsored terrorism, according to Pillar.[56] As of January 2011, the United States had designated the following countries as state sponsors of terrorism: Cuba, designated on March 1, 1982; Iran, January 19, 1984; Sudan, August 12, 1993; and Syria, December 29, 1979. Existing sanctions laws penalize persons and countries engaging in certain trade with state sponsors.[57]

SUICIDE AND SOCIETY

Justification for the Use of Suicide Warfare

Understanding Belief Systems outside the West

In an effort to understand Islam, it is important to examine a variety of practices that exist within the religion. David Aaron differentiates the practices of Islamist fundamentalism and Islamist political movements from those practiced by terrorists. These distinctions are similar to the one I drew in 2002 when I had completed my first book on the women of Afghanistan. I concluded that the Taliban had hijacked Islam. Their extremism was neither Afghan nor Islam. Aaron's work reflects my conclusion, in that the current voice of Jihad "is about a small group among the 1.2 billion Muslims on earth that carries out and promotes terrorism in the name of Islam."[58] Youssef Aboul-Enein and Sherifa Zuhur explored the Koran, the Islamic book of divine revelation, and *hadith*, Prophet Muhammad's sayings and deeds. The authors found that proper use of Islamic scripture discredits rather than supports the tactics of al Qaeda and other jihadist organizations.[59]

In *Female Suicide Bombers,* I stated that only by identifying sacred values in different cultures and understanding how they compete for people's affection can we fully understand suicide bombing.[60] This viewpoint reflects an aspect of C. Wright Mill's sociological imagination theory.[61] Talip Kucukcan puts forth this concept as well, "without a thorough analysis of social contexts of such acts, fighting terrorism and violence will not be effective and international relations will deteriorate further."[62] This philosophy reflects Durkheim's collective inclination, which is "a determined reflection of the society in which the individual lives."[63] Motives, then, are inspired by social conditions. This theory offers an ethics of form and allows the presentation of different cultures that employ suicide warfare, in the context of the power of the society in which those combatants live, of the terrorist group to which they may belong, and of their society as part of the larger global community.[64]

Talip Kucukcan found that most studies of terrorism fail to adequately address social roots of conflicts. He concluded that global economic imbalance or global inequalities and claims over equal share of the wealth are a basic cause of terrorism. "Local identities in many parts of the world became sharper and stronger that contributed to the sense of 'we' and 'them.' "[65] If this conclusion is accurate, then an important aspect of conflict theory is applicable. Anthony Oberschall defines it as purposeful interaction of two or more parties in a competitive setting that are likely to inflict damage, harm, or injury. He notes Lewis A. Coser's definition of social conflict conveys its meaning very well: "[It is a] struggle over values or claims to status, power, and scarce resources, which the aims of the conflict groups are not only to gain the desired values, but also to neutralize, injure, or eliminate rivals."[66]

Another significant social condition to consider is religion, according to Kucukcan. Religion as a social factor should be included in an analysis of terrorism because religious symbols and rhetoric are oftentimes used to justify acts of terrorism. Some of Kucukcan's examples include a Christian group bombing in 1995 of the Federal Office Building in Oklahoma City taking the lives of 168, Yigal Amir's killing of Izak Rabin because of a command from God, the extreme Islamists 9/11 attacks in the United States, and the 7/7 attacks in Britain. These acts of violence are evidence that religion should be taken seriously when we speak of collective identity.[67] Further, the interrelationship of society and religion is critical because "The role of religion symbolically embodies society itself. Religion's power is through representations. God, for example, is societally transfigured and symbolically expressed.[68] Society is the source of the sacred and it is society that defines what is sacred and what is profane."[69]

Understanding the belief systems other than those found in Western society is critical in understanding suicide warfare. In fact, what is meant by the term suicide warfare may differ depending on the participant. Often overlooked in theoretical discussions of these interrelationships is the use of language. If a use of language is what it recalls, then it has a social foundation.[70] Author of multiple works on terrorism, Richard Jackson had a valid point when he stated that he is uncomfortable with the notion that suicide warfare is labeled such. In an interview, he explained the terms suicide and warfare:

[T]he term "suicide" is culturally loaded and implies things about the individual committing the act that may not be correct, or will at least be culturally biased. I doubt they themselves would consider it "suicide," particularly those that are Muslim, as suicide is forbidden in Islam. Even the non-religious ones would not consider it suicide in a typical Western sense, but rather sacrifice or martyrdom on behalf of, or in the cause of, their people. Calling it "suicide warfare" functions therefore as a label that may misinform and misdirect attention from the real motives people have for sacrificing their lives.

[The notion of warfare] has a particular meaning in western society of total armed conflict of one society against another, when it is really just one specific strategy or tactic. In reality, as you know, groups tend to employ this particular strategy primarily in situations of asymmetry as a means of trying to create a greater psychological equivalence, and they often abandon it when it proves counter-productive or unpopular among their constituencies (as the PKK did in Turkey). That is, the broader struggle may continue while that particular strategy is abandoned. I fear that calling it "warfare" implies a totality of organized military and social conflict aimed at the complete defeat of the enemy. It is akin to mistaking ambushes or amphibious landings for "war": ambushes (like martyrdom operations) are a subset of the broader strategies employed in war (political struggle). I am also concerned that calling it "warfare" functions to justify the state's approach of launching a "war on terror" in response—and all the extra-legal, extraordinary measures that come with declaring a state of "war."[71]

Karunya Jayasena is correct in saying that defining terrorism is not merely a theoretical issue. To be taken into account are the fundamental factors that recur across the forms of terrorism and the fact that terrorism is a collective social phenomenon. Also, the definition must account for the fact that world systems and national politics are interconnected as causes of terrorism.[72]

When defining terrorism and suicide terrorism, it is important to understand the terms in the context of their relation to suicide warfare. Not all terrorism is suicide terrorism. Terrorism is a much broader phenomenon. Not all suicide warfare is suicide terrorism although suicide terrorism has been a part of the tactics of most of those who have used suicide warfare. A limitation of the use of "terrorism" as a part of the definition of suicide warfare is that, in most instances, "terrorism" and "terrorists" are pejorative terms ascribed by one side to the other in a dispute. The defining side then can treat the other side harshly and even kill them simply because they are defined as "terrorists." The other side might consider themselves positively. To paraphrase the old saying, "one person's terrorist is another person's freedom fighter." The definition of the combatants depends on where the individual stands within the conflict.

In attempting to understand cultures other than Western societies, Marie Breen-Smyth, School of Politics, University of Surrey, proposed using a critical approach. She stated, "A critical approach . . . would advance universal human security, not merely the security of the state; its mission would entail the establishment of human security in the broader sense of security, . . . to include all threats and obstacles to human actualization, not merely those posed by political violence."[73] In an interview, Breen-Smyth explained,

A great deal of what has gone before is from the point of view of the state and the problem solving approach that was used was one of how do we get these people to stop. Instead of asking why do human beings go to these lengths to attack our people or to do these appalling things? After 9/11, there were a whole group of people, mostly feminists I have to say, who wrote material of that nature saying when something like 9/11 happens, it's an opportunity to think about why this is happening, what we need to do next or who do we need to attack but how have we and the world gotten ourselves into the state whereby some people feel this is a justified act. How can we understand this first of all and then how can we move political relationships beyond that to somewhere where security is a global concern. It's not the security of the west vs. the east or security of the state vs. citizen, but everybody's security.[74]

CHAPTER 2

Suicide Warfare in Modern Conflicts

Suicide warfare is increasingly common in military conflicts globally. It is waged in two ways: as a defense and as an attack. In either case, the individual may use a variety of means, take many different approaches, and employ a range of weapons.

SUICIDE AS A DEFENSE

Suicide as a defense has been an instrument of individuals and groups in wars for thousands of years. Suicide as a defense occurs when a person kills herself or himself without attempting to kill or injure others. Weapons include swords, firearms, poisons, fire, and bombs. The common motivations for committing defensive suicide are to protest injustice, to avoid dishonor, to prevent being captured, and to avoid being tortured.

In December 2010, in Tunisia, Mohamed Bouazizi set himself on fire to protest being denied a way to earn his living. His self-immolation sparked worldwide protest, which was the beginning of the Arab Spring.[1] In Tibet, self-immolation has been used as a protest against the rule of China. From March 2011 to June 2012, 38 people set themselves on fire in Tibetan-inhabited areas of China in protest at what they say is religious and cultural repression by the Chinese authorities. Tibetans have long chafed under China's rule over the vast Tibetan plateau, saying that Beijing has curbed religious freedoms and their culture is being eroded by an influx of Han Chinese, the country's main ethnic group.[2]

In Japan, seppuku or hari-kari was ceremonial disembowelment and consists of plunging a short blade into the abdomen and moving the blade from left to right in a slicing motion. Seppuku was part of the samurai honor code and was used by samurai to die with honor rather than fall into the hands of their enemies (and likely suffer torture), or as a form of capital punishment for samurai who had committed serious offenses, or performed for other reasons that had brought shame to them.[3]

The mass suicide of the 960 Zealot defenders of Masada in the first century was an effort to avoid capture. After Rome destroyed Jerusalem and the Second Temple in AD 70, the Great Revolt ended except for the surviving Zealots, who fled Jerusalem to the fortress of Masada, near the Dead Sea. There, they held out for three years as Roman troops placed the fortress under siege. Masada is situated on top of an enormous, isolated rock; anyone climbing it to attack the fortress would be an easy target. Yet the Jews, encamped in the fortress, could never feel secure, as they saw the Roman Tenth Legion hard at work, constructing battering rams and other weapons. The Zealots at Masada were the group that had started the Great Revolt. In fact, the Zealots had been in revolt against the Romans since the year 6. More than anything else, the length and bitterness of their uprising probably account for Rome's unwillingness to let Masada and its small group of defiant Jews alone. In the end, all defenders committed suicide.[4]

In times when threat of capture or torture could face military personnel, they have been issued a pill that when taken, would produce death. The suicide pill contains cyanide and is ingested in order to end his or her own life quickly to avoid torture or painful death or to prevent leaking sensitive information if captured. The pills can be concealed and evade detection more easily than other methods of suicide.[5] Examples of the use of suicide pills are Francis Gary Powers, the American U-2 pilot who was shot down while flying over the USSR in May 1960 was given a tiny poison-impregnated needle hidden inside a fake silver dollar, but he did not use it;[6] and William Sterling Parsons and crew members of the B-29 Superfortress bombers sent to drop atomic bombs on Japan in World War II were issued lethal pills. All planes returned safely and the pills were not used.[7] During the Sri Lankan civil war (1987–2009), the Tamil Tiger suicide bombers wore potassium cyanide necklaces.[8]

The defensive weapon is, in some cases, a bomb. A Chechen female suicide attacker saw that she was not going to get to her target, the police station, and blew herself up. Even though eight people were killed by her action, her suicide was defensive.[9]

SUICIDE AS AN ATTACK

In World War II, when the Japanese military used kamikaze pilots as suicide attackers, they were the first in the modern era to do so (see Chapter 6). Since the 1970s, the use of suicide in war has become a common weapon in conflicts around the world.

Types of suicide warfare bear a relationship to the method of attack. A suicide attacker may employ a biological weapon. Court testimony documents that biological weapons are considered weapons of mass destruction (WMD). The relationship of group goals to the individual purpose and the societal context is a factor in the attacks success. The relationship demonstrates the acts of suicide bombers are not random or mindless, but are a tactic of war that reflects the goals of the organization.

Missions and Attacks

A mission is a specific task assigned to a tactical grouping, whereas an attack is an offensive use of force in order to achieve an objective (e.g., the capture of ground).[10] The Chechen rebels emerged in the early 1990s. At issue was the degree of autonomy Chechnya should have. Whether Chechnya should stay within the Russian Federation or whether it should form an independent nation was the contention and that it should form an independent nation was the primary mission of the Chechen rebels.[11] The rebels launched attacks to realize their mission, and in 2004, they held "the distinction of having killed the largest number, 170 in Moscow in October 2002 when they with a high percentage of women held hostages in the Theater Center. The police killed 129 captives and 41 rebels in a rescue effort."[12]

A group may have an overall mission as did the Chechen rebels. It may have additional missions that are designed to carry out one or more specific attacks. According to Luca Ricolfi, the concept of suicide mission is broader than that of suicide bombing. In suicide bombing, the mission success is entirely dependent on the attacker's death. Ricolfi's database, LUPA, includes only executed and certainly suicidal missions. Missions may result in foiled missions, failed missions, successful missions, and very high risk missions, which are almost suicide missions. Successful missions are categorized into certainly suicidal and probably suicidal.[13]

Suicide Attacks that Fail

Some attacks fail because the attacked authority intervenes with massive force. The basis of the Liberation Tigers of Tamil Eelam's (LTTE's) long-standing conflict was in the political and economic marginalization of the Tamils.[14] In May 2009, the Sri Lankan army decisively defeated the Tamil Tigers.[15] When the Chechen rebels held hostage the audience in the Dubrovka theater in Moscow in 2002, the Russian special forces injected a chemical agent in the building's ventilation system that killed theatergoers and rebels.[16,17]

Homeland Security found the most significant factors contributing to the success or failure of an attack occurred in the pre-execution phases.[18]

Other factors that sometimes contribute to the outcome of an incident are the location, method, and level of sophistication of attack.[19]

The Increase in Suicide Attacks

The U.S. Department of Defense views suicide attackers from the terrorism perspective. Suicide terrorism is "the calculated use of unlawful violence or threat of unlawful violence to inculcate fear; intended to coerce or to intimidate governments or societies in the pursuit of goals that are generally political, religious, or ideological."[20]

The *Deputy Chief of Staff for Intelligence (DCSINT) Handbook* states that although terrorists are versatile in method of attack, the suicide attack is becoming more prolific. Indications from the RAND database are that, despite the decline in the overall number of terrorist attacks, suicide terrorist attacks have increased. Of the 144 suicide bombings recorded since 1968, two-thirds occurred between 2001 and 2003.[21]

When a suicide attack is executed by an improvised explosive device (IED) or a vehicle-borne improvised explosive device (VBIED), the IED is placed on the attacker's person and is detonated where it will cause the most damage. The advantage is accessibility to a location, gaining close proximity to a person. The VBIED is the use of a vehicle the user has converted into a bomb. A vehicle-assisted attack offers the opportunity for a mass casualty event against a "soft" target, or the capability to penetrate a "hard" target.[22] A soft target is a "person or unit or vehicle which is vulnerable or unable to defend itself properly" as opposed to a "hard" target, which is a person or unit or vehicle "moving across ground in such a way as not to present an easy target to the enemy."[23] An example of a soft target may be a particular supply truck in a convoy. An example of a hard target is the suicide bomber who steered a hijacked truck loaded with the equivalent of six tons of TNT down the airport road in Beirut, Lebanon. The attacker smashed into the four-story barracks where more than 300 U.S. troops from a U.N. peacekeeping mission slept. The truck detonated what the Federal Bureau of Investigation (FBI) called the largest nonnuclear bomb in history.[24]

Assassination and Targeted Killing

Suicide attacks are used in assassinations and targeted killings. Assassination is the murder of well-known persons.[25] The LTTE sought an independent Tamil state. Usually, LTTE targeted senior political and military officials in Sri Lanka. It is the only organization that successfully assassinated two heads of state by suicide bombing. In May 1991, they assassinated Indian Prime Minister Rajiv Gandhi and in May 1993, they assassinated President Ranasinghe Premadasa of Sir Lanka.[26]

Targeted killing, according to Jason Fisher, is "the intentional slaying of a specific alleged terrorist or group of alleged terrorists undertaken with explicit governmental approval when they cannot be arrested using reasonable means."[27] Although not with the use of suicide bombing, such was the targeted killing on May 1, 2011, of Osama bin Laden, leader of al Qaeda and the 9/11 orchestrator. Reports indicated that he was unarmed when he was shot dead, which raised the issue of whether the killing was legal. Legality depends on whether bin Laden can be considered an enemy combatant.[28] U.S. Attorney General Eric Holder testified before the Judiciary Committee of Congress that the operation was "lawful, legitimate, and appropriate in every way."[29] Since bin Laden led the al Qaeda, an organization that conducted the attacks of 9/11 that killed thousands, he was a legal military target. Joshua Raines pointed out that the 9/11 attacks were "not the first time the U.S. had implicated bin Laden in attacks against U.S. interests. Previously the U.S. had linked him to the bombing of two U.S. embassies in Africa in 1998 and the explosion that rocked the U.S.S. Cole at a port in Yemen in 2000."[30]

According to the *International Business Times,* Obama justified the use of lethal force in the Authorization to Use Military Force Act of September 18, 2001.[31] The act permits the president to use "all necessary and appropriate force" against those nations, organizations, or persons he determines aided in the 2001 attacks. The actions are self-defense, "to prevent any future acts of international terrorism" against the United States. Presidential executive orders under this law do not include assassinating foreign political leaders.[32]

Bioterrorism

Suicide attackers have engaged in bioterrorism.[33] Usually, a disease such as anthrax is developed for use as a weapon. Anthrax is a disease of cattle and sheep and is transmissible to humans by touching infected skin, meat, or other parts of an animal. It causes pustules on the skin or in the lungs. Some nations are known to have developed anthrax for use as a biological weapon.[34]

A suicide attacker "could employ a biological weapons attack where both the plague and smallpox (piggybacking) is used," Jason D. Söderblom reported.[35] The report shows how difficult the containment of an orchestrated outbreak would be. Söderblom develops a scenario of committing a bioterrorism attack through the suicide attacker. To spread the pneumonic plague, for example, an infected suicide terrorist would not look out of place seeking treatment in any medical facility while he or she spread the plague. The suicide attacker would rely on the flu-like symptoms to prevent diagnoses as a pneumonic plague carrier. Spreading the virus in the hospital is easier than on a train, for example, because coughing would not be considered out of the ordinary. Another example might be the creation of a mass plague with a smallpox infection of patients and staff at hospitals that causes people to stay away from medical facilities. The infrastructure and economy of the city languishes. Means of delivery and venues for vaccines become difficult. Containment is near impossible when people are afraid that the situation is an enemy attack. When the people travel to other locations, they spread the virus further.[36] While Söderblom's theory is hypothetical, Carlos E. Sluzki's is not. Sluzki states, "boundaries between bioterrorism and other forms of terrorism can be at times blurred and filled with gray zones—as would be, for instance, a (until now hypothetical) case of a suicide-bomber carrying shrapnel tainted with anthrax or HIV virus."[37] His reasoning is that if it is thought that attacks will remain in the realm of speculation, it is wishful thinking.

Bioterrorism is demonstrated by the March 20, 1995, sarin nerve gas attack on the Tokyo subway system. Sarin gas is 500 times more toxic than cyanide gas and can be made from readily available chemicals. The attack was against trains passing through Kasumigaseki and Nagatachō, home to the Japanese government. Twelve people died from the gas attack, and 5,300 people became ill. The Japanese millenarian cult, Aum Shinri Kyo, was responsible. It hoped to hasten the apocalypse.[38]

Weapons of Mass Destruction

Controversy exists whether there is an accepted definition of WMD. W. Seth Carus believes that authoritative definitions do exist. The term first appeared in December 1937 in an address by the Archbishop of Canterbury.[39] In 1945, President Harry Truman signed a document defining "weapons adaptable to mass destruction."[40] In 1946, the phrase appeared in the first UN General Assembly.[41] In 1948, the words "weapons of mass destruction" became the preferred phrase. The term became integral to post–World War II disarmament diplomacy. The United Nations adopted a standard definition in 1948 that stated WMD are

atomic explosive weapons, radioactive material weapons, lethal chemical and biological weapons, and any weapons developed in the future which have characteristics comparable in destructive effect to those of the atomic bomb or other weapons mentioned above.[42]

That WMD can be chemical, nuclear, or biological is shown in the two court cases of Khalid Aldawsari and Najibullah Zazi. The cases will show explosives such as bombs are considered an aspect of WMD; therefore, laws and policy concerning WMD are applicable to suicide bombing. Control of WMDs is employed on national and international levels. U.S. law defines WMD in 18 USC §2332a as follows:

(A) any destructive device as defined in section 921 of this title (i.e. explosive device);

(B) any weapon that is designed or intended to cause death or serious bodily injury through the release, dissemination, or impact of toxic or poisonous chemicals, or their precursors;

(C) any weapon involving a biological agent, toxin, or vector (as those terms are defined in section 178 of this title); and

(D) any weapon that is designed to release radiation or radioactivity at a level dangerous to human life.[43]

The FBI adds, "WMD is often referred to by the collection of modalities that make up the set of weapons: chemical, biological, radiological, nuclear, and explosive (CBRNE, pronounced 'See-Burr-Nee'). These are weapons that have a relatively large-scale impact on people, property, and/or infrastructure."[44]

In recent years, charges in two cases involving suicide bombers were based on aspects of the U.S. law regarding WMD. In 2011, Khalid Aldawsari, a 20-year-old Saudi student, was charged with attempting to create bombs to be used in attacks on American targets, which is "one count of attempted use of a weapon of mass destruction, which carries a penalty of life in prison."[45] Prosecutors in Lubbock, Texas said that Aldawsari was more dangerous than a want-to-be bomber because he had the technical knowledge and the political motivation to carry out his attack. Aldawsari's journal revealed that he had planned to carry out attacks long before he came to the United States in September 2008, reported the *New York Times*. As of this writing, U.S. District Judge Donald E. Walter ordered a change in venue and that the trial date be changed to June 21, 2012.[46]

Similarly, in a Brooklyn federal court on February 22, 2010, Afghan-born Najibullah Zazi, 25, a Colorado airport shuttle driver, admitted plotting with al Qaeda to bomb New York City subways and other targets. His purpose was to avenge U.S. military action in Afghanistan. He was charged with conspiring to use WMD, to commit murder in a foreign country, and providing material support to a terrorist group. He faced the possibility of life in prison when sentenced on June 25.[47] To receive a lesser sentence, in April 2012, Zazi testified for the U.S. government in the trial of Adis Medunjanin. He testified that Medunjanin was his alleged co-plotter in a planned attack on the New York subway system.[48] The FBI definition of WMD and these two cases demonstrate the relationship between suicide bombing and WMD.

The counter proliferation initiative recognized the potential for terrorism using WMD, but their main concern was preparing for conflict with a WMD-armed state. Paul I. Bernstein et al. noted that, by 1995, after the first attack on the World Trade Center in New York City, the bombing of the Murrah Federal Office Building in Oklahoma City, and the Aum Shinrikyo sarin gas attack in Tokyo, anxiety increased about terrorists acquiring and using unconventional weapons. Soon after senior national security officials openly spoke about WMD, terrorism increased and became a major concern.[49]

The perceived belief that Iraq had WMD was the principle reason for the United States going to war in Iraq. However, in June 2003, the Senate Select Committee on Intelligence began a formal review of U.S. intelligence about the existence of Iraq's WMD programs and Saddam Hussein's actual use of WMD against his own people. In its review, the committee found the perceptions of WMD in Iraq to be faulty. They concluded, "Most of the major key judgments in the Intelligence Community's October 2002 National Intelligence Estimate, Iraq's Continuing Programs for Weapons of Mass Destruction, either overstated, or were not supported by, the underlying intelligence reporting."[50]

SUICIDE ATTACKS IN CONFLICTS

Modern suicide offensive attacks have existed since the war between Israel and the Hezbollah in Lebanon. The Hezbollah first used suicide bombing on April 18, 1983. They attacked the U.S. embassy in Beirut with a car bomb, killing 63 people, 17 were American citizens. Shortly thereafter on October 23, 1983, the Hezbollah attacked U.S. Marine Barracks with a truck bomb, killing 241 American military personnel stationed in Beirut as part of a peacekeeping force. A separate attack against the French military compound in Beirut killed 58.[51]

After the Hezbollah engaged in suicide bombing, other groups adopted the tactic beginning on July 5, 1987 with the Sri Lankan LTTE. The suicide attack killed 40 Sri Lankan troops at the Nelliyady army camp in the northern Sri Lanka.[52] From 1994 to 1996, the Palestinian Islamist group, Hamas, initiated a series of bombings on Israeli civilian busses to discourage the success of the Israel and Palestine peace process.[53] The Kurdistan Workers Party (or Partiya Karkeren Kurdistan) used it in Turkey on June 30, 1996. A young woman who was a Kurdish rebel disguised herself as a pregnant woman, and blew herself up in the middle of a military ceremony. She killed 9 soldiers.[54]

Evidence links al Qaeda to the February 26, 1993 World Trade Center in New York bombing. Six people were killed and over 1000 injured by a 500-kg bomb planted in the underground parking garage. Al Qaeda began planning the 1998 bombings of the U.S. embassies in Kenya and Tanzania and other attacks.[55] The al Qaeda suicide terror attack against the United States on September 11, 2001 hurled suicide bombing into a global threat with the potential for spreading to other parts of the world.[56] The 9/11 attack involved the hijacking of four planes: two crashed into the World Trade Center, one into the Pentagon, and one into the Pennsylvania countryside. Over 2,800 people were killed.[57]

Religious and secular Palestinian terrorist groups employed suicide bombing extensively in the second Palestinian intifada (uprising) that began in 2000. On June 2 and 3, 2000, the Chechen rebels conducted 5 suicide bomb attacks on police stations and Russian army bases in Chechnya, killing at least 54 people.[58] Whichever the group, Philip E. Kapusta noted the tactical advantages of the use of suicide bombers: "increased tactical flexibility and effectiveness, streamlined operational planning, less likelihood of intelligence leaks, expanded target sets, limited vulnerability, and increased publicity and psychological impact on the target population."[59]

Scope

The National Counterterrorism Center (NCTC) provides the Department of State with required statistical information to assist in its reporting requirements. They reported that most attacks in 2009 applied conventional methods such as armed attacks, bombings, and kidnappings. Sunni extremists used suicide militia style attacks in numerous large-scale attacks. Terrorists continued coordinated attacks that included secondary attacks on first responders at attack sites. They also continued to reconfigure weapons and other materials to create IEDs. They employed women and children to elude security countermeasures.[60]

In the center's 2010 report, suicide attacks decreased from 405 in 2008 to 299 in 2009. The reduction was attributed to declining violence in Iraq. A total of 13 countries experienced suicide attacks with Afghanistan having the highest number, 99, followed by Pakistan with 84, and Iraq with 82. For Afghanistan, the 2010 findings of the NCTC vary some from U.N. Assistance Mission in Afghanistan's (UNAMA's) for 2010, The number of IED attacks that occurred in Afghanistan was 1,129 compared to UNAMA's finding 940. Incidents of suicide attacks totaled 264 compared to 495. Civilians, military, and political were the category of victims that were frequently targeted.[61]

In their 2009 report, the NCTC provided the State Department with the following information related to suicide attacks:

- Attacks in Iraq, Afghanistan, and Pakistan accounted for about 60 percent of all terrorist attacks.
- Al Qaeda in Iraq used dual suicide bombers to target the residence of an antiterrorism police official and first responders and onlookers, killing 12 police officers, 24 civilians, and wounding 83 civilians and children.
- Attacks by female suicide bombers declined significantly from 2008, accounting for only 7 of the 299 total suicide attacks. Three of these attacks occurred in Iraq, two in Sri Lanka, and two in Russia.
- In Thailand, Muslim separatists used a woman and child to park VBIEDs in an effort to avoid suspicion and security procedures.[62]

The NCTC's tracking system revealed that of the number of terrorist incidents in 2011 when grouped by weapon, the most attacks were from the IED (277), followed by explosives (168) and the vehicle bomb (136). Respectively, these three attacks killed 2,670, 1,694, and 1,453; and wounded 6,793, 3,828, and 3,965. Included in the total victims results are the additional figures representing those individuals taken hostage. The total number of victims as a result from IEDs was 9,519, from explosives 5,578, and from vehicle bombs 5,461 (see Table 2.1).[63]

Table 2.1
Terrorist Attacks by Weapon, Worldwide, 2011.

Weapon	Attacks	Killed	Wounded	Hostage	Victims
Explosive	168	1,694	3,828	56	5,578
Firearm	38	518	874	56	1,448
Firebomb/incendiary	1	4	20	0	24
Grenade	4	111	208	40	359
Improvised explosive device	277	2,670	6,793	56	9,519
Missile/rocket	3	16	36	0	52
Mortar/artillery	2	65	109	40	214
Other	1	65	100	40	205
Rocket-propelled grenade	9	90	208	0	298
Vehicle bomb	136	1,453	3,965	43	5,461
Total	639	6,686	16,141	331	23,158

Source: NCTC, http://nctc.gov/.

Target selection includes research conducted through the use of the Internet followed by a preoperational surveillance of targets to determine their vulnerability and appeal, according to Stratfor, Global Intelligence. Terrorists generally, but not exclusively, attack soft targets or places that have symbolic value rather than hard targets or military targets, like supply lines. The reasons for this approach are that they attract more media attention, generate more casualties, and terrorists usually do not have arms to compete militarily.[64] In Afghanistan, Pakistan, and Iraq, insurgents frequently targeted the military. On May 13, 2011, a double Taliban suicide attack in Shabqadar near Peshawar, Pakistan, killed 66 paramilitary police recruits and wounded about 120 people. The Taliban said it was avenging the May 2, 2011, death of bin Laden.[65] The following examples that occurred in Iraq 2007 are three among many listed on the *Iraq Pipeline Watch*:

395. February 19—Iraqi insurgents deployed a suicide bomber in a road tanker north of Baghdad.

396. February 20—Six people were killed and 105 injured after a suicide IED detonated his device in a fuel tanker in the town of At Taji, north of Baghdad.

397. February 23—A VBIED incorporated into a road fuel tanker exploded in a market in the town of Buhayrat al Habbaniyah in the province of Anba. The explosion killed 40 people and injured 64.[66]

When targets are determined to be vulnerable and would further terrorist goals, the next phase, intelligence collection, begins, according to Homeland Security.

The Attack

Planning: Intelligence Gathering

Logistical planning is highly secretive and carefully done. Once the decision has been made to launch an attack, the organization gathers intelligence, assembles bomb material, and organizes the departure for the attack target selected, reported Assaf Moghadam.[67] Intelligence gathering can occur quickly or it can take a period of years, according to the U.S. Department of Homeland Security. The department stated, "There is no universal model for terrorist planning but experience and success have demonstrated traditional principles for plans and operations. Terrorist organizations exchange personnel and training and study methods and operational successes of other groups. Innovation is a proven key component of operational success."[68]

Gathering intelligence involves observing the selected facility's practices, procedures, and routines; the physical layout and activities at the target's residence and workplace; transportation and routes of travel for the individual and for the facility; and security measures around the target.[69]

Good quality intelligence and reconnaissance of the target is one of the most important factors in the success of suicide attacks, according to the *DCSINT Handbook*.[70] High priority is given to targets that show the most vulnerability. Before Congress, Bruce Hoffman testified that planning takes time. Planning for the August 7, 1998 attack on the U.S. Embassy in Nairobi took nearly five years. Twenty-seven months of planning preceded the October 12, 2000 attack on the USS *Cole*.[71]

Procurement of Parts and the Making of Devices

The methods for procuring weapons depend on the organization. Moghadam pointed out that in 2003, Egypt smuggled by sea or underground tunnels into the Gaza Strip most of the explosive materials that were used in suicide bombings in Israel. In 2002, Iran was believed to have supplied weapons to the Palestinians when Israel seized the ship *Karine-A* and discovered 1.5 tons of explosives.

Explosive devices are not always purchased, but are obtained in other ways. In 2005, the Congressional Research Service reported that, in Iraq, munitions for constructing IEDs may have come from a large supply of unused Iraqi military armaments that was collected and stockpiled in secret locations. In April 2003, Iraqi looters forcefully attacked the Al Qaqaa military weapons site south of Baghdad and reportedly took nearly 400 tons of powerful conventional explosives that after Iraqi forces had abandoned and was left unsecured by U.S. forces. It is not known when the munitions may have vanished from the site. There is some question whether Iraqi forces may have removed and relocated some explosives prior to the U.S. invasion.[72]

IEDs commonly used in suicide attacks include briefcase or backpack, package or object carried, vest or belt worn, handheld bomb or grenade, and car bombs loaded with 500 pounds of ammonium nitrate.[73] The disadvantage of a briefcase or backpack is that it can be seen and is carried in plain sight. Vests can be detected upon search, but are difficult to remove. The handheld explosive allows easy movement in a crowd. Most bombs can be detonated at will if events transpire that would act to prevent the attack.

VBIEDs have been used extensively. The attacks of 9/11 demonstrated the suicide terrorists' use of aircraft.[74] On August 24, 2004, two Black Widows of the Chechen rebels, Nagayeva and Satsia Dzhebirkhanova, blew up two Russian passenger planes killing 89 people.[75] Although several separate groups have included naval vessels as VBIEDs, the *DCSINT* stated that the most well known is the al Qaeda attack on October 12, 2000, on the USS *Cole* in the Yemen port of Aden, which killed 17 American sailors.[76]

Specific Target Selection

Choosing a target for actual operational planning includes the following: "does success affect a larger audience than the immediate victim(s), will the target attract high profile media attention, does success make the desired statement to the correct target audience(s), is the effect consistent with objectives of the group, does the target provide an advantage to the group by demonstrating its capabilities, what are the costs versus benefits of conducting the operation."[77] The U.S. Department of Home Security noted that, if a decision is made to continue, ongoing intelligence collection against the target takes place. If targets are not immediately selected, the collection of information may continue for future occasions with that target.

Pre-attack Surveillance and Planning

The attack information gathered focuses on the target's current patterns within days or weeks of the planned attack. Greater emphasis is placed on known or perceived vulnerabilities. The type of surveillance used depends on the target's activities. The information is used to conduct security studies and detailed preparatory operations; recruit specialized operatives; acquire a base of operations in the target area, such as safe houses and caches; design and test escape routes; and decide on type of weapon or attack.[78]

Rehearsal

The advantages of rehearsals are that they increase the chances of success, confirm planning assumptions, develop contingencies, and test security reactions.[79] The LTTE suicide attackers were trained in a separate camp, but the Tigers and Tigresses conducted full-dress rehearsals near their target.[80] Al Qaeda used one bombing as a dress rehearsal for another. Al Qaeda and Kashmiri terrorist groups, Lashkar-e-Taiba and Jaish-e-Muhammad, had developed close ties. Some liaisons predated 9/11. In late 1999, bin Laden, Taliban forces, and Pakistani intelligence agents were closely implicated in the Kashmiri terrorists' hijacking of an Indian airliner. The Indian Foreign Minister at the time, Jaswant Singh, has since described this operation as the "dress rehearsal" for 9/11.[81]

Homeland Security reported that rehearsals include "equipment and weapons training and performance, staging for final preparatory checks, deployment into target area, actions on the objective, escape routes." In addition, tests in the target area are needed to confirm "target information gathered to date, target pattern of activities, physical layout of target or operations area, and security force reactions such as state of alert, timing response, equipment and routes."[82]

Movement or Deployment to Target

The U.S. Department of the Army stated that the two main methods of employing devices are by person or vehicle. "A person-borne suicide bomb usually has a high-explosive and fragmentary effect and uses a command-detonated firing system such as a switch or button the wearer activates by hand. A vest, belt, or other specially modified clothing can conceal explosives with fragmentation. . . . A vehicle-borne suicide bomb uses the same methods and characteristics of other package or vehicle bombs, and is usually command detonated."[83] IEDs in Iraq caused about half of all the American combat casualties, including those service members killed in action and wounded. Two-thirds of vehicular borne explosives were detonated by suicide bombers.[84]

The *DCSINT* of the U.S. Department of Defense explained that there are many uses of VBIEDs. These devices can be employed without resulting in the death of the attacker. The army makes the distinction that the terrorist attack can succeed whether the attacker kills himself or herself or survives (see Chapter 1). The Muslim extremists attack in 1993 on the World Trade Center used an estimated 1,200 pounds (544 kg) of explosives. The explosives were put together and transported in a late-model Ford F-350 Econoline van rented from Ryder Truck Rental. On April 19, 1995, when Timothy McVeigh bombed the Alfred P. Murrah Federal Building in Oklahoma City, the bomb consisted of about 4,000 pounds of nitrate mixed with fuel and was carried in a standard moving truck.[85] McVeigh was not in the truck when the bomb exploded and killed 168 people. McVeigh was captured within hours of the attack. He was tried and sentenced to death and was executed on June 10, 2001.[86]

Assaf Moghadam found that the Palestinian suicide bomber was sometimes disguised as a religious Jew, an Israeli soldier, or a tourist. The attacker had little trouble crossing from the West Bank into Israel, but had more difficulty in crossing the border from the Gaza Strip to Israel.[87]

Members of the operational team normally provide the attacker with required accommodations, transportation, food, clothing, and security until he or she reaches the target.[88]

Detonation of Device: Execution of the Attack

Triggering methods for IEDs include a cell phone, a garage door opener, a child's remote-control toy, running over a rubber hose to produce enough air pressure to activate a switch for a mine, or manual triggering by concealed insurgent.[89]

The methods of insurgents to design and deploy IEDs include the following according to the Congressional Research Report:

- Coupling—It is a method of linking one mine or explosive device to another, usually with detonating cord. This technique is often used to defeat countermeasure equipment. A heavy mine roller will pass over the initial, unfused device and set off the second fused device. This in turn detonates the over passed device underneath the clearing vehicle.

- Boosting—Buried mines or other explosive devices are stacked on top of one another. The topmost explosives are nonmetal, and only the device buried deepest from the surface is fused. This reduces the probability of detection, and it increases the force of the blast.

- Daisy chaining—IEDs may be linked together along a roadway with trip wire or detonating cord. When the initial mine is detonated, the other mines are also detonated.

- Shaped charges—A cylindrical container is closed off at one end, packed with explosive, and capped by a conical piece of metal that becomes a molten projectile when the device is detonated. The shaped charge concentrates blast energy to punch through armor plating and then propels the molten metal into the vehicle's cabin.[90]

The *DCSINT Handbook* listed common applications of suicide VBIEDs, which include the use of a broken down car or truck parked along the route the intended victims use. The suicide bomber appears to be fixing a tire, or repairing an engine problem. The VBEID is detonated as the target comes into range; single-suicide VBEID against a target point such as a check point or multi-suicide VBEID against a complex or facility where one breaches security and the other detonates the explosive; and finally, the supported suicide VBIED versus a convoy makes use of another vehicle to provide reconnaissance as to the best target or control the speed of the convoy to allow for the VBIED to approach the target.[91]

Other methods have been used to detonate a device. The Chechen rebels' September 2004 attack on Beslan School No. 1 in Beslan, North Ossetia, a southern Russian Republic, employed female suicide bombers who openly disagreed with their leader, the colonel, about the children hostages. The women were killed when he detonated their bombs by remote control.[92] Likewise, a suicide bomb in Russia's Domodedovo Airport was remotely triggered by a cell phone. Authorities discovered melted circuit boards that implied a cell phone was embedded with the bomb. Remote control allows handlers to detonate the explosive device if attackers change their mind or become incapacitated.[93] In fact, the army warns of complications in attempting to apprehend a suspected suicide bomber:

- A pressure release switch can detonate the device as soon as the bomber is shot.
- A device could be operated by remote control or timer even after the bomber is incapacitated.
- Another person observes and gives a command that detonates the bomb.
- A second suicide bomber might be operating as a backup or to attack the crowd and assistance forces that normally gather after a detonation.[94]

Escape

In suicide attacks, support personnel and handlers require escape or evasion from attack responders.[95]

Exploitation

Publicity will achieve an intended effect. Prepared statements timed to media cycles and targeted audiences help exploit a successful operation. If the attack was unsuccessful, it is denied.[96]

Conflicts

The War in Afghanistan

The UNAMA found that the occurrence of suicide attacks in Afghanistan is relatively new. Until the assassination of Ahmad Shah Massoud on September 9, 2001, suicide attacks were considered alien. They began occurring in 2005 and 2006, but at first Afghans rejected the idea that Afghans themselves might be involved.[97] According to the NCTC, in 2009, the country with highest number of suicide bombings was Afghanistan with 99, followed by Pakistan with 84, and Iraq with 82.[98] In 2007, Monica Czwarno and Ana Marte acknowledged, "One of the most notable developments in Afghanistan over the past two years has been the dramatic increase in the use of suicide bombings as a strategic and tactical tool by the Taliban and al-Qaida."[99] A change in Afghan attitude is reflected in empirical data as well as the havoc and bloodshed the insurgents have caused. Two ways to measure insurgent destruction are by the number of attacks and their results and by the number of civilian casualties.

Attacks

In Afghanistan, the number of suicide attacks dramatically increased when U.S. forces began to expand their presence to the south and east of the country in 2006, Robert Pape reported. Twelve suicide attacks had occurred from 2001 to 2005 in Afghanistan when the United States had a relatively limited troop presence of a few thousand troops primarily in Kabul. By the end of 2001, troops numbered 2,500. The following two years, force levels remained about 10,000 and in 2004, rose to 17,000. Since 2006, over 450 suicide attacks have occurred and they are becoming more deadly. Troop levels averaged approximately 22,000 for most of 2006 and 2007, and continued to rise. Pape found that deaths from suicide attacks increased by a third in the year since President Barack Obama added 30,000 more U.S. troops in December 2009.[100] In addition, the Department of Defense released data that demonstrated that "insurgents in Afghanistan have answered the Obama administration's troop surge with a surge of their own, planting thousands of roadside bombs that caused more U.S. troop casualties last year than the prior eight years of the war."[101] In 2010, the bombs wounded 3,366 U.S. troops, or nearly 60 percent of the total IED-wounded since the war's start in late 2001. In 9 years of war, IEDs accounted for the death of 617 American troops with the majority of those deaths occurring in 2009 and 2010. In 2010, IEDs killed 268 troops accounting for more than 40 percent of all deaths caused by bombs during the war.

Civilian Casualties

A second method of measuring insurgent destruction is by the number of civilian casualties. In the first six months of 2010 compared with the same period in 2009, the UNAMA said that tactics of the Taliban and other antigovernment elements were responsible for a 31-percent increase in conflict-related Afghan civilian casualties. In addition to an intensified pattern of assassinations and executions, UNAMA reported other statistics related to insurgency caused deaths: "Improvised explosive devices (IEDs) and suicide attacks killed 557 Afghans and injured 1,137 in the first six months of 2010. IEDs alone accounted for 29 per cent of all civilian deaths in the period, including 74 children, a 155 per cent increase in IED-related deaths of children in the same span in 2009."[102] According to their report, the civilians assassinated and executed included teachers, nurses, doctors, tribal elders, community leaders, provincial and district officials, other civilians including children, and civilians working for international military forces and international organizations.

In 2011, UNAMA reported, "the tactics of Anti-Government Elements subjected Afghan civilians to death and injury with increasingly lethal results in 2011."[103] In 2011, the single greatest number of deaths was caused by IEDs that killed 967 civilians. Targeted killings caused 495 and suicide attacks caused 431. The number of civilian deaths from suicide attacks increased significantly in 2011. While the Taliban improved its messaging on protection of civilians in 2011, UNAMA confirmed that the Taliban continued to directly target civilians and use indiscriminate weapons (see Table 2.2).

Table 2.2
Afghanistan, Anti-Government Elements Deaths by Tactic, 2009–2011.

Year	Improvised Explosive Device (IED) No. (Percent)	Targeted Killing No. (Percent)	Suicide Attack No. (Percent)	All Tactics No. (Percent)
2009	796 (40.1)	220 (11.1)	967 (48.8)	1,983 (100)
2010	940 (49.1)	482 (25.1)	495 (25.8)	1,917 (100)
2011	967 (35.8)	495 (41.3)	431 (22.9)	1,893 (100)
Total	2,703 (NA)	1,197 (NA)	1,893 (NA)	5,793 (100)

Source: UN Assistance Mission in Afghanistan (UNAMA), *Afghanistan Annual Report 2011 Protection of Civilians in Armed Conflict*, February 2012, 3–4, 11 http://unama.unmissions. org/Portals/UNAMA/Documents/UNAMA%20POC%202011%20Report_Final_Feb%20 2012.pdf.

The Strategic Role of Suicide Bombing in Afghanistan

Suicide bombings in Afghanistan have served a number of strategic goals, according to Czwarno and Marte. First, the bombings underscored the inability of the Karzai government and the international coalition and security forces to guarantee the safety and security of the people. This inability led the people to believe that the international forces should withdraw. Rather than withdraw, the NATO forces changed strategies and tactics and began a counterinsurgency that affected their public diplomacy initiatives. One change was the use of more heavily armored vehicles to withstand suicide attacks. The heavier vehicles created a barrier between the forces and the civilian population. "Suicide bombing levels the playing field between a conventional militarily superior force and insurgent fighters,"[104] wrote Czwarno and Marte.

Suicide Attacks in the Iraq War

The Iraq Insurgency

On March 19, 2003, President George W. Bush announced that the military operations to disarm Iraq had begun. The reason Bush gave for starting the war was that Iraq threatened "the peace with weapons of mass murder."[105] The U.S. combat role in the war continued for seven years, until on August 31, 2010, President Barack Obama ended U.S. combat operations in Iraq.[106]

Groups

The Iraq insurgency consisted primarily of Sunni Muslims, but its membership represents diverse backgrounds including al Qaeda. According to *BBC*, Sunni groups targeted coalition forces and anyone working together with the United States in the rebuilding of Iraq. They have also waged attacks on Shia targets. These attacks include those associated with the Shia-dominated Iraqi government and civilian targets, including Shia shrines and festivals. In addition to the Sunni nationalists, the insurgency included al Qaeda in Iraq, Mujahideen Shura Council, and Ansar al-Islam. Shia militias included Mehdi Army and Badr Brigade. All groups have the common goal of attacking U.S. forces, but the other goals vary. Some formed militias in defense. Civil war was also a part of the insurgency.[107]

Al Qaeda in Iraq remains relevant since the coalition withdrawal from Iraq in 2009, stated the NCTC. High profile attacks in 2009 and 2010 demonstrate the group's significance and efforts to take advantage of the changes in the security. In addition, on August 15, 2011, they conducted attacks across 17 cities, killing more than 80 people and injuring hundreds. Al Qaeda in Iraq publicly eulogized Osama bin Laden after his death in May 2011 and reaffirmed their support for al Qaeda and Ayman al-Zawahiri.[108]

Attacks and Casualties

As in Afghanistan, insurgents in Iraq have caused havoc and bloodshed. Their destruction can be estimated by the number of attacks and their results and by the number of civilian casualties (see Table 2.3). Suicide attacks totaling 1,068 caused 12,885 deaths, according to Iraq Body Count. The highest numbers of both appear from 2005 to 2008, with 2007 being the highest with 275 suicide attacks causing 3,860 deaths.

The military began in June 2003 compiling figures on casualties resulting from insurgents according to the *New York Times*. A Defense Department 2006 bar graph indicated insurgents killed or wounded 26 Iraqi civilians and security forces a day in early 2004, and about 40 a day later that year. The number grew in 2005 to about 51 a day, and at the end of August to about 63 a day. From January 1, 2004 to September 16, 2005, the number killed was 25,902. No figures were provided for the number of Iraqis killed by American-led forces.[109] Hamit Dardagan compiled statistics for Iraq Body Count, a private British-based group that has tracked the number of Iraqi civilians killed since the war began. He reported

Table 2.3
Iraq, Number of Suicide Attacks and Recorded Deaths, 2003–2011.

Year[a]	Attacks	Killed
2003	13	116
2004	61	923
2005	232	2,294
2006	151	1,642
2007	274	3,860
2008	170	1,644
2009	65	1,094
2010	51	742
2011	51	570
Total	1,068	12,885

[a]All years begin with the month of January.

Note: Datasets filtered for any perpetrators in Iraq of suicide attack, killing one or more.

Source: Iraq Body Count, "Iraqi Deaths from Violence 2003–2011: Analysis and Overview," first published January 2, 2012, http://www.iraqbodycount.org/analysis/numbers/2011.

that "2010 averaged nearly two explosions a day by non-state forces that caused civilian deaths (685 explosions killing 2,649). As well as occurring almost daily, these lethal explosions can happen almost anywhere, with 2010's attacks occurring in 13 of Iraq's 18 governorates (administrative regions). Such non-state bombings were responsible for 66% of all Iraqi civilian deaths in 2010."[110]

The Iraq Body Count's 2009 violence profile indicates that anti-occupation activity continued to play a central part in the deaths of Iraqi civilians especially of police (1,193 or 25.5%) or government-allied targets. Weapon trends indicated that magnetic car bombs had changed from a rare to a common form of assassination (48 killed in 2008 and 186 killed in 2009). Summary executions, often involving torture, fell significantly from 2,227 in 2008 to 152 in 2009. The WikiLeaks logs add another 15,000 civilian deaths to the original statistics of Iraq Body Count.[111]

Between 2004 and 2009, *ABC* reported, the WikiLeaks documents totaled "109,032 deaths in Iraq, comprised of 66,081 'civilians'; 23,984 'enemy' (those labeled as insurgents); 15,196 'host nation' (Iraqi government forces) and 3,771 'friendly' (coalition forces). In a statement regarding the documents' release WikiLeaks confirmed, 'The majority of the deaths (66,000, over 60 percent) of these are civilian deaths. That is 31 civilians dying every day during the six-year period.'"[112] Iraq Body Count found 15,000 previously unreported deaths from WikiLeaks documents, which would raise its total from as many as 107,369 civilians to more than 122,000 civilians.[113]

Although airstrikes composed the majority of explosive deaths (64%) from 2003 to 2005, Iraq Body Count found suicide attacks accounted for 900 or 4.3 percent of civilian deaths and 3.4 percent accounted for nonsuicide attacks such as vehicle bombs or car bombs. Driver-controlled suicide vehicle bombs alone were usually car bombs, but some were other vehicles. In September 2004, a single 659-kilo bomb accounted for the majority of child deaths and increased the number of deaths from 9 to 19 percent. Except for this incident, drivers most often steered into their intended adult targets. Suicide attacks not vehicle-borne produced a lowered proportion of child casualties. Of 181 deaths resulting from these attacks, 162 were adults and 19 were children (10.5%).[114]

SUICIDE BOMBING OPERATIONAL PROCESS

One way to view the operational cycle for suicide bombing attacks is as a nine-phase process, according to *The Police Chief.* The cycle begins with identification and recruitment of bombers; proceeds with their training, target selection, purchase of needed parts, making of devices, final preparation, and movement to the target; and ends with the detonation of the device.[115] A suicide terrorist is usually the last link in a long organizational chain that includes many individuals. Merle Miyasato outlined six similar operations in the execution of an attack: target selection, intelligence gathering, recruitment, physical and spiritual training, preparation of explosives, and transportation of the suicide bombers to the target area.[116]

Identification

How a would-be warrior makes the transition from self-radicalization, or wanting to be a terrorist, to actually being one is that the drive to be a jihadist is as much internal as it is external, according to Brian Michael Jenkins. He stated, "There is no easily identifiable terrorist-prone personality, no single path to radicalization and terrorism."[117] Some self-radicalized jihadists become terrorists, but some do not. For those self-radicalized that do not find they have the will to become a terrorist, it may depend upon whom and whether they meet, along the way, a more determined zealot. Sometimes, becoming a terrorist is more happenstance.

Recruitment

Recruitment involves child bombers and women attackers who must be indoctrinated and trained. Paul Wood reported, "By one count there are more than 150 would-be suicide bombers between 13–17 years of age who have been intercepted by the Afghan security forces."[118] Female suicide bombers, like child bombers, can sometimes go undetected or evade the inspection and body searches of male security personnel and can therefore, complete their bombing mission more easily.[119] The tactic of using female bombers represents the evolution of weaponry.

Conventional wisdom has begun to give way to the fact that individuals willing to give their life for a cause are entirely normal (not psychotic), nationalistic, and, before 2000, religious, according to Mario Ferrero. She found that, in the case of Palestinian volunteers, recruiting organizations systematically screen out recruits who are psychotic as not dependable.[120] There is no one profile of a suicide attacker. Marta Sparago maintained that instead of assuming all terrorists are different and thus cannot be profiled, researchers should examine the groups themselves to see who is being recruited and why. Different groups possibly place different values on who is an ideal recruit. To one group, a recruit may be an asset. To another, a recruit may be a liability.[121]

When I asked Marie Breen-Smyth, School of Politics, University of Surrey, is there a general analysis that can be applied to all situations in which suicide warfare occurs, she said,

I don't think so. There are commonalities, probably, but as soon as you say that, up comes an exception. I really do favor analyzing things contextually. Without the context, it is really difficult to be sure that you are on the right track. While I do think there are commonalities, I also think people were very happy to say they are religious fanatics. And then, of course, somebody says, what about the Tamil Tigers, they were not religiously motivated. And people will say they are brainwashed. Then you find that that's not the case. It's very hard to make a general sweeping rule. Robert Pape talks about altruistic suicide using Erving Goffman's typology. He is saying basically that the way to understand it is to see it as an act on behalf of our people, our cause. And so, it is a self sacrificing act on behalf of the others. So, you can see that in some cases, but my guess is that that's not always the case. For example, it is not inconceivable that some people might have intellectual incapacity and not understand what they are letting themselves in for to keep them from doing it. Certainly, there are people that I know who have been forced to drive cars with bombs in them. They were forced at gunpoint and then there is a timer and it stopped and they can't get either of them. So, people have been forced to do it as well. So it is quite hard to generalize and be sure that you've covered all bases.[122]

It is important to learn why an individual would join a group in order to explain why that individual would carry out an attack, Breen-Smyth explained,

Once a person is in the group, then there is the process of socialization that goes on in all armed groups including state armies where people are trained to follow orders and do what they are told and unquestioned by and large. That's the kind of military discipline part that involves ideology, involves indoctrination with certain kinds of ideas, but it also involves an automatic following of orders with an unquestioning attitude about authority. Once you get from the underground groups, then the tactics of the group become enacted by the individuals in the group as a result of their inculcation into that kind of military command structure. For me, it's a mistake to ask the question why does this individual carry out a suicide attack, because you're missing out, it seems to me, one very important stage of questions which are to do with why would that individual join that armed group. And once you arrive at these reasons, it becomes much easier to explain why they carry out suicide attacks.[123]

Indoctrination and Training

Organizations use death as a source of legitimization to condition recruits. Julian Madsen explained, "The message is one of no going back. The group glorifies the act, infusing a culture of martyrdom that may include posters, songs, and flyers, and in doing so seeks to inspire others to join its ranks. Indeed, even before the bomber has struck, he is in many ways a living martyr."[124] Philip E. Kapusta found that framing suicide bombers as martyrs produces the required link between the organization making the strategic decision to employ suicide attackers and the recruits who must volunteer for and carry out the missions.

The Relationship of Military Presence and Suicide Campaigns

Robert Pape, a University of Chicago political science professor, said, "We have lots of evidence now that when you put the foreign military presence in, it triggers suicide terrorism campaigns, . . . and that when the foreign forces leave, it takes away almost 100% of the terrorist campaign."[125] Pape drew on a six-year study of suicide terrorist attacks around the world. The study begins with the first suicide terrorism attack of modern times, the 1983 truck bombing of the U.S. Marine Barracks in Beirut, Lebanon. The bomb killed 241 U.S. Marines.

More jihad activity is to be expected with the direct American military involvement in Iraq, Afghanistan, and Pakistan and the growing indirect involvement in Somalia and Yemen, maintains Brian Michael Jenkins. In analyzing wars and suicide attacks, Jenkins states,

There are no frontiers, no front lines, no home fronts. The battlefield is everywhere. There is no distinction between combatants and bystanders. It is also important to remember that these individuals believe that the entire Islamic community is the target of aggression by the United States, Israel, and other infidel powers. Armed defense, according to this view, is a necessary and personal duty. For some, the jihadist narrative can be compelling.[126]

The Attacks Continue

Suicide attacks continue in Somalia, Nigeria, Afghanistan, and Iraq, among others. It is an ongoing, viable weapon for groups engaged in today's asymmetrical warfare.

CHAPTER 3

Suicide Warfare and Policies of War

The policies that guide the conduct of a war reflect the conditions under which the war is fought. Policies change when the way war is waged changes. In the time when wars were fought by armies confronting each other on an open battlefield, the policies committed the combatants to wage war with honor. In the contemporary world, war is most often waged asymmetrically and often includes suicide warfare. The just war policy reflects the changed nature of war.

U.S. war policies have evolved from President George Washington's rules for waging battle with honor through President Barrack Obama's just war approach. The U.S. policy on war is based in the U.S. Constitution.

U.S. FOREIGN POLICY AND THE JUSTIFICATION FOR WAR

The U.S. Constitution grants powers to the president to use military force. Article II, Section 2 states, the

President shall be Commander in Chief of the Army and Navy of the United States, and of the Militia of the several States, when called into the actual Service of the United States.[1]

The constitution gives the president the right of the executive power and the duty to execute the laws,[2] but gives Congress alone the power to declare war.[3] The president as commander in chief of all U.S. armed forces has the authority to respond to imminent threats.[4]

History of U.S. War Policy

War with Honor

President George Washington (April 30, 1789–March 4, 1797) believed in waging war with honor. His rules of battle were don't assume you are welcome, cultivate local support, respect local religious practices, don't abuse prisoners, and withdraw if your objectives are unobtainable. Law and policy that we have today reflect these rules. Washington explained that the "cultivate local support" rule means "convincing them that we come, at the Request of many of their Principal People, not as Robbers or to make War upon them; but as the Friends and Supporters of their Liberties, as well as ours."[5] Today's Geneva Conventions provide a comparison to Washington's respect local religious practices rule. The conventions prohibit "indiscriminate attacks against those the law and professional Soldiers are sworn to protect—the innocents or those who are hors de combat,"[6] or out of combat.[7] A person hors de combat is

- anyone who is in the power of an adverse party;
- anyone who is defenseless because of unconsciousness, shipwreck, wounds, or sickness; or
- anyone who clearly expresses an intention to surrender, provided he or she abstains from any hostile act and does not attempt to escape.[8]

In addition to his rules, Washington held the belief that a foreign power could turn against America. In his farewell address, he warned against foreign entanglements: "Against the insidious wiles of foreign influence (I conjure you to believe me . . .)."[9]

President James Monroe (March 4, 1817–March 4, 1825) established the right to go into another state's territory to avert terrorist attacks when the host is unable or unwilling to protect citizens.[10] Preemption has a long tradition in American history, according to Melvyn P. Leffler. In 1904, President Theodore Roosevelt (1901–1909) followed up the Monroe Doctrine with a new corollary: "the right of the United States to intervene militarily in the western hemisphere to preserve order."[11] Leffler labeled this intervention, preemptive imperialism. Its purpose was to prevent potential European interventions and protect the national security of the United States. The United States intervened frequently in Cuba beginning in 1898, the Dominican Republic (1916–1924), Nicaragua (1912–1933), and Haiti (1915–1934).

Even before President George W. Bush (2001–2009) authorized the preemptive strike in Iraq on March 20, 2003, Deputy Secretary of Defense Paul Wolfowitz in September 2002 told a joint congressional committee, "This is not a game we will ever win on defense. We'll only win it on offense," Leffler reported.[12] Mary Ellen O'Connell's conclusions on preemptive strike are thought provoking and offer a legal point of view:

The Security Council action after September 11 [2001] can be cited to support anticipatory self-defense in cases where an armed attack has occurred and convincing evidence exists that more attacks are planned, though not yet underway.[13] By contrast, international law continues to prohibit preemptive self-defense or even anticipatory self-defense,[14] if that is understood to be different from responding to incipient attacks or ongoing campaigns. In other words, a state may not take military action against another state when an attack is only a hypothetical possibility, and not yet in progress—even in the case of weapons of mass destruction.[15]

In America, preemptive strike policy is not new.

Martin Van Buren (March 4, 1837–March 4, 1841) established the standard for justifiable anticipatory self-defense during the Canadian insurrection of 1837. When confronted with military threats, the commander in chief could legally exercise the standard. James A. Green explained that the correspondence between the United Kingdom and the United States in relation to the dispute over the sinking of an American ship, the *Caroline*, by British forces in 1837 provides the basis for international law concerning self-defense and represents the position of the customary limitations on self-defense actions today. The events post-9/11 have called the traditional view into question. Green stated, "States have found themselves faced with the unenviable problem of finding a balance between the need to adequately secure themselves against this threat and the imperative to ensure that any action taken in combating terrorist activities conforms to the principles of international law."[16] The use of force in Afghanistan (2001) and Iraq (2003) demonstrates the great difficulty in finding a balance. Green concluded that one lawful way to respond to international terrorism in some situations is to resort to the inherent right of self-defense as the United States did in Operation Enduring Freedom in Afghanistan.

Woodrow Wilson (March 4, 1913–March 4, 1921) and Franklin D. Roosevelt (March 4, 1933–April 12, 1945) made concerted efforts to stay out of the European War and supported isolationist policy, but both were drawn into major wars. Before 1914, the tradition of isolationism had been the cornerstone of American foreign policy.[17] Jonathan Zasloff believed that the foreign policy of that time "embodies the greatest disaster in American diplomatic history."[18] Traditional American isolationism reflected the viewpoint that the clearest option was to refrain from active U.S. involvement in global politics. Isolationists believed that, because the United States was protected by two oceans, the country easily could afford not to involve itself in world politics. During the 1920s, or the New Era, American leaders maintained that they did not accept isolationism. They preferred extensive engagement with Europe and the remainder of the world.

By the end of World War II (1939–1945), President Roosevelt had led the United States into an internationalist role. The desire of Americans for U.S. neutrality dropped when Hitler invaded Poland in 1939, and the desire for neutrality fell to the lowest point when the Japanese navy attacked the U.S. fleet at Pearl Harbor in 1941. The American public previously believed that "only neutrality would keep the United States clear of foreign entan-glements."[19] Aaron Xavier Fellmeth explained that internationalists lob-bied their points of view including aid to countries fighting fascists and dictators. During the period from the first loosening of the restrictions of the Neutrality Acts to the freezing of Japanese assets in July 1941, Roos-evelt and most Americans believed that the United States could fight wars and defend democracy abroad "without the loss of a single American life. The compromise wrought by these conflicting sentiments, unofficial aid coupled with official neutrality, finally resulted in inadequate aid and un-neutral neutrality."[20]

President Harry S. Truman (April 12, 1945–January 20, 1953) adhered to a policy of containment of communism and the Soviet Union. When World War II ended, U.S. international objectives shifted from efforts to defeat Nazism and fascism to a position of anti-Soviet and anticommu-nism. By early 1946, the Soviet Union was viewed as the primary threat to world peace, according to Mary L. Dudziak. Truman introduced an ap-proach to international relations that became known as the Truman Doc-trine. "Anticommunism would not be limited to foreign affairs. With the communist threat now perceived in global, apocalyptic terms, scrutiny of how domestic policies might interface with the struggle against world communism became a priority. The most direct way in which this mani-fested itself was the concern about communist 'infiltration' in American government," wrote Dudziak.[21]

Interventionist Policy

Presidents John F. Kennedy (January 20, 1961–November 22, 1963) and Lyndon B. Johnson (November 22, 1963–January 20, 1969) viewed the con-flict between communism and pro-Westernism as a challenge to the con-tainment policy.[22]

Shortly after his inauguration, John F. Kennedy authorized the contin-ued execution of the Eisenhower administration's plan to train Cuban ex-iles for an invasion of their homeland. The plan's goal was the overthrow of Castro and the establishment of a noncommunist government friendly to the United States. In an effort to disguise U.S. support, part of the de-ception involved landing on the Bay of Pigs in Cuba. On April 17, 1961, the invasion was launched. It was vigorously counterattacked and the inva-sion did not succeed. Some of the exiles escaped to the sea. The rest were killed or imprisoned by Castro's forces. One hundred of the members of Brigade 2506 (the name the exile group gave themselves) were killed. Approximately 1,200 surrendered. The Bay of Pigs was a failure for the Kennedy administration.[23]

In 1962, in order to prevent the Soviet Union from installing short- and intermediate-range offensive nuclear missiles in Cuba, President John F. Kennedy placed a blockade of ships around Cuba and imposed a quarantine on the island. If installed, the missiles could have reached most of the continental United States in minutes. The Soviets backed down and its ships turned back. Both countries agreed not to pursue nuclear war, but the arms race continued as the Soviets escalated the building of their military arsenal.[24]

Interventionism has existed since President Wilson's term, but international law changed during the Cold War, according to D. J. Lecce. The 1965 Dominican intervention illustrates that change. The Johnson administration's intervention in the Dominican Republic was condemned mainly because it did not have legitimate grounds. The communist threat in the Dominican Republic was more President Johnson's fear of a Cuba repeat than real. Lecce said of the intervention, "History's read of the Dominican intervention could have been very different if a viable communist threat existed in proof. With the Cuban missile crisis fresh in the minds of most Americans, many would agree that stemming the tide of communism in the Caribbean was a vital U.S. national interest. One worthy of unilateral military intervention."[25] The criterion for unilateral intervention becomes the protection of vital national security interests. "Legal justification of that intervention is a different issue," Lecce stated.

Efforts to contain communism in Vietnam ended when President Richard M. Nixon (January 20, 1969–August 9, 1974) ended the Vietnam War in 1973. This war produced a dislike for intervention,[26] but did not prevent Presidents Ronald W. Reagan (January 20, 1981–January 20, 1989) or George H. W. Bush (January 20, 1989–January 20, 1993) from implementing policies of intervention.

President James (Jimmy) E. Carter (January 20, 1977–January 20, 1981) followed a nonmilitary policy when Iranian militants who were protected by the Iranian government seized the U.S. Embassy in Teheran and held 86 Americans hostage. In response to the hostage crisis, Carter employed options other than the direct use of military force. The result was an agreement favorable to Iran, according to James P. Terry.[27]

President Ronald Reagan (January 20, 1981–January 20, 1989) had foreign policy challenges in Lebanon, Grenada, Libya, and in the Iran–Contra affair. After the Beirut bombings, Reagan ordered American troops to Lebanon as part of a second multinational force with France and Italy to enable the Lebanese government to resume full sovereignty over its capital. On October 23, 1983, in Beirut, Lebanon, a suicide bomber killed 283 marines in their barracks. Reagan reassessed his Lebanon policy,[28] and on February 7, 1984, ordered withdrawal of U.S. troops and when he went in, his policy was denounced as interventionist policy.

Reagan ordered the October 25, 1983 invasion of Grenada "as another step toward ridding the world of Communism."[29] Plans to invade Grenada were well underway before the October 23, 1983 Beirut bombings.

In 1986, President Reagan ordered an attack on Muammar Gaddafi in Libya after Gaddafi's terrorist organization attacked U.S. citizens in West

Germany. Reagan gave a new articulation of presidential prerogatives in combating terrorism, wrote Terry.[30] Reagan also faced scrutiny from the Iran–Contra affair, a secret arrangement in the 1980s to provide funds to the Nicaraguan contra rebels from profits gained by selling arms to Iran, in spite of the embargo against selling arms to Iran. During this affair, the Central Intelligence Agency (CIA) trained and assisted this and other anticommunist insurgencies worldwide.[31]

On August 2, 1990, Iraq on the command of Saddam Hussein invaded Kuwait. The George H. W. Bush administration (January 20, 1989–January 20, 1993) responded by ordering U.S. ground and naval forces to Saudi Arabia in an operation called Desert Shield. The U.K. military forces were part of a U.N.-sponsored coalition. On January 16, 1991 (ET), the coalition launched Operation Desert Storm to drive the Iraqi forces out of Kuwait. On February 28, 1991, Saddam Hussein was defeated.[32] President Bush's decision to commit forces underwent legal scrutiny, but "President Bush's adherence to the strictures of the congressional mandate for Iraq, as it had interpreted U.N. Resolution 678 (which authorized member states to use 'all necessary means' to implement prior Security Council Resolutions), both saved American lives and restored sovereignty in Kuwait," concluded Terry.[33]

Policy and Terrorism

President William J. Clinton (January 20, 1993–January 20, 2001) had an assertive multilateral foreign policy, Terry maintained. The resolution of the crisis faced by President Clinton and NATO in Kosovo in early 1998 is an example of a multilateral effort. Other examples include operations in Somalia, Rwanda, Haiti, and the former Yugoslavia. On August 7, 1998, when al Qaeda led by Osama bin Laden attacked the U.S. embassies in Nairobi, Kenya, and Dar es Salaam, Tanzania, Clinton responded with missile strikes in Sudan and Afghanistan. It is reported that he called off a missile strike in Afghanistan intended for bin Laden in 1999, and that he did not retaliate for the October 12, 2000, USS *Cole* attack in Yemen that killed 17 U.S. sailors and wounded 39 even though bin Laden took credit for the attack.[34]

After the attacks on America on September 11, 2001, President George W. Bush (January 20, 2001–January 20, 2009) launched the United States and its coalition partners into Operation Enduring Freedom in Afghanistan on October 7, 2001. This war was the U.S. response to the attacks of 9/11.[35] The response was led by a NATO coalition and that coalition still leads the conducting of the war. In 2002, citing the doctrine of preemptive war, Bush initiated the war in Iraq.[36] On September 17, 2002, Bush presented the case for preemptive self-defense in his National Security Strategy, now known as the Bush Doctrine (See Appendix A). He said, "While the United States will constantly strive to enlist the support of the international community, we will not hesitate to act alone, if necessary, to exercise our right of self-defense by acting preemptively against such terrorists, to prevent them from doing harm against our people and our country."[37]

One of the most public changes in the Bush administration's strategy was to the language of diplomacy. The language shifted to "a global struggle against violent extremism" from "the global war on terror."[38] Bush said, on August 1, 2005 at a White House meeting, that he had not been consulted about the change.[39]

Testing Presidential Powers

The president's power as commander in chief has been tested many times. According to Terry, the first test occurred during the administration of James Madison in the War of 1812. More recently, the George W. Bush and Barack Obama (January 20, 2009 to–) presidencies have been tested in Iraq and Afghanistan in the War on Terrorism, Middle East unrest, and Southwest Asian crises.[40] The Congressional Research Service wrote Obama's position at the beginning of his term, "Obama confronts a set of challenges more daunting perhaps than any chief executive has faced since the Great Depression and World War II. At home, the nation is in the second year of a recession that Obama warns may get worse before the economy starts to improve. Abroad, he faces the task of withdrawing U.S. forces from Iraq, reversing the deteriorating conditions in Afghanistan and trying to ease the Israeli-Palestinian conflict."[41] Since the beginning of his term, Middle East unrest can be added.

President Obama is committed not only to strengthening existing alliances, but also to developing relations with hostile nations, including Iran, according to Danica Curavic.[42] When Obama gave a speech at the University of Cairo in June 2009, "he reached out to the Muslim world, openly addressing American and Muslim relations and offering a hand of friendship, signaling a new direction in American foreign policy."[43] In February 2010, Obama nominated an ambassador to Syria. This nomination filled a position that had been left vacant for five years. In a campaign fact sheet, Obama noted the success of cultural diplomacy during the Cold War and said, "Artists can be utilized again to help us win the war of ideas against Islamic extremism."[44]

In spite of Obama's efforts to strengthen diplomatic approaches, the dangerous nature and increased unrest in the world during his term has made it mandatory that he continue the use of military force. The use of military force is exemplified in the expansion of the stealth war. In December 2009, a military campaign in Yemen began without notice and represented an example of bringing counterterrorism into the shadows.[45] Other examples include the drone-missile campaign in Pakistan, approved raids against al Qaeda operatives in Somalia, and dismantling terrorist groups in North

Africa. According to the *New York Times*, the clandestine approach has changed the CIA into a paramilitary organization and the Pentagon to be more like the CIA. The strategy provides a unique political landscape. Republicans in Congress have been reluctant to confront Obama for aggressively hunting terrorists, and many Democrats appear eager to support any move away from the long, costly wars begun by the Bush administration.

"The intellectual foundation for the morality, and international law, of the resort to violence is the just war doctrine," according to Thomas C. Wingfield.[46] Just war thinkers make a direct liaison between international law and just war in respect to the goal of peace. One philosopher, Michael N. Schmitt, stated, "international law is about morality."[47] Due to the changing nature of warfare and the threats to civilized societies, the just war theory is more relevant today than ever. Wingfield concludes how basic the laws of war are to peace: "Distinguishing between aggressor and victim, setting firm limitations on the exercise of moral violence, establishing standards of behavior more demanding than mere well-meaning, and accepting the conclusion that there are times when it is immoral not to fight, are the inevitable outcome of applying just war analysis to the topics of tyranny, democracy, and regime change."[48]

In his Nobel Peace Prize acceptance speech, President Obama said that part of the challenge is reconciling two seemingly irreconcilable truths, "that war is sometimes necessary, and war at some level is an expression of human folly"[49] (see Appendix B). The law makes certain aspects of war such as suicide attacks clear, but in other ways, the law is evolving. Opposition to suicide warfare, on the other hand, is strong.

Just War Theory

The criteria of the just war theory—*jus ad bellum*, the law on recourse to force, and *jus in bello*, the law governing the conduct of hostilities—have been undergoing change, according to Major Richard C. Anderson. The traditional criteria are that armed force is justifiable when these conditions exist: just cause, proper authority, right intention, reasonable chance of success, proportionality of ends, and last resort.[50] Anderson notes that Michael Walzer's work *Just and Unjust Wars* concludes "the recognition of inalienable human rights yields a comprehensive theory to shape our moral judgments regarding war."[51] The just war theory or the law of armed force is usually also classified into a second body of law, *jus in bello*, according to Carsten Stahn. Historically, a third concept of *jus post bellum*, the law after war, has had a traditional place in just war, but has remained at the outside edge of legal scholarship.[52]

Just War Theory in Western Societies

In 2009, President Barack Obama discussed the just war theory in his speech accepting the Nobel Peace Prize at Oslo, Norway. Obama added to

Walzer's criteria when he said, "I believe that force can be justified on humanitarian grounds, as it was in the Balkans, or in other places that have been scarred by war."[53] He said that over time, a rarely observed

concept of a "just war" emerged, suggesting that war is justified only when certain conditions were met: if it is waged as a last resort or in self-defense; if the force used is proportional; and if, whenever possible, civilians are spared from violence. . . . The capacity of human beings to think up new ways to kill one another proved inexhaustible, as did our capacity to exempt from mercy those who look different or pray to a different God. Wars between armies gave way to wars between nations—total wars in which the distinction between combatant and civilian became blurred.[54]

Shari'a Law in Muslim Societies

Just war theory is commonly applied to Western societies, and Shari'a law applies to Muslim societies. Shari'a law is derived from the Koran, as the word of God, from the Prophet Muhammad's life examples and from fatwas, the rulings of Islamic scholars.[55] Because acts of martyrdom are tactics to militarily engage the enemy, John Kelsay advocated that the acts must be evaluated either in terms of the criteria of the just war tradition or the Shari'a provisions governing armed conflict. Debates about these provisions are abundant among Muslim scholars. Ultimately, a martyr's intention is understood in relation to the target. Shaykh al-Azhar, the highest authority in Egyptian Islam, held that suicide is acceptable in self-defense as long as the attacker did not take the lives of women or children. Kelsay draws a parallel from Shaykh al-Azhar's philosophy to a saying of Muhammad, "When you fight, do not cheat or commit treachery. Do not kill or mutilate women, children or old men." Kelsay translates these philosophies as, "A just warrior never directly and intentionally targets civilians. In this matter, Shari'a parallels the just war tradition and its concern for discrimination or noncombatant immunity."[56]

Devout Palestinian Muslims have argued that one justification for the killing of civilians in Israel, their aggressor, is that no civilians exist there. Its society is militaristic in nature because all men and women are subject to the draft. Further, when children and the elderly are killed, it is by mistake, and their deaths are considered collateral damage. The superior military advantage of the opposition justifies these and other tactics. This justification was used by the Muslims that carried out the 9/11 attacks on the United States.[57] Youssef H. Aboul-Enein and Sherifa Zuhur stated, "Islamic radicals have defended attacks on civilians with several sorts of twisted logic."[58] Nonetheless, Osama bin Laden, in the October 1996 Declaration of War, justified his aggression as defensive aggression, declaring that the Islamic nation was under attack:

The people of Islam had suffered from aggression, inequality and injustice imposed on them by the Zionist-Crusader alliance and their collaborators to the extent that Muslims' blood became the cheapest and their wealth looted in the hands of enemies. Their blood has spilled in Palestine and Iraq. The horrifying pictures of the massacre of Qana, in Lebanon are still fresh in our memory. Massacres in Tajikistan, Burma, Kashmir, Assam, Philippines, Somalia, Chechnya and In Bosnia-Herzegovina took place, massacres that send shivers in the body and shake the conscience.[59]

Some groups justify suicide in seeking nationalistic or political goals. Groups seeking nationalistic goals include the Palestinians, Kongra-Gel, Chechens, and Tamil Tigers. The Palestinians seek an independent state. Israel's agreement to have a Palestinian state has fluctuated. The Palestinians argue that the use of suicide warfare is defensive in that they perceive they are protecting their homeland. In order to defend Palestine, they must go on the offensive. Either way, the warfare is in the name of nationalism. According to John L. Esposito, "increased Israeli violence, brutality, and targeted assassinations reinforced the belief among many Palestinians and Muslims that so-called suicide bombers were committing not an act of suicide but one of self-sacrifice, engaged in resistance and retaliation against Israeli occupation and oppression."[60]

The Kongra-Gel (formerly Kurdistan Workers' Party, PKK [Partiya Karkerên Kurdistan], and KADEK) sought to establish an independent, democratic state in southeast Turkey, northern Iraq, and parts of Iran and Syria. It is characterized as a secessionist secular Islamic movement whose campaign began in 1984. The Chechen rebels began their quest for independence from Russia in 1991, and the Liberation Tigers of Tamil Eelam founded in 1976 has been fighting for a homeland from Sri Lanka.[61]

Nationalism

Nationalism, a philosophy with political value or vision for the future, is embroiled with other issues that help define or confuse. The difficult issue, terrorist or freedom fighter, surfaces in discussions of nationalism. Edward Marks maintained that this concern is particularly true with the prominence of national-liberal movements seeking nationalism as a prime political value.[62] Marks suggested that one way to address the issue is to turn the expression around to say, "One man's freedom fighter is another's terrorist. Disapproving of a particular act of violence as terrorism, like any other unjustified act, therefore becomes subject to the principle once coined for the question of determining pornography: you recognize it when you see it."[63] Further, the concept of just war is sometimes used by those groups who are in a weaker position, therefore justifying their tactics. Thus, they implicitly admit that certain acts are extreme but justify them as all that is available.

"Globally, a tide of nationalist movements and re-awakened self-identity by ethnic minorities has surged. The sweep of nationalist movements has created world-wide social instability, precipitated by calls for complete independence," noted Edward T. Canuel.[64] Recent examples included the civil war in Bosnia, a resurgence of Russian nationalism, religious chauvinism in Poland, and the self-determination drives of Palestinian groups in the occupied territories. Canuel believed that universally accepted definitions, or conceptualizations of nationalism, and the rights of self-determination are nonexistent. Furthermore, failing to confront the issue of nationalism is ultimately without value.

Robert A. Pape argued that nationalism motivates suicide bombers: "Contrary to popular perception, suicide bombers are not overwhelmingly motivated by religion, despair or the promise of an afterlife, but by nationalism. . . . The use of suicide terrorism is . . . a strategic method aimed toward securing nationalist goals."[65] Pape believed that Islamic fundamentalism is not the main motivation of suicide terrorism. Rather, he said, "Nearly all suicide terrorist attacks are committed for a secular strategic goal—to compel modern democracies to withdraw military forces from territory the terrorists view as their homeland."[66]

Shift in Framing the Laws of War

Ganesh Sitaraman notes the importance of remembering the context for formulation of the laws of war: "The laws of war were created with an assumption that conventional war's strategy—kill or capture the enemy— was the route to victory."[67] Regardless of tactical innovations such as the absence of uniforms and a networked enemy structure, the War on Terror keeps the same strategy: to win, simply kill or capture all the terrorists. Counterinsurgency forcefully rejects the kill/capture strategy. Counterinsurgents follow a win-the-population strategy that is aimed at building a stable and legitimate political order. Winning the population involves protecting the population, providing essential services, building political and legal institutions, and fostering economic development. "Killing and capturing the insurgents is not the primary goal, and it may often be counterproductive, causing destruction that creates backlash among the population and fuels their support for the insurgency," Sitaraman stated.

An important disconnect exists between counterinsurgency and the laws of war and roots that disconnect in the strategic differences between counterinsurgency and conventional warfare, Sitaraman argued. The principle of the laws of war is based on a strategic foundation that no longer applies, making many of its rules problematic for the age of counterinsurgency. Also, the debate on legal issues related to the War on Terror has been myopic and misplaced. Legal scholars have missed a major shift in military circles: "Military strategists have rejected the war on terror approach and now interpret global threats as an insurgency that requires a win-the-population strategy for success. This shift in framing not only expands the set of topics legal scholars interested in contemporary conflict must address, but also re-quires incorporating the strategic foundations of counterinsurgency when considering familiar topics in the war on terror legal debates."[68]

JUSTIFICATION FOR OPPOSING SUICIDE WARFARE

The justification for opposing suicide warfare is in international and national laws. The *U.S. Code* addresses terrorism and suicide bombing. The discussion in Chapter 1 laid out the specific points of *U.S. Code* Title 22, Ch. 38, Para. 2656f(d).[69] U.S. policy also justifies its opposition to suicide warfare (see Chapter 1).

U.S. Policies in 2012

"In practice, the pressures and demands of the actual waging of war have a way of relegating policy purpose to the background. All too often, policy may seem to serve war, rather than war serve policy," stated Colin S. Gray.[70] Gray includes four elements in strategy: use made of force and the threat of force for the goals of policy; the relationship between means and ends; constant dialogue between policy-maker and soldier, that is, troops must be able to execute policy and if they are so effective, policy may fall behind; and, finally, if the point of warfare should slowly disappear from view due to military events, politics must rule. When the four factors are mixed, they become the core of strategy: the instrumentality of the threat or use of force.

Counterterrorism Policy

In the mid-2000s, most of the terrorism research had focused on the suicide bombers, rebels, terrorists, and their organizations as the evil perpetrators, according to Claudia Brunner. She stated, "Rarely does state power come into critical view in this literature."[71] The focus was acceptable counterterrorism literature. In 2006, when I wrote *Female Suicide Bombers*, as a sociologist, I believed to achieve an understanding of suicide warfare, the participants should be presented in the context of the power of the society in which they live, of the group of which they are a member, and of the society as part of the larger global community. In part, I accomplished the feat. Left unsaid, at the time, was that this effort was not easy to achieve. Even though I was a sociologist with my theoretical base, due to external pressures, it was not uncomplicated to include positive or structural comments about the Palestinian bombers or negative comments about Israel, for example. This omission was noted by Brunner who reviewed my book. She commented that I had freely criticized the United States' Cold War enemy, Russia, but not U.S. allies.[72] Thus, I found of particular interest

Amentahru Wahirad's review of Richard Jackson et al.'s book *Critical Terrorism Studies: A New Research Agenda*. Wahirad notes the authors' assessment of the literature that claims objectivity when it "nearly always fails to even question or consider what is going on within the communities where terrorists arise . . . terrorism is used to discredit, . . . demonize, . . . denounce, . . . shut off debate, . . . etc."[73] Although the book addresses all terrorism acts rather than only suicide warfare, in an interview, I asked Richard Jackson what position he held on assessment of the literature on balanced treatment of terrorism. He said that a real blind-spot exists when it comes to questions around Israel and to talking to terrorists. Israel is taboo because of organized attacks launched against academics or journalists who publicly criticize or imply wrongdoing on the part of Israel. The terrorist taboo goes back to the 1970s when terrorism studies and counterinsurgency studies began. Terrorism was conceived as a means to understand and defeat the enemy. In addition to this primary motive for many scholars, there is also a broader discourse that has grown up around terrorism in which terrorists are perceived as evil and inhuman. Jackson explained the effects of this view on scholars and counterterrorism experts:

There is consequently a ritualistic determination to not be "contaminated" by empathy for the terrorist; talking to them risks developing such empathy and should thus be avoided. An example of this taboo at work is the review by Alex Schmid of our book on the Perspectives on Terrorism website[74] in which he criticizes us for not making a stronger denunciation of the evils of terrorism—as if that is one of the main purposes of terrorism scholarship! The point is that denouncing the evils of terrorism functions to remind the scholar of their true purpose and avoid developing any empathy for a group or individual who would feel driven to employ violence in that way.

The point is that there is a failure of both scholars and counter-terrorism practitioners to try and understand terrorists and the communities they emerge from in their own terms and within their own subjectivity. I suggest that anyone who purports to be a "terrorism expert" should be required to have at least talked to some of those he/she calls "terrorists." Certainly, the field would benefit greatly from much more research which involved actually talking to terrorists to find out what they think they are going to achieve and why they have chosen to use violent strategies. More generally, it might even generate the basis for dialogue with those groups and individuals, which in turn could lead to non-violent solutions to their grievances and conflicts.[75]

Another point made in Wahirad's review was that the literature is silent on nonviolent alternatives. I asked Jackson to expand on these alternatives for peaceful resolution:

An argument I hope to make in a forthcoming paper is that all the knowledge needed to resolve conflicts involving terrorism already exists in the fields of conflict resolution and peace studies, among others [paper since published].[76] In some ways, it already exists within terrorism studies itself. For example, after the

Pentagon's Defense Science Board stated in the late 1990s that there is "a historical correlation between U.S. involvement in international situations and an increase in terrorist attacks against the United States," an article entitled "Does U.S. Intervention Overseas Breed Terrorism?" by Ivan Eland set out to examine the historical record. Eland concluded after extensive research that "The large number of terrorist attacks that occurred in retaliation for an interventionist American foreign policy implicitly demonstrates that terrorism against U.S. targets could be significantly reduced if the United States adopted a policy of military restraint overseas."[77] In other words, the Pentagon and terrorism and security scholars know that one of the main drivers or causes of terrorism directed at the US is due to foreign military intervention and that the resolution of terrorism may simply involve withdrawal of U.S. forces from foreign soil. My contention would be that they also "know" from the analysis of previous cases that there is no military solution to terrorism, but that processes of reform and dialogue are necessary to resolve the conflicts and grievances which make some groups turn to terrorism. In fact, there is a growing literature now which has examined the impact of violent counter-terrorism tactics like targeted assassination and found that it has no impact at all on reducing subsequent terrorism.

The fact that this "knowledge" is largely "unknown" in terrorism studies is because it is subjugated, which is a process described by Foucault whereby knowledge which threatens to destabilize the dominant narratives of the discourse (e.g., that terrorism is caused not by "evil" but by rational political demands) is denigrated and suppressed, usually by arguing that it is naïve, unscientific or lacking in scholarly authority. Thus, within terrorism studies, the knowledge of peace scholars regarding how to resolve political conflict through dialogue and reconciliation is ignored and dismissed because it contradicts the dominant narratives of terrorism being and exceptional kind of evil which threatens the whole world (instead of a tactic of political conflict that can best be resolved through dialogue and reform).[78]

Domestic Policy Relationship to Foreign Policy

The United States has several activities to prevent terrorism within the country (see Chapter 1). One effort is denying terrorist safe havens enabling them to train recruits and plan operations. The relationship of domestic policy to foreign policy becomes clear, for example, when we recall the discovery of Osama bin Laden's compound in Pakistan where he played an active role in al Qaeda in focusing on attacking the United States. Jacquelyn L. Williams-Bridgers reported that the U.S. State Department has annually identified terrorist safe havens since 2006 through its *Country Reports on Terrorism.* The views of the National Security Staff and National Counterterrorism Center are incorporated in these reports. The State Department's identification of safe havens is required by the Intelligence Reform and Terrorism Prevention Act of 2004. In August 2010, the State Department identified 13 safe havens.[79] In addition to the State Department's responsibilities, U.S. agencies such as the Departments of Defense and Justice address safe havens. The Department of Homeland

Security does not include specific language but has a goal "to protect the homeland from dangerous people."[80]

The Law Regarding Prisoners of War

The 1949 Geneva Conventions III, Article 4 describes the categories of prisoners of war. These categories include members of the armed forces and militias or volunteer corps that form part of the armed forces; other militias and members of other volunteer corps, including organized resistance movements that are a party to the conflict and operating in or outside their own territory, even if the territory is occupied, provided that there is a responsible command; a distinctive and recognizable sign that can be seen from a distance; carrying of arms openly; and carrying out their operations in accordance with the laws and customs of war.[81] The Additional Protocol I to the 1977 Geneva Conventions provides protection to the revolutionary. The armed forces treatment of prisoners is also outlined in Article 44, and of particular importance is that an armed combatant must be visible and distinguish himself or herself and carry arms openly.[82]

Torture Law

Torture is against national and international laws. The *U.S. Code* defines punishment for committing torture.[83] The *U.S. Code* also refers to it as "Standards of Conduct for Interrogation."[84] The U.S. Patriot Act that "establishes equivalent sanctions for conspiracy and the underlying offense in cases of . . . torture committed overseas under color of law, 18 U.S.C. 2340A"[85] makes it illegal on the domestic level. Internationally, in 1994, the United States ratified the 1984 U.N. Convention against Torture. Article 1 prohibits torture stating:

"Torture" means any act by which severe pain or suffering, whether physical or mental, is intentionally inflicted on a person for such purposes as obtaining from him or a third person information or a confession, punishing him for an act he or a third person has committed or is suspected of having committed, or intimidating or coercing him or a third person, or for any reason based on discrimination of any kind, when such pain or suffering is inflicted by or at the instigation of or with the consent or acquiescence of a public official or other person acting in an official capacity. It does not include pain or suffering arising only from, inherent in or incidental to lawful sanctions.[86]

In May 2012, a new court decision resulted from a lengthy lawsuit by rights groups, primarily the American Civil Liberties Union. These groups sought records related to detainee mistreatment. The three-judge panel of the U.S. Court of Appeals for the Second Circuit in New York upheld the Obama administration's claim that cables describing the CIA's use of waterboarding and a photograph of a high-value detainee, Abu Zubaydah, who was subjected to repeated waterboarding, were exempt from disclosure under the Freedom of Information Act.[87] This decision is one of deference that lacks logic even though the government's claims of national security and secrecy were perceived by the *New York Times* overwrought.

Detention

"Does International Humanitarian Law recognize these persons [unprivileged belligerents] as combatants, noncombatants, civilians, criminals—or an entirely new category of person?" asked Harrold J. McCracken.[88] The question represents a centuries long debate about properly handling persons who are not members of a sovereign's military, or do not conduct themselves in agreement with recognized standards of military operations. The *Independent Panel to Review the Department of Defense (DoD) Detention Operations* report stated that although there is not a label for the persons who do not comply with specified conditions and thus fall outside the category of those persons entitled to enemy prisoner-of-war status, in law of war conventions, "the concept of 'unlawful combatant' or 'unprivileged belligerent' is part of the law of war."[89]

Harrold J. McCracken maintained the controversy surrounding the debate is demonstrated in the proper handling of some terrorists. Detainees of Guantanamo Bay detention facility (often referred to as GTMO) Khalid Sheikh Mohammed, Walid Muhammed Salih, Mubarak bin Attash, Ramzi bin al-Shibh, Ali Abdul Aziz Ali, and Mustafa Ahmed al-Hawsawi were tried in U.S. federal courts. On the other hand, U.S. military commissions tried the alleged mastermind of the October 12, 2000, USS *Cole* bombing, Abd al-Rahim al-Nashiri, and four other GTMO detainees. In determining the appropriate jurisdiction, Attorney General Eric Holder considered the nature of the offense, location of the offense, identity of the victims, and manner of the investigation.[90]

The international community has recognized individuals who are not lawful combatants, but has not defined exactly who they are or the treatment they should receive when captured, McCracken maintained. Questions arise: Does a person captured on an active battlefield in Iraq or Afghanistan, but is not a member of a recognized sovereign's military organization, receive different treatment than a person who makes an improvised explosive device? Do those persons involved in cyber security attacks or the financing of terror receive dissimilar handling? What is the standard of treatment? Are the Geneva Conventions accorded? Should the interrogation techniques of the conventions, not used in domestic law enforcement, be followed?[91]

The Authorization for the Use of Military Force (AUMF) authorizes the president to use "all necessary and appropriate force against those nations, organizations, or persons he determines planned, authorized, committed, or aided the terrorist attacks that occurred on September 11, 2001, or harbored such organizations or persons,"[92] with the clear goal of preventing further attacks, according to Robert Chesney, 2009 advisor to the Detention Policy Task Force. President Bush's declaring of al Qaeda responsibility for 9/11 and the Taliban's harboring most of al Qaeda's leadership in Afghanistan was clear. What isn't clear is the scope of AUMF such as which groups and against which individuals does AUMF authorize detention. Congressional hearings addressed these and other issues.

In 2011, Michael B. Mukasey, U.S. attorney general (November 9, 2007–January 20, 2009), testified that no clear policy existed on how to deal with captured detainees. Options included holding them aboard naval vessels, sending them to third countries that will accept them, bringing them to the United States for trial in civilian courts, or releasing them because there is no other option. In addition, Mukasey testified that no sound policy exists on who U.S. troops are to detain, on what standards, where, and for what purpose. Important intelligence opportunities can be wasted and dangerous terrorists returned to the fight. The use of drones that permit lethal strikes does not allow taking advantage of the intelligence value of detainees.[93]

Prosecution

Prosecution of detainees is part of the debate. Civilian criminal prosecution and/or trial by military commission or use of military detention consistent with the law of war are lawful options to try detainees in certain circumstances. Chesney testified in 2011 that there should be flexibility in the method of detention and that more than one method should be pursued.[94] Former deputy assistant attorney general, Office of Legal Counsel, U.S. Department of Justice, Steven A. Engel testified that the 9/11 attacks took the United States by surprise and it has taken time for the legal framework to catch up. The traditional laws of war are based on conventional international armed conflict or, in some cases, civil wars. These laws provide "clear answers to who may be detained, how they must be treated, and where they should be prosecuted. None of these questions is self-evident when it comes to the War on Terror."[95]

The executive branch has developed a legal framework that has been partially tested by the courts, but the framework is incomplete because Congress needs to do more, Engel testified. He maintained the Detainee Treatment Act of 2005 and the Military Commissions Acts of 2006 and 2009 did not provide a comprehensive legal framework. The Detainee Treatment Act is designed to provide humane treatment, but also did away with the ability of Guantanamo Bay prisoners to challenge their detention in federal court.[96] The Military Commissions Act enacted in 2006 authorized "trial by military commission for violations of the law of war, and for other purposes,"[97] and, among other changes, the amended version in 2009 replaced the term "unlawful enemy combatant" with "unprivileged enemy belligerent." One way an individual is an unprivileged enemy belligerent is membership in al Qaeda, whether or not the member has taken part in or supported hostilities against the United States. The Taliban is no longer named in the new definition.[98]

In December 2010, Congress had voted to prohibit prosecution of Guantanamo detainees in U.S. federal courts. Amnesty International, who favored prosecution in federal courts, said this action would effectively prevent the closing of the facility.[99] Mukasey testified in favor of prosecuting detainees on the basis of Military Commissions Act that prescribes trial before military commissions for those accused of acts of terrorism as well as a detention facility is available at Guantanamo Bay, Cuba. Security and evidentiary problems will exist in federal courts, particularly if the detainee has been removed from an active battlefield.[100] Part of Mukasey's objection is reflected in his testimony:

For starters, human beings have spent the last several hundreds of years trying to civilize the laws of war. We have devised rules such that combatants who wear uniforms, carry their arms openly, follow a recognized chain of command, and do not target civilians, may be confined in humane conditions for the duration of hostilities. It seems downright perverse to tell people who violate every one of these rules that they are entitled to even better treatment, to appointed counsel, to a trial in a courtroom that they can use as a platform to spread their views.[101]

In 2011, the House Committee on Armed Services, when considering the National Defense Authorization Act (NDAA) of fiscal year 2012, took a significant step ahead in providing answers to these questions. Rep. Eliot Engel (D-NY) testified that the act would make clear that the armed conflict on terror continues and would verify that the enemy includes those who "are part of, or are substantially supporting, al-Qaeda, the Taliban, or associated forces that are engaged in hostilities against the United States or its coalition partners."[102] Engel testified that this step ratifies the understanding of this conflict that the executive branch of President Obama and President Bush has developed in fighting this war and makes clear who can be detained and targeted.

The controversy about the NDAA revolves around Section 1039 that would prevent the administration from relocating detainees at Guantanamo into the United States. It also prevents the administration from transferring any detainee in the War on Terror to the United States. The proposed language in Section 1039, if passed, would extend to the case of Abdulkadir Warsame, the al-Shahab member detained on a U.S. warship before being transferred to the United States for a civilian prosecution. Section 1039 prevents that alternative by requiring the U.S. military to hold Warsame outside the United States, at Guantanamo Bay or somewhere else. The Obama administration objects to Section 1039 on the basis of separation of powers. The administration contends that Section 1039 challenges executive branch authority "to determine when and where to prosecute detainees, based on the facts and the circumstances of each case and our national security interests."[103]

In addition to defining the status of detainees, the issues of where to send them when captured, how to prosecute them, and what techniques to use when interrogating detainees, particularly of al Qaeda prisoners, are unresolved. Between October and December 2003, Iraqi prisoners at Abu Ghraib prison in Iraq and other sites were abused by U.S. soldiers and members of the intelligence community. The *Independent Panel* characterized the unauthorized abuses as "acts of brutality and purposeless sadism."[104] The panel reported that the United States was in a different kind of war with a different kind of enemy. Those captured were no longer a homogenous group of enemy soldiers.

President George W. Bush determined that the Geneva Conventions did not apply to conflicts with al Qaeda or Afghanistan and the Taliban, and that they were unlawful combatants and did not qualify for prisoner-of-war status.[105] He later qualified that position and contended that the policy would be "consistent with the principles of Geneva."[106] John Hagan, Gabrielle Ferrales, and Guillermina Jasso pointed out that these abuses included "breaking chemical lights and pouring the phosphoric liquid they contained on detainees; pouring cold water on naked detainees; beating detainees with a broom handle and a chair; threatening male detainees with rape; allowing a military police guard to stitch without anesthetic the gaping wound of a detainee who was injured after being slammed against the wall in his cell; sodomizing a detainee with a chemical light and perhaps a broom stick; using military working dogs to frighten and intimidate detainees with threats of attack, and in one instance biting a detainee."[107] Abuses of al Qaeda by CIA interrogators at other overseas cites included enhanced interrogation techniques such as noise, stress positions, isolation, and waterboarding, a technique utilized to coerce prisoners during interrogations employing the use of water to cut off oxygen and to create both the sensation and fear of drowning. The concern of Hagan et al. was broader than just perpetrators and victims of torture. Rather, they were concerned with the broader effects of the George W. Bush administration's interpretations of torture law on important individual legal decision-makers such as the Iraqi judges' thinking about the meaning and acceptability of torture.

Although waterboarding was used during the Bush administration, the case of Khalid Shaikh Mohammed, the mastermind of the 9/11 terrorist attacks, demonstrates that it may not have been an effective technique. The killing of Osama bin Laden rekindled the torture debate. Khalid Shaikh Mohammed underwent waterboarding 183 times. He frequently misled interrogators about bin Laden's courier's identity.[108] Waterboarding was also used in the Obama administration. CIA Chief Leon Panetta reported that intelligence acquired from waterboarded detainees was used to find al Qaeda leader Osama bin Laden and kill him.[109]

President Obama issued Executive Order 13491 that revoked all previous executive directives, orders, and regulations inconsistent with 13491
including, but not limited to, those issued to or by the CIA from September
11, 2001 to January 20, 2009 concerning detention or the interrogation of
detained individuals. The executive order to ensure lawful interrogations
included that prisoners be "treated humanely," and forbade "violence to
life and person, murder of all kinds, mutilation, cruel treatment, torture,
outrages upon personal dignity," and "humiliating and degrading treatment." These terms referred to the same terms in Common Article 3, and
were to have the same meaning.[110] The president issued two other orders.
Executive Order 13492 instructed the prompt and appropriate disposition
of detainees at Guantánamo and closure of the facilities at Guantánamo.
These actions would further the national security and foreign policy interests of the United States and the interests of justice.[111] Executive Order
13493 reviewed detention policy options and created a task force to conduct a review of the federal government's lawful options with respect to
apprehension, detention, trial, transfer, release, or other disposition.[112] In
2011, Defense Secretary Robert Gates said closing the U.S. prison at Guantanamo Bay was very remote due to the intense congressional opposition
to transferring suspected terrorists to the United States.[113] Equally controversial is Obama's position on the Bush administration rendition policy,
the transferring of prisoners to countries that practice torture. In 2009, the
Obama administration announced that it would continue the Bush policy,
but with oversight protections to insure torture was not used.[114] Some reports indicate rendition continues. Fueling the controversy is the assertion
that, in 2011 in Afghanistan, at least 20 secret prisons still actively torture
"short-term transfer" detainees.[115]

Traditional Rules and Principles of Warfare

Although irregular warfare differs from regular combat in some ways,
it is not at all distinctive from the perspective of the essence of strategy.
War is war, and strategy is strategy, Gray maintained. There are no new
or old wars, there are only wars. But if America's future strategic history
includes irregular enemies, it will be necessary to have a clear understanding of the distinctive character of the irregular strategic challenge especially terrorism and insurgency, Gray stated. The traditional American
way of war in some ways encourages a less optimal military approach to
the challenges by irregular enemies. The American way is deeply based
in history for good reasons, Gray stated. But in 2006, it demonstrated that
mind-set and doctrine have not effectively adapted to irregular warfare,
because the American way had not fully adapted including the depen-
dence on technology, the reliance on firepower, and the emphasis on U.S.
casualty avoidance. Strategy must rule all of warfare, regular and irregular. The traditional American way of war was intended to defeat regular

enemies, and did not strongly address the strategic effect and political consequences of military action.[116]

The 2010 Strategic Studies Institute's Strategy Conference recognized that the security strategy debate has been ongoing since the end of the Cold War. Differences of opinion center on whether the nature of war has changed and, if so, what that means for nations as they prepare for future security challenges and as their military and civilian leaders come to grips with the changed meaning of war.[117] Steven Metz and Phillip Cuccia reported that recently, international law and conventions have made great efforts to formalize the rules governing war (see Chapter 1). This single set of normal rules and law was derived from Western tradition and aimed to transcend cultural differences. Global challenges exist to the domination of Western norms and rules. Nonstate antagonists have proliferated that are little bound by these laws and conventions and that also appear to have made the legal and treaty regime ineffective. "The best legal system on earth matters little if it is consistently ignored."[118] Legal means and treaties have focused principally on conventional warfare between nation-states. Tests to existing traditional rules include the new participants in war including private military and security firms; new technology such as unmanned aerial vehicles, robotics, and nonlethal or nondeadly weapons; and new methods of war such as cyber war.

The panelists at the Strategy Conference were asked to respond to the question, "Do current rules of war need to be completely revamped or would a modification be sufficient?" Metz and Cuccia reported that the panelists differed in their responses. Dr. Albert Pierce spoke to the principles of war and proposed modifying the traditional just war theory to include an adequate ethical framework. The traditional ethical principles for war addressed the decision to go to war (*jus ad bellum*) and the conduct of the war (*jus in bello*). President George W. Bush advocated and employed the preemptive strike as a justification for war. President Obama has advocated just war theory. Pierce understood that sometimes preemptive use of force is better than preventative warfare: "[It] was legitimate but required a manifest intent to injure, a degree of active preparation that makes that intent a positive danger, and a situation where waiting or taking action other than the use of force greatly magnified the threat—as opposed to preventative war which had much less stringent requirements."[119] Pierce believed that discrimination and proportionality, the traditional standards for the conduct of war, remain important. Just because the principles may be more difficult to apply in a "war amongst the people," does not make the principles unnecessary.[120] The important thing is to make certain that an understanding of the principles spreads to the operational and tactical levels.

The way Osama bin Laden was killed in Pakistan in May 2011 raised issues about targeted killing. The use of targeted killing within nations that are not at war with the United States is a crucial issue that needs further ethical analysis. At present, there is no consensus on the ethical or legal framework for targeted killing or high-value targeting in American counterinsurgency and counterterrorism operations. Pierce believed the modifications would apply to nations that utilize targeted killing such as Russia, Israel, and the United States.[121]

It is difficult for me to envision the effect of Pierce's suggestions in the case of the targeted killing of bin Laden. Not knowing all that the government knew in the planning and execution of the operation that killed bin Laden leaves unanswered whether Pierce's modifications may have been implemented. Perhaps in the bin Laden case, the stakes were so high that most nations were just relieved that he was gone, but in less high-profile cases, would ethical considerations be of more concern? Is it a matter of in one case, the justness is relevant and in another case, justness is not, at least when the same criteria are applied? Pierce's ethical considerations would be derived from the answers to a series of questions: What type of actions qualify someone to be a legitimate target of official killing? Would terrorist financiers be valid targets? What is the required burden of proof and level of intelligence? Are supporters and family members also legitimate targets or do they have noncombatant immunity? When bin Laden was killed, was the killing of bin Laden's son legitimate? And what is the role of the government where the target is located? Did the U.S. inform Pakistan in advance of the raid on bin Laden's compound?[122] Pierce's suggested modifications are thought provoking.

Other legality issues surface when the Obama administration had a secret document that legalized the killing without trial of Anwar al-Awlaki, American-born radical Muslim cleric hiding in Yemen. A missile from a drone attack took his life on September 30, 2011.[123] A legal document issued by the Department of Justice in about June 2010, before al-Awlaki's death, justified the legal killing on grounds that "if it was not feasible to capture him, because intelligence agencies said he was taking part in the war between the United States and Al Qaeda and posed a significant threat to Americans, as well as because Yemeni authorities were unable or unwilling to stop him."[124] Evidence against al-Awlaki is not analyzed. Distinguishing between regular and irregular warfare, in part, depends on understanding traditional warfare. Policy-makers and military personnel must deal with irregular and regular warfare. Frank G. Hoffman calls this combination of approaches in warfare a fusion of war forms or hybrid threats. These threats will be combined in the same force and battle space. States will not necessarily employ only regular warfare and nonstate actors will not be identified with solely irregular warfare.[125] Whatever the type of war waged, the cause of war is changing from wars waged by evildoers and never by a democracy-oriented force to enemies "eager to die for radical ideological, religious, or ethnic causes; enemies who ignore national borders and remain unbound by the conventions of the developed world—who leave little room for negotiations or compromise."[126]

The new wars with their new causes, methods, and philosophies were not in the thinking of traditionalists upholding the long-standing American way of war.

International Law and Violence

The Lieber Code is the basis for everything contained in the modern laws of war today, according to Gregory P. Noone et al. President Abraham Lincoln commissioned Dr. Francis Lieber to write a code for Union forces during the American Civil War. The Lieber Code was the first time a government issued policy to its troops in the field. It became General Order No. 100 for the Union Army, and contains 48 articles (Articles 48–80 and 119–133) regarding prisoners of war.[127]

The law of war is a combination of customary and conventional international laws with exclusively Western interpretations of justness, necessity, proportionality, and chivalry, according to David P. Cavaleri. The current version of the law of war is codified in the 1949 Geneva Conventions, and has evolved over time as changing environments and important geopolitical events dictated. Cavaleri stated that it is not unexpected that "a public debate has emerged about the law of war's applicability to the asymmetric nature of the Global War on Terror within the common operating environment."[128] Cavaleri, himself, held that the law of war does not need revising to face the War on Terror. Three documents are the foundation for the law of war, according to Cavaleri: the Hague Convention of 1907 that regulates the methods and means of warfare, the four Geneva Conventions of 1949 that established unbreakable protections for specific categories of war victims, and the 1977 Protocols to the 1949 Geneva Conventions that expand upon the 1949 convention.

The 1949 Geneva Conventions were intended to address wars between states; War on Terrorism was not considered.[129] The Geneva Conventions are included in a collection of four separate conventions and two 1977 protocols, and one in 2005.[130] The conventions and protocols address specific areas pertaining to the protection of the wounded, sick, shipwrecked, prisoners of war, civilians in time of war, and victims of international and noninternational armed conflicts.[131]

Common Article 3 of the Geneva Conventions discusses internal armed conflicts and the principles the two additional protocols (1977) to these conventions.[132] Important international law principles relevant to the violence in Iraq are found in these three sections relating to internal armed conflicts. For example, in 1977, Common Article 3 provided the minimal protections that include prohibitions on inhumane treatment of noncombatants, including members of the armed forces who have laid down their arms.

Explicitly forbidden acts include "murder of all kinds, mutilation, cruel treatment and torture; taking of hostages; outrages upon personal dignity, in particular, humiliating and degrading treatment," and extrajudicial executions. The sick and wounded must be collected and cared for.[133]

Conflict activates the law of war regardless whether it is international or internal or recognized by all parties. The activation standard is outlined in Article 2 of all four 1949 Geneva Conventions. Whether both parties recognize the war or are members of the convention, the party belonging must still abide by the rules.[134] What does this mean in relationship to the capture of terrorists? Have they in all cases accorded the principles of the Geneva Conventions because the United States recognizes the conventions? Or do terrorists or unlawful combatants have no lawful existence other than as criminals?

In contrast to Cavaleri's position that the law of war does not need modification, McCracken argued for a new international convention to deal with unprivileged belligerents, also described as unlawful enemy combatants, terrorists, spies, and brigands. He believed that the War on Terror "has showcased a gap in international law."[135] The individuals responsible for the 9/11 attacks did not conduct themselves according to the generally accepted principles for the conduct of warfare. McCracken proposed that the international community has to respond to this shift. Humanitarian law already provides the foundation for this change. Leadership's lack of recognition of the shift includes not acknowledging the legitimacy of this method of warfare to appropriately deal with the unprivileged belligerents. He concludes, "Without this movement forward, the UB [unprivileged belligerents] will continue to hide in the shadows, both practically throughout the world and metaphorically in the world of International Humanitarian Law."[136]

Controversial, in recent years, is the use of waterboarding on detainees. Its use was spotlighted after the recent killing of Osama bin Laden when CIA Chief Leon Panetta said that intelligence collected from waterboarded detainees was used along with other sources to find al Qaeda leader Osama bin Laden and kill him. Because waterboarding, multiple intelligence, and years of work preceded the killing, it is difficult to say whether the waterboarding that took place years ago singularly led to bin Laden's location. The persons subjected to enhanced interrogation were 9/11 mastermind Khalid Sheik Mohammed and the 20th hijacker Mohammad al-Qahtani. The policy was authorized by President George W. Bush who said in 2010, "We used this technique on three people, captured a lot of people and used it on three. We gained value; information to protect the country. And it was the right thing to do as far as I'm concerned."[137]

United Nations

U.N. law includes 12 universal legal instruments concerning the prevention and suppression of terrorism adopted between 1963 and 1999 and 5 regional conventions from 1971 to 1999.[138] In addition to those universal instruments, three U.N. actions are important to note: U.N. Charter and Resolutions 2625 and 3314.

U.N. Charter, Article 2, Paragraph 4 states, "All Members shall refrain in their international relations from the threat or use of force against the territorial integrity or political independence of any state, or in any other manner inconsistent with the Purposes of the United Nations."[139]

Resolutions 2625 and 3314 helped clarify the U.N. Charter. Resolution 2625 of October 24, 1970, "Declaration on Principles of International Law Concerning Friendly Relations and Cooperation among States in Accordance with the Charter of the United Nations" puts forth a set of principles to assure behavior is lawful and in accord with a code of conduct. States are to refrain from the threat or use of force against the territorial integrity or political independence of any state; to use peaceful means so as not to endanger international peace, security, and justice; not to intervene within the domestic jurisdiction of any state; to cooperate with one another; to abide by equal rights and self-determination of peoples; to abide by sovereign equality of states; and shall fulfill their obligations in accordance with the charter.[140]

Resolution 3314 of December 14, 1974, "Definition of Aggression" provides seven acts, regardless of a declaration of war, that qualify as acts of aggression by one state against another. The acts are invasion or attack that result in annexation by the use of force; bombardment of armed forces of a state or use of any weapons; blockade of ports or coasts; attack on land, sea, or air; use of armed forces of one state while in another shall not stay beyond the termination of the agreement; a state that allows its territory to be used by another state, shall not allow it to be used by that other state to commit an act of aggression against a third state; and sending armed bands, groups, irregulars, or mercenaries to carry out acts of armed force against another state that are so severe as to amount to the above six acts.[141]

The traditional rules of warfare continue to be pressured by counterterrorism and by the rules applied to the wars in Afghanistan and Iraq, including prisoners of war, intelligence gathering, the emergence of asymmetric warfare, the lawful distinction between insurgents and terrorists, and relevant international law and policy. The slowly changing just war theory has been affected by the change to asymmetric warfare with suicide attacks having a significant role.

CONCLUSIONS

The question of whether the current laws of war are suited to the War on Terror remains part of the debate. To me, because new types of fighters are present in warfare, distaste for their methods, particularly in the case of suicide bombers, is understandable. Viewing the method as a tactic of war with the goal to rack up military victories helps to ameliorate the aversion.

Thus, I believe the new fighters should be included in the laws of war, because, like it or not, they are a part of current warfare. In matters of the treatment of prisoners of war, I believe that when a country is a signatory to laws that prohibit torture and require humane treatment, that country should abide by those laws of war regardless of whether the enemy is a signatory. I suspect a change in these two aspects of the laws of war will come only with consternation. If the laws appear to be working, the stakes for change may appear too high, the risk too great. As one researcher found, anyone who knew that the person being waterboarded could supply valuable information in killing terrorists who in turn could kill you, you would not object. On the other hand, Cavaleri concluded, "Until Congress ratifies a revision to the law of war, Geneva 1949 remains the legal standard of conduct for all U.S. Armed Forces regardless of the operational environment."[142]

CHAPTER 4

Strategies of Suicide Warfare

STRATEGIES

The strategies and tactics of groups that employ suicide warfare depend on the context in which they are used. The contexts include countries like the United States, Israel, Iraq, and Afghanistan. They include terror, jihads, insurgency, defense, and finance. The strategies are adapted to the situations in which they are used and by whom they are used. In all cases, suicide warfare is effective, if not sufficient to enable the perpetrators to prevail. In all cases, the strategies provoke powerful and even more effective responses.

Strategies of Terror

The suicide warfare strategies of terror are dependent on the context in which they are used. Charles Tilly wrote, "Terror is a strategy, that strategy involves interactions among political actors, and that to explain the adoption of such a strategy we have no choice but to analyze it as part of the political process."[1] Tilly advocated dispositional explanations such as motives, emotions, decision logics, and cultural templates including ideologies are not sufficient cause for terrorism, but rather relational explanations must be a primary consideration. Relational reasoning includes that individuals, groups, and networks employ the recurrent strategy of intimidation that is relational and corresponds to asymmetrical deployment of threats and violence against an enemy. This strategy connects to other forms of political struggle within the same settings and populations. Lastly, coercion specialists ranging from government employees to bandits employ terror under certain political circumstances and with more devastation than nonspecialists.[2]

Jessica Stern stated that terrorists do not fight on traditional battlefields. Instead, they fight among civilians and increase the risks of collateral damage. She believed Islamist terrorists provoke opposing governments to react in ways that appear to demonstrate that these governments want to humiliate or harm Muslims. "Guantanamo, Abu Ghraib, and 'extraordinary rendition' have become for Muslim youth symbols of the United States' belligerence and hypocrisy," according to Stern.[3]

The beginning of wisdom is to recognize terror as a strategy, wrote Tilly. The main factors in strategy include a one-sided situation with either a powerless people against a powerful opponent or in reverse a powerful people such as armies and governments against powerless people, a goal to employ threats of or actual violence with immediate damage, and a break with political routines where the violence occurs.[4]

Dispositional reasons should be factored into the strategy of suicide bombers, but it is the relational that is key, wrote Tilly. This position is my thesis as I examine the interrelationship of the culture, the military, and the individual used as a weapon. In Durkheim's theory of collective consciousness, the motives of individuals apt to commit suicide bombings are interrelated with the social conditions wherein they occur. This collective inclination is itself a determined reflection of the structure of the society in which the suicide bomber lives. Sociological imagination provides insight into which values are sacred. Conflict theory enables us to see the common characteristics of the core of how groups struggle for power while constrained by resources. The combined theories of Emile Durkheim and C. Wright Mills along with Lewis A. Coser's conflict theory allow us to factor in dispositional or motive explanations while enabling relational explanations as well. This threefold theoretical approach makes sense when, in *Female Suicide Bombers*, I reported that some early Palestinian bombers may have had personal reasons for becoming a suicide bomber, but societal conditions, including oppression from Israel, created the opportunity. In turn, the strategy of the groups that use suicide bombers was to rack up military victories.[5]

Surprise and Terror

Individuals, usually nonstate, engaged in violent actions against other persons, usually state, are generally thought of as terrorists because they have a political agenda. As a rule, they are at a disadvantage in weapons and numbers. But they do have one strategic advantage; they operate underground and with surprise attacks. "The terrorist strategy is mainly focused on creating psychological impact and effects," wrote Ronald

Meinardus.[6] This focus often involves killing innocent civilians. Their strategy is to shock and intimidate groups or individuals, and provoke a reaction. The reaction sought is often realized through media reaction. Meinardus believes that terrorism would be inconceivable if it were not for the global media.

Insurgent Strategies

The Department of Defense defines insurgency as "the organized use of subversion and violence by a group or movement that seeks to overthrow or force change of a governing authority. Insurgency can also refer to the group itself."[7] Eli Berman and David Laitin define insurgency as "a technology of rebellion by guerilla warfare which has been very successful in surviving for decades in a large number of countries and in challenging regime domination in those countries."[8] Insurgency has been connected to a variety of ideologies: communism, nationalism, religious fanaticism, and no ideology at all. The authors inferred that the tactic of suicide attacks is used when conditions are not favorable to conventional insurgency, attacks in which the attacker does not face certain death and sometimes little risk. Suicide attacks are more likely to be favored when the religions of the perpetrator and target differ.

"The 'success' of an insurgency is measured by the number of occupying force's casualties that leads to the overall demoralization of the force," according to Nicholas Corbett.[9] Corbett does not compare post-Soviet insurgency in Afghanistan to Iraqi insurgency, but rather the Afghan mujahideen anti-Soviet insurgency in Afghanistan to the insurgents in Iraq. Still, he makes some relevant points. He maintained they differ most in war casualties and in the role of suicide warfare. The Iraqi insurgency is less successful because of their unsustainable tactic of suicide warfare.

Due to religious reasons, the mujahideen did not use suicide warfare as much in Afghanistan as in Iraq. Rather, the Arab volunteers to the insurgency advocated suicide attacks. That the mujahideen were reluctant to attack bridges and trade routes would indicate they had a postwar mentality rather than one that envisioned the afterlife. A suicide attacker can only be dispatched once, therefore, suicide warfare is not a sustainable tactic.[10]

Further, Corbett indicates political science theory reveals that a group that resorts to violence has an ultimate goal to share in power in order to control resources. One means used to build support for insurgencies is to appeal to people's ethnic or religious identities. This reasoning is not unlike Lewis A. Coser's definition of social conflict theory or Durkheim's collective inclination. But I differ with Corbett when he singles out suicide warfare as a method of violence wherein the attacker cannot benefit from the action.[11]

That conclusion can be interpreted to mean the attacker will not be alive to benefit from the act. That the attacker will not live does not matter to most suicide attackers. What matters is attaining the group's goal,[12] and that the promised afterlife is condoned by a hadith.[13] Corbett's research indicated that postmortem rewards for suicide warfare seemed tailored to men.[14] In *Female Suicide Bombers*, I explained Raphael Israeli's interpretation of a Koran passage that links self-sacrifice and bravery in battle with paradise for men and women alike:

> The prophet Muhammad motivated his followers not to fear battle by describing the next world as a better one. The tradition involves the Angels Munkir and Nakir who question all deceased Muslims before they enter Paradise. Martyrs bypass this interrogation, enter heaven directly, and are spared the trials on resurrection day. A Hadith specifically says, in part, the *shahid* (male martyr) will be pardoned by Allah, admitted to paradise, marry beautiful women and be spared the tomb and will not be submitted to judgment. For the female martyr, marrying beautiful women is not generally an attraction of paradise, but being recreated as a virgin in paradise is.[15]

Strategies of Islamic Organizations

Islamic militant organizations have developed suicide bombing over the years resulting in it becoming an effective strategic weapon, maintained Gabriel Ben-Dor and Ami Pedahzur. Ben-Dor and Pedahzur compared the effectiveness of Islamic and non-Islamic suicide bombing. The effectiveness of Islamic organizations is reflected in the suicide attacks in Israel, Lebanon, Tunisia, Indonesia, Egypt, Kenya, and the United States. The authors call suicide bombers "the main force multiplier" of Islamic terrorism.[16] They advocated that while groups such as the Sri Lankan Tamil Tigers and the Kurdistan Workers' Party employed suicide bombing, it was the Islamic groups who made it a valuable strategic weapon. The reason is that the tactic of the Islamic terrorists is that they are closely related to their selection of targets, random passersby, citizens at entertainment centers, or on public transportation, as opposed to nonrandom targets such as politicians, government bodies, or military and police officers. Ben-Dor and Pedahzur found that from 1992 to 2002, not including the years 1995, 1996, and 1999, dead and injured victims numbered higher than any other form of terrorism.[17]

Islamic Organizations and Global Jihad

Three core principles compose jihadists' strategic vision, according to Devin R. Springer, James L. Regens, and David N. Edger. Expressed in Osama bin Laden's 1998 fatwa, the first principal contains a crucial concept: that jihad is an individual religious obligation in defense of Islam. It is every Muslim's duty to take part in war either by fighting, supporting, or promotion. This standard provides the motivation for the collective action espoused by Durkheim by bringing leaders together to achieve goals while molding popular support through religious values. The second core attribute of the strategic vision is geographically far-reaching, a protracted, unvarying state of warfare. Springer et al. wrote that, in the jihadists' minds, protracted means decades or centuries, not months or years. The third core principle is that the jihadists represent a revolutionary leading position and example for the Muslim world. This principle is to create a critical mass of mujahideen within the Muslim population who can restore the caliphate and extend its boundaries to include the world that represents their desire to inextricably unite the political and religious. *Al-Khilafah* or caliphate is a unified system of temporal authority of a successor to the Prophet Muhammad over the community of believers.[18]

Al Qaeda realized they were not close to either having a mass following or taking over any Muslim country. Therefore, they focused on the immediate concern of how to defeat the United States, overthrow U.S. allies in the Muslim world, and how to destroy Israel. Bruce Riedel wrote of a three-pronged strategy as well: The first was to wear down the United States and its allies with the wars in Iraq and Afghanistan; second, to consolidate their safe havens in South Asia while authorizing new al Qaeda franchises such as the Zarqawi network in Iraq and al Qaeda in Mesopotamia, all across the Muslim world; and third, to build an infrastructure of supporters in the West, particularly Europe, to stage raids into the West.[19]

The shared core principles are quite different from implementation, wrote Springer et al. Three competing elements compete with these principles: first, ethnic and territorial resistance movements such as the Chechens or Hamas; second, religious nationalists such as the Egyptian Islamic Jihad or the Algerian GIA; and third, the radical al Qaeda movement that focuses internationally, specifically on Western governments that support local regimes seeking to establish a religious based state. Springer et al. categorizes these competing elements the near enemy and the far enemy, and that the shift from the near to the far was a fundamental change in strategy borne out of necessity. However, all jihadists did not accept the change, for example, the Muslim Brotherhood in Egypt and the Hamas in Israel and occupied territories. Attacks that represented this shift include the 1998 bombings on the U.S. embassies in Kenya and Tanzania and the 2000 USS *Cole*. In addition, other strategy variations occurred. Targeting of the far enemy in a local setting, that is a jihadist thinks globally but acts locally, also happens, for example, the Saudi branch of al Qaeda's May 12, 2003 suicide car bombings in Western housing compounds in Saudi Arabia. The goal of these attacks was to control territory to restore the caliphate. Examples include Afghanistan, Iraq, or Somalia in the 1990s.[20]

Al Qaeda's goal to establish the Islamic caliphate is outlined in seven phases. It first appeared in 2005 when a reporter, Fuad Hasnin, wrote the book *Al-Zarqawi: Al-Qaeda's Second Generation*. The seven stages are a stated timetable spread over a period of 20 years. It began in 2000, with the preparations for the 9/11 attacks, and is intended to end in 2020. Stages 1–5 include the steps to establish Islamic caliphates throughout the Arab world. Stages 6 and 7 confront the international community, within bin Laden's structure of the war between the powers of faith and the powers of the heretics, to impose Islam. This plan ends in 2020 (see Appendix C).[21]

Jihadists Tactic of Suicide Attacks (Martyrdom)

Jihadist suicide attacks often occur in a variety of locations at the same time with mass casualties. Al Qaeda emphasizes reliance on suicide attacks and refer to them as martyrdom operations in their statements and literature, reported Springer et al. Jihadists cloak suicide terrorism in a religious mantel thus enabling them to pursue their strategic goal of forcing Western democracies to withdraw military forces from areas of conflict. The Koran does not mention suicide, but it is forbidden in the hadith, a collection of statements and actions of the Prophet Mohammad. On the other hand, martyrdom is praised both in the Koran and in the hadith. By defining suicide bombing as martyrdom, radical Islamists have provided a religious justification for it. The prohibition of suicide does not apply in a suicide attack because suicide is motivated by selfishness out of fear and desperation as opposed to martyrdom acts that are altruistic. In addition, Abu Ubayd al-Qurashi reported that the al Qaeda's use of asymmetric strategy cannot be employed by the defenders. The martyrdom bombs caused a reduction in the U.S. military effectiveness and an evaporation of the U.S. sense of security.[22]

Al Qaeda

Two very important world events occurred in 2011 that have strongly affected al Qaeda's strategy and tactics: the revolutionary unrest in the Arab world and the killing of al Qaeda leaders, including Osama bin Laden. Peter Knoope and Anno Bunnik believe some effects were evident as developments unfolded in the Arab world. Primarily, the revolts in Egypt and Tunisia demonstrated "the bankruptcy of al Qaeda's strategy and tactics."[23] Part of the reason that al Qaeda did not cause the Arab unrest that resulted in change was because it did not consider these corrupt oppressive regimes as the near enemy. The citizens in the region demanded effective change calling for social justice, better employment opportunities, less corruption, and more political freedom. Jihad was neither the instigator nor the answer. This unrest did not occur in the name of God. Knoope and Bunnik contend that the failure of al Qaeda's strategy over the last decade has prompted the confrontations between the citizens and the governments in Tunisia, Egypt, Libya, Yemen, and Syria.

The big question is whether al Qaeda adjusted its strategy after bin Laden was killed. One view is that these revolutionary groups who were not "organized under one roof" brought down long-ruling, powerful dictators, wrote Moshe Covo and Gilad Zahavi. Al Qaeda, on the other hand, with its hierarchical organization, reciprocal relationships, organized system of the seven stages (also called the 2020 plan), and clear ideology had fallen short of its goal to bring down oppressive regimes. Defenders of al Qaeda organizational policy argued that the mujahideen should help the insurgents in these regions in a way that accelerates the bringing down the tyrannical governments.[24] In Ayman al-Zawahiri's June 8, 2011 eulogy for bin Laden, he said al Qaeda supported the Muslim people's blessed uprisings and that al Qaeda is their partner in one campaign against America and its allies. Like themes appeared in the announcement of al-Zawahiri's appointment as bin Laden's successor published by al Qaeda's general leadership in June 2011. Other similar themes are also available on the Internet.[25]

Along with avenging bin Laden's death, al Qaeda is paying more attention to near enemies and these factors translate into the possibility of more attacks, Covo and Zahavi reported.[26] The chaos in the Arab countries and the substantial release of security detainees and escaped prisoners provide opportunity and a place to maneuver in these countries against foreign targets, wrote Cove and Zahavi. In Yemen, the organization will do everything possible to take advantage of the turmoil, but in the long run, al Qaeda in the Arabian Peninsula (AQAP) will not succeed in Yemen because its message is counter to the goals of most of the population. A longer-term goal is to be aware of the extent that al Qaeda affiliates can continue to follow a common strategy and doctrine without bin Laden. Their media output is a good indicator of at least their intentions, according to Michael W. S. Ryan.[27]

So, how will al Qaeda plan its attacks without bin Laden? Not only did he establish al Qaeda, but also turned the idea of a global Islamic caliphate into an operational plan, became a role model and representative of a jihadist vision shared by millions, and established a global jihad terror network with al Qaeda as its center. "Bin Laden's assassination does not affect the capabilities of these organizations [global and regional jihad] and, in fact, only raises their motivation to perpetrate revenge attacks," concluded Boaz Ganor.[28] A mega attack is likely due to the desire for revenge and perhaps bin Laden may have left behind instructions for such an attack should his life end. Despite high motivation, al Qaeda's capability may not be sufficient to stage a large-scale attack.

The strategic change in the organization will be apparent in its new leadership, according to Murad Batal al-Shishani. These leaders include Egyptian jihadist Ayman al-Zawahiri; Egyptian commander Saif al-Adel; and other Shura council members (the governing council of the organization) Abu Yahya al-Libi (a.k.a. Hassan Muhammad Qaid, killed in 2012), Abu Abdulrahman Attiya al-Libi (a.k.a. Jamal Ibrahim Shtelwi al-Misrati), Abdul Majid Abdul Majid, and little known Abu Khalil al-Madani.

Nonetheless, the organization will continue relying on its ideology. It will be more collective than hierarchical in nature, concluded al-Shishani. Zawahiri is likely to focus on the near enemy, but this concentration may depend on the popular movements in the Arab world. A need exists to develop a military ideologue.[29]

Insurgents

The strategy of insurgents that has emerged, however chaotic, is fairly typical for insurgents opposing outside occupiers. Steven Metz and Raymond Millen gave three parallel and interlinked tracks of the insurgency: destabilize the existing government, alienate the population, and cause counterinsurgent casualties. Key changes in current insurgencies are they are linked to a wider, but asymmetric, global conflict; opponents are a major power and a transnational insurgent terrorist network; dedication of extensive amounts of time to fund raising independent of sponsors; development of terrorism, strategic intelligence, and regional and global linkages without state effort; shift in ideology with one based on transnational, radical Islam on the rise; and a change in the nature of psychological warfare due to transparency that results from information technology, globalization, and the international flow of people.[30]

Jihadist Insurgencies

The jihadist understands the principles of asymmetrical warfare, wrote Springer et al. In 1996, bin Laden acknowledged the imbalance of power between the jihadists' armed forces and its enemy forces:[31]

[I]t must be obvious to you that, due to the imbalance of power between our armed forces and the enemy forces, a suitable means of fighting must be adopted, i.e., using fast moving light forces that work under complete secrecy. In other words, to initiate a guerrilla warfare, where the sons of the nation, and not the military forces, take part in it. And as you know, it is wise, in the present circumstances, for the armed military forces not to be engaged in a conventional fighting with the forces of the crusader enemy (the exceptions are the bold and the forceful operations carried out by the members of the armed forces individually, that is without the movement of the formal forces in its conventional shape and hence the responses will not be directed, strongly, against the army) unless a big advantage is likely to be achieved; and great losses induced on the enemy side (that would shake and destroy its foundations and infrastructures) that will help to expel the defeated enemy from the country.[32]

Patrick Porter describes jihadists as not a centralized body or a directed arm of one power, but represent various scattered groups. Central direction and unified command structures are also lacking. The insurrections in Iraq are examples of the variety for they are part Islamist, Sunni supremacist, confessional and ethnic civil war, and criminal activity. Making use of the Internet and media, the multifaceted insurgency cohesively grows, changes, and inspires other attacks while "enabling insurgents to copy one another's martyrdoms as a worldwide conversation."[33]

The success of the jihadist strategy depends on their capability to sustain a conflict with a stronger force that has technological advantages in conventional warfare. It is doubtful that asymmetrical warfare can curtail superior military technology, particularly airpower. The strategy of prolonged conflict, however, can wear down military force through reducing its morale as well as public support.[34]

Strategies of Suicide Bombers in Iraq, Afghanistan, and Pakistan

Iraq

No suicide bombers existed in Iraq until the coalition entered the war, but as Pape reported, the number of suicide attacks dramatically increased whenever U.S. forces expanded their presence (see Chapter 2). Mohammed M. Hafez, however, contends that this correlation is not the cause of ongoing suicide attacks, but rather al Qaeda's pragmatism and its organizational adaptability and evolution. First generation jihadists did not employ suicide bombing as a key component in their strategy in the Soviet–Afghan war. The second generation understood the Palestinians use of suicide bombing in Lebanon and in Palestine. Special recognition and religious legitimacy became acceptable reasons to participate in suicide bombing, according to Hafez.[35] In Iraq, the intent of salafi-jihadi terrorism was to incite a secular civil war in Iraq and have the United States withdraw because it found the situation untenable. A U.S. pullout would permit al Qaeda to establish a base and move toward a true Islamic state or caliphate. The logic of promoting suicide tactics in Iraq was to set off sectarian violence that would pull the hesitant Sunni population into the conflict, then establish the conditions for foreign jihadis to operate freely among the host Sunni population.[36]

Most suicide attacks in Iraq were aimed at Shia noncombatants. The Sadr (Muqtada al-Sadr) militia conducted the Shia response to the suicide bombing campaign. The Shia militia used covert death squads and employed abductions, torture, and extrajudicial murder against everyday Sunnis, wrote Hafez. Al Qaeda or Sunni groups promoted suicide attacks through writings, ritual, and ceremony to cultivate a cult-like status for martyrs. Fanaticism is deeply rooted in the Saudi Wahhabi doctrine and *Takfiri* extremism. Sunni suicide bombers have volunteered as martyrs and come from outside Iraq.[37]

The Iraq insurgency followed Metz and Millen's three parallel and interlinked tracks, but the authors concluded that a positive dimension is missing from the strategy of the very young and immature Iraqi insurgency. In 2004, it had not created the impression that the government or occupier could not create a stable or just society and, in turn, it could, nor had the insurgency a vision of the kind of nation it would create should it expel the coalition.[38]

Suicide bombing was an integral part of the Iraq war. Nicole Stracke conducted a study of 550 of confirmed suicide bombing operations between March 2003 and December 2006. She found that suicide attacks on U.S. military and civilian targets in Iraq were low when compared to the number of overall suicide attacks that have occurred since the U.S. invasion. She also found that suicide bombing attacks on soft targets increased from March 2003 to February 2007.[39]

Afghanistan

The insurgency in Afghanistan consists of conflict between different groups and powerful figures, and the global insurgency focused on radical Islam, wrote Metz and Millen. Because bin Laden viewed the United States as a deterrent in creating Islam's historical caliphate, he sought to challenge, humiliate, and psychologically dominate it. In an effort to duplicate the Soviet–Afghan conflict, the decade of attacks ending with September 11, 2001 was al Qaeda's effort to draw the United States into Afghanistan. Al Qaeda's success led to a temporary setback for the organization resulting in the loss of Afghanistan as a base of operations. In 2004, the Afghan insurgency lacked the characteristics of success. Primarily, it was unable to formulate an ideology that communicated the worthiness of their return to power. Violence had not subsided, the Afghan people were weary of war, and viewed the al Qaeda and Taliban as unsuccessful in bringing about peace.[40]

The Taliban in Afghanistan

In 1999, Ahmed Rashid indicated that neighboring countries were in Afghanistan, such as militants from Pakistan, Iran, and the Central Asian republics, and China's predominantly Muslim Xinjiang province. He wrote, "the dangerous behavior of Afghanistan's new leaders is no longer a local affair" and that "thousands of foreign radicals now fighting alongside the Taliban in Afghanistan are determined to someday overthrow their own regimes and carry out Taliban-style Islamist revolutions in their homelands."[41] In addition, the insurgency flourished with bin Laden serving as an ideological mentor and the backing of Pakistan and Saudi Arabia entered the foreign–national mix that joined the Taliban. The support of the mix is from outside Afghanistan. The Taliban are largely Pushtun, the largest ethnic group, and are Sunni fundamentalists. The Taliban are the self-ordained true leaders of Afghanistan who represent pure Islam.[42] The Taliban and al Qaeda's utilization of suicide bombing is one method the groups use to commit their violence (see Chapter 2).

Stanley A. McChrystal states that the Taliban strategy is shared by their allies, al Qaeda, because they can function as a network. He explained, "The Taliban not only enjoy the typical insurgent advantage of working on home ground, but they have also learned to use 21st century information technology. This allows them to function as a network rather than as a traditional army, a strategy which is shared by their allies in the Islamic terrorist group al Qaeda."[43]

The Taliban have completely changed, reported Vahid Mojdeh, a former Taliban foreign ministry official who watches the movement. They have dropped their international agenda of spreading the Islamist revolution, and instead are focused on Afghanistan. Another change is that their policies are more sophisticated. The Taliban represent a new generation familiar with computers and cell phones. The Taliban have developed a plan for civilian governance of regions they control. They are now accepting ideas from those people who had been in the movement of the late Afghan guerrilla leader, Ahmed Shah Massoud. One such idea is that people behind the front lines should be safe, according to Haroun Mir Vahid Mojdeh, director of Afghanistan's Center for Research and Policy Studies.[44] Recruitment for suicide bombings takes place in madrassas or Islamic schools. Pupils who are emotional are prime candidates. The Taliban provide these pupils with a fake suicide belt to be replaced with a real belt when the student no longer displays fear. The students say good-bye to their families, and then disappear, according to Mojdeh. The Afghan National Directorate for Security estimates that, in the guise of religious education centers, at least 1,000 mobile insurgent training centers are in Pakistan's seven tribal agencies. These centers are in "lawless zones beyond the writ of the central government," according to Roy Gutman.[45]

In July 2009, Mullah Mohammed Omar issued a new code of conduct that included instructions such as to avoid civilian casualties, not to attack or harm prisoners, suicide bombings should be used only on high and important targets, and every fighter is to win over the local population by treating them well and behaving well themselves.[46] According to the *New York Times*, issuing a code and enforcing it are not the same. The new public relations campaign combined with relatively less cruel behavior may have abated some of the anger at the insurgency, but the most important aspect in their increasing popularity is the ineffectiveness of the central government and Afghans' resentment of foreign troops. The Taliban still relied on intimidation through night letters, threatening conversations, and assassinations. People feared the Taliban.[47] Attacks in 2011 also indicated no change had taken place. In Kabul, on September 13, 2011, Taliban launched an attack on the U.S. Embassy and the headquarters of the NATO-led foreign forces. They fired missiles from a partially constructed multistory building. In addition, three suicide bombers targeted police buildings in other parts of the city. It is believed that the Haqqani network was responsible. Haqqani is one of three Taliban-allied insurgent factions and responsible for introducing suicide bombing to Afghanistan.[48] In August 2011, Taliban militants shot down a U.S. helicopter, killing 30 U.S. special forces, mostly Navy SEALs, and 8 Afghans.[49] Lastly, the safe haven of Pakistan was not to be underestimated in the Taliban's success.[50]

In 2011, on the occasion of Eid, the end of Ramadan, Mullah Omar issued a message that Ahmed Rashid refers to as "the longest and by far the most forward-looking political message he has ever sent, offering the Taliban's latest views on several central issues."[51] Omar stated that the Taliban are not interested in monopolizing power. For the first time, he admits that the Taliban have negotiated with the Americans about the release of prisoners rather than a political exchange of ideas. This admission sent a clear message to his fighters that future political talks were a possibility and, at the same time, indicated to the Americans that Omar may in time broaden the scope of the dialogue and include those already participating. Omar wanted immediate withdrawal of NATO and U.S. forces. Rashid views this message as a hopeful sign that talks and a negotiated settlement to end the war are possible. One hopeful sign of progress for negotiations with the Taliban was that the gulf state of Qatar was hosting a Taliban office. The office enables the West to begin formal talks to end the war in Afghanistan, according to Brendan Trembath.[52] Attacks continue in 2012. One of the latest involved three suicide bombers who overtook a hotel in Kabul, killed three security guards and engaged in a lengthy gun battle.[53]

The Taliban's pressure on major carriers to turn off their signal towers is just one part of a broader shift in their strategy that has concentrated on intimidation, carefully selected assassinations, and a degree of spectacular assaults, according to Alissa J. Rubin. Although the Taliban and the Haqqani network sometimes avoid large-scale combat with NATO forces, they have effectively undermined peace talks with the Afghan government in an effort to pave the way for a gradual return to power as the American-led forces begin reducing military operations.[54]

Examples of the Taliban's broader strategy include the September 13, 2011 rocket attack on the American Embassy that was seen as a shift in the conflict to the cities where a NATO airpower response is less likely for fear of harming civilians, according to Rubin. Suicide bombing is ongoing. On September 20, 2011, a Pakistani turban suicide bomber killed Professor Burhanuddin Rabbani at his home in Kabul. Rabbani was chairman of President Karzai's High Peace Council with the task of negotiating with the Taliban. Two men arrived claiming to be from the Taliban. The Inter-Services Intelligence–backed Haqqani network was suspected to be responsible. Peace talks with the Taliban were temporarily suspended until a new peace strategy was worked out.[55] The Taliban's asserted support of education and business development combined with projecting an image that they are more open to the world, they hope to play a prominent role in Afghanistan's future.

In May 2011, two events signify the Taliban were not yet receptive to the idea of peace talks. Taliban attacks followed President Obama's visit with troops and signing of a strategic partnership agreement with President Hamid Karzai.[56] The second event involved the assassination of a former high-ranking Taliban, Arsala Rahmani, who was working on reconciling Afghanistan's insurgency with the government, reported Chris Blake and Rahim Faiez. The strategic timing of the shooting sent a message of disapproval for peace efforts since on the same day, Kabul had announced it was gradually assuming the lead from the U.S.-led coalition for providing security in the country. The Taliban deny responsibility for the attack, but had said they would target the peace process.[57]

Pakistan

Pakistan is becoming the fifth largest country in the world with a rapidly developing nuclear program, according to Peter Bergen. He believes that Pakistan presents a major foreign-policy challenge. The idea that a terrorist could access nuclear weapons is difficult to imagine, but the idea that a terrorist could set off a nuclear attack or cause a Mumbai Two is to be considered.[58] Pakistan's record combating terrorism is mixed. It should be remembered that the Taliban is not an indigenous movement that started from southern Afghanistan, Haron Amin contended. The Taliban did not just come out of some sort of a spontaneous combustion theory, but that they were created in Pakistan.[59]

Pakistani performance in the War on Terror hasn't always met the expectations of the United States. Pakistan's inability to defeat the terrorist groups within its country is due to many factors going beyond its lack of motivation, wrote Ashley J. Tullis. In fear of its strategic needs with India going unmet, President Pervez Musharraf cut his initial ties with the Taliban to maintain U.S. support regarding issues with India, but failed in other counterterrorism efforts.[60]

Although it is difficult to say how many terror groups operate in Pakistan, the Council on Foreign Relations lists five major groups:

1. Sectarian—Sunni Sipah-e-Sahaba, Lashkar-e-Jhangvi, and Shia Tehrik-e-Jafria are active within Pakistan.
2. Anti-Indian—Lashkar-e-Taiba, Jaish-e-Muhammad, and Harakat ul-Mujahadeen. They function with the supposed support of the Pakistani military and the intelligence agency Inter-Services Intelligence.
3. Afghan Taliban—The original Taliban movement.
4. Al Qaeda and its affiliates—The organization led by Osama bin Laden and other non-South Asian terrorists believed to be well established in the Federally Administered Tribal Areas (FATA). Additional foreign militant groups are located in FATA: Islamic Movement of Uzbekistan, Islamic Jihad Group, Libyan Islamic Fighters Group, and Eastern Turkistan Islamic Movement.
5. Pakistani Taliban—Groups consisting of extremist outfits in the FATA.[61]

Robert A. Pape and James K. Feldman divided the Pakistan suicide campaign into two phases: from 2002 to 2005 and 2006 to present day. The emerging relationship of the two countries during the first period was militarily autonomous, and the number of suicide attack rates was low (12). Although their target was Shiite civilians, the broader objective of the sectarian suicide attacks was to damage the Pakistani government. Lashkar-e-Jhangvi conducted most sectarian attacks until Musharraf banned the group. Al Qaeda then reached out to the alienated groups.[62]

During the second period, from 2006 to present day, the United States dominated the relationship with Pakistan, and wanted Pakistan to take serious action against the militants. In so doing, the United States moved 100,000 troops from Pakistan's eastern border with India to fight militants in western Pakistan. Pape and Feldman called the situation indirect occupation of Pakistan by the United States. Musharraf eventually fell from favor and resigned in August 2008. Of the 206 suicide attacks, 62 percent were directed at military targets in the tribal areas.[63]

In 2012, Pakistan continues to produce and export Islamist extremism and terrorism, but there was a decrease in overall fatalities through 2011, according to the South Asia Terrorism Portal. Fatalities caused by suicide attacks sharply declined, but the reduction in the total number of such attacks was not as sharp. In 2011, 41 suicide attacks caused 628 fatalities compared to 2010 when 49 attacks causing 1,167 fatalities. The FATA continues to be the most volatile region.[64]

Previous years demonstrate that although no suicide attack took place in Pakistan until 2001, Pakistan has had to bear the brunt of the War on Terror in its country, reported *Individualland*. At the end of 2009, 200 suicide attacks had occurred and about 500 bomb and improvised explosive device (IED) explosions. Casualties for the 8-year period totaled 25,000. Most in Pakistan's society do not support suicide bombing. In 2010, a survey within FATA revealed that 57.1 percent condemned suicide bombing, whereas in 2009, 42 percent had viewed suicide bombing as never justified. Respondents (41%) saw terrorist attacks as the main threat to their life. The poll in 2010 also revealed dislike for Pakistani Taliban, but not Afghan Taliban.[65]

Strategies of Female Suicide Bombers

Public discourse tends to be reductionist in nature by accentuating only certain elements of female attackers' reality, wrote Melissa Finn.[66] These narratives either describe such attributes as the attackers' beauty, piety, or purity, or characterize them negatively as social outcasts, defective, manipulated, exploited, or forcibly recruited. Early bombing attacks by women were often characterized with insufficient dispositional explanations such as motives, emotions, decision logics, and cultural templates. Early in my own research for *Female Suicide Bombers*, I sometimes found that predominately personal motives such as acquiring honor for her or family were attributed to women who bomb. If she acted solely on these personal motives, suicide may be termed Durkheim's anomie. Motives were also inspired by social conditions such as honor to country. To be so tightly integrated into one's society that women commit suicide, Durkheim labeled as altruistic and noted that it also applies to people who seek to be martyrs. Anomie can overlap with altruism. Durkheim believed that suicide could not be explained by its form alone, but suicide must be related to social concomitants.[67] In *Female Suicide Bombers*, I concluded that an ethics of form was needed in the examination of the female suicide bomber and made the effort to present women with empathy and more than a history. To achieve this goal, I chose to "present the female suicide bomber in the context of the power of the society in which she lives, of the terrorist group of which she is a member and of her society as a part of the larger global community."[68]

Whatever the reasons that women bomb, "the use of women as suicide bombers has been a strategic choice used by contemporary terrorist groups to attain their political goals," wrote Karunya M. Jayasena.[69] From 1985 to 2010, the U.S. Customs found that 262 women suicide bombers in their attacks resulted in higher casualties than the same number by men. The reason for more casualties is because women are able to get closer to their target.[70] In 2011, in *Women in Combat*, I concluded,

So, regardless of the conflicting ways women are perceived within their organizations or from without, women combatants are highly successful at their assigned task, suicide bombing. Men alone cannot win the war and since this phenomenon is war, the men and women who recruit women, are highly aware of women's ability to meet the organization's need in combat.[71]

Exploiting women for their personal reasons is part of a terror group's strategy. Jayasena noted Fighel's findings that the Palestine Islamic Jihad (PIJ) exploits and knows that the period of mourning is an ideal time to approach women. Feelings for revenge are at a peak and the PIJ manipulates the personal grief to serve the organization's own agenda.[72]

Patterns of Women Who Bomb

In 2010, the U.S. Customs Office of Intelligence and Operations Coordination found the following patterns in female suicide bombers:

- The majority of female suicide bombers are young, primarily between the ages of 17 and 24; however, the overall range in age for female suicide bombers is from 15 to 64.
- Female suicide bombers come from various educational, religious, social, and personal backgrounds.

- Education plays a role, with the more educated females such as lawyers, paramedics, or students accounting for the greatest percentage of suicide attacks.
- Most tend to be of average economic status and are rarely impoverished.
- Some may be dishonored through sexual indiscretion, or unable to produce children.
- Some appear motivated by revenge or grief of losing husbands or children as in the woman who killed 15 people in Diyala province on December 7, 2008. Her two sons joined al Qaeda in Iraq and were killed by security forces.[73]

Lindsey O'Rourke conducted a study across the groups of the five conflicts that took place from 1981 to July 2008. She sought to explain variation in utilizing women in regard to the specific coercive strategy of suicide attacks. She found, "female suicide attacks are more likely to inflict casualties and are more lethal at both the individual and team levels."[74] Further she found that women compared to men offered many tactical advantages. The favorable position of women attackers is demonstrated by the greater lethality of their attacks, the greater frequency of assassination attacks, and the increased public fury and media coverage they generate. Interestingly, O'Rourke noted, "This effectiveness results from the gender norms of the societies where [female suicide] attacks take place; such norms enable female attackers to achieve greater surprise and concealment."[75] The superior effectiveness influenced secular and religious terrorist organizations to utilize women at the service of the groups' strategic goals.

Primary groups involved in conflicts that employed women early include the Syrian Social Nationalist Party versus Israel and the South Lebanon Army, the Kurdistan Workers' Party versus Turkey, the Liberation Tigers of Tamil Eelam (LTTE) versus Sri Lanka, the Chechen separatists versus Russia, and those groups related to the Palestinian–Israeli conflict such as al-Aqsa Martyrs Brigade, the Palestinian nationalists, the PIJ, and the Hamas (see Part II).

LTTE Tigresses

Of these groups, the LTTE perpetrated the most attacks with women. The Black Tigresses prepared women for suicide bombing and represented 30–40 percent of the attackers.[76] Recruiters selected women to bomb for their mental stability over tactical military competence. They had to be highly motivated to complete the mission. Once chosen, they were trained in camps separate from the others. Part of the training was that the Tigers and the Tigresses conduct a dress rehearsal near the proposed site of the attack and study films of past operations.[77] LTTE is the only organization that has assassinated two heads of state by suicide attacks. Indian Prime Minister Rajiv Gandhi was killed by a woman, Dhanu, in May 1991 and President Primadassa of Sri Lanka was killed in May 1993 by a later identified male attacker as Babu.[78]

Black Widows

The Chechen rebels hold the distinction of having killed the largest number, 170, with a high percentage of women participants, the Black Widows, in 2002, when the rebels held 700 hostages in the Moscow theater. In 2004, five attacks were attributed to the Chechen rebels. An attack on a school in Beslan, North Ossetia–Alania, Russia, resulted in the death of about 326 children and adults on September 1, 2004.[79] The Black Widows remain active. On March 28, 2011 in Moscow's metro, two women thought to be Chechen rebels blew themselves up, killing about 35 people and injuring 100.[80]

Women Attackers: Al Qaeda in Iraq and Afghanistan

Al Qaeda recognized the strategic value of women attackers in 2003, later than the earlier groups.[81] Insurgents in Iraq accounted for about a dozen women attackers between 2003 and December 2007, and approximately 27 between January and July 2008, a period of relative decline for suicide attacks in general, according to O'Rourke.[82] Women had previously attacked in Iraq and Israel, but in 2010, security officials were warned the use of Western looking women for al Qaeda attacks was imminent.[83] In Iraq, female bombers had been able to get to their targets despite multiple layers of security. The reason being the culture forbids male policemen or checkpoint guards from searching women who therefore have easy passage because they can go unchecked. Culture also frowns upon employing women in security forces, thus allowing them to enter high-value targets such as police stations and markets.[84] Afghan culture also forbids men searching women. In August 2011, a woman carried out an attack at a checkpoint near Peshawar, Pakistan, complicating security efforts. In December 2010, a bomber wearing a burqa killed more than 40 people in a food distribution center in Bajaur tribal region near the Afghan border. It is believed that the Taliban were behind these attacks.[85]

In the past, explosive devices were primarily concealed on women. These devices were equipped with a simple toggle or push button switch that if it failed, it could be remotely detonated. Small pieces of metal were used and the device was worn close to the body. New strategy involves surgical breast implants filled with explosives.[86]

Strategic Responses to Suicide Warfare

Differences in Traditional and Irregular Warfare

According to Rear Admiral (RADM) D.M. Williams, Jr., U.S. Navy (Retd.), former commander, Naval Investigative Service Command, in the

War on Terror, the enemy "does not abide by rules of warfare that have evolved over centuries. They neither recognize nor respect what constitutes a legitimate target and what does not." He contrasts state-based military action and suicide bombers:

The military functions under a recognized chain of command at the direction of a state. In the case of terrorists, for the most part, that frequently is not the case. They may be acting independently or if they are sponsored by or acting on behalf of some state, that is frequently difficult if not impossible to prove. The UN Charter recognizes the right of self defense—a defense of necessity. Thus, the military functions under a body of rules that requires targeting discretion. You are only allowed to attack military objectives. You don't attack churches. You don't attack hospitals. You don't attack civilians. If you look at the object of terrorist attacks, they are precisely the opposite of that. Indiscriminate killing is their touchstone and hallmark. Innocent civilians and children are specifically targeted and killed. They don't really care. You can cite any number of examples of that from terrorist attacks; the bombing of airliners, the World Trade Center, the Kenyan embassy, the IRA killing of Lord Mountbatten, the Mumbai attacks, and a number of bombings in Iraq that are directed at civilian targets. All of those involved incidents where the people being attacked are civilians that have no connection to combat.[87]

Asymmetric Warfare and Modular Defense

In 2001, Timothy L. Thomas wrote that very few people understood asymmetry's formal definition. One of the reasons was that the 1998 joint doctrine did not define asymmetry.[88] The 2000 joint doctrine defined symmetrical and asymmetrical as "the engagements with the enemy may be symmetrical (if the U.S. force and the enemy force are similar), or asymmetric if forces are dissimilar."[89]

Inherent in the concept of irregular warfare is asymmetric warfare. Natural tension exists between the role of doctrine and the nature of asymmetry. Clinton J. Ancker, III, and Michael D. Burke stated, "The implicit premise is that asymmetric warfare deals with unknowns, with surprise in terms of ends, ways, and means. The more dissimilar the opponent, the more difficult it is to anticipate his actions."[90] Doctrine, or philosophy, should communicate concisely how the U.S. Armed Forces carry out military operations. It should provide a way to think about asymmetry. If known how an opponent planned to exploit dissimilarities, specific doctrine to counter his actions can be developed. Uncertainty, however, is not separable from the nature of warfare. Asymmetry increases uncertainty, according to Ancker and Burke.

In 2008, the first major update of the Field Manual 3-0, *Operations*, was released. This manual is the army's keystone doctrine used to prepare the military force to have a mindset to deal with uncertainty quickly and effectively. It marks a shift from earlier manuals in that it contains more specific doctrine, stated Ancker and Burke.[91] Lt. Gen. William B. Caldwell, IV, the commanding general of the U.S. Army Combined Arms Center at Fort Leavenworth, Kansas commented about the 2008 manual:

We're not teaching soldiers what to think in the school and centers; we're teaching them how to think, how to think critically and how to think creatively. There is no way that we can properly prepare soldiers for the challenges and diversity of the threats they will face on the battlefield today. They are too diverse. The asymmetrical threats are absolutely unpredictable and will continue to be in the 21st-century battlefield. Therefore, we must ground soldiers in the principles and the art of creative and critical thinking. That has been what we are pushing back into the school houses.[92]

The importance of the reasoning powers of soldiers is demonstrated at several points in the field manual. For example, the enemy may combine traditional, disruptive, catastrophic, and irregular capabilities, as they seek to "create advantageous conditions by quickly changing the nature of the conflict and moving to employ capabilities for which the United States is least prepared."[93] Military leaders must have the ability to operate across this range of conflict and flexible enough to adapt when necessary. Most importantly, leaders need an offensive way of thinking that permits them to see opportunities in challenges and act on them. Responses to hostile asymmetric approaches must be fielded across the force in weeks not months to be adapted often and innovatively as the enemy adapts to counter the newfound advantages.[94]

Key in this discussion is irregular threats that the enemy poses utilizing unconventional, asymmetric methods and means to counter traditional U.S. advantages. The manual states, "A weaker enemy often uses irregular warfare to exhaust the U.S. collective will through protracted conflict. Irregular warfare includes such means as terrorism, insurgency, and guerrilla warfare. Economic, political, informational, and cultural initiatives usually accompany and may even be the chief means of irregular attacks on U.S. influence."[95]

Offensive and defensive operations put utmost importance on employing the lethal effects of combat power against the enemy. Speed, surprise, and shock are vital considerations. The side better able to combine them defeats its opponent rapidly and with fewer losses. In the offensive phase of Iraqi Freedom in 2003, the combination of operations collapsed the organized resistance. Asymmetric capabilities along with speed and operations security contribute to the element of surprise. However, it is the shock operation that slows and disrupts enemy operations. Shock results from applying overpowering violence with enough speed and magnitude that it slows and disrupts enemy operations. Although usually transient, shock may paralyze the enemy's ability to fight. Threatening to use overwhelming violence can also produce shock. The manual states, "Shock is often greater when generated with asymmetric means. Joint forces create opportunities to increase it by using capabilities against which the enemy has limited defense. Surprise and speed magnify the effects of shock."[96]

In 2010, the Joint Chiefs revised for the third time Joint Publication 3-0, *Joint Operations* publication. This publication provides doctrine and is the basis of the joint operations series. Unlike the 1998 doctrine, it includes asymmetric warfare as a vital part. In fact, it stresses throughout that irregular warfare favors indirect and asymmetric approaches, even though it may utilize the full range of military and other capabilities to wear down an opponent's power, influence, and will. Terrorism is one form of irregular warfare that occurs alone or in combination with other forms such as insurgency, disinformation, propaganda, or organized criminal activity. The form depends on the opponent's capabilities and objectives. According to *Joint Operations*, "What makes irregular warfare irregular is the focus of its operations, a relevant population and its strategic purpose to gain or maintain control or influence over, and the support of that relevant population through political, psychological, and economic methods. Warfare that has the population as its focus of operations requires a different mindset and different capabilities than warfare that focuses on defeating an adversary militarily."[97]

Historically, the use of asymmetric warfare has provided the leverage needed to prevail in many cases. Examples include operations against German efforts to reinforce its forces in Normandy, attacks against Japanese surface reinforcement of Guadalcanal, and the allied maneuver in Europe in 1944 to reduce German submarine bases and V-1 and V-2 launching sites. Today, new technologies permit small groups to use asymmetric methods to threaten the United States directly or indirectly with criminal activity, terrorism, or armed aggression on a transnational scale with relative ease and with little cost.[98]

A more recent example of the use of asymmetric warfare is the Iraqi insurgency's suicide campaign. Domenico Tosini focuses in particular on the campaign of al Qaeda and its allies against Iraqi civilians, who are Shiite, rather than attacking occupying forces. In fact, Tosini stated that since the overthrow of Saddam Hussein in 2003, Iraq has become a "theatre of a asymmetric warfare conducted by a multifaceted Sunni insurgency" (see Chapter 2).[99] The components of the insurgency included the foreign terrorists who relied heavily on car bombs, the main insurgency in the Sunni triangle (north and west of Baghdad), and the Shiite uprising.[100] One of the crucial factors that contributed to the decision-making of al Qaeda and its allies was their radical opposition to the new political regime that the Anglo American occupiers chose along with the highly asymmetric nature of the warfare between al Qaeda and the occupying forces. Much of al Qaeda's effectiveness was due to the impact of suicide attacks, militarily, emotionally, and symbolically. Suicide attacks against coalition forces, however, became difficult because American soldiers became more effective in defending themselves. Thus, violence against the population, specifically, vigilantism against the Shiites, became an alternative way to put pressure on the occupying forces and the puppet regime. It also put pressure on Iraqi civilians not to collude with the occupiers. Tosini concludes, "Using unconventional methods, including suicide bombings against civilians, instead of fighting the enemy directly, is part of their strategic gamble."[101]

Culture and Asymmetric Conflict

"Culture is crucial, both ours and theirs, . . . irregular wars are won or lost in the minds of the local people. If we do not understand what is in those minds, what they value and how much they value it, success secured against terrorists and other insurgents will most likely be only temporary," wrote Colin S. Gray.[102]

The U.S. military, especially the Army and Marine Corps, has taken on numerous initiatives to factor culture into mission planning at tactical, operational, and strategic levels. Service school curricula and training situations increasingly include cultural courses and factors, stated John W. Jandora. One current use of asymmetric conflict involves jihadism and recognizes a concept of center of gravity. This theory departs from the conventional systemic approach. The concept did not apply to resistance in Iraq or treatment of al Qaeda, and focused on contrast of culture to clarify jihadism.[103] Jandora and Gray strike a responsive chord in me. In Chapter 1, I stressed the need to understand belief systems of cultures and groups that have utilized suicide as a weapon. An important aspect of that understanding is identifying sacred values in different cultures and understanding how they compete for people's affection is the center of suicide warfare. Cultural points of view are evident in international attempts to define terrorism, especially in military conflict. Examining the social forces in the jihadist community helps understand cultural differences that could lead to more American warfare successes.

Two social forces that offset one another in the jihadist community are tribalism and clientelism, Jandora stated. Both outside the American experience, the terms produce disdain. Tribalism involves kinship groups that accomplish their minimal economic chores and defend itself yet small enough that members can remain in contact and proportional to the supply of food.[104] Tribalization then is "the self-legitimation of the kin group and its intent and endeavor to optimize its collective self-interest. Self-legitimation is conviction that the tribe is the beginning and end of loyalty, identity, obligation, purpose, status, honor, past, and future—exclusiveness relative to society at large."[105]

The self-legitimization of the kin group then is what Durkheim described as common beliefs and practices learned make the individual the personification of the collective consciousness. And this collective inclination is itself a determined reflection of the structure of the society in which the individuals live, in this case, Afghanistan or Iraq.

The tribe may have its own militia or certain members may go away to join a state militia, but they remain loyal to their tribe. This loyalty remains in effect until self-alienation occurs. At this point, the second social force, clientelism, sets in. Members then cease to act like tribesmen and become loyal to the authority of new leadership. The leader offers religious salvation in return for loyal service. Service is based on volition, not obligation, as is the case with tribalism. Jandora concludes that the jihad leadership attracts self-alienated individuals and genuine outcasts by justifying and facilitating jihad.

In 2005, Jandora found that, because of doctrinal discord, neither the person nor the legend of Osama bin Laden is the center of gravity in jihadism. The Taliban do have unity of doctrine (Deobandist) and a high degree of ethnic homogeneity (Pashtun). While they are loyal to al Qaeda, they are also loyal to their tribes and that causes a loss in membership to the movement. Jandora concludes whatever method the U.S. military uses to combat jihadism, it must factor culture into the mission plan.[106]

In 2006, Gray believed the need for greater cultural awareness of enemies and allies had been accepted. The real problem and greatest challenge is with America and its culture. While some transformation of U.S. forces has taken place, Gray believed that transformation in a preferred way of war that expresses enduring cultural realities may not be possible. America's strategic culture reflects American historical, social, ideological, and material realities. Gray posed a provocative question, "Of the two problems is the more serious, the strategy deficit or the cultural hindrances to adaptation to meet irregular foes?"[107]

The social forces at work in asymmetric conflict are culture, the military, and the individual. Marie Breen-Smyth, School of Politics, University of Surrey, explained that the wider culture determines the participants in a war and the goals of war, but that the military provides the ideology to indoctrinate the individual who then carries out the suicide attack to realize the larger society's political goals. She explains,

I'm saying the culture within organizations, as the youth culture in the sociological sense. The military's culture is within an organization and the ideological tell is backdropped on that where you believe that what you are doing is justified and there is an ideology that you are pursuing as a result of that. I think that is one component. I think it's a military culture that we are talking about. The wider political culture, the armed group or the organization that uses suicide warfare is located in that wider political culture whereby that organization deems that the only way to achieve their political goals is by the use of violence. So, the wider culture contributes that piece to the overall configuration of the armed group or versus the states or whomever they are fighting. Then the individual is in the organization acculturated into this ideology and into the military command structure in a way that allows them to follow orders and to see that they are doing their part of the overall political process which is on their part to carry out the suicide attack.[108]

Modular Defense

In 2004, Secretary of Defense Donald H. Rumsfeld defined the modularization of the army. He "advocated not just adding more divisions, but focusing on creating smaller, self-contained, interchangeable brigades that would be available to work for any division anywhere. The Iraq war was fought in the context of the Global War on Terror and was void of the linear battlefields of past wars."[109] In addition, the defense was to permit forces to be assigned, for example, in other hot spots such as Korea. Tosini stated that al Qaeda's battlefield is everywhere. "Warfare is taken away from the monopoly of states, and becomes the business of nonstate organizations, small cells, and even lone bombers."[110] Unconventional methods assist the weak in defeating the strong, "and the first rule of unrestricted warfare is that there are no rules, with nothing forbidden."[111]

The army offers background issues that explain the reasons for the creation of modular units to met global requirements. These issues include the inabilities of a fixed formation to support diverse requirements, the change in modern land operations, a shift in communications and command and control systems, and the evolution of tactical operations to distributed and noncontiguous forms.[112]

The risks in participating in protracted irregular warfare activities in multiple locations are straining the capacity and reducing the readiness of the joint force to conduct major conventional combat operations and sustain its other long-term global commitments, according to the Department of Defense.[113] Methods that alleviate the risks include increasing the ability of leaders to operate across the spectrum of conflict, pursuing technological advances to increase asymmetric advantages, and dedicating force structure to establish a persistent presence that may be useful to avoid violent conflict in total and/or to shape the environment.

Does the Coalition Fight Fair When It Engages in Asymmetric Warfare?

One of the problems with the initial lack of definitional understanding was that respected publications emphasized "that if an opponent does not fight the way we expect, then we automatically label his fighting technique asymmetric."[114] The United States has global military supremacy, thus almost any opponent could consider that the U.S. and coalition forces do not fight fair when, for example, they use long range, precision weapons or when they use drones to target opponents. Thomas stated, "The most asymmetric and least-discussed element is values. Operating principles, individual, social group and national values all play a role in the information age. There is always a lack of symmetry in values, even between two people."[115] Entirely different principle beliefs and ideologies may propel logic in other cultures. For example, some societies may consider it easier to attack the Western psyche or will to fight than to encounter it on the battlefield where a challenge between technologies may exist. Thomas concludes that asymmetry is when two unlike systems interact, each within its capabilities.

Suicide Bombing as an Example of Asymmetric Warfare

Preventing a hijacking of an airliner is less difficult than catching a suicide bomber before he or she strikes, according to the *Dossier*. Deterrence is unlikely to work since usually the attacker is destined to die, and, as long as there is a supply of attackers, the same tactic can be used again and again. Suicide attacks have an impact because they strike "directly at the heart of civilian society: the bomber could be almost anyone on the street, and if one target appears too secure, the bomber can simply select another."[116] Defense against suicide attacks is difficult. The Palestinians have said that since military power is unequal, the suicide bombers are "our tanks and F-16s," the *Dossier* reported. Israel has retaliated against the infrastructure of the Palestinian authority, but has not been successful in preventing suicide attacks.

Strategies of Financing Terror

The World Bank stated that the financing of terrorism is a simple concept: "It is the financial support, in any form, of terrorism or of those who encourage, plan, or engage in terrorism."[117] It adds that defining terrorism is less simple. Terrorist financing often involves money laundering and both transactions often display similar features, mostly having to do with concealment. The Financial Action Task Force on Money Laundering sets the standard for anti-money laundering. It defines the term as " 'the processing of . . . criminal proceeds to disguise their illegal origin' in order to 'legitimize' the ill-gotten gains of crime."[118] Fighting funds and charity aid add to the complexity of the financing of terror.

Financing terror is an intricate issue with laws and conventions against it such as the U.N. Convention for the Suppression of Terrorist Financing, and efforts to track financing of terrorist networks through such means as the U.S. Treasury Department Terrorist Finance Tracking Program (TFTP). Many issues complicate the tracking program. In the case of al Qaeda, the Central Intelligence Agency (CIA) detailed the extent of the problem in April 2001. The CIA reported, "Usama Bin Ladin's financial assets are difficult to track because he uses a wide variety of mechanisms to move and raise money[;] . . . he capitalizes on a large, difficult-to-identify network with few long-lasting nodes for penetration."[119]

U.N. Convention for the Suppression of Terrorist Financing

On December 9, 1999, the General Assembly adopted the U.N. Convention for the Suppression of Terrorist Financing.[120] The convention prohibits, in part, "any person(s) from directly or indirectly, unlawfully, and willfully providing or collecting funds with the intention that they should be used, or in the knowledge that they are to be used, to carry out an act that constitutes an offense under one of the nine treaties listed in the annex. It shall not be necessary that the funds were actually used to carry out an offense."[121]

U.S. Treasury Department Terrorist Finance Tracking Program

After 9/11, the U.S. Department of the Treasury initiated the TFTP to identify, track, and pursue terrorists and their networks.[122] On August 1, 2010, an agreement between the European Union and the United States went into force on the transfer and processing of data for purposes of the TFTP. Since then, the program has provided valuable lead information that has assisted in the prevention of attacks and the investigation of many high-profile and violent attacks and attempted attacks, such as the attacks in Mumbai in 2008, the liquid bomb plot against transatlantic aircraft in 2006, the bombings in London in 2005, the Madrid train bombings in 2004, and the Bali bombings in 2002.[123]

The 2004 report *National Commission on Terrorist Attacks upon the United States* focused on al Qaeda financing. The report found al Qaeda was funded, in the amount of approximately $30 million per year, by diverting money from Islamic charities and using well-placed financial facilitators who collected money from intentional and unintentional donors, mainly in the Gulf region. The organization was not funded by bin Laden, drug trade, diamonds, the U.S. government, or a foreign government. After 1996, al Qaeda made use of money movers or bulk cash couriers, but supporters and operatives utilized banks. The Taliban received about $20 million a year, and the cost of 9/11 was approximately $400,000–$500,000. Operations money was used for training and camps, creating networks and alliances, and supporting jihadis and their families.[124]

Before and after 9/11, al Qaeda raised money from many different sources using a core group of financial facilitators to move money through its organization using an array of conduits, including couriers, and financial institutions.[125] Al Qaeda also made significant use of hawalas, a method that employs money brokers (hawaladars), to transfer funds primarily in the Middle East, North Africa, the Horn of Africa, and South Asia. This method does not use a negotiable instrument or other commonly recognized methods for the exchange of money. Other methods that are utilized to settle include "settle a preexisting debt, pay to or receive from the accounts of third parties within the same country, import or export goods (both legal goods, with false invoicing, or illegal commerce, such as drug trafficking) to satisfy the accounts, or physically move currency or precious metal or stones."[126] Hawalas are not criminal, but some of their characteristics make criminality amenable.

In addition to an al Qaeda focus, Roth et al. presented a case study of the Somali community and al-Barakaat. Somali immigrants looked for safe, quick, and effective ways to move money earned in the United States to their destitute families and homes in devastated and conflict-ridden Somalia. Because Somalia lacked a banking system and central bank, the safe and convenient international wire transfer system was not an option. Therefore, in 1985, the al-Barakaat network of money remitters with headquarters in the United Arab Emirates was established. A money remitter

collects money from an individual at one point and pays it to another in another location, charging a fee for the service. The money itself does not actually move; rather, the originating office simply sends a message to the destination office, informing it of the amount of money and the identity of the sender and of the recipient. The destination office then pays the ultimate recipient. To settle, money is periodically wired in aggregate amounts from the originating office's bank account either to a central clearing account owned by the money-remitting company or through correspondent bank accounts. The central office, in turn, settles with the destination office.[127]

Western Union and Money Gram are examples of money remitters in the United States.

Fighting Funds

In 2011, the United States and Pakistan were involved in a billing disagreement over billions of dollars that Washington paid Islamabad to fight al Qaeda and other militants along the Afghanistan border. The United States perceived Pakistan as having a mixed record against militants and rejected more than 40 percent of Pakistan's claims for payment that included military gear, food, water, housing, and other expenses.[128] The *Congressional Research Service* noted, "By this account, Pakistan has 'routinely' submitted 'unsubstantiated' or 'exaggerated' claims, and denial rates have climbed from less than 2% in 2005 to 44% in 2009."[129] In spite of the disagreement and Pakistan's security services' complicity and incompetence in circumstances surrounding bin Laden's death, U.S. national security interests in Pakistan and the region are inextricably linked to a stable Pakistan. Thus, tighter foreign aid and accountability measures are in order. Although the United States allocates fighting funds domestically as well, the case of Pakistan illustrates the challenges these funds present.

Charity Aid

As of July 2005, the U.S. Executive Orders 13224 and 12947 designated 41 charities that support terrorist activity. In addition, several foreign terrorist organizations, also designated under Executive Order 13224,

Immigration and Nationality Act, have operated under names that appear as potential fund-raising fronts for terrorist activities. The U.S. Treasury's lists of charities and organizations are part of the larger group of individuals and entities designated under the executive orders, or the Antiterrorism and Effective Death Penalty Act of 1996, and appearing on the Office of Foreign Assets Control's *Specially Designated Nationals List*. The U.S. Treasury's list also represents a shortened list.[130]

After the earthquake in October 2005 affecting Pakistan and India, the United States suggested close attention be paid to guidelines concerning charity. The guidance was issued because of the remoteness of the areas of need, weak to nonexistent government regulation or oversight of the charitable sector, and the ongoing presence of militant groups in the region. The result was a typology and examples of the activities of militant groups and terrorists in the area. Terrorist abuse of the charitable sector can take many forms, including the following:

1. establishing front organizations or using charities to raise funds in support of terrorist organizations;
2. establishing or using charities to transfer funds, other resources, and operatives across geographical boundaries;
3. defrauding charities through branch offices or aid workers to divert funds to support terrorist organizations; and
4. leveraging charitable funds, resources, and services to recruit members and foster support for terrorist organizations and their ideology.[131]

The example of charity funding related to the 2005 earthquake was discovered when innocent Pakistani residents of Britain transferred about $10 million to the charity for Pakistan earthquake relief. Millions were diverted from the charity and eventually used to prepare for the attacks in an alleged plot to blow up airplanes traveling to the United States, according to Joshua Partlow and Kamran Khan. Authorities focused on the renamed Jamaat-ud-Dawa (JuD), a Pakistani charity that is a front for Lashkar-e-Taiba and is an Islamic militant group.[132] In December 2008, the U.N. Security Council declared the group's charity affiliate, JuD, a terrorist organization, requiring Pakistan to close it down. Lashkar-e-Taiba was blamed for the November 2008 Mumbai massacre. In 2009, JuD's flags flew over a relief effort for refugees from the Swat Valley, under the name Falah-e-Insaniat [Human Welfare] Foundation.[133] Based on news reports, the group does meaningfully assist in disaster areas, particularly large-scale calamities.

The Hamas's use of charity aid included the al-Islah charity sending gifts to families commemorating their suicide bomber relatives, and the Tulkarn charity and the International Relief Fund for the Afflicted and Needy for health, education, and welfare projects. To support families of Hamas suicide attackers, the Hamas charity committee usually paid rent for temporary housing for families of attackers whose homes the Israeli forces destroyed in an attempt to prevent families from encouraging their members from becoming part of terrorists groups. In 2003, the Jenin charity in cooperation with the Hamas-associated Committee for Humanitarian Aid in Israel and the Union of Good in Saudi Arabia allotted $18,000 a month for one rental project. Matthew Levitt describes the act of rebuilding houses as a dichotomy. On the one hand was Israel destroying the same Palestinian homes to deter them from allowing their members to participate in terrorism, and on the other was the Hamas building the homes to give the Palestinians incentive to join or to support the organization.[134]

RECENT PATTERNS AND TRENDS IN STRATEGIES OF SUICIDE WARFARE

"Behind the public leadership of al Qaeda and its franchises, there is a depth of strategic thinking that buoys the movement, and it remains intact," wrote Christopher Heffelfinger.[135] He stated that although U.S. counterterrorism efforts had considerably weakened al Qaeda, it remained a decentralized movement. In the past 10 years, the organization had changed from a hierarchy into something much more diffuse, had a greater presence online, and did not depend on senior leaders in Pakistan for orders. Heffelfinger suggests that while senior leaders were targeted, no evidence exists that there were fewer jihadis targeting the United States. Drone warfare encouraged AQAP to leave Waziristan and Afghanistan and operate in Yemen. This group had increased lethality.

The National Intelligence Council's "Global Trends 2015" predicted several tendencies including a continuing greater lethality in terrorist attacks; more diverse, free-wheeling, transnational networks, as opposed to state-supported, that are enabled by information technology and that will seek safe havens; state-supported terrorism will decrease or desist due to regime changes; weak states could drift toward cooperation with terrorists; and terrorist tactics will become more and more sophisticated and designed to achieve mass casualties.[136] In addition, many acts of terrorism will be directed at the United States and its overseas interests. Acts will be based on perceived ethnic, religious, or cultural grievances. U.S. military and diplomatic facilities abroad are likely to include U.S. companies and American citizens. The most likely groups are Middle East and Southwest Asian based.

Robert Pape described two waves of terrorism research: violence that happened in the 1970s–1990s in countries other than the United States and the 9/11 attacks. In earlier years, terrorism had often been looked upon "as a persistent, but modest menace comparable to individual acts of violence associated with domestic criminals. 9/11 increased the fear of another large scale, direct attack usually connected with acts of war."[137]

Pape's research supports the thesis of this book because he distinguishes between the focuses of the two waves of terrorism research. Usually, the first wave emphasized single causal factors. The second wave considers factors that operate at different levels of analysis across strategic, social, and individual levels of causes for terrorist events. This approach increases our understanding.

Some of Pape's findings in years prior to 2009 include women who bomb, leadership decapitation, and the relationship between democracy and terrorism. Lindsey O'Rourke's study demonstrated female suicide attackers are likely to carry out attacks for secular groups, implying that religion may be dampening the number who become suicide attackers. The women are over the age of 24 and committed to the traditional norms of their society. This dedication implies "efforts to westernize traditional societies with military power are likely to backfire."[138] Jenna Jordan's data on leadership decapitation suggests beheading is only successful against terrorist groups that are less than 10 years old. Older groups and religious groups respond with more vigor and lethality. Risa Brooks's study implies that in a very few cases would democracy yield a reduction in the incidence of terrorism.

Most European plots seem to be independent. The most serious plots are apt to have extensive operational connections to groups that operate outside of Europe, according to Lorenzo Vidino. Vidino's study also found that contrary to common portrayals, little evidence indicates that al Qaeda and affiliated organizations that operate outside of Europe conduct direct efforts to recruit European Muslims. More significant is the formation of a linkage between self-radicalized individuals or clusters based in Europe and al Qaeda and like-minded groups, with the self-radicalized initiating the linkage. Vidino analyzed all plots against Europe between 2006 and 2010 and found that this linkage is frequently the factor that determines the level of the plot's sophistication. He pointed out that Europe has not experienced a completely successful attack since 2005, but that attacks planned by individuals and networks with operational ties to groups operating outside of Europe are usually more elaborate, professional, and potentially lethal than those devised by independent individuals and networks. Usually, the factor determining this difference is the training in handling explosives received overseas.[139]

A RAND report noted that the early terrorist groups were more ethnic/nationalist, separatist, and ideological, and that a variety of other groups have become a part of the scene. The newer and larger organizations have more amorphous religious and millenarian aims, less cohesive organization, and more diffuse structure and membership, as was seen in the Kenya and Tanzania bombings. Early groups claimed credit and stated intelligible demands. Later groups were vague such as defending holy places with a goal of pursuing U.S. forces and/or interests anywhere. The new motivations and different capabilities bring increased lethality.

Organizations have shown little deviation from traditional patterns using the gun and the bomb, weapons that lack sophistication. Although traditional terrorists will continue to kill in the 1s and 2s, or at most the 10s and 20s, rather than utilizing weapons of mass destruction (WMD), new types of terrorists may evolve that will use WMD.[140]

The Office of the Director of Intelligence reported on a wide range of statistical attack data including incidence, attackers, types of attacks, victims and targets, and location. Over 11,500 terrorist attacks occurred in 72 countries in 2010, with approximately 50,000 victims, including nearly 13,200 deaths. The number of attacks increased by almost 5 percent over 2009, but the number of deaths decreased for a third year in a row, dropping 12 percent from 2009. Over 75 percent of the world's terrorist attacks and deaths occurred in South Asia and the Near East. South Asia had the largest number of reported attacks in for the second year in a row and had the largest number of victims for the third consecutive year.[141]

The Director of Intelligence report focused on suicide bombers and included attackers who actually died in the attack. In June 2010, Algeria witnessed its first suicide vehicle-borne improvised explosive device (VBIED) since September 2008. Sunni extremists were responsible and have been responsible for 60 percent of all worldwide terrorist attacks. These attacks caused about 70 percent of terrorism-related deaths, an increase from nearly 62 percent in 2009. Two of the largest suicide attacks involved the Islamic State of Iraq (ISI). The ISI was responsible for the attack by three suicide bombers on April 4, 2010 in the Mansur and Al Karkh districts, Baghdad, Iraq. VBIEDs that were detonated near the Egyptian, German, and Iranian embassies killed 42 and wounded approximately 250. The ISI was believed to be responsible for the second large suicide attack that took place on July 7, 2010 in the northern Azamiyah district of Baghdad. An IED detonated near a group of Shia pilgrims making their way to the Imam Musa al-Kadhim shrine, killed between 29 and 48 pilgrims and several Sunni civilians and wounded between 133 and 315 pilgrims and several Sunni civilians.[142]

In 2010, bombings, including suicide attacks, caused about 70 percent of all deaths. Suicide bombings continued to be the most lethal type of terrorist attack, killing about 13.5 percent of all terrorism-related deaths. Sunni extremists carried out 93 percent of all suicide attacks in 2010. Suicide attacks declined for a second consecutive year, from 299 in 2009 to 263 in 2010, just under 2 percent of all terrorist attacks in 2010.[143]

In Afghanistan, a disturbing trend is the Taliban's utilization of women and children as suicide attackers. Using children "represents a new and dangerous evolution of the insurgent threat in Afghanistan, with militants taking advantage of the facts that young boys are easily impressionable and can be either persuaded to carry out such attacks voluntarily or forced to do so by threats to themselves or their families."[144]

The U.S. State Department 2010 report indicated that al Qaeda remained the greatest terrorist threat to the United States. Even though its core in Pakistan became weaker, al Qaeda kept its capability to conduct regional and transnational attacks. Together al Qaeda and Afghanistan and Pakistan–based militants contributed to the threat al Qaeda posed. Danger remained high from Lashkar-e Tayyiba, Tehrik-e Taliban Pakistan and like groups, and the Haqqani network. In addition, al Qaeda affiliates have grown stronger and have a greater share of the propaganda effort. The state department calls it a troubling trend that English-speaking militants are more and more connected to each other through online sites, for example, on militant discussion forums and video-sharing platforms. Al Qaeda continued to be politically marginalized as its constituency decreased. The 2011 revolutions in the Arab world left the possibility that the resulting chaos would give an opening to terrorists. The Hezbollah and Hamas continued to play destabilizing roles in the Middle East.[145]

CHAPTER 5

Effects of Suicide Warfare

Suicide as a weapon in warfare has effects, sometimes devastating effects. Despite its frequent use and immeasurable effects, suicide warfare has not yet enabled the attackers to prevail in their conflict with the attacked. The suicide attacks on the United States on September 11, 2001 caused 3,000 deaths, thousands wounded, and hundreds of millions dollars damage. They also produced the war in Afghanistan that caused thousands of military and civilian deaths, tens of thousands of injuries, and more than a trillion dollars spent. Al Qaeda and the Taliban have been greatly affected by the conflict that resulted from the 9/11 attacks. The Taliban were driven from power in Afghanistan and even though they have returned as an insurgent force, they are not close to returning to power. Al Qaeda has had major setbacks. A majority of its top leaders have been killed, including al Qaeda leader Osama bin Laden.

Suicide warfare affects the societies in which it occurs and the societies in which it originated. The United States and the world experienced massive change after the 9/11 attacks. In 2011, on the 10th anniversary of the attacks, media analyses chronicled the changes. National Geographic television marked the 10th anniversary of the 9/11 attacks by detailing events of that day as well as events that occurred over the last decade.[1] The Rachel Maddow and Richard Engel documentary "Day of Destruction, Decade of War" reviewed in depth the U.S. domestic and international responses to the events of 9/11.[2] The suicide attacks of 9/11 produced far-reaching change, including greatly increased counterterrorism expenditure and infrastructure and the wars in Afghanistan and Iraq, and the treatment of prisoners of war. The Office of Homeland Security (OHS) was established with a strong antiterrorism mandate. The social climate became less trusting and more defensive.

Although most who were killed on 9/11 were non-Muslims, Muslims have borne the brunt of the attacks because most of the responses have occurred in predominantly Muslim countries. Suicide attacks in the countries produce a great loss of human life, much destruction, and ongoing threat of violence. According to the National Counterterrorism Center, Somalia had the largest number of terrorist attacks in 2010 that had 10 or more deaths. Iraq and Pakistan had the next largest number of attacks with 10 or more deaths. Iraq and Pakistan had the same number but the attacks in Iraq produced more fatalities.[3]

EFFECTS OF SUICIDE WARFARE
IN THE UNITED STATES

"Tuesday, September 11, 2001 dawned temperate and nearly cloudless in the eastern United States. . . . For those heading to an airport, weather conditions could not have been better for a safe and pleasant journey," begins the *9/11 Commission Report*. Among the travelers were Mohamed Atta and Abdul Aziz al Omari, hijackers of American airlines flight 11 that crashed into the north tower of the World Trade Center. Other hijackers on three other aircraft were also boarding for flights. The 9/11 attack involved the hijacking of four planes. Two crashed into the World Trade Center, one into the Pentagon, and one into the Pennsylvania countryside. More than 2,800 people are killed. These attacks were the first by suicide bombers within the U.S.[4]

Weather conditions did not change, but the nature of the journey for passengers aboard those flights did. It changed also for those of us who watched helplessly the events unfold on our television screens. A new and untested journey for the United States was about to unfold, most notably in counterterrorism efforts and its escalation into different kinds of war.

The United States Response to 9/11

Counterterrorism

From 2001 to 2011, the United States witnessed much change. The long wars brought surprises, some of America's own making, wrote Brian Michael Jenkins and John Paul Godges. After America invaded Iraq, al Qaeda killed Muslims in Iraq and elsewhere that provoked a powerful worldwide backlash against al Qaeda among Muslims. These events, the global economic crisis, America's financial difficulties, and the revolutions in North Africa and the Middle East, will impact future American counterterrorist policy and strategy.[5] In the final analysis, "the emphasis on counterterrorism as war has had at least one additional, lasting effect," according to Jenkins.[6] Before 9/11, the United States had rejected assassination of terrorist leaders. In 2011, the country accepted routine use of drones, missiles, and special operations to kill terrorist leaders even outside of the conflict zone. The American people seemed more willing to accept preemptive and modular warfare because they view war as protecting the home front.

Expenditure of Funds and Human Life and Escalation into War

Expenditure of Funds

The killing did not stop on the day of 9/11. The wars in Afghanistan and Iraq added hundreds of thousands more. In addition to the lives lost, counterterrorism efforts have cost billions of dollars. The new national security infrastructure created included the $3.4 billion, Department of Homeland Security (DHS) headquarters, the National Counterterrorism Center, the joint use intelligence analysis facility, the National Reconnaissance Office, military bases, prisons, rebuilding the Pentagon, and the Ground Zero recovery efforts, according to Engels and Maddow.[7]

The Congressional Research Service report concluded the cumulative costs of the wars in Afghanistan and Iraq through fiscal year 2011 totaled $1.28 trillion dollars. The more than a trillion dollars spent does not include war-related spending on the Veterans Administration and the State Department/U.S. Agency for International Development.[8] The Eisenhower Study Group stated, "These wars were financed almost entirely by borrowing adding more than $1.3 trillion dollars to the national debt."[9] The large increase in military spending and debt in turn impacted interest rates, jobs, and investment.

Expenditure of Human Life and Escalation into War

In 2011, the Eisenhower Study Group revealed that, in the 10 years since 9/11, 225,000 people had been killed, and $3.2–4 trillion had been spent or obligated. Direct war casualties were about 225,000 dead and about 365,000 wounded in the Iraq and Afghan wars as of June 2011. The great majority of the casualties were civilians in these countries. Since 9/11, over 2 million American troops have been deployed to Afghanistan and Iraq. Those groups who have suffered loss of life include over 6,000 troops, 2,300 U.S. contractors, over 20,000 U.S. allies, including Iraqi and Afghan security forces and other coalition partners, and the 8756 Afghan and 3520 Pakistani military and police. The number of refugees and displaced persons for the 3 countries totaled 7,815,000. Torture and detainment of prisoners remain problematic.[10] Western forces experienced some of the civilian deaths; however, a West Point study revealed that the majority of al Qaeda's victims were Muslims. Only 15 percent of the fatalities resulting from al Qaeda attacks between 2004 and 2008 were Westerners.[11]

The Eisenhower Study Group reflects only the 10 years since 9/11 and only those casualties related to Afghanistan, Iraq, and Pakistan. Stephen M. Walt selected low-end estimates for Muslim fatalities and his figures present the best case for the United States. Overall in 11 categories that included Iraq and Afghanistan, the United States has killed about 30 Muslims for every American lost. His categories include the Embassy/Marine bombings in Lebanon in 1983 where 300 U.S. soldiers and diplomats were killed, and no data were available for Muslim fatalities. Another category included Desert Storm (1990–1991), the total U.S. fatalities numbered 293. Muslim casualties were 56,000 military and 3,500 civilian (not including postwar deaths).[12]

While the number of American casualties in the armed conflicts since 9/11 does not come close to matching the carnage of the two world wars, the Korean War, and the Vietnam War, the length of the conflicts since 9/11 is unparalleled. Although America's involvement in Iraq ended in December 2011, the involvement in Afghanistan has a 2014 timetable for U.S. total withdrawal, these conflicts continued for a long time, 8 years and 10 years, respectively.

Difficulties in suppressing the insurgencies in Iraq and Afghanistan have made the public and certainly the political leadership more cautious about committing to new military engagements that require troops. The support for the effort that brought down Libyan leader Moammar Kadafi was limited to air and naval power.[13]

In 2011, the Heritage Foundation reported that, from 1969 to 2009, approximately 5,600 people lost their lives and more than 16,300 were injured as a result of international terrorism directed at the United States. From 2001 to 2009, homegrown terrorist attacks of all kinds against the United States numbered 91, while international terrorist attacks totaled 380. International terrorists preferred method of attack against the United States was bombings (68.3 percent), while the domestic terrorists preferred method was arson (46.2 percent). The result or effect was that law enforcement thwarted about 39 terror plots since 9/11. Intelligence and law enforcement communities are better able to follow leads in local communities than they were before.[14]

Military doctrine has modified because American armed forces were unprepared for the type of warfare that broke out in Afghanistan after the Taliban were overthrown and in Iraq following the defeat of Saddam Hussein's conventional forces. Officers were faced with relearning how to engage and fight an insurgency, sometimes influenced by military prejudices and historical ignorance on the part of many of their own senior commanders, wrote Jenkins (see Chapter 3).[15] In addition to change in military doctrine, the troops who patrol on foot in bomb fortified areas in Afghanistan are affected. Troops know "they might lose a leg, or two, if they step in the wrong place. But for young men in their prime, most unmarried and without children, the prospect of losing their sexual organs seems even worse," Christopher Torchia reported.[16] Blast panties or ballistic boxers that end above the knee were issued to the Marines. The clothing cannot stop shrapnel, but it protects against infection. The tightness compresses body tissue and offsets the effect of a blast wave that separates skin from muscle.

Improvised explosive device (IED) strikes, finds, or interdicts in Sangin, Helmand province averaged five a day. Approximately 1 in 10 IEDs hits a target. Sixteen Marines in the American battalion had died and approximately 160 had been injured during a 7-month deployment. Of those injured, about 90 were sent home because of the severity of their wounds. One lost both testicles, four lost one testicle, and two had penis injuries. The U.S. military's Landstuhl Regional Medical Center in Germany treated 134 servicemen with one or more amputated limbs through July 31, 2011, about 80 percent of the number who had suffered similar injuries in 2010. Ninety of the 134 also suffered genital injuries. Almost all the troops were injured in Afghanistan, Torchia reported.

Homeland Security

A major effect for the United States was the formation and growth of the DHS. In response to the terrorist attacks of 9/11, Executive Order 13228, issued on October 8, 2001, established two units within the White House to determine homeland security policy. The OHS was to develop and implement a national strategy to coordinate federal, state, and local counterterrorism efforts to secure the country from and respond to terrorist threats or attacks.[17] Its objectives are to prevent terrorist attacks within the United States, to reduce America's vulnerability to terrorism, to minimize the damage, and to recover from attacks that do occur.[18] The OHS became the DHS on November 25, 2002. The department was given responsibility for counterterrorism, border security, preparedness, response, recovery, immigration, and cyber security.[19]

The economic effect of this response to the 9/11 attacks has risen each year. In 2004, the DHS budget totaled $36.2 billion. In fiscal year 2011, its budget was $98.8 billion. DHS has more than 200,000 employees and is the 3rd largest Cabinet department, after the Departments of Defense and Veterans Affairs.[20] Since DHS was established, the total of its budgets has exceeded $500 billion. The United States has not been attacked successfully within its borders in over 10 years, in part, because DHS has done its job effectively. The existence of DHS and the level of monies expended are both effects.

Change in Social Climate

Fear and Prejudice

"For a couple of years, our reasonable fears spilled over here and there into panicky overreach, leading to un-American excesses," wrote Kurt

Andersen.[21] As a nation, we calmed down and free political discourse began again. But one result of fear is prejudice. Andersen pointed out that the real change is reflected in American prejudice against Muslims because before 9/11, it was insignificant. Examples of this change were in the summer of 2010 Ground Zero mosque controversy and the 2011 anti-Sharia law movement.

But have Americans calmed down? Jenkins believed that in the 10 years after 9/11, the mood of the country had changed profoundly. For sure, the post–Cold War era ended harshly on September 11, 2001. History was from this time forth to be divided into pre-9/11 and post-9/11. Response to terrorism became the dominant issue in American defense, foreign policy, and American politics. The country reorganization included homeland defense, the land of the fearful, or the home of the brave. The U.S. DHS grew to the third largest body in the federal government. Executive authority was extended, security became a national preoccupation, and nation's commitment to American values was tested.[22]

Laws that Changed the Social Climate

9/11 had a lasting impact on the daily life of most Americans when laws were passed that intruded into their privacy. The intrusions became the new normal. In November 2001, Congress passed and President Bush signed the Aviation and Transportation Security Act that created the Transportation Security Administration (TSA). The TSA became responsible for the security of all modes of transportation. It took charge of all security officers from commercial airports, and provided 100 percent screening of all checked luggage for explosives. In March 2003, the agency was moved from the Department of Transportation to the DHS as part of the Homeland Security Act of 2002.[23]

When flying was the travel choice, citizens could expect intrusions that included "bag and suitcase contents scrutinized; shoes off, jackets off, luggage locks and lighters gone; liquids limited to tiny containers; laptops out of their bags; explosive detecting swabs; metal detectors like we used to have but also puffer machines; and body scans—and really detailed body scans."[24] Jenkins explained that for many, passenger screening is their only contact with government security procedures. As measures have become more intrusive and intimate, some resisted, such as, to the full-body scans and new pat-down procedures.[25] But at the onset of tightened security, Maddow explained that the public knew about the preflight intrusions, but it did not know intrusion that was kept secret. In 2002, President Bush expanded collecting foreign communications to include U.S. eavesdropping on its citizens within the country. This expansion was kept secret until the *New York Times*[26] exposed it in 2005, according to Maddow. She reported that items subject to secret government inspection included bank accounts, credit cards, e-mail, phone calls, business records, and library records. The intrusion powers were previously reserved for America's spies abroad, for the black arts of the intelligence world were put in the hands of law enforcement. The Eisenhower study reported that although some Muslims and people of South Asian descent have been interrogated at airports, fingerprinted or deported for visa problems, none had been cited for terrorism.[27]

Although President George W. Bush made it clear that the war on terrorism was not a war on Islam, in 2002, the U.S. profiled foreigners arriving from designated Arab and Muslim countries, according to Jenkins. The U.S. developed new measures to examine foreigners already in the country. This procedure was to uncover sleeper cells within the country. Men who were between the ages of 16 and 45 from these countries and without legal permanent resident or refugee status were required to register. Jenkins found that between 2002 and 2003, 85,000 men registered; deportation proceedings were initiated against over 13,000 and 2,870 were detained for various violations, the number deported is not known; 11 were suspected of ties to terrorists, but none were charged; the number of people suspected of terrorist activity and arrested on lesser charges is unknown, but those who were not citizens were deported; and widespread discrimination reports forced a reduction in the program in 2003 and suspended in 2011.[28]

From the Homeland Security Act of 2002 came the Uniting and Strengthening America by Providing Appropriate Tools Required to Intercept and Obstruct Terrorism Act of 2002, known as the USA Patriot Act. According to Engels and Maddow, the Patriot Act "tears down many of the walls constructed over the years between law enforcement and spying, walls designed to protect American citizens from being spied on by our own government, walls designed ultimately to protect the presumption of innocence."[29]

Effects on Media

A purpose of suicide attacks is to acquire media exposure because the terrorist group is confident that the media will interpret the bombing as a sign that that the situation is getting worse, according to Clara Beyler. The first use of women as bombers, for example, offered a new media dimension. Byler noted that Cherif Bassiouni found that suicide bombers perform their acts in the most dramatic manner in order to gain media attention and make the most of impact. Reliance on media coverage takes place in the planning and execution phases. The reporting furthers the bombing "objective of producing a social impact that would not otherwise occur."[30] Beyler stated that terrorist organizations had made excellent use of the media. For example, the media coverage of the Israeli-Palestinian terrorist organizations gave the new dimension of gender to a continuing conflict. Organizations manipulate female participation in the conflict.

They intend to use the image of a female suicide bomber to distort worldwide public opinion. Beyler stated, "The media becomes a victim of this strategy by describing female bombing actions as the only way for these women to express their frustration; a testimony of utter despair."[31]

In the post-9/11 era, James Castonguay characterized the mainstream media as having "uncritically embraced the Bush administration's Orwellian nightmare of civil and human rights abuses, militarism, isolationism, and anti-intellectualism, while also actively promoting the 'war against terror' for ratings and profit. The currently unprecedented level of concentration of media ownership in the hands of a few transnational conglomerates and the existence of a military-industrial-media-entertainment network further facilitates the implementation of a Cold War logic of 'us' against 'them' in the context of the Manichean rhetoric of good versus evil (doers)."[32] The cultural production of the War on Terror involves an assortment of media. Castonguay noted that fictional programming is often overlooked, but when the United States attacked Afghanistan, Warner Brothers tried to "put a real face on the war against terrorism." The conservative family drama *7th Heaven* (1996) presented an emotional memorial with the real widow and son of a U.S. Marine killed in Afghanistan. By constructing a companion website on its sister company, TurnerLearning.com, Warner Brothers assumed an educational role. While mainstream media censored the torture and murder of Daniel Pearl, for example, various websites made it available. Castonguay concludes that the emergence of medias' multiple meanings of the War on Terror text was severely controlled and with little room for negotiation.

The effect of 9/11 on the mainstream media was restrictive. One incident of silencing the media is shown in an interview, Dan Rather, former anchor on CBS Evening News, remarked on the journalistic acquiescence to the Bush administration prompted a strong response from host Bob Garfield:

Dan Rather: Well, I couldn't get stronger, . . . that this is time for us, and I'm not preaching about it—George Bush is president, he makes the decisions and [breaking up], you know, as just one American, wherever he wants me to line up, just tell me where.

Bob Garfield: Yikes! Suspending journalistic independence in the name of patriotism, before a live studio audience. Alas, this declaration of submission foreshadowed two years of the media's largely uncritical acceptance of Bush administration's claims leading to the Iraq War, and beyond—the phantom weapons of mass destruction, for example.[33]

Garfield believed that misleading information from Vice President Dick Cheney and other administration figures held much of the U.S. media captive. For example, the press would go along to reiterate fantasy accounts of battlefield bravery. When the weapons of mass destruction were not found, when Abu Ghraib pictures appeared and when civil liberties were threatened, the quiescent media were finally returned to perform their real patriotic duty. But until that return, "in the emotionally charged post-attack environment, the country and the media and most of the political establishment were prepared to follow a president confidently riding the wave of national fury . . . or at least to get out of the way," wrote Tom Farer.[34]

A known example of restricting the media occurred in Operation Desert Storm (1991). Secretary of Defense Cheney warned of a shutdown of battlefield news, "We cannot permit the Iraqi forces to know anything about what we're doing."[35] But the blackout was short lived, and at issue is the right of the press and the public under the First Amendment of the U.S. Constitution to demand access to American military operations. David A. Frenznick concluded that even though the First Amendment does not guarantee unlimited access to the battlefield, press restrictions should be adapted to achieve a legitimate purpose and to provide as much media access as is possible.[36]

In the Iraq War (2003–2010), military censorship and media outlets' self-censorship occurred in the first five years according to Naomi Spencer. The military and the Bush administration had imposed rules barring photos of flag-draped caskets and documentation of casualties where identifiers such as faces and ranks were visible. Further, the number of embedded journalists was drastically reduced. Spencer noted that the journal *Editor & Publisher* found that at the beginning of the war, 770 journalists accompanied U.S. forces compared to in 2008, only a dozen embedded journalists continued and about half were photographers.[37] Some journalists were disembedded, while others were forbidden to be in a combat zone. Spencer stated that during the siege in Basra, hospital and health officials were forbidden from talking to independent journalists. She wrote, "American media dutifully reported Pentagon talking points, referring to killed civilians—even when children were counted among the dead—as 'terrorists,' or at best 'collateral damage.' "[38] Spencer believed that the suppression of the truth is an expression of the larger crime of the war. Military censorship and the self-censoring of the media reveal the immense increasing militarization of American political life.

So, whether some media presented misinformation or incomplete information on or shortly after 9/11 is one question. Second, if the media engaged in these types of information sharing? Then third, why did it? These are questions for which we may never know the answers. A probable and palatable answer is that the media controlled information because they were told to do so and that they were told to do so for national security reasons.

I remember my own 9/11 media experience. At my home in Midwest United States, I stared at a blank TV screen and listened to white noise until I finally heard a newscaster say that President Bush along with his staff were at undisclosed locations. Although we would later learn that

Bush wanted to go back to the White House and speak to the American people, I felt a leadership void in the middle of this crisis. New York City Mayor Rudolph Giuliani filled that void in the wake of 9/11 when he said that if citizens wanted to do something, to go fly their American flag. I immediately flew our flag.

Loss and Continuance of Life

Men and women in uniform continue to give their life or their quality of life to protect freedom. The use of coercive interrogation techniques that were equivalent to torture and the systematic prisoner abuse at Abu Ghraib prison challenged American values. Yet, tradition of religious tolerance proved strong when presidents have said that the wars on not wars on Islam. Yet in 2011, religious assimilation in the United States is resisted, wrote Jenkins. He concludes, "The objective of terrorism is to create terror. The 9/11 attacks certainly created a state of alarm. They made the country very edgy, if not fearful, but they did not bring down the republic, imperil America's democracy, or destroy individual liberties."[39]

EFFECTS OF SUICIDE WARFARE
IN MUSLIM COUNTRIES

Expenditure of funds, escalation into war, and loss of life are definitely effects of suicide war, particularly in Muslim countries, the larger society. But there are effects on those people faced with continuance of life. What happens when their homeland is destroyed or when they stay within their homeland and encounter a life with day-to-day violence or the threat of violence? Terrorist organizations not only affect their targets, but on communities composed of individuals as well. Much of their warfare takes place within civilian populations. These are only some of the effects of suicide warfare in Muslim countries.

Destruction of Homeland

The Eisenhower group found that the natural resources of forests and water supplies in the homelands of Afghanistan and Iraq have been ravaged by fuel emissions and oil. Wildlife has also been affected. Air, soil, and water pollutions are sometimes at a toxic level from war operations. Because drought has resulted due to deforestation and global climate change, dust is a chief problem. Military vehicles moving across the landscape make the dust problem worse. These conditions promote poor health. For example, in Fallujah, Iraq, considerably elevated rates of cancer were found in 2005–2009 compared to rates in Egypt and Jordan. Fallujah's infant mortality rate was 80 deaths per 1,000 live births, much higher than rates of 20 in Egypt, 17 in Jordan, and 10 in Kuwait. In ages 0–4, the ratio of male births to female births was 860–1,000 compared to the expected 1,050 per 1,000.22.[40]

Social Milieu: Ongoing Threat of Violence

From 2002 to 2007, the Pew Global Attitudes Project undertook a study to find out how America is perceived abroad and with global attitudes toward the U.S.-led war on terrorism. Since the study began, Pew interviewed approximately 110,000 people in 50 countries. They found that although anti-Americanism is a global phenomenon, it was plainly strongest in the Muslim world. In 2006, in all five predominantly Muslim countries, less than one-third held a favorable view of the United States. The Iraq War caused the spread of anti-Americanism to parts of the Muslim world where the United States had been comparatively popular. For example, Indonesia's favorability rating dropped from 61 to 15 percent between 2002 and 2003. In Turkey, it fell from 52 percent in the late 1990s to 15 percent by 2003. After Iraq, many in Muslim countries began to view the United States as a threat to Islam, according to Pew. A perceived loathing for the United States turned into fear and loathing. A 2005 Pew study revealed that "in all five majority Muslim countries, solid majorities said they worried that the U.S. might become a military threat to their country. This includes 65% in Turkey—a longstanding NATO ally."[41]

The War on Terror has been unpopular in Muslim countries, because it is viewed as an American campaign specifically against unfriendly Muslim governments. In 2006, while these countries disliked the United States, they viewed Osama bin Laden favorably, according to PEW. In 2011, Rohan Gunaratna and Karunya Jayasena found that operational counterterrorism needed to be supplemented with strategic counterterrorism to correct misled ideologies. Their study describes "the factors and drivers that are correlated to an increase or decrease in support for al Qaeda and its leader, Osama bin Laden."[42] In so doing, a measured insight was gathered for the increase or decrease in the U.S. efforts, Gunaratna and Jayasena wrote. Their study concluded that there were two reasons correlated to increase in support for al Qaeda and bin Laden. First, since 2003, opposition to U.S.-led War on Terror has noticeably increased. Many Muslims considered the U.S.-led War on Terror as a factor in their economy deteriorating. And they were not supportive of drone attacks that targeted extremist leaders because they believed the attacks were carried out without the approval of their governments. Many Pakistanis held that United States and NATO should withdraw their troops from their country, because Pakistanis supported their own country's army to fight terrorism. Second, an absence of consciousness about political conditions that give rise to terrorism and increase support for extremist ideologies has lead to the rise of extremisms.[43]

Table 5.1
Confidence in Osama bin Laden*

Country	2003 (%)	2005 (%)	2006 (%)	2007 (%)	2008 (%)	2009 (%)	2010 (%)	2011 (%)	Pct Point Change	
									Since March 2011	*Since October 2011*
Palestine territory	72	—	—	57	—	52	—	34	-38	—
Indonesia	59	36	35	41	37	25	25	26	-33	+1
Egypt	—	—	27	18	19	23	19	22	—	+3
Pakistan	46	52	38	38	34	18	18	21	-25	+3
Jordan	56	61	24	20	19	28	14	13	-43	-1
Turkey	15	6	4	5	3	2	3	3	-12	0
Lebanon	19	4	—	2	2	4	0	1	-18	+1

*Based on Muslims only.

Source: "On Anniversary of bin Laden's Death, Little Backing of al Qaeda Survey Report," *Pew Research Center*, April 30, 2012, http://www.pewglobal.org/2012/04/30/on-anniversary-of-bin-ladens-death-little-backing-of-al-qaeda.

Source Note: The Pew Research Center bears no responsibility for the interpretations presented or conclusions reached based on the analysis of the data.

However, in 2012, one year after bin Laden's death, the Pew Research Center's new survey of Muslim publics showed al Qaeda as widely unpopular. Pew conducted their survey from March 19 to April 13, 2012 and found that majorities expressed negative views of al Qaeda in Egypt (71%), Jordan (77%), Pakistan (55%), Turkey (73%), and Lebanon (98%). Support for bin Laden before his death had declined considerably in Muslim publics worldwide. Muslims in Jordan, Indonesia, Pakistan, and the Palestinian territories experienced a steep decline. In Pakistan, 13 percent held a favorable view of al Qaeda, 55 percent had an unfavorable view, and about 31 percent had no opinion. In 2011, 34 percent expressed confidence in bin Laden.[44]

The Pew Research Center found that before bin Laden's death, Muslim support had diminished significantly. The most noticeable decline occurred in Jordan. In 2005, 61 percent said that bin Laden would do the right thing in world affairs, but in 2006, after suicide attacks in Jordan's capital, Amman, the percentage plunged to 24 percent. In 2011, just 13 percent expressed confidence in him. Although the support of Muslims in Indonesia, Pakistan, and Palestinian territories declined sharply over time, in 2011, 34 percent of Palestinians remained more supportive than other publics (Table 5.1).[45]

EFFECTS OF SUICIDE WARFARE IN ALL COUNTRIES

Effects of Failed Attempts

Perhaps nowhere is the effects of the ongoing threat of violence more real than in reports of attempts to self-explode. On December 22, 2001, al Qaeda shoe bomber Richard Reid attempted to detonate explosives hidden in his sneakers on an American Airlines flight from Paris, France, to Miami, Florida. Passengers thwarted his plan and the plane landed safely in Boston, Massachusetts. On October 4, 2002, Reid pleaded guilty to terrorism charges and on January 30, 2003, he was sentenced to life in prison at the nation's supermaximum security prison in Florence, Colorado.[46] The shoe bomber resulted in a new requirement of all airline passengers departing from an airport in the United States having to pass through airport security in socks or bare feet while their shoes are scanned for bombs. In 2011, passengers registered for a trusted traveler program under development may be allowed to omit the shoe screening earlier than the general public, according to TSA officials.[47] In 2012, this requirement was modified for passengers 12 years of age and younger and 75 years and older. They are allowed to leave their shoes on during security screening.[48]

Another well-known failed attempt is the al Qaeda Christmas bomber, Abdul Farouk Abdulmutallab. On December 25, 2009, he detonated 80 g of explosives sewn into his underwear to try to destroy passenger jet flight 253 as it came in to land at the Detroit airport. On October 12, 2011, he pleaded guilty in federal court in Detroit to all eight of the charges. The charges included attempting to use a weapon of mass destruction and conspiring to commit an act of terrorism. Had he been successful in exploding the pentaerythritol tetranitrate, or PETN, over 300 people would have been killed.[49] On February 16, 2012, a federal judge imposed four life sentences on Abdulmutallab, who expressed no remorse.[50]

Various Groups' Effects of Suicide Attacks

To evaluate the effects of various groups' usage of suicide bombing in an armed conflict, know the enemy is a necessary step, according to Lee Hamilton. In other words, what effects can an organization produce? Fear? Defeat? Principal themes in this knowing are to examine who will want to engage U.S. military forces, to understand organizational models, and to determine likely capabilities based on their affiliation with other terrorist groups or sovereign governments. Knowledge and situational awareness improves the ability for U.S. military forces to minimize the effects of terrorist activity. According to the *Military Guide to Terrorism in the Twenty-First Century*, "A terrorist organization's structure, membership, resources, and security determine its capabilities and reach."[51] Engagement in armed conflict requires some forethought of possible outcomes, but what are possible effects of organizations outside the conflict zone?

The organizational structure of a group affects its strengths and weaknesses. Knowledge of the structure of particular groups assists in understanding their capabilities. In general, factors that influence type of group include hierarchical or networked structure, stage of development, national or international agendas, and number of cells. The category of the organization also indicates under what circumstances an organization might be effective. For example, domestic groups operate within their own country. An international group, such as Hezbollah, has cells worldwide, and has executed organized activities in several countries, while primarily focused on events in Lebanon and Israel. Transnational groups, such as al Qaeda, operate internationally, but are not bound to a specific country or region. Al Qaeda thus conducts operations all over the world. Their goals affect many countries whose political systems, religions, ethnic compositions, and national interests differ.[52]

Other types of groups will affect a different audience, and may or may not be of concern to counterterrorism activities in all audiences. For example, the Chechen rebels are often referred to as the Chechen separatists. At issue was the amount of independence Chechnya should have and whether Chechnya should stay within the Russian Federation or whether it should form an independent nation. Likewise, Tamil separatism has been a part of Sri Lanka since it gained independence from India in 1948.[53] The effect these two movements may be of little concern to counterterrorism efforts in other parts of the world, but on Russia and on India, the effects have demanded attention (see Chapters 8 and 9).

Targeted Killing and Assassinations

An increasing number al Qaeda leaders were targeted and killed in 2011 and 2012 including Osama bin Laden, Atiya Abdul Rahman (al Qaeda's second-in-command), Fazul Abdullah Mohammed (al Qaeda operative in East Africa), and Anwar al-Awlaki (an American-born cleric in Yemen; see Chapter 10). What happens to the organization when confronted with the unexpected death of a leader. Bruce Hoffman stated, "Terrorist groups become cornered animals. When wounded, they lash out. Not only in hopes of surviving, but also to demonstrate their remaining power and continued relevance."[54] Al Qaeda's statement of May 6, 2011, as translated on CNN, corroborates bin Ladin's death reflects Hoffman's conclusion, "The soldiers of Islam in groups and as individuals will continue to plan and plot without any fatigue, boredom, despair, surrender or indifference until you receive from them a cunning misfortune that will gray the hair of the child even before he gets old."[55]

Retribution and revenge is the direct effect of the organization on society when its leadership is targeted and killed. Hoffman offered past patterns in other organizations, for example, the January 5, 1996, killing of Hamas field commander, Yahya Ayyash. The Hamas's response occurred 40 days later with the first of 4 bus bombings that continued for 2 months. The 2004 Israelis assassination of Shaykh Ahmed Yassin, the founder and leader of Hamas, and a month later, Abdel Aziz Rantisi, his deputy and successor. The Hamas responded by building a stronger organization. The U.S. capture of Saddam Hussein in 2003 led many to believe that the insurgency in Iraq would end. The insurgency responded by escalating for another four years. The killing of the leader of al Qaeda in Iraq, Abu Mus'ab al-Zarqawi, in 2006 hindered al Qaeda in Iraq, but the killing did not spell disaster for the group because as it still persists.

So, while the targeted killing and assassination of organizational leaders may beget more killing, counterterrorism experts, policy-makers, and political leaders must weigh the balance of such killing: Will more destruction take place with organizational leaders dead or alive? Or is the answer elusive, but the stakes too high to not target them? Does the power of the organization regroup thus keeping terrorism and its effects ongoing? Hoffman believed that where al Qaeda is concerned, whether it can continue to move forward, proving it can survive the death of its leader "is surely the most pressing question of the moment."[56]

Yet, the answer to possible effects of terrorist groups in general is through combining an assessment of the intentions of various groups with their capabilities, according to R. Kim Cragin and Sara A. Daly. Most significantly they point out that "groups are the most vulnerable to counterterrorism activities when they go through periods of transition, especially if actions taken against them magnify the pressures forcing the evolution."[57] The authors note Hoffman's insights on the difficulty of predicting the path of terrorism: "The terrorist campaign is like a shark in the water: it must keep moving forward—no matter how slowly or incrementally—or die."[58] And the organization is a critical key to terrorism moving forward thus keeping an effect of its terror on societies.

Prisoners

Domestic prisoners and prisoners of war have been directly affected by acts of terror. In both cases, prisoners are often recruited by terrorist organizations. Mark Hamm reported, "The radicalization of prisoners is a problem unlike any other faced by correctional administrators today—or at any other time in history. It grows in the secretive underground of inmate subcultures through prison gangs and extremist interpretations of religious doctrines that inspire ideologies of intolerance, hatred and violence."[59] Radicalization and extremist activity in prisons along with radicalized mosques and educational establishments, primarily universities, was increasingly emphasized as an area of concern in the United Kingdom and Europe in the aftermath of the attacks in Madrid in 2004 and on the London transport network in July 2005.

Imprisoned Muslim youth are vulnerable to radicalization because they may be experiencing a crisis of self-understanding that challenges or destroys self-conception, according to Greg Hannah, Lindsay Clutterbuck, and Jennifer Rubin. This experience could produce acute feelings of rejection by the native or adopted society. A coping mechanism could be the adoption of a new self-identity or belief. The acceptance may be achieved by adopting a new belief structure, religious or not religious, and then assimilated into a new, inclusive and frequently protective, group identity. Hannah et al. contend radicalization is difficult to assess and counter because officials may not be forthcoming with needed information needed to work toward rectifying the situation.[60]

Prisoners of War

Abu Ghraib Prison

Images of prisoner abuse in Iraq appeared over the web yet today. CNN is one example that shows the photos of abuse at Abu Ghraib stating they "became an emblazoned image, an icon of war and people at war, gone wrong."[61] The video opens with President George W. Bush remarking that Abu Ghraib was one of the United States' biggest mistakes so far. In 2003 and 2004, the United States collected large numbers of Iraqis and put them in Abu Ghraib. In April 2004, abuses of Iraqi prisoners began that included having prisoners disrobe in front of all, prisoner officials including women and other prisoners, and having their pictures taken in what one prisoner called shameful poses. U.S. Congressional hearings were held. In 2004, the U.S. Senate held hearings.[62] In 2006, Abu Ghraib was transferred to the Iraqi government. In 2009, the prison was renamed to Bagdad Central Prison. Eleven U.S. soldiers were convicted and some went to prison.

The Issues

The government released a report that revealed the abuses at Abu Ghraib prison were not due solely to acts by rogues of low military-ranking individuals, but that they also occurred at Guantánamo, and with some sanction from the highest ranks. Diane Marie Amann referred to these incidents as the dark underbelly of the U.S. detention policy since September 11, 2001. She maintained, "In the first years after the attacks of September 11, 2001, key actors did not see—did not acknowledge or accommodate—[the] lush landscape of law."[63] The lush landscape included the 1949 Geneva Conventions on the laws of war and constitutional law, congressional enactments, and treaties. It also included other examples for actions such as historical values on which U.S. law is established, international declarations, and the views of like-minded governments and bodies (see Chapter 3).

The neglect of key actors included the executive branch that singled out the constitution's commander-in-chief clauses as ample basis for its contention that the president benefited from plenary power to combat terrorism as he saw fit. The Supreme Court justices' agreement on what laws mattered came after the detainees were in military custody. Because the executive's pronouncement that Geneva law did not apply at Guantánamo, the military became uncertain whether any rules applied. Many types of failures are at fault, for example, lack of success in planning and training and the failure to acknowledge and accommodate potentially relevant laws, concluded Amann. The field is influx and prisoner abuse represents a conflict within a conflict, which according to Amann opens the way for reform, and hopefully no repeats of Abu Ghraib.[64]

Counterterrorism

Since the strategy of suicide warfare entails great asymmetry, groups engaging in this approach are always at a massive disadvantage in relation to their opponent, stated Richard Jackson. Based on interviews with groups who employ suicide warfare, Jackson learned that if they could use more sophisticated weaponry, they would. Human bombs are the cheapest and best tactic against a superior enemy they cannot face on an open battlefield. He explained,

[T]he best way to stop a group or movement from employing a particular violent strategy is to either resolve the deeper political conflict that is being fought over, or to convince the protagonists to move the struggle from the military to the political realms. Either way, this requires that dialogue becomes the primary mode of managing conflict, both to discover the issues being contested and the grievances driving it, and to draw out potential non-violent solutions.[65]

Generic solutions do not exist, according to Jackson. Every conflict is fought over specific issues of concern to a particular group and nation, and obstacles to overcome to achieve peace will be specific. He provided examples:

In some cases, such as Palestine or cases of foreign military occupation, a major part of the solution has to be the reform, redress and restitution of historical injustices and grievances. You can't expect the victims of injustice to simply accept their fate and surrender their struggle. In other cases, the obstacles to direct dialogue will be too great and intermediaries will have to be employed instead, or historical grievances will require symbolic and real processes of reconciliation. In all cases, recognition of a legitimate set of grievances, a willingness to engage in genuine reform and restitution, and open dialogue and trust-building will be needed to make progress. I would recommend this for any and all of the current conflicts in the world where terrorism and political violence is currently employed.[66]

Jackson believed that if a society had elements within it that objected to suicide warfare, steps can be taken to prevent it through peaceful movements and groups that exist in every society and in every conflict. He illustrated with Hamas,

I met a member of Hamas at a summer school I was teaching at, and she was working within the movement to try and convince them that non-violent struggle would be more effective and more moral. It was a revelation to know that there are committed peace activists in Hamas working to build coalitions and transform the movement from within. The European Platform for Conflict Prevention has a wide range of publications which document the official and citizen-based groups working for peace in all the world's conflict zones. It is a fascinating list of activities that is rarely, if ever, noted by the media or diplomats. My view is that if the Israeli and US governments, for example, worked with the Palestinian peace groups, or the Afghan and Iraqi peace groups, and helped to strengthen their position and used them as a conduit for dialogue, instead of employing excessive military force and treating every member of Hamas or the Taliban as an "enemy combatant" to be killed or rendered, they would make much quicker and more genuine progress towards peace.[67]

The much broader problem is "the global culture of violence in which war and military force are viewed as legitimate and useful ways of achieving political goals," Jackson believed. For example, "It is very difficult to convince Hamas activists not to engage in violence when they see the U.S., Israel, the U.K. and the U.N. using excessive force whenever they want to take land from their neighbors, secure their borders, overthrow a dictator they no longer want to be allied with or prevent human rights abuses.

Until we can de-legitimize the use of violence by anyone and everyone as a means of solving political conflict, peace groups trying to convince oppressed groups to stop using violence will face a difficult task."[68]

Conflict and its many effects remain. The difficult task of working for peace is ongoing and reflected in the findings of the Center for Systematic Peace. The center found that the general global trend in armed conflict is continuing to decrease in the early years of the 21st century, but they warn that some countertrends should be acknowledged. Most relevant include the escalation of long-standing disputes or rivalries, most notable Israel versus Palestine; separatism, the Tamil Tigers and the Chechen separatists; controlling world oil reserves, the Iraq War; and Islamic antiglobalism. The Islamic antiglobalism's "full course and effects of the still emerging war on terrorism will have on the global system are not yet fully known. Nearly two-thirds of new wars since 2001 have taken place in Muslim-majority countries or involved Muslim minority groups."[69] In other words, some effects of terrorism may remain unchanged while other effects will evolve, but in majorly Muslim countries.

PART II

Case Studies

The case studies in Part II examine conflicts that had significant use of suicide warfare: Japan's kamikaze pilots, Hezbollah and Palestinian conflicts with Israel, Sri Lanka and the Tamil Tigers, Chechen separatists, and al Qaeda. Suicide warfare has not been confined to these conflicts.

In 19th-century Japan, Miyabe Teizo led the *Inin-Shishi Ronins* in close quarters battle suicide attacks against legitimate forces and authorities of the Shogun. In the early 20th century, Muslim Malays (*Moros*) conducted chaotic suicidal tactics that included frantic close combat knife-fighting with American soldiers in the Philippines.[1]

Early groups in modern times are the Syrian Socialist Nationalist Party (SSNP/PPS) sometimes referred to as the Syrian National Party and the Kurdistan Workers Party. The SSNP/PPS Party "was an important landmark in the ecumenical movement of Syrian nationalism."[2] It organized the first suicide attacks conducted by women in Lebanon in 1985. Women took part in 5 out of 12 attacks. In Turkey, 66 percent (14 out of 21 suicide attacks) were carried out by women.[3]

The Kurdistan Workers Party began in 1984 to create an independent Kurdish state. It is now known by the name Kongra-Gel (KGK). Since 2010, the KGK has repeatedly extended its unilateral cease-fire of October 2006, but continues to take an active defense posture against Turkish military operations, and is active in northern Iraq and southern Turkey. In both cases, nationalism spurred suicide warfare.[4]

Groups in Somalia and Nigeria are using suicide warfare. Al-Shabaab is the militant youth wing of the Somali Council of Islamic Courts. In the second half of 2006, al-Shabaab took over most of southern Somalia. Between December 2006 and January 2007, the Somalian government and Ethiopian forces defeated the organization, but it has continued its violent insurgency in southern and central Somalia. Although al-Shabaab's goals are nationalistic in nature, its leadership is linked to al Qaeda.[5]

Al-Shabaab has claimed responsibility for various types of suicide attacks in Mogadishu and in central and northern Somalia. Usually, they target Somali government officials and allies of the Transitional Federal Government (TFG). In October 2008, al-Shabaab was likely responsible for five coordinated suicide car bombings that simultaneously hit targets in two cities in northern Somalia. About 26 people were killed and 29 were injured. Ugandan officials have accused al-Shabaab of carrying out the twin suicide bombings in Kampala, Uganda, on July 11, 2010 that killed over 70 people.[6]

In Nigeria, Boko Haram uses suicide attack in its battle with the Nigerian government. The conflict pits the Islamic against the Christian. The Islamic Boko Haram believe they and not the Christians should have been given control over the government. The targeting of Christians is seen in the suicide attack when a bomber in a vehicle detonated explosives near a church on Easter morning, April 8, 2012, in Kaduna. Approximately 38 people were killed.[7] In the past, Boko Haram had attacked international targets, as it did on August 26, 2011 with a suicide attack on the U.N. headquarters in Abuja. According to David Cook, the most significant changes to Boko Haram's operations are discontinuing such high-profile operations with international implications and increasing the attacks on Nigerian Christians and the Nigerian security. Boko Haram's goal of creating a Shari'a state remains constant, but the way to achieve it is undergoing change.[8]

PERSPECTIVES ON SUICIDE WARFARE

Suicide warfare is viewed from differing perspectives and these perspectives are intensely debated in the literature, according to Murad Ismayilov. It is important, he contends, to distinguish among the perspectives: the motivation for a political decision to launch a martyrdom campaign, the strategic level of analysis and factors motivating individuals to serve as suicide bombers, and the individual and structural levels of analysis. Ismayilov states that social scientists classify martyrdom operations into two groups: rational choice theories that operate at a strategic level regard terrorist violence as inherently rational action perpetrated by purposeful agents and irrational models operate at an individual level of martyrs or a structural level of a broader society in which those martyrs exist, ascribe it to psychological or social causes.[9]

A pathway perspective model, advocated by Paul Gill, includes the structural and situational procedures that facilitate and encourage recruitment of suicide bombers. Prospective bombers experience four major stages on their path to suicide bombing: broad socialization processes and exposure to propaganda, experience with catalysts, previous ties with friends or family, and in-group radicalization. Gill illustrates the model with bombers who act against a state within that evidences no widespread conflict or bombers who left their birth state to bomb in another state. He highlights the slight differences in bombers from Palestine, Tamil, Chechnya, and Lebanon.[10] These differences will be shown in Chapters 7–9.

My perspective focuses on the interrelationship of culture, the military, and the individual as a weapon. Durkheim's collective inclination dovetails with conflict theory that demonstrates that common characteristics of the core of how groups struggle for power while constrained by resource. Causes of war over a variety of reasons demand rational strategic action. The examination includes the historical context, the organization, the military, the individual as a weapon, and outcomes.

Marie Breen-Smyth notes that in "a significant proportion of recent literature on terrorism,"[11] disparity is created when the literature focuses solely on 9/11. Recent literature is moving toward state-centrism, wrote Breen-Smyth. She finds that troublesome because the terrorist is defined as a security problem and inquiry is restricted to gathering information and data that would solve or eliminate the problem as the state defines it. "This focus ignores the roots of terrorism and the contribution of the state itself to the creation of the conditions in which terrorist' action by non-state actors occurs."[12] Each group I address in Part II, I view as nationalistic in origin as opposed to the misnomer, terror. The Japanese kamikazes represented a state military action; the Palestinians, the Tamil Tigers, and the Chechen rebels wanted to gain control in their homeland. Bin Laden aspired to have al Qaeda create a caliphate as a homeland.

CHAPTER 6

Japan's Kamikaze Pilots

Suicide warfare has been an increasing strategy in modern warfare. The first extensive use of suicide as a weapon was in World War II when Japan employed kamikaze pilots against the U.S. Navy. Kamikaze means divine wind in Japanese[1] and has been a part of the Japanese culture since 1281 AD. The great Mongol leader Kublai Khan organized a fleet and set sail to overpower the Japanese islands. Success was likely, but a typhoon on the coast destroyed and scattered the Mongol ships. The Japanese people interpreted this storm as heavenly protection. Since then they have attributed the saving of the empire to the kamikaze, the divine wind.[2]

HISTORICAL CONTEXT

It is significant that the Japanese attributed their deliverance from Kublai Khan to the divine wind, to the kamikaze. The Japanese are a religious people. Japan has a unique combination of a great variety of religious traditions within Japan. Religion in Japan reflects a long history during which various religious beliefs and practices—some indigenous, some imported from other places—have been adopted and adapted to Japanese culture.

The ancient indigenous folk religion, later formalized as Shinto, was based on feelings of awe toward the sacred powers (*kami*) that brought life to the earth and human community. Shinto, or "the way of the gods," is practiced by about 83 percent of the population. Shinto originated in prehistoric times as a religion with a respect for nature and for particular sacred sites, each associated with a deity, or *kami*. A complex polytheistic religion developed.

After 1868, Shinto and Buddhism were forcefully separated. Emperor Meiji made Shinto the official religion known as State Shinto by merging Shrine, Folk, and Imperial Household Shinto. Under Meiji, Japan became a moderate theocracy, with shrines under government control. Shinto soon became a reason for Japanese nationalism. After Japan took over Korea and Taiwan, State Shinto became the official religion of those countries as well. During World War II, the government forced every subject to practice State Shinto and admit that the emperor was divine. Those who opposed the Imperial cult were persecuted.[3]

In the 6th century AD, Buddhism was introduced into Japan. It both influenced Shinto beliefs and practices and also incorporated Shinto elements. Both Confucianism and Taoism migrated to Japan, impacting Japanese culture, religion, philosophy, and politics. Japanese religion adopted Chinese Buddhist rituals, Taoist storytelling and divination, as well as Confucian concepts of piety and ancestor veneration. New popular schools of Buddhism formed in Japan, taking on a structure of their own. Pure Land, Zen, and Nichiren Buddhism all developed in Japan, with the Nichiren school taking on a uniquely Japanese character.[4]

In the 16th century, Christianity was introduced in Japan by Jesuit missionaries, including Francis Xavier. In response to this missionary activity, some Japanese led a resurgence of the ancient traditions of Shinto, Buddhism, and Confucianism. These complex, hybrid Japanese religions continue to play a significant role in Japanese culture, although there is also a sense that, as in other contexts, much of the religious and spiritual heritage unique to Japan is being swallowed by modern secular life.

THE CONFLICT

Suicide warfare was not used at Pearl Harbor. It was not used until kamikaze pilots attacked American ships in the Battle of Leyte Gulf on October 25, 1944.

Attacks

In 1971, Nicolai Timenes, Jr., authored a study on the U.S. defense against kamikaze attacks. The study maintained that the kamikaze were "initially employed in an attempt to neutralize carriers so that they could be engaged and destroyed by other forces, the kamikazes soon became the primary Japanese weapon, and their use continued and intensified during the campaigns for the Philippines and Okinawa."[5] In the Philippines, kamikazes attacked in small groups. At Okinawa, they employed more mass attacks to overwhelm defenses. Kamikazes per plane were less effective even though they used more planes and caused more damage. Reasons for the ineffectiveness included reduced pilot experience levels, inferior aircraft, and new American defensive tactics.

At the end of the Okinawa campaign, the allies prepared for their final assault and the Japanese readied for their defense. Timenes assessed this time in battle: "The resources available for kamikaze attacks-given the limited training and technological requirements—were impressive, and invading forces would surely have suffered great casualties had not the events at Hiroshima and Nagasaki been decisive."[6]

One of the major reasons for introducing the kamikaze attacks was the high rate of attrition the Japanese aircraft suffered in attacks on American ships and installations, stated Timenes. The Japanese hoped that each succeeding operation might be decisive. Therefore, they were willing to accept heavy attrition. When attrition and strategic position made operations more costly, the Japanese became more desperate. High attrition led to the consideration of conventional missions as one way trips, so that resorting to kamikaze tactics appeared reasonable.[7]

By the Battle of the Philippine Sea, U.S. Naval aviators had 2 years training and over 300 hours flying time before flying from a carrier in combat. The three Japanese air groups' average experience had reduced to 100 hours. Pilots trained for kamikaze missions had 30–50 flight hours. Japan began the war with 10 aircraft carriers (9 fleet carriers), and the United States had 7 with 3 in the Pacific. Timenes stated that the number, characteristics, and fate of Japan's aircraft carriers were difficult to establish.[8]

The first kamikaze attacks were not designed to be decisive, but to only to cause temporary incapacitation in order to destroy by other means U.S. carrier forces. Timenes, giving the American perspective, stated that the kamikaze strategy was based in "cynicism and contempt for the value of life and hope which underlie the calculation of per-sortie effectiveness and the command decision which followed. It is no less unacceptable for the reasonableness of the calculation."[9] The Japanese adopted these tactics when it must have been apparent to the high command that they were losing the war. Over 2400 Japanese naval aviators died in suicide attacks, stated Timenes.

Combatant Zero fighter planes, modified to carry 250-kg bombs, flown by regular pilots of one of the better combat squadron, carried out the first kamikaze attacks. Later, novice pilots trained for kamikaze were used for suicide missions. As training levels diminished, suicide tactics were simple. Early attacks employed five or six aircrafts: three kamikazes and two or three escorts. Later, at Okinawa, massed attacks were used. The escorts, whose primary mission was to decoy interceptors, were ordered not to engage if it might result in their falling behind the kamikaze aircraft. When kamikazes and escorts were both Zeros, this instruction meant that escorts could not be aggressive. Carriers were the primary targets with the aim point an elevator.[10]

In the Okinawa campaign, Japanese pilots flew 1,900 kamikaze sorties in addition to many more conventional sorties, reported Timenes. Total Japanese combat losses included 3,000 aircraft, and total losses to all causes were 7,000 aircraft. Even though more sorties were flown resulting in more damage to Allied ships when compared to Leyte, the Japanese effectiveness was reduced due to lower Japanese training levels, inferior aircraft, and improvements in American tactics and equipment.[11]

In addition to the Zeros, two other aerial kamikaze vehicles were employed. The first was the MXY7 Ohka weighed 2,600 pounds with a final rocket-powered speed of 390 mph. The other was the D4Y4 Model 43, Special Strike Bomber that was the fastest dive-bomber of World War II with a long range. It was adapted for kamikaze missions, and had only one pilot and with a 1,800-pound bomb, reported Max Gadney.[12]

One of the kamikaze's offensive tactics included the high dive that involved the pilot diving out of the sky from about 20,000 feet. At the end, he increased the angle to 45–50 degrees. The allies developed a defensive tactic, "The Big Blue Blanket," by deploying a screen of radar picket ships and destroyer escorts far from the carriers. This positioning gave advance warning to fighters on constant patrol above the carrier group. The ships on the outer edge suffered heavy losses, explained Gadney. Some of the other tactics involved skimming the waves, flying 50 feet above the sea, ascending to 1,500 feet at the last minute, and dive down on the target; bluff flying with approaching escorts and bombers until the last minute; and prime target: carriers, as aim for the central flight deck elevator, make the carrier useless. A triple blow tactic included bombing, crashing, and fire. First, the plane released bombs just before the crash. Then the plane crashed into the hangar level that contained fuel, planes, and munitions, resulting in fire at the crash with fuel tanks exploding sending burning gasoline into the ship.[13]

Leyte Gulf and Okinawa

The exact number of kamikaze flights is not known but the estimates include 7,465 kamikazes flew to their deaths; 120 U.S. ships were sunk, with many more damaged; and 3,048 Allied sailors were killed and another 6,025 wounded.[14]

During the Leyte Gulf conflict, suicide aircraft sunk 16 vessels and damaged about 90 others. American losses consisted of 2 carriers, 3 destroyers and 5 transports, 23 damaged carriers, 5 battleships, and damaged were 23 carriers, 9 cruisers, and 28 destroyers and destroyer escorts. Japanese losses comprised more than 700 suicide army pilots and about 500 air fleet pilots. About 1,200 pilots died in all. At the end of the Leyte campaign, 68,000 Japanese had been killed and 3,500 U.S military were killed and 12,000 wounded. The Okinawa campaign saw 900 Japanese air raids. About 4,000 Japanese planes were destroyed of which 1,900 were kamikaze. About 35 American vessels were sunk and more than 300 damaged.[15]

The U.S. Navy compiled results by months for planes that arrived within gun range of ships. The Japanese made the strongest suicidal effort during April 1945, but of the planes taken under fire by ships only 35 percent were suicide planes. Other planes bombed, torpedoed, harassed, or snooped, according to the navy.[16] The total number of suicide planes increased from 376 (24%) in the Philippine campaign to 408 (31%) in the succeeding 3 months. The number of Japanese planes within U.S. gun range that antiaircraft (AA) killed increased from 256 in the Philippine campaign to 312 in the next 3 months. The number of times Japanese suicide planes hit decreased from 120 to 96 (see Table 6.1).

Table 6.2 represents the successes of the United States against suicide and nonsuicide planes. The navy report points out that AA successes

Table 6.1
Japanese Planes within U.S. Gun Range of Ships by Month, 1944–1945 and 1945.

Campaign Dates	Leyte Gulf, Philippines (October 1944–January 1945)	Okinawa, Japan			Total	
		February 1945	March 1945	April 1945	February–April	Both Campaigns
Total planes	1,616	123	219	978	1,320	2,936
Suicide planes	376	18	42	348	408	784
Nonsuicide planes	1,240	105	177	630	912	2,152
Suicide antiaircraft kills	256	10	32	270	312	568
Nonsuicide antiaircraft Kills	206	7	38	108	150	356
Suicide hits	120	8	10	78	96	216
Nonsuicide hits	41	1	10	6	17	58

Note: Figures represent the number of suicide planes and include not only those planes that definitely attempted to crash into ships but also a proportion of the planes shot down by antiaircraft before they demonstrated their intentions. This proportion is determined by separating the uncertain kills according to the ratio of known suiciders to known nonsuiciders.

Source: U.S. Department of the Navy, Naval History and Heritage Command, *Anti-Suicide Action Summary*, COMINCH P-0011 (Washington, D.C., August 1945), Table 1, 1, http://www.history.navy.mil/library/online/Anti_Suicide_Action_Summary.htm#I.

Table 6.2
U.S. Successes against Japanese Planes, 1944–1945 and 1945.

Campaign Dates	Leyte Gulf, Philippines (October 1944–January 1945)	Okinawa, Japan (February–April 1945)	Total
Suicide kills	256	312	568
Nonsuicide kills	206	150	356
Total kills	462	462	924

Source: U.S. Department of the Navy, Naval History and Heritage Command, *Anti-Suicide Action Summary*, COMINCH P-0011 (Washington, D.C., August 1945), Table 2, 2, http:// www.history.navy.mil/library/online/Anti_Suicide_Action_Summary.htm#I.

increased only against suicide planes. Reasons for this effectiveness on the part of the U.S. ships were lack of surprise due to alertness and destroyer radar pickets' early warning, obsolete Japanese aircraft, and ships employing open fire at long range.[17]

Table 6.3 demonstrates that even though the scale of the Japanese suicidal effort increased more than 50 percent for February–May, 1945 over October–January, 1944–1945, their efficiency dropped. Hits and damaging near misses occurred in 45 percent of the crash attempts, compared to 54 percent for the earlier period. According to the U.S. Navy, "Even more startling is the fact that 27 suicide tries were required to sink a ship in February-May as compared with 14 in October-January."[18] During the April antisuicide campaign, over twice as many suicide planes made crash attempts on U.S. surface forces as in any earlier month, yet the Japanese scored just 27 percent hits as compared with 37 percent in October–January and 34 percent in October–May.

The last suicide attack occurred after the Japanese surrendered when the kamikaze forces led a flight of 11 planes on an attack against U.S. ships at Okinawa from April 1 to June 22, 1945 during World War II (see note of Table 6.3).[19] The final phase of the U.S. Pacific engagement in World War II involved the fighting forces landing in Okinawa. The forces secured two air bases and staging areas that commanded the island, according to G. Miki Hayden. Things were bad thus far in the conflict. The United States fought from muddy trenches and the Japanese from underground extensive man-made tunnels. The Japanese had resolved never to surrender that led to denial of their true position. They signed 4,000 kamikaze recruits to sink the ships that were a lifeline to U.S. soldiers, then surround and kill all of them. In spite of the courageous spirit of the Japanese, they could not defeat U.S. forces. Approximately 77,000 civilians and about 207,000 people died in the 3 month battle on Okinawa.[20]

Table 6.3
U.S. Antiaircraft Successes on Suicide Planes that Made Crash Attempts and Japanese Successes in Scoring Hits and Damaging Near Misses.

Campaign Date	Suicide Attempts	Hits on Ships	Damaging Near Misses	Nondamaging Misses	Antiaircraft Successes	Ships Sunk
Leyte Gulf, Philippines						
October 1944–January 1945	326	120	57	149	206	23
Okinawa, Japan						
February 1945	17	8	2	7	9	1
March 1945	35	11	7	17	24	1
April 1945[a]	288	78	43	167	210	11
May 1945[a]	171	68	16	87	103	6
Total of Okinawa	511	165	68	278	346	19
Total of both campaigns	837	285	125	427	552	42

[a]April and May figures are based on data from action reports and are incomplete. Dispatches, which give a reasonably accurate record of damage but not of misses, indicate that the following numbers of suicide planes scored hits and damaging near misses, and sank ships as follows:

Month	Suicide Planes	Ships Sunk
April	12	15
May	98	10
June	18	3

Source: U.S. Department of the Navy, Naval History and Heritage Command, *Anti-Suicide Action Summary*, COMINCH P-0011 (Washington, D.C., August 1945), Table 3, 3, http://www.history.navy.mil/library/online/Anti_Suicide_Action_Summary.htm#I.

Suicide Boats and Suicide Frogmen

Kamikaze pilots were not the only weapon of suicide warfare used by Japan. By September 1945, suicide boats filled the gap due to fewer planes. Along with suicide boats, the Japanese employed suicide frogmen or human mines. Three groups of suicide boats dropped depth charges alongside the enemy ship leaving the crew a slim chance to escape. But with the navy boat, there was no chance to escape. Its bow was loaded with 660 pounds of high explosives set to detonate when contact with the ship occurred. Some boats also had two rockets on both sides of the cockpit. The tactic was straightforward: make a multidirectional attack on an anchored enemy convoy. The difficult part was stationing the boats, night navigational problems in inclimate weather, and vulnerability to enemy fire due to gas engines. While the suicide boats were taking over from the kamikaze pilots, the Japanese executed suicidal assaults on the ground on enemy tanks. Infantry formations organized their suicide squads to attach demolition charges to the sides of tanks. Another method involved loading the space under trucks with explosives with protruding firing pins that would cause the truck to explode on contact.[21]

THE CULTURE

The national emperor system is a combination of religious and political authority, according Kenneth J. Dale. Until 50 years ago, the Japanese emperor was deified as *kami* (divine) and followed with respect. The self-sacrifice of the kamikaze, wind of god pilots, and the citizens exemplified these values. "This system, though revised, is still strongly influential today!" and there exists a "social/cultural phenomenon of group solidarity which nobody wants to break," wrote Dale.[22] John Orbell and Tomonori Morikawa analyzed materials written by 661 kamikaze pilots and 402 rank-and-file members of the Japanese military, all of whom died. They concluded that concern for family and religious motivation had a characteristic role in persuading the kamikaze pilots to carry out their suicide missions, and the fact that pilots mentioned them reflects widely shared cultural values.[23]

THE MILITARY

Onishi Takijiro, a navy vice admiral, created the *tokkotai* (kamikaze) operations toward the end of World War II when the American invasion of Japan became apparent. The types of weapons included the use of airplanes, gliders, and submarine torpedoes. None was provided with a way to return to base, wrote Emiko Ohnuki-Tierney. Not a single military academy officer volunteered to sortie as a pilot. They viewed it as a meaningless death mission. The total kamikaze consisted of 4,000 teenage and enlisted pilots and about 1,000 university students whom the government graduated early in order to draft them. The students represented about 85 percent of the officers who died. Once on the base of the Japanese state-supported military, draftees suffered corporal punishment on a daily basis. Recruits who had felt patriotic found their enthusiasm for fighting destroyed. Since they had no choice in mission, they died whether or not they supported an emperor-centered ideology.[24]

Rikihei Inoguchi and Tadashi Nakajima shared Admiral Ohnishi's philosophy that was summarized in a presentation to his staff after the organization of the Kamikaze Corps:

> In blossom today, then scattered;
> Life is so like a delicate flower.
> How can one expect the fragrance
> To last forever?
>
> (Ohnishi, of the Kamikaze Special Attack Force)[25]

Inoguchi and Nakajima believed Ohnishi had dedicated his life to the Kamikaze Corps at its inception and would have taken his own life even if Japan had won the war.

Axell and Kase noted that the existence of a May 1945 suicide manual, *Basic Instructions for To-Go Flyers,* has not been published in its entirety in the West nor has it received much attention in Pacific war literature.[26] My own search on the Internet and in the Defense Technical Information Center turned up only extractions from the information found in Axell and Kase.[27] The manual includes exact information on how to damage a ship, what to do and think approaching a target and informs the pilot that he will see the expressionless face of his mother during the final moments, and finally, after the crash, pilots will become *kami*, gods, and be with their friends. Some other instructions were if a pilot cannot locate a target, he should return to base; be intent at the last moment on sinking the ship and all the cherry blossoms at Yasukuni Shrine, Tokyo will smile brightly at the pilot; remain calm, don't give up, observe the ship's position and the terrain and AA positions as well as smokescreens; and how to fly through enemy radar screens.

The Cherry Blossom

The key to comprehending how young, intelligent men submitted to military ideology is their "misrecognition of the aesthetics strategically deployed by the government," stated Ohnuki-Tierney.[28] She explains that misrecognition is the "absence of communication, whereby parties in a given context fail to realize that they are talking past each other, deriving different signification from the same symbols and rituals."[29] The Japanese military government was not unlike the other societies in efforts to aestheticize its military actions. Since the beginning of the Meiji period (1868–1912), the Japanese did so by choosing the cherry blossom as the central symbol. Although everyone enjoys the cherry blossom, its meaning varies depending on the level viewed. On the individual level, it represented the life cycle, while in the abstract, it is the subversion of the norm such as the masquerade or the geisha. On the collective level, each social group had its own way of viewing the blossom. From the blossom's vital societal position, the Japanese military expertly used it to symbolize the soldiers' sacrifice for the emperor qua through Japan. Ohnuki-Tierney explained that the cherry blossom symbolized the Japanese soul, an "exclusive spiritual property of the Japanese that endowed young men with a noble character, enabling them to face death without fear—'Thou shalt die like beautiful falling cherry petals for the emperor.'"[30] The activation of the blossom's aesthetics of the flower reached its height with the kamikaze. The aircraft displayed on both sides one cherry blossom painted in pink on a white background, and the names of the corps had Japanese terms for cherry blossom. High-school girls waved blossomed branches while pilots took off with blossom branches attached to their helmets and uniforms.

The Samurai

In addition to the cherry blossom symbol, the samurai custom required "there was a time to live and a time to die, then now was the time for Japan's airmen to die . . . trailing clouds of glory," according to Peggy Warner and Denis Warner.[31] From January to October 1944, the Japanese Navy lost 5,209 pilots, 42 percent of the total in the service. The use of the kamikaze pilots increased and their tactics included diving into Allied ships without bombs, use of unmodified mortar shells instead of bombs, and loading cockpits with grenades. By November 1944, most of the suicide planes were used up.[32]

Fear

The Japanese state-supported military employed fear, a valuable tactic, to assist them in their suicide missions. In 1945, William L. Worden wrote that only recently had the U.S. Navy removed the subject of suicide divers from their secret list. Initially, the navy had not allowed war correspondents to refer to them or describe their attacks because thus far, they had not found a meaningful defense. Worden stated, "It [the Navy] was afraid to have them mentioned which was precisely what Tokyo wanted Americans to believe."[33] Once the navy lifted the shroud of secrecy, the kamikaze myth was debunked, and the pilots were no longer the menace that they were.

THE INDIVIDUAL AS A WEAPON

John Orbell and Tomonori Morikawa's study concluded that coercion was a likely but not the major reason that pilots participated in kamikaze attacks even though it was not mentioned in the materials they evaluated.

Drawing from other reasons where coercion might have played a role, their top three findings included the following. The first figure represents the kamikaze and the second, the rank and file: honorable or beautiful death 78.8 percent ($n = 521$) and 60.0 percent ($n = 225$), mentions of war effort 52.5 percent ($n = 347$) and 29.4 percent ($n = 118$), and doing it for country 49.2 percent ($n = 325$) and 35.8 percent ($n = 144$). Percentages dropped markedly for other reasons.[34]

The kamikaze had a particular mindset, according to Albert Axell. The kamikaze pilots had an ordinary background and little experience of under 100 hours of flying time. Some were of the Christian faith, and were passionate advocates of Japanese righteousness. Everything in the embattled world was black or white. Japan was pristine white. The added incentive of self-sacrifice was that they would be respected as gods. Before a final mission, the pilots were blissful, especially during their last 24 hours.[35] Some original pilots wore black uniforms, said good-bye to friends on the airfields, attended funeral services for themselves, and took off to die for the emperor.[36]

Surviving diaries and letters reveal normal young men who enjoyed life and possessed a sense of duty to their country, according to Mario Ferrero. They were also skeptical or critical of the military control and the nationalist politicians who had brought Japan to the brink of disaster. They were not blind fanatics. In light of this mindset, what were the reasons they accepted and obeyed the contract? Ferrero stated that the few weeks spent in training and moral preparation were intense, and it was under these circumstances that men would sign a martyrdom contract. Attention was given to details of ordinary things. Their written last thoughts revealed they were grateful for and appeased by small joys of camaraderie and the true reckoning with one's soul that such a compressed last stage of life had forced on them, or rather allowed to them. In addition, in these last days before their mission, pilots were frequently allowed to freely indulge in heavy drinking and sex, not normally available to them in Japan's society.[37]

In addition to carrying the Bible and his mother's photograph on his last flight, Hayashi Ichizo also took with him Kierkegaard's *The Sickness unto Death,* according to Ohnuki-Tierney. Hayashi had committed long portions of it to memory. The primary theme of the work is despair in relation to suicide. Hayashi was deeply attached to life, but possessed an equally deep obligation to defend his homeland. He often reached a state of despair. Kierkegaard's work offered Hayashi a way to consider self, life, and death within Christianity's framework. Although he faced death directly, Hayashi rejected Kierkegaard's view that despair leads to suicide. Instead, he sought philosophical and religious perspectives to lead him from despair and self-destruction. In the end, he turns to his family, homeland, cultural traditions, Christianity, and European and Japanese literature and philosophy. He does not fully rely on the emperor-centered and militaristic state ideology.[38]

Inoguchi and Nakajima also shared a series of letters and diary entries written by kamikazes, some who were preparing for their last flight. Most individuals write that flying the suicide mission is an opportunity to fulfill their destiny for their homeland, and most letters close with the word "Farewell." Part of an excerpt of the last entry from the diary of Ensign Heiichi Okabe reads:

> What is the duty today? It is to fight.
> What is the duty tomorrow? It is to win.
> What is the daily duty? It is to die.
> We die in battle without complaint.[39]

OUTCOMES

Military Outcomes

The kamikazes caused great damage to primarily American carriers and destroyers in the Leyte Gulf and off Okinawa. Of the 15 destroyers lost in 1945, 12 were lost to kamikazes. But they did not succeed in helping Japan win the war. The kamikazes did not achieve their objective of destroying the U.S. fleet nor did they prevent the occupation of the Philippines and Okinawa. "But they did extract a terrible price," Timenes concluded.[40] Timenes noted the conclusion of the U.S. Strategic Bombing Survey in its volume on *Japanese Air Power* found suicide planes were the most effective weapon the Japanese had against surface vessels. In 10 months of a 44-month war, these planes caused 48.1 percent of all warships damaged and 21.3 percent of all ships sunk. But the Japanese suicide effort was costly during those 10 months. Two air arms expended 2.550 planes that achieved 474 hits on all types of surface vessels with an effective rate of 18.6 percent.

Societal Outcomes

Japanese society did not universally approve the kamikaze operation. The basis of societal discord with the kamikaze suicidal attacks was the protracted period during October 1944 to August 1945 that the assaults persisted, Inoguchi and Nakajima wrote. The sustained aspect of the attacks was without historical precedent. The Japanese people severely criticized the system and its leaders. After the war, mostly the uninformed, adamantly denounced the kamikazes. Those militarily inclined or able to observe military function observed realities of war: conventional tactics were useless and to defeat the enemy by any means, destruction is inevitable, and the bravery of the kamikaze.[41] However, society also responded in positive ways. By the end of the Leyte campaign, suicide was no longer a ritual but a "deeply emotive part of the national psyche," wrote Warner and Warner.[42] Tokyo newspapers conveyed awards for those pilots who had died in suicide attacks. The government organized the group, One Hundred Million in Rage Destroy the Anglo-Americans. The group trained civilians how to use hand grenades and bamboo spears. Girls who worked in factories pledged themselves to the kamikaze spirit by wearing rising sun towels around their heads.

CONCLUSION

Ohnuki-Tierney's treatment of the kamikaze reflects my effort to capture suicide warfare as a result of culture, the military, and the individual as a weapon. She stated, "An aesthetics is assigned to the symbols that stand for the most cherished values of the people—their land, their history, idealism, and the moral codes of purity and sacrifice. People respond to this aesthetics, interpreting it in terms of their own idealism and aesthetics, while the state can use the same aesthetics and symbols to co-opt them."[43] "Everybody hates death, faces death. But only those, the believers who know the life after death and the rewards after death, would be the ones who will be seeking death."[44]

CHAPTER 7

Hezbollah and Palestinian Conflicts with Israel

Since the 1980s, suicide warfare has been a part of the ongoing conflicts involving Israel. Hezbollah used it in Lebanon. Al-Fatah, Hamas, and other Palestinian groups used it in the Palestinian territories and in Israel. The common denominator in all cases was opposition to the existence of Israel.

The continuing conflicts have fueled the flames of Islamic radicalism in countries throughout the Middle East. Islamic radicalism "is a political response to the deepening economic, social, political, and cultural crisis in the Muslim World," stated Alan Richards.[1] High unemployment and increasing poverty caused by rapid demographic growth, educational changes, government policy failure, and rapid urbanization had alienated large segments of Muslim youth. Richards is correct that people were seeking a political response to a problem.

The sustained presence of societal distress on the scale manifested contributes to, not causes, the continued appeal of Islamist radicals. Richards points to the failure of Arab states to resolve the Palestinian circumstances and the inability of Pakistan to ease the plight of Kashmiri Muslims as contributing to the youth considering regimes illegitimate. Nationalism has not vanished, but has been assimilated into the Islamists' discourse.[2]

LEBANON AND THE HEZBOLLAH

Lebanon is one of the most complex and divided countries in the region, according to *BBC*. Sometimes, it is on the periphery of the conflict over the creation of Israel, and at other times, it is at the center. From

1975 to 1990, Lebanon began to right itself from the effects of the Civil War. In 2006, war again broke out. In January 2011, the government collapsed. Five months later, a new government was formed with Hezbollah dominating the cabinet. Lebanon is a mountainous region with a western coastal region. The literacy rate is high and the culture is mercantile.[3] Lebanon borders the Mediterranean Sea between Israel and Syria. It is about 0.7 times the size of Connecticut. Natural resources include limestone, iron ore, salt, water-surplus state in a water-deficit region, and arable land. Major ethnic groups include Arab 95 percent and Armenian 4 percent of a population of 4,140,289, Muslims comprise 59.7 percent, and Christians 39 percent.[4]

Historical Context

The causes of the Lebanese Civil War (1975–1990) were seeded in Lebanon's history, stated Faten Ghosn and Amal Khoury. Conflicts and compromises of the French colonial period (1920–1943) involved domestic factors that were directly related to the political confessional system that governed. In addition to a weak government, other elements that preceded the Civil War included domestic tensions concerning the political structure, power-sharing, exploitation of sectarian differences, economic inequalities and disparities, along with external/regional conflicts related to Israel and Palestine.[5] Syria's proximity to Lebanon was also a factor prior to the war. Changing demographic trends exacerbated the nation's situation. Palestinian refugees had made Lebanon their home after Israel became a state in 1948.[6]

The United Nations Relief and Works Agency (UNRWA) registration system provides survey data that is inaccurate given the massive emigration of Palestinians, according to Jad Chaaban et al., but it enables for the first time an accurate estimate of the total number of refugees living in Lebanon. Of the 425,000 refugees registered with UNRWA since 1948, 260,000–280,000 currently resides in Lebanon. Over half live in camps (62%) compared to 38 percent living in gatherings, mainly in camp vicinity.[7]

The early fighting was primarily in south Lebanon, which was occupied by the Palestine Liberation Organization (PLO), and later occupied by Israel. Syria and Israel were significantly involved in the war. Israel invaded Lebanon in 1978 in the Litani Operation, but withdrew under pressure from the United Nations. In 1982, Israel invaded Lebanon in Operation Peace for Galilee. They forced out the PLO, and when a bomb killed Lebanon's president, Bahir Gemayel, the Phalangist militia killed 900 Palestinian civilians at the Shabra and Shatilla refugee camps.[8]

Hezbollah or Party of God was founded in 1982 in response to the Israeli invasion of Lebanon. It could be argued that its attacks were in defense.[9]

Hezbollah was forming before that, but that is when it crystallized, according to Max L. Gross, an intelligence analyst who followed them at the time. Gross gives insight on how much was known about Hezbollah at the time:

The public had not known very much about [Hezbollah] until the bombing of the barracks: our barracks, the French barracks, and the Israeli barracks on that famous day, October 23, 1983. It was quite a spectacular thing. We had sort of thrown up the terrorism warning, but, as they said, there were so many warnings. You didn't know which was which, or what their targets were. We did have information that they were preparing car bombs and truck bombs in this place in eastern Lebanon, but where they were going to use them, we had no idea. Whether this was a true or false report, you didn't know that either. Once the bombings took place we were able to put together the story how it had happened. Then, of course, the upshot was, "Why didn't you know this ahead of time?" There had been a bombing of our embassy on April 18, 1983, and it was a suicide bombing, a van drove up under the canopy and exploded itself.[10]

Suicide bombing was a very new tactic that Hezbollah had developed far enough where "they could sacrifice their own lives for the larger cause which was basically to get the United States to withdraw from Lebanon which it did in 1984. Their tactics worked," stated Gross.

Again in July 2006, the Hezbollah had, as they had twice before, captured a couple of Israeli soldiers.[11] Israel retaliated with a heavy offense on Lebanon raising concern on the part of Presidents George W. Bush and Jacques René Chirac and Prime Minister Anthony Charles Lynton "Tony" Blair, for high civilian casualties. In the G-8 Summit press briefing, Secretary of State Condoleezza Rice responded that the primary goal was to end the violence, but in at least five different instances, Rice defended Israel and said that Israel had a right to defend itself. She also faulted the Hezbollah for launching the attacks against Israel when the Lebanese government was unaware.[12] On July 13, 2006, President George W. Bush supported Israel's right to defend itself. On July 21, 2006, Rice ruled out a ceasefire.[13] At the time, analysts speculated that when Rice delayed her departure to negotiate peace, it was to allow Israel more time to conduct its aerial war.[14]

When asked how Hezbollah has changed over the years, Gross replied that since 1995, they appear to have ceased using suicide bombings. From July 12 to August 14, 2006, the 34 days war between the Israelis and Hezbollah took place in Lebanon. "What we learned is that Hezbollah had collected a lot of rockets that could hit Israel, and Israel couldn't stop it. They are fighting in a different way now and also they've transformed themselves into a political party in Lebanon and they're struggling politically as well as militarily: militarily against Israel and politically within Lebanon, so their whole way of thinking how to achieve their goals has evolved."[15]

Organization

Hezbollah, a powerful political and military organization in Lebanon, consists primarily of Shia Muslims. It surfaced in the early 1980s with Iran providing financial backing. The organization began its effort to drive Israeli troops from Lebanon. Hostility to Israel continues to be the party's defining platform since May 2000, according to *BBC*.[16] In addition to arms and money from Iran and Syria, Hezbollah has an international infrastructure involving it in weapons trafficking, money laundering, and drug trade, according to Brian A. Jackson et al. It provides monetary support for charities in Lebanon that, in turn, provide new recruits and political support in elections. The organization's hierarchical structure and its religious nature give its leaders a high degree of control. Top officials' strategic decisions for change were easily translated throughout the organization. In a variety of ways, Hezbollah demonstrated its ability to adapt. Suicide bombings revealed this ability to store knowledge, for years if needed, and reapply it when the situation dictated.[17]

The Military

From 1983 to 1988, Hezbollah engaged in 19 (of its total of approximately 30) suicide attacks, according to the RAND Terrorism Chronology.[18] One of Hezbollah's most successful suicide attacks took place in Beirut, Lebanon on October 23, 1983. The attacks caused President Ronald Reagan to withdraw U.S. forces on February 7, 1984. French and U.S. fatalities numbered 241 and the wounded totaled 81. The Hezbollah destroyed the buildings housing the U.S. Marines' peacekeeping force with a truck full of explosives at 6:20 a.m. Most of the dead had been asleep when the explosion took place. Explosive material used was similar to TNT in the amount of 1000 kilos. According to RAND, U.S. officials have said privately that the bombing is attributed to a militant, pro-Iranian Shiite Moslem group known as Hezbollah, the Party of God, a breakaway group from the main Shiite Amal, headquartered in a Syrian-controlled part of Lebanon. The group's Lebanese leader, Hussein Mussawi, denied responsibility but praised the attacks.[19]

When Hezbollah adopted the tactic of suicide bombing in 1983 with its attack on U.S. and French peacekeeping forces in Beirut, Lebanon, the uniqueness of their method caught the world's attention toward the newly formed group. Daniel Helmer considers Hezbollah's use of suicide bombing worth systematic study because of factors that distinguished it from any other group of the 1980s: "[t]he specific, rational choice of suicide bombing as a militarily effective, theologically justified means to achieve political ends."[20]

Clearly, political reasons gave rise to the tactic of suicide bombing, but Hezbollah formed the doctrine of self-martyrdom within the framework of the highly politicized Shi'ite legal system coming from Iran, according to Helmer. Even though Hezbollah had ties to revolutionary clerics and Ayatollah Ruhollah al-Musavi al-Khomeini, suicide bombing doctrine was different from Iranian martyrdom. So Muhammad Hussein Fadlal-lah, Hezbollah's spiritual guide and a supporter of suicide bombings, de-veloped a theological argument based on the politicization of martyrdom that prevailed over Shi'ite prohibitions against suicide. Even though the theological justification of suicide bombing based on rational thought within the scope of radical Shi'ite jurisprudence was in place before He-zbollah sent out its first suicide bombers, the real reason Hezbollah used the tactic was that it could bring about political change. Therefore, they carefully timed suicide bombings so that their enemies would pay signifi-cant military and political costs.[21]

After justifying suicide attacks theologically, the group compared the military and political consequences of bombings to other tactics. Un-derstanding of the capabilities of suicide bombing as a weapon and the political goals it might help attain, Hezbollah then timed suicide bomb-ing operations to make their enemies pay significant military and political costs, wrote Helmer. Political justification was that they would follow the Islamic revolution and not accept any other government in Lebanon con-sidering America, Israel, and France enemies. They believed that judicious use of suicide bombing was necessary in order to prevent diminishing returns: for example, loss of too many bombers, development of Israeli familiarity with the tactic, and cessation of political benefits or not bring-ing the desired number of casualties.[22]

Hezbollah designed its first suicide attack on April 18, 1983, on the U.S. Embassy, to forestall the Israeli–Lebanese peace treaty. The treaty came to fruition much later. When Hezbollah's enemies would not leave, they bombed the barracks. "By establishing a clear political objective, Hezbol-lah was letting the allies know it sought specific goals through the use of this weapon," stated Helmer.[23]

By the end of 1985, Hezbollah had driven out the multinational force and forced the Israel Defense Forces (IDF) to withdraw from parts of Lebanon. From mid-1985 to November, Hezbollah, trying to hasten Isra-el's pullback and eject it altogether from Lebanese soil, performed about 12 suicide bombings. Bombers executed their attacks from the backs of donkeys. The political and military message was that attacks would con-tinue until Israel withdrew totally. Beginning in 1986, Hezbollah achieved the greatest possible military effect when it combined guerilla warfare with suicide bombing, Helmer stated.[24]

In 2000, when the last Israeli troops left Lebanon, it was a major suc-cess of the Islamic Resistance, Hezbollah's military arm, according to *BBC*. Hezbollah's popularity then reached its highest point.[25] In 2005, Robert A. Pape characterized Hezbollah as a mainstream political party that had abandoned suicide attacks and virtually discarded terrorism, and since the early 1990s, had become essentially a mainstream political party.[26]

In 2006, Hezbollah was a central force in a war with Israel that followed the capture of two Israeli soldiers, stated *BBC*. Israel launched an intensive air campaign and invaded southern Lebanon. Hezbollah fought the invasion and forced Israeli armed forces out of Lebanon. A truce was agreed to,[27] but most analysts believe Hezbollah won the war.

The Individual as a Weapon

Regardless of the individual's motivation or trigger, organizations provide the mechanism for recruitment of would-be suicide attackers. Organizations provide logistical support and market suicide bombing as part of a culture of death, which holds self-sacrifice for the community and its cause desirable, wrote Nicola Pratt. But, we can learn what factors motivate an individual by observing the organization's methods. For example, Paul Gill noted the model of focusing, in part, on two distinct processes, the organization and the individual, permits "why and how leaders of terrorist organizations socially construct a 'culture of martyrdom' and under what conditions audiences become susceptible to such narratives."[28] Pratt noted Ami Pedahzur's example of Hezbollah's celebration of suicide bombing to attract support and recruits. It put up very large images in public places of its first suicide attacker, 15-year-old Ahmad Qasir. In November 1982, Qasir drove a vehicle loaded with explosives into an Israeli military compound in Tyre, Lebanon. The commemoration of his death aided the recruitment of other suicide attackers.[29] Hezbollah commemorates the anniversary of Qasir each year.[30]

Hezbollah plays on a theme part of which is idealistic. Gross explains, "There are many assertions that they use coercive techniques. If someone's family is poor, the family is offered large amounts of money if their child will do this. There are a variety of techniques that are a combination of idealistic appeal versus coercive measures to make [a child] really go along with it."[31]

Hezbollah trained everyday fighters in its own camps and sent elite troops to Iran for specialized training. In the late 1970s, they trained most of the core fighters in Palestinian camps and, after setting up its own bases, provided assistance in return.[32]

Organizations provide the public with moral justifications for suicide bombing and facilitate the creation of a culture of martyrdom. To legitimize suicide attacks, most organizations used leaders who are revered, such as Osama bin Laden, or an authority figure who most likely is a religious leader. Hezbollah, as well as Hamas, al Qaeda, Islamic Jihad, Iraqi, and Afghan, insurgents relied on Sheikh Ahmad Yassin, Sayid Muhammad Hasayn Fadlalla, and Shaikh Yusuf Qardawi, according to Gill.[33]

Scholarly works on why a person responds to suicide bombing have put forth a variety of reasons, but they agree that all suicide bombers share common characteristics (see Chapters 1 and 2). No suicide bomber has acted alone, but with an organization that coordinates, designs, premeditates, and organizes the attack. The second common characteristic lies in the immediate social environment rather than a personality flaw. Gill explained the relationship among the individual, the organization and its military agenda, and the society:

Under conditions of threat, societies accept the proclamations of authoritarian charismatic leaders as authentic and resort to authoritarian mindsets. Threat salience coupled with, and caused by, surrounding political conditions facilitate support for suicide bombing. The individual, in search of a positive identity, joins the terrorist organization with the support of a surrounding community. Experiencing catalysts and recruitment through pre-existing familial and friendship ties drive the process of becoming a suicide bomber forward. Within the group, the new recruit radicalizes further. Relevant norm internalization, group polarization, group conformity, group identity overriding individual identity, the use of multiple bombers and other techniques are used by group leaders to facilitate the individual becoming a suicide bomber.[34]

Gill applied aspects of this model to Hamas, Hezbollah, al Qaeda, Islamic Jihad, Iraqi, and Afghanistan insurgents; Tamil Tigers; and Kurdistan Workers' Party.

Outcomes

Gross describes the Hezbollah of today:

Their current party is within Lebanon but they still maintain a military force to counteract Israel. And in a way, I think they are successful. They showed in 2006 that they can hurt Israel, and everything I read suggests that they have collected even more rockets. So, Israel is a bit hesitant to do anything in Lebanon because Hezbollah has the capability of striking back. Within Lebanon they are a formidable group. They still remain armed. The Lebanese in cooperation with the international community disarmed all of the other militias in Lebanon, but they didn't disarm Hezbollah, which argued that they needed to remain armed in order to counter the Israeli threat in southern Lebanon, which the Lebanese armed forces were unable to do (or wouldn't do). The unresolved issue of the legal status of the Shebaa farms [Lebanese and involving certain villages and adjacent land on the eastern side of Alsheikh Mountain occupied by Israel] remained the potential flashpoint of conflict. So, it's an extra legal; it's not army; it's not police forces; it's a militia. They are armed and they say that they are providing the defense against Israel which the Lebanese army can't do. The Lebanese don't push it too hard. That's part of their being formidable. Of course, from the Israeli perspective, this is an intolerable situation which is why there's so much tension now in the air with these threats of imminent war. But I think the Hezbollah's army itself and all these rockets which are capable of hurting Israel as kind of a deterrent. It's not that they are threatening Israel per se, but they are trying to keep Israel from attacking Lebanon.[35]

In early 2011, Israel advised its citizens of a number of Hezbollah plots against Israeli interests in Turkey, Azerbaijan, Georgia, and Cyprus.[36] On June 13, 2011, Hezbollah gained control of the Lebanese government when they dominated the Cabinet following a five-month period in which Lebanon was without a functioning government. Lebanon's allies, Syria and Iran, benefit from Hezbollah's rise to power in turbulent times, Israel does not.[37] The Arab Spring has presented new issues for Hezbollah. In February 2012, Hezbollah denied allegations that it supports the Assad regime when it had supported other revolutions in the Arab Spring. Syria had permitted shipments of weapons from Iran to Hezbollah in South Lebanon, on the border with Israel, to pass through its country, according to Moni Alami. Hezbollah has taken advantage of the turmoil in Syria to acquire advanced weapons systems, such as long-range rockets and Russian-made air-defense systems. Alami wrote that, according to reports in *The Jerusalem Post* that quoted Western intelligence assessments, the threat of another civil war is at stake.[38]

In July 2011, the U.N. Special Tribunal for Lebanon indicted four Hezbollah members for the assassination of former Lebanese Prime Minister Rafiq al-Hariri. The car bomb killing took place in Beirut on February 14, 2005.[39]

THE PALESTINIAN–ISRAELI CONFLICT

Hamas and Palestinian Factions

At the heart of the Israeli–Palestinian conflict are the Gaza Strip and the West Bank. The Gaza Strip borders the Mediterranean Sea between Egypt and Israel. The Gaza Strip is a little more than twice the size of Washington, D.C. The only ethnic group represented is Palestinian Arab. Their religion is predominately Muslim, mainly Sunni (99.3%) and a very small number of Christians (0.7%). The Gaza Strip's estimated population as of July 2012 was 1,710,257. The West Bank is situated west of Jordan and east of Israel, and is slightly smaller than Delaware. Its population is 83 percent Palestinian Arabs among other ethnicities and 17 percent Jewish inhabitants out of an estimated total population of 2,622,544 as of July 2012. Approximately 311,100 Israeli settlers lived in the West Bank in 2010, and about 186,929 Israeli settlers lived in East Jerusalem.[40]

Historical Context

The Palestinian and Israeli conflict began over 3,000 years ago. The Old Testament of the Bible records that the Israelites started conquering and settling in the land of Canaan on the eastern Mediterranean coast in 1250 BC. The basis of conflict can be traced to the historic claim to the land between the eastern shores of the Mediterranean Sea and the Jordan River.[41] The modern conflict between Israel and Palestine (1948–present) has

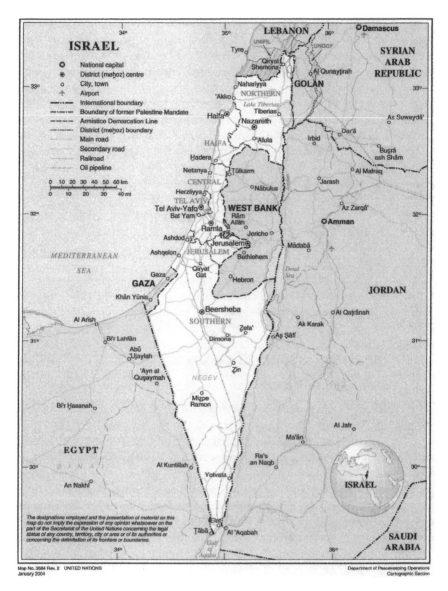

Map No. 3584 Rev. 2   UNITED NATIONS
January 2004

Department of Peacekeeping Operations
Cartographic Section

resulted in four major wars since World War II. As a result of the 1967 war, Israel remains the occupying power over large portions of Palestinian territory not allocated to it by the United Nations in 1947.[42] In February 2005, the Israeli government voted to disengage from the Gaza Strip. All settlements and military bases in Gaza were dismantled. On September 12, 2005, Israel declared an end of its occupation that had endured since

Israel captured the territory in 1967, but "Israel continues to control Gaza through an 'invisible hand': control over borders, airspace, territorial waters, population registry, the tax system, supply of goods, and others. Gaza residents know that their ability to use electric lights, to buy milk, or to have the garbage collected depends on decisions made by Israel. At times, soldiers operate in the streets of Gaza, but even after they leave, Israeli control over the lives of Gaza residents remains constant," according to Sari Bashi and Kenneth Mann.[43]

Hamas

Of the Islamist groups outside of the global jihad, Hezbollah ranks first for having the most capability and Hamas (Harakat al-Muqawama al-Islamia) or the Islamic Resistance Movement is second, reported Angel Rabasa et al. Hamas's basic objective is to establish a Palestinian Islamic state in Israel proper, in the West Bank, and in Gaza. Suicide bombings directed at Israel to secure a state has been one part of their two part strategy. The second part is the requirement that the group pursue its Islamic agenda through al-Fatah and the Palestinian Authority. To accomplish this objective, Hamas abstained from Palestinian National Authority elections in 1995. As an alternative, Hamas focused on municipal elections in the Palestinian territories.[44]

Organization

To accomplish its objectives, Hamas depends on its relationship with local Palestinian communities and the Palestinian diaspora. Hamas is a practical organization that opposed Saddam Hussein's overpowering Kuwait even though Arafat supported Hussein. As a result, the Gulf States gave monetary support to Hamas. In addition, at the beginning of the second intifada, Hamas, al-Fatah, and the Palestinian Authority united against Israel. In 2004, violence resulted among Hamas, al-Fatah, and the al-Aqsa Martyrs' Brigades. Israel had withdrawn and Hamas indicated it was prepared to govern, and the al-Aqsa Martyrs' Brigades had started to challenge al-Fatah.[45]

The National Consortium for the Study of Terrorism and Responses to Terrorism (START) indicates that Hamas was an outgrowth of the Muslim Brotherhood, an Egyptian Sunni, Islamist, religious movement that strives for broad social, moral, and political reforms based upon Islam. In 1973, Sheikh Ahmed Yassin, Hamas founder and spiritual leader, established al-Mujamma' al-Islami (the Islamic Center), an umbrella organization overseeing Muslim Brotherhood activities in the Gaza Strip.[46] Rabasa et al. noted that the center was registered with the authorities of the Israeli military who administered the Gaza Strip in 1978. In 1983, the spiritual reformist group ceased and focused on educational and charitable activities. It also considered launching militant activities against Israel. In 1988, after the beginning of the first intifada, the organization became known as Hamas, which means "zeal" in Arabic, with a military branch, al-Qassam. All of these activities made Hamas a credible player in the political and militant arenas.[47]

After the outbreak of the first Palestinian intifada, Hamas was recognized as the political arm for Muslim Brotherhood. Hamas members began advancing the uprising. In August 1988, Hamas released its official charter[48] dedicated to creating an Islamic state in the territory of Palestine, which included all of Israel and Palestinian territories. Because the land of Palestine has been endowed to Islam, it was all Muslims' duty to liberate Palestine with a violent jihad.[49]

The Military

In May 1989, the Israeli government through a series of arrests assumed leadership of Hamas. Leadership handover became a characteristic of Hamas, wrote Rabasa et al. In 1994, two years after former Israeli Prime Minister Yitzhak Rabin deported 400 Palestinian activists to southern Lebanon, Hamas committed its first suicide bombing on a bus in Afula, killing 8 and wounding 44. The attack was not only directed at Israel, but was also intended to undermine the secular Palestinian Authority.[50]

When filtering in the *CPost* database for 10 organizations that employed suicide bombing in the Palestinian Resistance versus Israel campaign from 1981 to October 14, 2011, a total of 158 attacks killed 799 and wounded 5,212 from 1994 to 2008. Suicide attacks began in 1994, and were the most frequent during 2001–2004, that is during most of the al-Aqsa or second intifada. From 2009 to 2011, they were not employed (see Table 7.1). Of the 10 groups, Hamas conducted the most attacks, 74, killed the highest number of people, 540, and wounded the most, 3.268 (see Table 7.2). All attacks either occurred in Israel, 102, or in the Palestinian territory, occupied, 56. Israel's casualties numbered 730 killed and 4,924 wounded while the occupied Palestinian territory casualties numbered 69 and 288, respectively.[51] Of these groups, Hamas, Palestinian Islamic Jihad (PIJ), al-Aqsa Martyrs' Brigade, and the Popular Front for the Liberation of Palestine (PFLP) are the most important groups, and share the goal of Palestinian nationalism and method to attain their goal through suicide attacks. The groups differ as to what the borders should be, according to Robert A. Pape and James K. Feldman.[52] These groups have not attacked, but cooperated with each other. Palestinian militants comprise two basic groups: secular and religious nationalists. The most active secular nationalists are al-Fatah, the PFLP, Tanzim, Force-17, and al-Aqsa Martyrs' Brigade. Religious nationalists include Hamas and PIJ.[53]

Table 7.1
Suicide Attacks and Casualties by Year, Palestinian Resistance versus Israel Campaign, 1994–2011.*

Campaign Period	Attacks	Killed	Wounded
First Period			
1994	5	40	236
1995	7	64	295
1996	3	61	220
1997	5	28	397
1998	2	1	30
1999	0	0	0
Total	22	194	1,178
Al-Aqsa or Second Intifada			
2000	2	1	10
2001	29	116	953
2002	52	240	1,692
2003	24	153	780
2004	15	59	337
2005	7	28	230
Total	129	597	4,002
2006–2011			
2006	3	4	6
2007	1	3	2
2008	3	1	24
2009	0	0	0
2010	0	0	0
2011	0	0	0
Total	7	8	32
Total of all years	**158**	**799**	**5,212**

*Statistics represent groups that appear in Table 7.2.

Source: Adapted from Suicide Attack Search Database, *Chicago Project on Security and Terrorism (CPOST)*, October 14, 2011, http://cpost.uchicago.edu/search.php.

The groups involved in the Palestinian versus Israel conflict used the belt bomb in 97 (60.6%) attacks and the car bomb in 27 (16.9%). Other weapons were used in 20 (12.5%) attacks. These figures represent attacks in which the weapon used was known. The weapon used was unknown

Table 7.2
Suicide Attacks and Casualties by Group, Palestinian Resistance versus Israel Campaign, 1994–2008.

Group	Attacks	Killed	Wounded
Hamas	74	540	3,268
Palestinian Islamic Jihad	40	157	878
Al-Fatah	30	62	616
Al-Aqsa Martyrs' Brigade	10	65	378
Popular Front for the Liberation of Palestine	9	22	266
Unknown	7	20	163
Islamic Holy War	6	53	376
Fatah al-Islam	1	0	2
Popular Resistance Committees	1	0	2
Tanzim	1	0	1
Total	179	919	5,950

Source: Adapted from Suicide Attack Search Database, *Chicago Project on Security and Terrorism (CPOST)*, October 14, 2011, http://cpost.uchicago.edu/search.php.

in 26 (10%) attacks. The percentage killed by these methods was comparable to the method used. The belt bomb killed the most people, 579 (69.1%), and the car bomb killed 93 (11.1%). The target of most attacks 105 (65.6%) was civilians of which 729 (86.5%) were killed and 4,896 wounded. The next most attacks 53 (33.1%) targeted security, killing 101 (12.0%) and wounding 477 (see Table 7.3).[54]

Pape and Feldman reported that although the Israeli–Palestinian conflict has endured a number of years, suicide attacking did not appear until 1994 (see Table 7.1). They divide the attacks into three time frames: 1994–1999, 2000–2005, and 2006–2012.[55] The authors assigned sub-campaigns for the 1994–1999 time frame that demonstrate operational strategy.

1994–1999

Early suicide attacks from 1994 to 1999 as outlined by Pape and Feldman were to force the Israelis to comply with the Oslo Agreements and to stop Israel from targeting the Hamas leadership.[56] The Oslo Agreements (1993 and 1995) offered Israel and Palestine a road map to peace, whereby the two countries were to benefit from trade agreements. However, the past 60 years "unequivocally indicates that neither side is seriously interested in such an outcome," concluded Charles K. Rowley and Jennis Taylor.[57]

Table 7.3

Suicide Attacks and Casualties by Weapon and Target, Palestinian Resistance versus Israel Campaign, 1994–2011.*

	Attacks (Percent)	Killed (Percent)	Wounded (Percent)
Weapon			
Airplane	0 (0)	0 (0)	0 (0)
Belt bomb	97 (60.6)	579 (69.1)	3,689 (69.4)
Car bomb	27 (16.9)	93 (11.1)	552 (10.4)
Other	20 (12.5)	77 (9.2)	493 (9.3)
Unknown	16 (10.0)	89 (10.6)	578 (10.9
Total	160 (100)	838 (100)	5,312 (100)
Target Type			
Security	53 (33.1)	101 (12.0)	477 (8.9)
Political	1 (0.6)	0 (0.0)	3 (0.0)
Civilian	105 (65.6)	729 (86.5)	4,896 (91.1)
Other	0 (0.0)	0 (0.0)	0 (0)
Unknown	1 (0.6)	13 (1.5)	0 (0)
Total	160 (100)	843 (100)	5,376 (100)

*Statistics represent groups that appear in Table 7.2.
Source: Adapted from Suicide Attack Search Database, *Chicago Project on Security and Terrorism (CPOST)*, October 14, 2011, http://cpost.uchicago.edu/search.php

The first Oslo Accord marked the most important political result or achievement of the first intifada or uprising from 1987 to 1993. Since the Oslo Accord, the two governments had been officially dedicated to a two-state solution. Unresolved issues remained. The status and future of the West Bank, Gaza Strip, and East Jerusalem were a primary concern because these areas were the proposed State of Palestine. The nature of a Palestinian state and the outcome of the refugees were to be settled. Security issues for Israel and Palestine had to be resolved. The agreements were unacceptable at the second or the al-Aqsa intifada that started in 2000 and ended in 2005.[58] The Declaration of Principles that evolved from the Oslo Agreements outlined the mutually agreed-upon general principles regarding the five-year interim period of Palestinian self-rule. Israel and Palestine agreed to recognize each other.[59] This time marked frequent and widespread violence within Israel and in the West Bank and Gaza. Suicide bombings caused more fatalities than any other tactics from 2000 to 2009, accounting for 43 percent of the total, reported Jonathan Schachter.[60]

The Subcampaigns

Pape and Feldman devised four subcampaigns for each time frame that demonstrate operational strategy.

Subcampaign No. 1, 1994 Attacks—When the IDF failed to withdraw by the March 1994 deadline, Hamas conducted the April 6 and 13 attacks in Israel. When on April 18, 1994, the Israeli legislature voted to proceed with the Gaza–Jericho agreement; it withdrew on May 14, 1994. Hamas did not conduct three out of five announced attacks. Pape and Feldman wrote that this change is significant in that Hamas's change in operations was based on desired outcome.[61] In 2006, Robert J. Brym and Bader Arajthe found that the timing of suicide attacks varied with Robert A. Pape's findings at the time. Pape's results were that suicide attacks were timed to maximize the achievement of strategic or tactical goals. The analysis of participants of Brym and Arajthe concluded that most suicide bombings were revenge or retaliatory, and were advertised as such.[62]

Subcampaign No. 2, 1995 Attacks—Hamas and PIJ attacks that took placed from October 1994 to August 1995 were to force Israel to withdraw from the West Bank. The withdrawal took place in December 1995, and the attacks ceased. The operational pattern was one of "action–reaction," Pape and Feldman concluded.[63]

Subcampaign No. 3, 1996 Attacks—Hamas conducted four 1996 attacks to avenge Israel's targeted assassination of Hamas leader, Yahya Ayyush. These attacks caused 58 Israeli lives. Pape and Feldman reported that Palestinian support for suicide attacks was at its lowest, 5 percent. Because of the lack of support and the Palestinian Authority's concentrated effort to curb militant groups, no attacks were conducted for a year.[64]

Subcampaign No. 4, 1997 Attacks—Three attacks from March to September 1997 killed 24 Israelis. After the attacks of March and July 1997, Israel tried to target the assassination of Hamas political bureau chief, Khaled Mash'al, in September. Hamas responded with capturing Israeli agents and another attack on September 4, 1997, proclaiming the attacks would continue until the release of Hamas members from Israeli prisons. When Israel released Hamas leader Sheikh Ahmed Ysasin on October 1 in exchange for Israeli agents, Hamas did not continue attacks, except for two, until the second or al-Aqsa intifada.[65]

The Al-Aqsa or Second Intifada

On September 28, 2000, Ariel Sharon and hundreds of Israeli police went to what the Jews call the Temple Mount and the Arabs call Haram esh-Sharif. This attack marked the beginning of the second intifada. Palestinian and Israeli violence prevailed, and the Camp David Agreements of July 11–25, 2000, for final status talks, were never realized. Palestine supporters see the conflict as an illegitimate military occupation of Palestine, supported with military and diplomatic assistance from the United States. Israel supporters view the conflict as a campaign of terrorism by Palestinian groups such as Hamas, PIJ, and al-Fatah, supported by other states in the region and most of the Palestinians. Each group believes that the Geneva Conventions and the U.N. Charter support its view.[66]

Hamas engaged in unarmed violent rebellion and did not employ suicide attacks in the first intifada from 1987 to 1992. In the second or al-Aqsa intifada from 2000 to 2005, Hamas's campaign turned to armed rebellion and large-scale suicide bombing, according to Pape and Feldman.[67] After the al-Aqsa intifada in 2000, Hamas included shopping malls, cafés, and pedestrian markets in its targets. While the organization stated the reason for its use of suicide bombing was to retaliate against Israeli assassinations, 59 percent of Palestinians indicated in 1996 opinion poll that the Palestinian Authority should do something to stop the attacks, reported Rabasa et al.[68] Tactical models contribute to the proliferation of effective styles of unconventional warfare. Although models vary in different conflict zones, Hamas has used ambulances as a cover for bombs or logistical support. It was the first to use suicide vests against Israel, wrote Rabasa et al.

Three Turning Points

Brym and Araj presented three turning points in the history of the second intifada. Heightened repression by Israeli forces sharply increased the cost to Palestinian insurgents of using alternative tactics at each of three turning points. The turning points included the first use of suicide bombing: during the second intifada in 2000; by a secular Palestinian organization in 2001; and by al-Fatah, the leading secular, nationalist Palestinian organization in 2002.[69] These firsts, or turning points, made it clear that a connection often exists between suicide bombings and Israeli assassinations of Palestinian organizational leaders, according to Brym and Araj. This connection, then, one could reason, is similar to Pape and Feldman's conjecture that the bombings during the first period were ones of "action–reaction" in nature.

The First Suicide Bombing of the Second Intifada—In September 2000, the first riot of the second intifada occurred outside of al-Aqsa Mosque. Israel aggressively responded by firing ammunition into the crowd. The rioting spread fast. At the end of the year, 319 Palestinians, 43 Israelis, including 22 civilians had been killed. Out of Israel's extreme repression, the PIJ changed its tactics and launched the first suicide attack of the second intifada. PIJ issued a press release that suggested the bombing was a reaction to the killings in the first days of the intifada.[70]

The First Suicide Bombing by a Secular Organization—On August 27, 2001, the Israeli forces assassinated Abu Ali Mustafa (Mustafa Zubari), the secretary general of the PFLP. This assassination was the first to involve the head of a militant organization. In response, the PFLP shot and killed a Jewish settler, assassinated the far-right Israel minister of tourism, Rehavam Ze'evi, and, on the same day, October 17, 2001, conducted the first suicide bombing by a secular, nationalist organization. Only the bomber was killed, and two Israeli soldiers were wounded.[71]

The First Suicide Bombing by Fatah, al-Aqsa Martyrs Brigade (AMB)— Israeli armed forces assassinated a folk hero and leader of the AMB militia, Raed al-Karmi, on January 14, 2002. They detonated a high-powered bomb beside his house in Tulkarem in the West Bank. The AMB retaliated and ambushed some Israeli soldiers killing one and wounding another. Other violent attacks took place over a period of two weeks, followed by the suicide attack on January 27, 2002, on a busy Jerusalem street corner during lunch hour. The bomber and one Israeli were killed, 11 wounded, and 150 others affected.[72]

In early December 2003, Ariel Sharon announced Israel's withdrawal of troops and settlements out of Gaza and part of the West Bank.[73] According to Pape and Feldman, suicide attacks began to decline right away, but noticeably, so after, the withdrawal process was complete in September 2005 (see Table 7.1).[74]

2006–2012

Although the Hamas were elected as the governing unit in January 2006, suicide bombing did not increase. The low level of attacks can be attributed to Israel's withdrawal. From 2004 to 2009, the intifada aftermath and a fragile peace framed a period of less suicide bombing, according to Pape and Feldman (see Table 7.1).[75]

Strategies

Public support for suicide bombing increased in 2004, making the bombings a method of recruitment for the Palestinian community's militant Islamic organizations, according to Mia Bloom. They served to attack the enemy, Israel, and to provide legitimacy to groups who competed with the Palestinian Authority for leadership. Groups using suicide bombing were more popular, and saw their organizational profile enhanced.[76]

Hamas suicide attack on March 14, 2004 in the Israeli port of Ashdod marked a potentially dangerous shift seen in the emerging Hamas–Hezbollah nexus, according to Rabasa et al. Hamas had killed more in other attacks, but this attack demonstrated its ability to hit more strategic targets. It also demonstrated Hezbollah's willingness to help Hamas select targets and plan attacks.[77] Two 18-year-old male bombers performed the attack: one employed a car bomb and the other used a belt bomb. The attack killed between 10 and 11 and wounded 18 and 20.[78]

In 2004, Mia Bloom wrote that the strategy of suicide bombing is to delegitimize the state of Israel. Part of the goal has been to force Israel to retaliate massively and betray democratic principles, compel Israel to "rip off the mask of legal justice, and show it to be the ravening beast that the Palestinians claim it is."[79] If Israel failed to hold the high ground in the face of suicide bombing, then it hands the victory to the Palestinians. Pape and Feldman also believe the primary impetus for beginning the use of suicide attacks is Israel's occupation and their changing cultural, political, and military influence on the West Bank and Gaza from the mid-1980s on.[80]

Andrew H. Kydd and Barbara F. Walter believed that Hamas's war is one of attrition strategy against their colonizer, Israel. This strategy is particularly true during the second intifada. The goal was to destroy Israel and establish a Palestinian state through persuading Israel that Hamas was strong enough to impose considerable costs if Israel continued its policy. A war of attrition is won or lost based on three variables: "the state's level of interest in the issue under dispute, the constraints on its ability to retaliate, and its sensitivity to the costs of violence."[81] The first variable is unlikely to occur for Israel has not withdrawn, and will not allow itself to become an Islamic state. Israel possesses the military means to commit genocide against the Palestinian people or to force them into exile to neighboring Arab countries. But Israel depends on and does not wish to lose the support of Europe and the United States, who would not be in agreement. Thus, their disapproval is a definite constraint on Israel's ability to retaliate. At the same time, this constraint makes attrition strategy more favorable and less costly to the Palestinians.

The Individual as a Weapon

The majority of the attackers in the organizations in the Palestinian Resistance versus Israel campaign were male, 164 (92.1%). Women were 10 (5.6%) and unknown, 4 (2.2%). The victims of the attacks were primarily men, 784 (95.1%). Women were 40 (4.9%). Of the known attackers, 56 were Muslim (NA); occupation was primarily professional, 21 or skilled worker, 23; with most 32 having a post-secondary education followed by those attackers with a secondary education, 18 (see Table 7.4).[82] It is not easy to draw an accurate profile of attackers because not much was known about attackers and their backgrounds. There were large numbers in the one hundreds representing the unknown categories. When we combine the empirical data and interviews and other research data, we broaden our knowledge about the attackers.

When I wrote *Female Suicide Bombers,* a school of thought existed that Palestinian bombers were in despair and/or they became bombers for religious reasons. Although I maintained attacks were a tactic of war, only

Table 7.4
Suicide Attackers, Attacks, and Casualties by Gender, Religion, Occupation, and Education, Palestinian Resistance versus Israel Campaign, 1994–2011.*

	Attackers (Percent)	Attacks (Percent)	Killed (Percent)	Wounded (Percent)
Gender				
Male	164 (92.1)	147 (91.9)	784 (95.1)	4,845 (79.2)
Female	10 (5.6)	10 (6.2)	40 (4.9)	425 (7.0)
Unknown	4 (2.2)	3 (1.9)	0 (0)	21 (0.03)
Total	178 (100)	160 (100)	824 (100)	6,115 (100)
Religion				
Muslim (NA)	56 (31.5)	53 (32.3)	354 (43.0)	2,134 (40.3)
Muslim (Other)	1 (0.5)	1 (0.6)	19 (2.3)	52 (1.0)
Muslim (Sunni)	8 (4.5)	8 (4.9)	31 (3.7)	160 (3.0)
Unknown	113 (63.5)	102 (62.2)	421 (51.0)	2,945 (55.7)
Total	178 (100)	164 (100)	825 (100)	5,291 (100)
Occupation				
Professional	21 (11.8)	20 (12.3)	147 (17.8)	872 (16.5)
Skilled	23 (12.9)	22 (13.6)	176 (21.4)	1,212 (22.9)
Student	5 (2.8)	5 (3.1)	13 (1.6)	17 (0.3)
Unemployed	3 (1.7)	3 (1.9)	2 (0.2)	12 (0.2)
Unknown	115 (64.6)	101 (62.3)	432 (52.4)	2,774 (52.4)
Unskilled	11 (6.2)	11 (6.8)	54 (6.6)	404 (7.6)
Total	178 (100)	162 (100)	824 (100)	5,291 (100)
Education				
Postsecondary	32 (18.0)	32 (19.5)	205 (24.8)	1077 (20.4)
Primary	3 (1.7)	3 (1.8)	22 (2.7)	136 (2.6)
Secondary	18 (10.1)	17 (10.4)	135 (16.4)	897 (16.9)
Unknown	125 (70.2)	112 (68.3)	463 (56.1)	3,181 (60.1)
Total	178 (100)	164 (100)	825 (100)	5,291 (100)

* Statistics represent groups that appear in Table 7.2.
Source: Adapted from Suicide Attack Search Database, *Chicago Project on Security and Terrorism (CPOST)*, October 14, 2011, http://cpost.uchicago.edu/search.php.

recently has that single approach been rethought. "Under conditions in which getting from point A to point B is increasingly obstructed by an arbitrary power, martyrdom operations are one means of taking back control," according to Lori Allen.[83] Socioeconomic status differs among bombers, but a faith together with conviction motivates bombers. Religion creates bravery and a sense of justice.

I. W. Charney noted the findings of Amira Hass, an Israeli reporter for *Haaretz*. Haas lived among the Palestinians for many years. Her reports on the Palestinian experiences were sometimes too much for some, according to Charney. Hass observed:

The claim that personal despair pushes the suicide bombers arouses sharp opposition among Hamas [a leading Palestinian fundamentalist group] operatives. . . . The sense of national purpose, a sweeping rage [at Israel], and a patriotic wish to advance the battle for independence are the main motivations.[84]

Earlier research tends to attribute personal reasons to an individual to attack. Brym and Araj found that much of Palestinian suicide bombing was explained by the desire to retaliate against Israeli killings of Palestinians. Conversely, much of Israeli killings of Palestinians was explained by the desire to retaliate for suicide attacks.[85] Anat Berko and Edna Erez interviewed seven incarcerated, failed suicide bombers. Four initiated contact with the organization, while the other three were approached by recruiters. Of the four who initiated contact, one was an experienced terrorist who had marital problems that included his wife's family, and following a divorce, he decided to become a martyr. The other three were women. The first woman's father refused to allow her to marry a particular man who could not meet his dowry requirements. She decided to retaliate by being a bomber. She felt useless and was interested in the promise that a *shahida* would be one of the 72 virgins. Another young woman was a refugee who was bored with her life. A third woman wanted to avenge her brother's death by IDF.[86]

Allen responded to customary conceptions of despairing Palestinian bombers. In 2002, Palestinians reported that the resistance to the occupation and sacrifice for the cause were normal, but that even though it was a desperate situation, resistance was highly praised and everywhere commemorated in Palestine. So, here we see the relationship of the individuals to the society in which they live as one of motivation.[87] Reasons to bomb during the mid-period were not always personal problems, but a mixture of religious and nationalism. In *Female Suicide Bombers*, I examined the accounts of failed female suicide bombers to determine why they agreed to bomb. Manuela Dviri, a journalist, playwright, and writer, whose son Jonathan was killed in 1998 by a Hezbollah rocket, interviewed failed female bombers in an Israeli jail. One 20-year-old woman, Ayat Allah Kamil, said that she became a martyr because of her religion. She claimed male martyrs would be welcomed into paradise by 72 beautiful virgins, and that a woman martyr "will be the chief of the 72 virgins, the fairest of the fair."[88] Common elements Dviri found among the women she interviewed were that women prisoners of the Hamas jihad agreed that they were part of a war, that outside was a battlefield, and that they must fight back as long as their people were being "slaughtered." When Dviri asked what their dreams were for the future, one prisoner, Kamil, responded, "Of the world becoming Islamic, a world in which we will all live in peace, joy and harmony, all of us. . . . And you'll be able to remain Jewish, whatever you want; it doesn't matter, but in an Islamic world."[89]

Outcomes

In an interview, Marie Breen-Smyth, School of Politics, University of Surrey, analyzed the status of the Palestinian case. She explained,

The alienation from the Israelis, is so complete on the part of Palestinians that any group that is fighting Israel is going to have an easy time in terms of recruitment, that's the first thing. Second, there is an argument made by people who support military action against Israel that there is no such thing as an Israeli civilian because of conscription. So, these are the two things I would point to in relation to the Palestinian case that are specific to the Palestinian case . . . in terms of the Palestinian case, certainly the comprehensive political alienation of Palestinians means that armed groups enjoy support. Israelis are fairly comprehensively hated. In Northern Ireland where I am from there was a mixture of Jews. There was no love lost certainly, but the depth of the alienation of the Palestinian case and it has gone on for so long now, is actually something that is going to mean that violence will be supported in the absence of political solutions.[90]

In 2005, the United States designated Hamas a foreign terrorist organization.[91] But the Palestinian elections on the January 25, 2006, gave Hamas an absolute majority (74 seats out of 132) in the Palestinian Legislative Council. Voter turnout was 77.7 percent. Hamas had provided basic services to the people. Major reasons for Hamas's victory included Fatah's lack of ability to provide basic services, many corruption scandals in the Palestinian Authority, high unemployment, and Hamas's successes in providing services to the poor. In spite of the expressed will of the people, some countries including the United States said they would not negotiate with or recognize Hamas until it either disarmed or recognized Israel or both.[92] The Bush administration largely abandoned Palestine's democracy focus after the Hamas victory in the January 2006 Palestinian parliamentary elections.[93] The refusal to negotiate with a government elected by its people is not a usual policy of the United States, who encourages countries to employ a democratic process.

In January 2012, an elusive election was on the horizon. The May 4 date seemed uncertain as Hamas and al-Fatah appeared reluctant or unprepared or both. Fatah had not begun to look for a candidate, and was addressing its need to clean its own house. Hamas popularity appeared to have waned and the organization has been globally shunned. Some believe if Fatah is not victorious, it could be its demise. But public opinion polls may not be accurate, and people may be reluctant to openly express support for Hamas, according to Karin Laub and Mohammed Daraghmeh.[94] In March 2012, Hugh Naylor reported that the election may be delayed until June. Hamas and Fatah still had not settled their disagreements.[95] On May 20, 2012, Hamas and Fatah signed an agreement that paved the way for elections and a new unity government for the West Bank and the Gaza Strip. "The new agreement essentially takes steps to carry out the previous one, particularly the registering of new voters in Gaza and the formation of an interim government," according to the *New York Times*.[96] Both are to begin May 27, 2012.

On September 23, 2011, Palestinian President Mahmoud Abbas submitted a letter[97] to the United Nations for statehood. The reaction of Israel and the United States was not favorable. Israeli Prime Minister Benjamin Netanyahu said only direct negotiations could bring peace, and the United States said it would veto the request should it come to a vote.[98] President Obama has opposed Palestinian statehood through methods other than talks between Israel and Palestine. Helene Cooper saw Obama's position as "throwing the weight of the United States directly in the path of the Arab democracy movement even as he hailed what he called the democratic aspirations that have taken hold throughout the Middle East and North Africa."[99] Further, Obama's challenge was how to address the incongruities of the administration's position: committed to peace from the beginning, now unable to get peace negotiations underway; and opened the door to Palestinian state membership at the United Nations last year, now indicating a veto to that membership. I understand that this issue is not only difficult for most, but it must also be very difficult for the president because Israel is our ally. My opinion on most issues related to this conflict is that the United States should support its allies, but not blindly. Israel may need strong encouragement from the United States to not occupy or oppress territory that is not theirs.

CHAPTER 8

Sri Lanka and the Tamil Tigers

The Tamils are a minority in Sri Lanka. They were long established in the north and east of the island. When Britain ruled Ceylon, they brought in Tamil laborers from India to work the coffee and tea plantations in the central highlands. The majority Buddhist Sinhalese resented what they saw as British favoritism toward the mainly Hindu Tamils.[1] After Sri Lanka gained independence in 1948, the Sinhalese gained power and passed laws that negatively impacted the Tamils. A civil war ensued. During the war, the Liberation Tigers of Tamil Eelam (LTTE, also known as Tamil Tigers) used suicide warfare beginning in 1987.

HISTORICAL CONTEXT

The Tamils' liberation aspirations have existed for more than a century. The most recent embodiment of those aspirations came in 1985 when LTTE put together a liberation charter to present to the government delegation when the two sides met in Thimpu, the capital of Bhutan, on August 12. The charter consisted of four principle demands: "recognition of the Tamils as a distinct nationality; recognition of a Tamil homeland in Sri Lanka; recognition of the Tamils' right to self determination; [and] full citizenship rights for all Tamils who regard Sri Lanka as their home."[2]

In 1948, Sri Lanka gained its independence from the British. The Sri Lanka parliament passed an act that disenfranchised Tamils of Indian origin. In 1972, Velupillai Prabhakaran, Tamil Tiger leader, formed the Tamil New Tigers (TNT). In 1976, the TNT became the LTTE. It launched its first

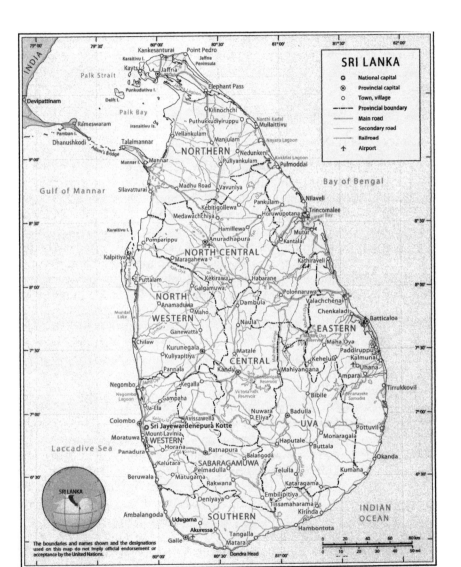

SRI LANKA

- ○ National capital
- ◉ Provincial capital
- ○ Town, village
- –·–·– Provincial boundary
- —— Main road
- —— Secondary road
- —— Railroad
- ✈ Airport

INDIA

Palk Strait

Devipattinam

Rāmeswaram

Pamban I.

Dhanushkodi

Adam's Bridge

Palk Bay

Kankesanturai
Point Pedro
Karaitivu I.
Jaffna Peninsula
Kayts
Jaffna
Punkudutivu I.
Delft I.
Elephant Pass

Kilinochchi
Puthukkudiyiruppu
Nanthi Kadal
Mullaittivu

Vellankulam
Nayaru Lagoon

Manjulam

Talaimannar
Mannar I.
Mannar
Madhu Road
Vavuniya
Silavatturai

NORTHERN
Nedunkeni
Puliyankulam
Kokkilai Lagoon
Pulmoddai

Gulf of Mannar
Bay of Bengal

Kebitigollewa
Pankulam
Nilaveli
Medawachchiya
Horuwupotana
Trincomalee
Koddiyar Bay
Hamillewa
Mutur
Pomparippu
Anuradhapura
Kantalai

NORTH CENTRAL
Kalpitiya
Maragahewa
Kathiraveli
Kala Oya
Kekirawa
Puttalam
Galgamuwa
Habarane
Polonnaruwa
Valachchenai
Anamaduwa
Dambula
Chenkaladi

NORTH
WESTERN
Maho
Naula
EASTERN
Batticaloa
Mundal Lake
Ganewatta
Maha Oya
Chilaw
Kurunegala
Matale
Paddiruppu
Kuliyapitiya
Kalmunai
Pannala
Kehelula
Uhana
Kandy
CENTRAL
Mahiyangana
Amparai
Negombo
Kegalla
Tirrukkovil
Negombo Lagoon
Gampaha
Bibile
Ja-Ela
Nuwara Eliya
Badulla
Colombo
Avissawella
UVA
Sri Jayewardenepura Kotte
Pottuvil
Mount Lavinia
Haputale
Monaragala
Moratuwa
WESTERN
Horana
Buttala
Panadura
Ratnapura
Balangoda
Okanda
Kalutara
SABARAGAMUWA
Telulla
Kumana
Beruwala
Pelmadulla
Kataragama
Matugama
Rakwana
Embilipitiya
Ambalangoda
Deniyaya
Tissamaharama
INDIAN OCEAN
Udugama
SOUTHERN
Kirinda
Akuressa
Hambontota
Laccadive Sea
Galle
Tangalla
Matara
Dondra Head

Karaitivu I.

SRI LANKA

The boundaries and names shown and the designations used on this map do not imply official endorsement or acceptance by the United Nations.

0   20   40   60   80 km
0 10   20   30   40   50 mi

79° 00'   79° 30'   80° 00'   80° 30'   81° 00'   81° 30'   82° 00'

9° 00'
8° 30'
8° 00'
7° 30'
7° 00'
6° 30'

Map No. 4172 Rev.3   UNITED NATIONS
March 2008

Department of Field Support
Cartographic Section

suicide attack on July 5, 1987. In 1983, the civil war began, and in 2009, the conflict ended. In 2012, a cease-fire is in place between the Buddhist Sinhalese majority and the mostly Hindu Tamil minority. The 2001 census provisional data indicated the breakdown of ethnic groups as follows: Sinhalese 73.8%, Sri Lankan Moors 7.2%, Indian Tamil 4.6%, Sri Lankan Tamil 3.9%, other 0.5%, and unspecified 10%.[3] The LTTE had been fighting for a separate homeland for minority ethnic Tamils since the civil war began. They accused the Sinhalese-dominated government of discrimination. The fighting took place in areas with Tamil majorities in the north and the east of the country.

ORGANIZATION

The LTTE is the national freedom movement of the people of Tamil Eelam. It is a political organization and a military power. And even though the Tamil minority is mainly Hindu and the Sinhalese majority is chiefly Buddhist, the conflict is not religiously motivated. The Tamils were the favored party under British colonial rule, but at the end of the colonial rule, they became an ethnic and political minority group. Examples of discriminatory behavior toward the Tamils included making Sinhala the only official language and giving preferences to Sinhalese in university admissions and government jobs.[4] This marginalization led to the founding of LTTE in 1976.[5]

Velupillai Prabhakaran, its charismatic leader, formed the LTTE as an underground guerrilla group. It has had the support of the Tamil masses. In 1983, its insurgency against the government began, and the women's fighting commando unit, Birds of Freedom, was formed.[6] Karunya M. Jayasena noted, "LTTE had one of the deadliest and well organized networks of female suicide bombers in the entire world until their local operations were defeated in 2009. [LTTE's] suicide unit, also known as the 'Black Panthers' had both men and women."[7] A central governing committee, headed by Prabhakaran, oversaw the two prongs of the organization: political and military. Specific subdivisions it controlled included an amphibious group, the Sea Tigers; an airborne group, the Air Tigers; an elite fighting wing, the Charles Anthony Regiment; a suicide commando unit, the Black Tigers; and a highly secretive intelligence group, an international secretariat. The LTTE is the only terrorist group that once had its own military, according to the South Asia Terrorism Portal and Institute for Conflict Management. On January 10, 2008, the Federal Bureau of Investigation reported that the LTTE was one of the most dangerous and deadly extremist outfits in the world.[8] Dearing noted that Robert I. Rothberg recognized the group as de facto state within a state.[9] Throughout the conflict, LTTE received external funding from Tamil expatriates in India and the West.[10]

THE CONFLICT

The resentment of the Sinhalese against the Tamils erupted in the 1980s when the Tamils were pressing for self-rule. During the civil war, the LTTE in 1987 began to engage in suicide warfare. The parties agreed to and then violated agreements to end the war. In 2009, the Tigers were defeated.

The 26-year civil war (1983–2009) is described as having four phases of armed conflict between the Sri Lankan Army (SLA) and the separatist Liberation Tigers of Tamil Eelam. These phases were called the First, Second, Third, and Forth Eelam Wars. The wars illustrated that suicide warfare was used alongside other tactics. The First Eelam War (1983–1987) started when a LTTE ambush killed 13 soldiers causing anti-Tamil riots that resulted in the deaths of several hundred Tamils.[11] But the first LTTE's suicide attack occurred in 1987 when a truck bomb that was detonated at an SLA post in Nelliyadi. The number of casualties has been reported as 20–100 killed and 12–27 wounded.[12] Table 8.1 is based on *CPost* data that contains the highest numbers. Therefore, in the first attack on 1 individual resulted in 100 deaths. After the first war, Indian intervention (1987–1990) resulted in no suicide attacks during that time (see Table 8.1). At the end of the first war, a cease-fire was put in place, the July 29, 1987 accord (the Indo-Lanka Accord).[13] There were no suicide attacks during the Indian intervention from 1987 to 1990.

The Second Eelam War (1990–1994) followed when intervening Indian troops left after a three-year period, and after getting mired in fighting in the north. Violence escalated between the SLA and separatists. On March 2, 1991, the LTTE carried out its first suicide operation in the capital of Colombo. The attack killed the Deputy Minister of Defense, Ranjan Wijeratna. On November 16, 1992, the Tigers launched the next high-profile target suicide attack on Sri Lanka Navy Commander Vice Admiral W.W.E.C. Fernando. He was killed after he visited India to establish naval cooperation that may have resulted in hindering the arrival of LTTE's supplies. In this attack, a Tiger wore a suicide jacket and rode a motorcycle alongside the commander's vehicle and leaped onto the vehicle, killing the commander, his bodyguard, and driver.[14]

On May 1, 1993, a suicide bomber assassinated President Ranasinghe Premadasa. Peace talks were in process. President Premadasa had demanded that Sri Lankan security forces reoccupy the Jaffna peninsula that the Tigers occupied. The LTTE opposed this position and therefore assassinated him.[15]

The Third Eelam War (1995–2001) began when rebels sank naval craft.[16] In December 2001, the Government of Sri Lanka (GSL) and LTTE declaration of unilateral cease-fires was issued and in February 2002, GSL and LTTE signed a cease-fire agreement sponsored by peace-process facilitator Norway. In February 2006, GSL and LTTE renewed their commitment to the agreement at talks in Geneva. The cease-fire remained in effect from 2002 to 2005.[17] No suicide attacks were carried out during this period (see Table 8.1).

The Fourth Eelam War (2006–2009) began with the Mavil Aru operation in July 2006, and concluded with the defeat of the Tigers in May 2009. The Mavil Aru operation involved fierce fighting near the disputed Mavil Aru sluice gates in the Kallar area of Trincomalee district. Forty LTTE cadres and seven SLA personnel were killed. SLA launched a military operation targeting LTTE positions that kept the sluice gate of the Mavil Aru anicut (irrigation channel) closed. Water could not flow into thousands of Sinhalese, Muslim, and Tamil villages. Security forces launched campaign Mission Watershed, which was supported by air cover.[18]

"With the fall of Mullaitivu, the Tigers lost their 'Kingdom,'" according to Ajit Kumar Singh. Earlier, on January 2, 2009, the SLA had conquered Kilinochchi town, in effect the capital of the likely Tamil *eelam* (homeland). Since July 18, 1996, LTTE had controlled Mullaitivu. When the LTTE had overrun the last army camp there, the SLA experienced a major catastrophe. Over 1,000 soldiers were killed and the Tigers gained a large supply of weapons that included long-range artillery and mortars.[19] The Fourth Eelam War ended in May 2009 with the defeat of the Tamils.

From 1987 through October 14, 2011, the LTTE was responsible for 102 attacks that resulted in 1,504 deaths and 3,585 wounded. These figures represent attacks in the LTTE campaign that took place within Sri Lanka except for one in India in 1991 (See Table 8.1).[20] The LTTE suicide campaign was the longest running suicide campaign as of 2010, according to Robert A. Pape and James K. Feldman.[21]

Table 8.1
Suicide Attacks and Casualties by Year in India and Sri Lanka, LTTE versus Sri Lanka Campaign, 1987–2011.

Year	Attacks	Killed	Wounded
1987	1	100	27
1988	0	0	0
1989	0	0	0
1990	2	9	0
1991	5	62	135
1992	1	4	0
1993	3	242	60

(*Continued*)

Table 8.1
(Continued)

Year	Attacks	Killed	Wounded
1994	4	85	2
1995	9	126	74
1996	11	218	1,463
1997	2	17	100
1998	7	116	345
1999	11	73	168
2000	15	123	304
2001	7	49	24
2002	0	0	0
2003	0	0	0
2004	0	0	0
2005	0	0	0
2006	7	172	229
2007	5	9	26
2008	11	82	428
2009	1	17	200
2010	0	0	0
2011	0	0	0
Total	102	1,504	3,585

Source: Adapted from Suicide Attack Search Database, *Chicago Project on Security and Terrorism (CPOST)*, October 14, 2011, http://cpost.uchicago.edu/search.php.

Suicide attackers not only used belt and car bombs, but also other weapons, and in some attacks, the weapon was not known. "Other" weapons were used in the most attacks 36 (35.3%) and produced 528 (34.7%) deaths. The weapon was unknown in 29 (28.4%) attacks, but unknown weapons produced the least number of people killed, 235 (15.4%). The car bomb was used in 12 (11.8%) attacks and caused 448 (29.4%) deaths and 1,892 wounded. The belt bomb was used in 26 (25.2%) attacks and caused 326 deaths (21.2%) and 581 wounded persons.[22] Security targets represented 72 (69.9%) of the attacks, killing by far the most, 976 (63.3%). Thirteen (12.6%) attacks were on civilians. These attacks killed 284 (18.4%) and wounded 2,249 (see Table 8.2).[23]

Table 8.2
Suicide Attacks and Casualties by Weapon and Target in India and Sri Lanka, LTTE versus Sri Lanka Campaign, 1987–2011.

	Attacks (Percent)	Killed (Percent)	Wounded (Percent)
Weapon			
Airplane	0 (0.0)	0 (0)	0 (0)
Belt bomb	26 (25.2)	326 (21.2)	581 (15.7)
Car bomb	12 (11.7)	448 (29.1)	1,892 (51.2)
Other	36 (35.0)	528 (34.4)	619 (16.8)
Unknown	29 (28.1)	235 (15.3)	603 (16.3)
Total	103 (100)	1537 (100)	3,695 (100)
Target Type			
Security	72 (69.9)	976 (62.8)	781 (21.2)
Political	18 (17.3)	295 (19.0)	654 (17.7)
Civilian	13 (12.6)	284 (18.2)	2,249 (61.0)
Other	0 (0)	0 (0)	0 (0)
Unknown	1 (1)	2 (0)	23 (0.1)
Total	104 (100)	1,557 (100)	3,707 (100)

Source: Adapted from Suicide Attack Search Database, *Chicago Project on Security and Terrorism (CPOST)*, October 14, 2011, http://cpost.uchicago.edu/search.php.

In the war, male attackers numbered 108 (52.2%) and they committed 55 attacks that produced 894 (57.2%) deaths and 2,070 (58.1%) wounded. Women attackers numbered 37 (17.9%) in 28 attacks that caused 303 (19.4%) killed and 403 (11.3%) wounded. The gender of 62 (30%) attackers was unknown. The number of attacks was 30 and resulted in 366 (23.4%) killed and 1,088 (30.6%) wounded. Most attackers practiced the Hindu religion, 172, but their occupation and education were unknown (see Table 8.3).

Table 8.3
Suicide Attackers, Attacks, and Casualties by Gender, Religion, Occupation, and Education by Groups in India and Sri Lanka, LTTE versus Sri Lanka Campaign, 1987–2011.

	Attackers (Percent)	Attacks (Percent)	Killed (Percent)	Wounded (Percent)
Gender				
Male	108 (52.2)	55 (48.7)	894 (57.2)	2,070 (58.1)
Female	37 (17.9)	28 (24.8)	303 (19.4)	403 (11.3)

(Continued)

Table 8.3
(Continued)

	Attackers (Percent)	Attacks (Percent)	Killed (Percent)	Wounded (Percent)
Unknown	62 (30)	30 (26.5)	366 (23.4)	1,088 (30.6)
Total	207 (100)	113 (100)	1,563 (100)	3,561 (100)
Religion				
Hindu	172 (83.1)	99 (91.7)	1,340 (85.7)	3,244 (91.1)
Unknown	35 (16.9)	9 (8.3)	223 (14.3)	317 (8.9)
Total	207 (100)	108 (100)	1,563 (100)	3,561 (100)
Occupation				
Unknown	207 (100)	102 (100)	1,563 (100)	3,561 (100)
Education				
Unknown	207 (100)	102 (100)	1,563 (100)	3,561 (100)

Source: Adapted from Suicide Attack Search Database, *Chicago Project on Security and Terrorism (CPOST)*, October 14, 2011, http://cpost.uchicago.edu/search.php.

CPOST Note: "Please note, the results include all attacks in which attackers of the selected gender were involved—attacks committed by multiple attackers of both genders (or 'unknown') will result in multiple genders being reported, not just those that have been selected."

The LTTE has conducted the longest run of suicide attacks of any group. The Tigers are known for attacking high-ranking officials. It is the only organization that succeeded in assassinating two heads of state: Indian Prime Minister Rajiv Gandhi, 1991 and Sri Lankan President Ranasinghe Premadasa, 1993. Two dozen high-ranking officials included members of parliament or the central committee and other government officials and candidates for public office. In addition, they invented the suicide belt and pioneered the use of more women in suicide attacks.[24]

PEACE EFFORTS

On February 21, 2002, the GSL and Tamil Tiger rebels agreed to a permanent cease-fire as part of a Norwegian initiative to end almost two decades of civil war. On November 21, 2006, the Tokyo Donors Conference Co-Chairs, United States, European Union, Japan, and Norway issued a joint statement that condemned the systematic cease-fire violations by both the GSL and LTTE. They urged both parties to immediately cease hostilities. The government abrogated the fragile cease-fire agreement in 2008.[25]

CULTURE

Structural considerations within society played a part in the formation of the Tamil Tigers, concluded Matthew P. Dearing. Those limitations included the encouragement of ethnic outbidding instituted Sinhalese and Buddhist elites keen on recreating a Sinhalese-only state; the May 1972 constitution changed Ceylon into Democratic Socialist Republic of Sri Lanka; the constitution protected the 1956 language policy; the 1976 Sixth Amendment to the constitution prohibited political parties and individuals from speaking for a Tamil separate state, thereby marginalizing the Tamil's from the democratic process; and the 1979 Prevention of Terrorism Act that condoned torture, seize, and imprison anyone without benefit of trial.[26]

THE MILITARY

Several factors must be in place for a successful suicide attack, such as surveillance of the target, research, and a support network (see also Chapter 2). India and Sri Lanka signed a peacekeeping agreement on July 29, 1987 resulting in Indian soldiers being assigned to Sri Lanka to maintain peace. On October 10, 1987, the LTTE declared war on the Indian government and the peacekeeping force. During the Indian Peace Keeping Force (IPKF) occupation (July 29, 1987–March 24, 1990), the LTTE had no way to keep a close watch or have safe houses where the force was deployed. "This is the main reason why there were no suicide operations during the deployment of the IPKF," according to Rohan Gunaratna.[27] On the other hand, windows of opportunity to infiltrate Colombo, the capital, occurred when there were peace talks between the LTTE and the GSL. The opportunity arose because levels of security dropped during the peace talks that made more difficult the monitoring of the formation of sleeper cells and the transport of weapons, Gunaratna explained.

The Tamil Tigers changed their strategy when it launched its first suicide attack on July 5, 1987. The SLA had arrested most of the LTTE leadership in 1981, and made significant military inroads, according to Jonathan Fine. Initially, the Tigers had provided their fighters with a poison capsule to avoid interrogation. From 1981 to 1987, they began to employ explosive-laden trucks, but the driver jumped out of the vehicle before the explosion. According to Jonathan Fine, this type of attack was imprecise; hence, beginning in 1987, they conducted suicide bomb attacks.[28]

Some of the reasons for LTTE's major attacks demonstrate that they coincided with political events. On May 21, 1991, a woman, Thenmuli Rajaratnam a.k.a. Dhanu, killed India's prime minister, Rajiv Gandhi, in Madras (Tamil Nadu), India. She detonated her explosive vest after bowing down at Gandhi's feet during an election rally. Table 8.1 represents attacks in Sri Lanka only, so this attack is not reflected. When controlling for all locations, CPost database reflected that the attack killed 14–15. Gandhi opposed LTTE.[29] On May 1, 1993, a LTTE suicide bomber assassinated President Ranasinghe Premadasa. At issue was that Premadasa had demanded that security forces of Sri Lanka reoccupy the Jaffna peninsula, which was occupied by the Tamil Tigers, stated Gunaratna. A male, Kulaweerasingham Veerakumer, killed from 24 to 30 and wounded from 0 to 60, according to *CPost*.[30] In 1995, the security forces launched another campaign to recover the peninsula, and the LTTE preempted that effort by destroying oil storage facilities in Colombo with suicide bombers. In 1996, the LTTE attacked a central bank. The protection fighters used to escort the suicide bombers were captured and revealed considerable information. This attack represented a degree of failure for the LTTE, according to Gunaratna.[31]

The United States labeled the LTTE a terrorist group under provisions of the Anti-Terrorism and Effective Death Penalty Act of 1996 and redesignated the group in October 2003.[32] The first designation took place a week before a revenge attack on the Colombo World Trade Center on October 15, 1997.[33] Operatives who did not perish in the attack blew themselves up. Azmat S. Hassan adds that the LTTE waged primarily a guerilla war, but they have also engaged government forces in frontal attacks even though the SLA outnumbered and outgunned them. The LTTE's most notable attack occurred in 1996 on an army base near Colombo that destroyed a garrison of 1,200 soldiers.[34] The media has also labeled LTTE terrorists and consequently, it makes it more difficult to have a potential role as a neutral mediator, according to Jayasena.[35]

THE INDIVIDUAL AS A WEAPON

The overriding reason of the Tamil Tigers is the spirit of nationalism. Because they seek a homeland, the LTTE seems more like insurgents than terrorists. The LTTE mirrors a civil war, and their decision to employ suicide attacks is strategic, according to Pape and Feldman.[36]

I believe women fight for the same reasons as do men, and in the case of the LTTE, they fought for a homeland. Both men and women have personal reasons for being willing to be suicide attackers. Some want a better society in which to live. For LTTE women, additional reasons existed in their patriarchal society. Jayasena noted Balasingham's premise that the LTTE recruited women with the ideological indoctrination that they would have an opportunity to create a new society that allowed women equal human rights, self-respect, and honor. Jayasena explained, "They were told that they will be liberated from the structures of oppression embedded in their society. Since many of these women were not satisfied with the social status quo, they easily persuaded to join the national conflict."[37] Danu, who killed Indian Prime Minister Rajiv Gandhi, had four brothers who had been killed in the conflict and she had also been gang-raped.[38]

Lisa Kruger found that, in early cases of suicide bombing, LTTE men and women were "motivated to participate in the group's terrorist activities for similar reasons. Similarities are rarely recognized since reporting tends to focus on rape and women's emancipation as the main motives."[39] Men and women share motivations of nationalism, revenge for suffering, oppression, poverty, and educational restrictions. But elements pertinent to women may also motivate them such as oppression of women and the desire to redeem oneself from incidents of sexual violence.

But what of the young people who leave home to join the LTTE? Hector N. Qirko found that Tiger recruits were less than 15 years of age when they left a home and community environment of opposition and criticism, especially females. Their training was demanding and explicitly organized around kinship roles. For example, respectful forms of address expected within families were used. Among cadres, older brother, older sister, or younger brother signified relationships. Young female members were addressed as mother. Velupillai Pirapaharan, their leader, was referred to as *Annan* (elder brother). Each member pledged daily support to Pirapaharan. Uniforms were worn in training, parading, and missions. In actual except suicide missions, uniforms were not worn. Members chosen for suicide cadres, the Black Tigers, went through additional intensive training in small, isolated groups. Recruits who wished to leave the organization were required to complete two or three years of punishment service. Group identification and bonding were key influences in recruitment. Qirko introduced the concept of induced altruism as a factor in recruiting. Suicide terror organizations were usually tightly structured around practices to maintain and reinforce commitment though the manipulation of kinship-recognition cues.[40]

Tracing commitment-reinforcing organizational practices that are instituted on the individual should be enlightening, concluded Qirko. He stated, "If the forces at work with respect to engendering commitment parallel those of religious institutions, it is when organizations grow from small groups in direct contact with charismatic leaders to larger ones where members are likely to be less related in terms of kinship and community that practices exploiting cognitive biases are developed."[41]

OUTCOMES

Between January and May 2009, 20,000 ethnic Tamils died at the hands of the Sri Lankan Army. In Britain, journalists and news presenters expressed outrage over the ethnic cleansing. Although they uttered such lines as "the massacre took place . . . ," they omitted three crucial words: with British weapons.[42]

So begins Tim Coles description of the "ethnic cleansing" of the Tamils. His research produced various reports such as human rights, the Red Cross, and Commission of the European Communities, which indicated crimes against humanity on the part of the GSL. The *Sunday Times* reported that the government cornered the Tamils in an area about the size of Hyde Park with tens of thousands of civilians. Although the Tigers ultimately accepted defeat in 2009, the war was so bloody that in desperation, they threatened mass suicide by cyanide, and threatened to activate their network of underground cells throughout the government controlled parts of the country if their leadership was killed.[43]

Sri Lanka troops surrounded Tiger rebels on this tiny piece of land in northeastern Sri Lanka when the Tigers conceded defeat. This event brought to an end what appeared at the time to be close one of Asia's longest civil wars. The armed struggle for a separate homeland for Sri Lanka's Tamil minority lasted 26 years. Selvarasa Pathmanathan posted on the Tiger website, *Tamilnet*, "This battle has reached its bitter end . . . to save the lives of our people is the need of the hour. Mindful of this, we have . . . announced to the world our position to silence our guns to save our people."[44]

The GSL forces declared victory over the LTTE in May 2009 and left approximately 300,000 displaced persons. As of May 2010, an estimated 68,000 remained in the displaced persons camps.[45] In 2011, a panel of experts advising Secretary General Ban Ki-moon on accountability issues in the final stages of the conflict found credible reports of war crimes committed by the government and Tamil rebels. The report accuses the government of large-scale shelling of no-fire zones such as hospitals, a U.N. hub, food distribution lines, and near Red Cross ships that came to pick up wounded civilians. It accused the Tamil Tigers of recruiting children, holding civilians as human shields, using them as forced labor, and exposing them to danger.[46]

The U.N. report also recommended that the secretary general conduct an international investigation into the allegations. But Ban Ki-moon's spokesperson has said that Ban would not investigate unless the GSL consented or a U.N. body such as the Security Council, the Human Rights Council, or the General Assembly asked him to do so.[47] Before this report was released, the GSL warned that the public release of the report on alleged war crimes committed as the civil war was ending could harm postwar ethnic reconciliation.[48] It is unlikely that the GSL will consent, reported Jim McDonald.

The number of casualties in Sri Lanka's civil war has been difficult to determine because many figures only reflect the last part of the war. The Council on Foreign Relations stated that about 70,000 have been killed in the nearly two decades of fighting.[49] The GSL reported the death toll of the final phase of the war in the northern part of the country at 9,000.[50]

The United States designated the LTTE as a terrorist group in November 2007. It froze the U.S.-held assets of the charitable organization, Tamils Rehabilitation Organization. In February 2009, the United States froze the assets of the Maryland-based Tamil Foundation, on suspicion that they were funneling money to the LTTE.[51] Mathew P. Dearing noted Claudia Brunner's statement that conflict that takes the form of suicide attacks occurs in very precise contexts of asymmetric power relations.[52] In Sri Lanka, the attacks occurred under a very organized militant organization that came because of limited protection provided to Tamils from the state. The West can often misinterpret relationships. The West can often misinterpret perceptions other societies have with Western-established institutions, wrote Dearing.

On August 18, 2011, the U.S. Department of State reported that overseas groups of the LTTE continued to procure weapons, while the LTTE diaspora remained persistent in supporting the organization financially. Although the LTTE suffered a military defeat, its international network of financial support continued. In 2012, the LTTE violence appears to be over, but with an "unfortunate ambivalence, on the part of both the country's majority Sinhala and minority Tamil leaderships," according to the South Asia Terrorism Portal and Institute for Conflict Management.[53]

CHAPTER 9

Chechen Separatists

In recent years, the Chechen separatists have used suicide warfare against Russia in an effort to gain independence as a republic. The separatists are called rebels because Chechnya is a republic within the Russian Federation. Geographically, the Russian Federation is the largest country in the world, even after the breakup of the Soviet Union in 1991. What the rebels want is a republic that is not a part of the federation. The Chechen's struggle is a classic case of small against huge.

HISTORICAL CONTEXT

The Chechnya republic is located in the southwestern part of the Russia Federation on the northern side of the Greater Caucasus range. Chechnya is bordered on the north by Russia, on the east and southeast by the Dagestan republic, on the southwest by the country of Georgia, and on the west by the Ingushetiya republic.[1] The historical basis for the current day struggle for an independent Chechnya lies in the 19th-century Chechen resistance to the Russian conquest of the Caucasus. Again in 1944, the Soviet Union's Premier Josef Stalin deported almost the whole Chechen population of about 400,000 people to Central Asia. Many perished there.[2]

THE CONFLICT

Chechnya declared independence from Russia in November 1991 when the Soviet Union collapsed. Fourteen regions became independent

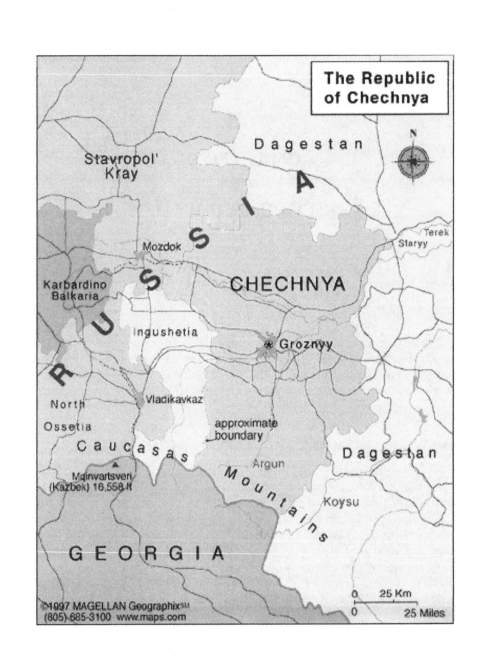

The Republic of Chechnya

Stavropol' Kray

Dagestan

N

Mozdok

Terek
Staryy

CHECHNYA

Karbardino
Balkaria

Ingushetia

✱ Groznyy

North

Vladikavkaz

Ossetia

approximate
boundary

Dagestan

Caucasas

Argun

Mqinvartsven
(Kazbek) 16,558 ft

Mountains

Koysu

GEORGIA

0   25 Km

0   25 Miles

©1997 MAGELLAN Geographix℠
(805) 685-3100 www.maps.com

nations, but not Chechnya. Chechen President Dzhokhar Dudayev declared Chechnya independent, and presided over the drawing of a secular constitution in 1992.

The First Chechen War (December 1994–August 1996)

Russian President Boris Yeltsin refused to recognize Chechnya's independence. Yeltsin sent troops into the country to restore Moscow's control in 1994.[3] Yeltsin's act caused the First Chechen War (December 1994–August 1996) that ended with the signing of the peace agreement, the Khasavyurt Accord. The agreement called for the withdrawal of Russian troops and three years of quasi-independence for Chechnya.[4] The Chechen separatists wanted independence, and they almost obtained it after 1996, according to *BBC*.[5] The accords stipulated that the two countries were to resolve Chechnya's final status by the end of 2001.

The Second Chechen War (August 26, 1999–April 16, 2009)

Aslan Maskhadov, who became president in January 1997, shifted from nationalism to radical Islam.[6] Peace negotiations delayed Chechnya's political status for five years. But Russian domination continued, and in 1999, the Second Chechen War began. The second war began after one event. In August 1999, the Chechen forces of Shamil Basaev and Amir al-Khattab, an Islamic extremist of Saudi origin, invaded Dagestan to create the Confederation of the Mountain Peoples of the Caucasus, according to Emma Gilligan. The ostensible purpose of Basaev and Khattab was to set up a Wahhabist, a fundamentalist Islamic state, in the Caucasus, wrote Mark Kramer.[7] The Russians held that their operation was to get rid of international terrorists. Gilligan stated that this Russian pretext led to years of continued state-sponsored violence.[8]

Russia recaptured the Chechen capital of Grozny in February 2000, taking back its control over Chechnya. After using conventional war strategy in the first war, the Chechen separatists' suicide campaign began in 2000 (see Table 9.1). Robert A. Pape and James K. Feldman suggest, the increased suicide attacks in the years of 2003 and 2009 can be attributed to the counterterrorism campaigns of the Russian forces and the Russian-backed Chechen President Ramzan Kadyrou.[9] Since the end of the second war, Chechen separatists activity has lessened, according to the Council on Foreign Relations. But in 2008, violence markedly increased in the North Caucasus. The council noted that a report by the Center for Strategic and International Studies found that "incidents of violence rose from 795 in 2008 to 1,100 in 2009, and suicide bombings quadrupled in 2009, the majority of which occurred in Chechnya."[10] In February 2003, the United States had designated the Chechnya-based groups as terror-ists: the Special Purpose Islamic Regiment (SPIR) led by Movsar Barayev, Chechen warlord and leader of armed Chechens, carried out hostage-taking operations; the Islamic International Peace Brigade (IIPB); and the Riyadus Salikhin Reconnaissance and Sabotage Battalion of Chechen Martyrs. Shamil Basayev, Chechen rebel leader with Aslan (Khalid) Ali-yevich Maskhadov, commander and third president, created the last two groups.

In 2006, human rights estimates were that 200,000 civilians had died and many had been wounded, crippled, widowed, and orphaned, accord-ing to Ekkehard Maass. Grozny was in ruins, and museums, libraries, three theatres, valuable art collections, the university, and the oil institute had disappeared. Refugees by their hundreds of thousands were suffering indescribable misery. Maass's categorization of Russian human rights' vi-olations is extensive and unpleasant. The list addresses general and indi-vidual violations in Chechnya. General violations include bombardment and shelling of civilian and refugee targets, deployment of internation-ally proscribed weapons including chemical weapons, creation of con-centration camps and torture centers, purges of farmsteads and villages, and targeted destruction of cultural monuments including mosques and churches.[11]

Individual violations of human rights that Maass included are arbitrary arrests and abductions; torture; beatings; electrical shocks; mutilation; burning with cigarettes and irons; tying up; sterilization of women by benzene exposure; rape of women, men, and children; killing; shooting; slow stabbing; beating; suffocation; throttling; ejection from helicopters; corpse mutilation; scalping; amputation; head boiling; hostage-taking; and trafficking with the living and the dead.

ORGANIZATION

Aslan Maskhadov became president in 1997. In 1999, Moscow branded him a terrorist. Chechens had launched a wave of bomb attacks and Russia accused Maskhadov as having lost control. Fierce fighting ensued and a pro-Moscow administration was set up. Maskhadov was killed on March 8, 2005. Maskhadov not only believed in an indepen-dent Chechnya, but also did more than any other negotiator to bring peace, reported *BBC*. Abdul-Khalim Saydullayev succeeded him, but he and Basayev were killed in 2006.[12]

At the time of these killings in 2006, the Chechen opposition faced the most critical situation since the beginning of the war, stated Raven Heal-ing. The Kremlin openly financed many Chechen military divisions loyal to Russia. Thousands of Russian soldiers were still in Chechnya. If a fam-ily member joined the resistance, a whole family or village was punished. People were frightened and did not support the rebels. In these crucial circumstances, Doku Umarov became the leader of the rebels. He gave the state a new name, Caucasus Emirate. In so doing, he replaced the plan of Chechen national independence because the mujahideen of the other republics were not eager to fight and die for Chechen independence. Under the banner of Islam rooted in a unitary Caucasian state, their loyalty was possible. The rebels did not accept Umarov's decision, but did not openly confront Umarov because they did not want Russian domination. In the summer of 2010, a split occurred within the rebels. The schism centered on a wider jihad rather than a narrower struggle for Chechen independence.[13]

The internal group dynamics of the fractured Chechen resistance movement and Russia's counterterrorist policies influenced the rebels to use suicide attacks, according to Jeff Collins. Groups were formed that identified the schism.[14]

Special Purpose Islamic Regiment (SPIR) and Islamic International Peacekeeping Brigade (IIPB)

The SPIR under the command of Arbi Barayev and the Islamic battalions led by the Ahkmatov brothers defined the split. At the beginning of the second war, conventional attacks were used, but overwhelming Russian attacks captured cities including Grozny as well as the countryside. At this time, the more radical group of the rebels began guerilla warfare. Some of the radicals believed terrorism was the best way to achieve their cause. Thus, suicide attacks grew out of the need to influence.[15] No suicide attacks were conducted during the first Russian–Chechen conflict (see Table 9.1).

Russian counterterrorist policies were very effective: For example, within the Chechen society, Russia manipulated the interclan rivalries and schisms and awarded support in exchange for their loyalty. Both groups became weakened so much so that the Chechens launched the three-day siege of the Dubrovka theater in Moscow on October 23, 2002. The rebels intended the theater to be a suicide mission that would raise funds from Middle East donors, to get news coverage, to undermine Russian society's sense of security, and to obtain a cease-fire, wrote Collins. The IIPB played a role in this seizure, according to Robert W. Kurz and Charles K. Bartles.[16]

Riyadus Saliheyn Martyrs' Brigade (also Transliterated Riyadus Salikhiin)

The Riyadus Saliheyn Martyrs' Brigade promotes radical Islamic doctrine (Wahhabism). According to Kurz and Bartles, the organization is believed to have strong ties to al Qaeda. The group employed the Black Widow suicide attackers, for example, in the August 2004 airline and subway bombings. The group's primary goal is an independent Chechnya rather than a religious objective. Because the *Riyadus* descended from the SPIR and the IIPB, it may be the result of the marriage of these two groups, wrote Kurz and Bartles. Two men and one woman launched their first attack employing a truck bomb on December 27, 2002, destroying the headquarters of the pro-Russian Chechen government, killing 72, and wounding 200.[17] Also in 2002, the group was responsible for Moscow's Dubrovka hostage crisis that also involved suicide attackers.[18]

Dzhennet and Ingush Jama'at Shariat

Robert W. Kurz and Charles K. Bartles noted two other groups within the Chechen organizational structure. The Dagestani insurgency in the North Caucasus formed in 2002 under the name Dzhennet (paradise). Their objectives are to rid the region of Russia, destroy all opponents of Sharia, and create an independent Dagestan under Islamic law. The Ingush Jama'at Shariat, a Muslim separatist group consisting of militants from Ingushetia and possibly Chechnya, has the goal of creating an Islamic state independent from Russia. The group is among the most militant and their language is extreme, violent, and of strict religious nature.[19]

The Chechen separatists did not succeed in creating new governmental or societal structures, nor did they create a modern political military organization to carry out their struggle for independence. These organizations had only a slight role impact and were not a product of the struggle. Individuals rather than organizations played leading roles. The Chechen revolt must be considered a rebellion rather than a revolution, concluded James DeFronzo.[20]

Black Widows

Shamil Basayev created the Black Widows, the women's arm of the Chechen separatists. Their name reflects that they have usually lost their husbands, brothers, or close relatives in the wars. The year 2004 was a bloody year. Black widows blew up two passenger planes that took off from the Moscow airport, bombed the Moscow metro twice, and took part in the siege of Beslan's School Number One. Hundreds of innocent civilians, including children, lost their lives. This strike was sophisticated, and women who openly disagreed with the leader concerning the use of children as hostages were killed when he detonated their bombs by remote control. In 2002, 18 women dressed in black wore black explosive belts and worked with 32 men to seize the Dubrovka House of Culture in Moscow. This attack marked the first time in the history of female suicide warfare that such a team was established. It signaled a shift from and individual action to a group structure. The Black Widows conducted a Moscow metro bombing in 2010.[21]

THE MILITARY

From 2000 to October 14, 2011, the *Chicago Project on Security and Terrorism (CPost)* reported that the Chechen separatists (including the Riyadus Saliheyn Martyrs' Brigade, also transliterated Riyad us-Saliheyn) conducted 35 attacks, killing 590 and wounding 1,432. Their greatest number of attacks (7) occurred in 2003, but more people died (141) in 2004 (see Table 9.1). Although no attacks are listed for January 1– October 14, 2011, the *New York Times* reported that in August 2011, two suicide bombers killed seven police officers and an emergency services employee. The attacks occurred in a heavily populated area of Grozny near a local parliament building.[22] On January 24, 2011, an explosion occurred at the international arrivals hall at Moscow's Domodedovo Airport, killing about 31 people and wounding approximately 170.[23] The conflict continues.

Table 9.1
Suicide Attacks and Casualties by Year in Russia, Chechen Separatists* versus Russia, 2000–2011.

Year	Attacks	Killed	Wounded
2000	5	123	255
2001	2	13	0
2002	2	76	200
2003	7	132	400
2004	4	141	171
2005	0	0	0
2006	0	0	0
2007	0	0	0
2008	1	1	11
2009	7	40	186
2010	6	58	187
2011	1	6	22
Total	35	590	1,432

* Includes the group, Riyadus Salikhiin Martyrs' Brigade, also transliterated Riyad us-Saliheyn.

Sources: Adapted from Suicide Attack Search Database, *Chicago Project on Security and Terrorism (CPOST)*, October 14, 2011, http://cpost.uchicago.edu/search.php; for the August 30, 2011 attack in Grozny, see "Triple Suicide Bombing Kills Police in Chechnya on Eid," *BBC News*, August 31, 2011, http://www.bbc.co.uk/news/world-europe-14726122.

The Chechen wars were part of a calculated state strategy primarily motivated by racial prejudice that indicates the wars were more than a byproduct of civil war, according to Gilligan.[24] In 2006, Maass wrote,

Terrorist attacks which harm civilians have always been condemned by the Chechen government. They discredit the struggle for independence and endorse the Russian propaganda which sells the Russian war on Chechnya to the rest of the world as a war on international terrorism.
The only effective way to end this kind of terrorism is to end the war.[25]

During the second war, Chechen guerrillas numbered about 1,600–1,800 compared to Russian troops and police of 90,000. Yet, the Chechens outmaneuvered their opposition by turning tactical advances into strategic gains. They were able to cause enough damage to "create the appearance of an endless, unwinnable war," according to Kramer.[26] The Chechens who had employed only conventional methods during the first war, engaged in suicide warfare in the second war (See Table 9.1).

The car bomb was the most used weapon. It was used in 15 (42.9%) attacks and killed 301 (50.5%). The second most used weapon was the belt bomb, 12 (34.3%). Yet, of these weapons, the least number of people killed was by airplane, 90 (15.1%; see Table 9.2).[27]

Security targets were involved in 22 (64.7%) of the attacks and killed the most, 262 (44.9%). Attacks on civilians were 7 (20.6%). These attacks killed 210 (36.0%) and wounded 365 (25.8%).[28]

Table 9.2
Suicide Attacks and Casualties by Weapon and Target in Russia, Chechen Separatists* versus Russia Campaign, 2000–2011.

	Attacks (Percent)	Killed (Percent)	Wounded (Percent)
Weapon			
Airplane	1 (2.9)	90 (15.1)	0 (0)
Belt bomb	12 (34.3)	179 (30.0)	585 (40.4)
Car bomb	15 (42.9)	301 (50.5)	833 (57.6)
Other	4 (11.4)	13 (2.2)	4 (0)
Unknown	3 (8.6)	13 (2.2)	25 (1.7)
Total	35 (100)	596 (100)	1,447 (100)
Target Type			
Security	22 (64.7)	262 (44.9)	651 (46.2)
Political	5 (14.7)	112 (19.2)	394 (28.0)
Civilian	7 (20.6)	210 (36.0)	365 (25.8)

(Continued)

Table 9.2
(*Continued*)

	Attacks (Percent)	Killed (Percent)	Wounded (Percent)
Other	0 (0)	0 (0)	0 (0)
Unknown	0 (0)	0 (0)	0 (0)
Total	34 (100)	584 (100)	1,410 (100)

* Includes the group, Riyadus Salikhiin Martyrs' Brigade, also transliterated Riyad us-Saliheyn.

Source: Adapted from Suicide Attack Search Database, *Chicago Project on Security and Terrorism (CPOST)*, October 14, 2011, http://cpost.uchicago.edu/search.php.

Small Chechen detachments employed hit and run attacks after lying in wait for Russian troop convoys. The ambushes frequently began with the detonation of roadside bombs followed by heavy gunfire when all types of weapons were used. The intent of the ambush attacks was to produce constant, high-level psychological stress and to weaken morale. The Chechens were very successful in launching ambush attacks. Other tactical successes are credited to the Chechens. During the mine war, they used improvised explosive devices (IEDs), and evaded Russian defenses by using mine-sniffing dogs. The Chechens became quite sophisticated in using explosives. They were skilled in concealing and detonating them by means of a radio signal. The Chechens experienced success in shooting down Russian aircraft and helicopters.[29]

Early in the second war, the Chechen rebels carried out car and truck suicide bombing attacks against Russian troops and facilities. At first, the attacks were usually against small groups such as Russian soldiers at a checkpoint. They continued with dozens of smaller attacks until the fall of 2004 when they shifted their target to military facilities. In addition to military targets, the rebels targeted the pro-Russian government in Chechnya, and increasingly spread to other parts of the North Caucasus. A planted IED enabled them to assassinate President Ahmad-Haji Kadyrov on May 9, 2004. These attacks against the pro-Russian government from August to September 2004 were intended to deter other Chechens from cooperating with Moscow and to prevent Putin's efforts at "Chechenization," the devolution of power to local authorities, according to Kramer.[30]

As the Chechen rebels took the war to Russia, they escalated to taking hostages. On October 23, 2002, they held hostage the Dubrovka Theater, and in September 2004, the Beslan school in North Ossetia. That Chechen *shahidin* were still present in Moscow came as a psychological blow to a city that was already on edge, according to Kramer. Logistics may have prevented the Chechens from taking their war too far away from Chechnya. They struck near targets because of the close associations to their own conflict in Chechnya, noted Kurz and Bartles.[31]

Although the attacks on the Beslan school and Dubrovka Theater were primarily hostage taking operations, some believe the Beslan assault (September 1–3, 2004) was planned as a suicide bombing attack. Evidence indicated that some suicide bombing occurred. In the Beslan attack, improvised explosives were positioned throughout the school, according to the U.S. Army.[32] In addition, authorities found a shredded black belt and bloodied camouflage utility vest in the hall next to cafeteria where a female suicide bomber detonated herself. Female suicide bombers who openly disagreed with the colonel, the leader whose name was Ruslan Tagirovich Khuchbarov, about the children hostages were killed when he detonated their bombs by remote control.[33] According to the U.S. Army, no professional negotiators were on hand when the rebels handed Ruslan Aushev a handwritten note dated August 30, 2004. Allegedly, the note was from Shamil Baseyev. Demands remained focused on the removal of Russian forces from Chechnya.[34] The date of the demands, August 30, indicates that if a reasonable response had been professionally negotiated, the Beslan attack on September 1, 2004, might not have occurred (see Appendix D).

In the Moscow House of Dubrovka hostage-taking attack (October 23–26, 2002), suicide bombing appeared to be the last resort, but was an option not taken. When the 41 armed Chechen rebels took control of Moscow's Dubrovka Theater, Chechen warlord Mosvar Barayev announced to an audience of about 800 that Russian forces must immediately leave Chechnya. He told the crowd that the rebels did not plan to return home because "theirs was a suicide mission."[35] Interestingly, a woman survivor reported to Radio Free Europe/Radio Liberty's Tatar-Bashkir service: "Everybody saw the gas and everybody realized what was happening. [The hostage takers] had enough time to blow up everything, but they purposely didn't do it. It is very strange. I do not know why [they didn't do it]."[36] And finally, when the Russian forces arrived, the male rebels left the theater to deal with them, but the women were left behind to detonate their bombs that they had no authority to do so on their own.[37]

Before September 2004, rebel attacks had increased throughout the region of North Ossetia and neighboring Ingushetia against the Russian government. These operations demonstrated a growing boldness in Chechen operations. "However, a significant spike in organization and planning occurred for the June 2004 attack on the Ingushetia capitol of Nazran and several towns and villages along a main highway in the republic," the U.S. Army reported.[38] These multiple raids demonstrated the rebels' ability to infiltrate and transit Ingushetia and conduct attacks. Border control seemed ineffective.

After a long hiatus (see Table 9.1), the separatists in 2009 resumed attacks far from Moscow in the mostly Muslim North Caucasus region that includes Chechnya, Ingushetia, and Dagestan. Andrew Osborn stated that their goal was to create an Islamist caliphate along Russia's southern spur. In addition, Russia had been experiencing more successes against them and so the separatists were motivated to resort to their most deadly and desperate tactic, suicide attacks. In March 2010, after prominent Islamist rebel fighters had been killed, analysts believe the Black Widows may have been sent into battle in revenge. Human rights groups add the reason of the Russian ill-treatment of Chechen women.[39] Attacks in 2010 and 2011 had high-value targets: the Moscow subway, parliament in Gronzy, and a densely populated area near the parliament. These targets posed a direct challenge to Chechnya's president, and indicated that the insurgency campaigns were designed to discredit him.[40]

THE INDIVIDUAL AS A WEAPON

Twenty-six (51.0%) male attackers in 22 (56.4%) attacks resulted in 259 (45.4%) deaths and 808 (69.0%) wounded. Females represented 18 (35.3%) attackers and unknown, 7 (13.7%). Women attackers conducted 14 attacks that killed 260 (45.6%) and wounded 428 (31.8%). The religion of most attackers was unknown, 36 (70.6%), as were the occupation, 45 (88.2%), and education, 48 (94.0%; see Table 9.3).[41] Although more males conducted more attacks than females, female attackers conducted more than one-third and the number killed by the attacks were the same as the male attacks. It is understandable that the religion, occupation, and education of the attackers were unknown because the process of recruitment did not focus on making public this information, and the Russian government did not recognize attackers.

Table 9.3
Suicide Attackers, Attacks, and Casualties by Gender, Religion, Occupation, and Education by Groups, Chechen Separatists* versus Russia Campaign, 2000–2011.

	Attackers (Percent)	Attacks (Percent)	Killed (Percent)	Wounded (Percent)
Gender				
Male	26 (51.0)	22 (56.4)	259 (45.4)	808 (60.0)
Female	18 (35.3)	14 (35.9)	260 (45.6)	428 (31.8)
Unknown	7 (13.7)	3 (7.7)	51 (8.9)	110 (8.2)
Total	**51 (100)**	**39 (100)**	**570 (100)**	**1,346 (100)**
Religion				
Muslim (NA)	11 (21.6)	8 (22.8)	100 (17.5)	329 (24.4)
Muslim (Other)	4 (7.8)	3 (8.6)	45 (7.9)	181 (13.4)
Unknown	36 (70.6)	24 (68.6)	425 (74.6)	836 (62.2)
Total	**51 (100)**	**35 (100)**	**570 (100)**	**1,346 (100)**

(Continued)

Table 9.3
(Continued)

	Attackers (Percent)	Attacks (Percent)	Killed (Percent)	Wounded (Percent)
Occupation				
Professional	3 (5.8)	3 (8.3)	53 (9.3)	235 (17.5)
Skilled	1 (2.0)	1 (2.8)	6 (1.0)	6 (0.4)
Unknown	45 (88.2)	31 (86.1)	422 (73.9)	1,105 (82.1)
Unskilled	2 (4.0)	1 (2.8)	90 (15.8)	0 (0)
Total	51 (100)	36 (100)	571 (100)	1,346 (100)
Education				
None	1 (2.0)	1 (2.8)	6 (1.1)	20 (1.4)
Postsecondary	2 (4.0)	2 (5.6)	44 (7.7)	117 (08.6)
Unknown	48 (94.0)	33 (91.6)	520 (91.2)	1209 (90.0)
Total	51 (100)	36 (100)	570 (100)	1,346 (100)

* Includes the group, Riyadus Salikhiin Martyrs' Brigade, also transliterated Riyad us-Saliheyn.

Source: Adapted from Suicide Attack Search Database, *Chicago Project on Security and Terrorism (CPOST)*, October 14, 2011, http://cpost.uchicago.edu/search.php.

CPOST Note: "Please note, the results include all attacks in which attackers of the selected gender were involved—attacks committed by multiple attackers of both genders (or 'unknown') will result in multiple genders being reported, not just those that have been selected."

Motivation for Becoming a Suicide Bomber

The assertion is incorrect that women were likely to be radicalized Muslim women in the North Caucasus, and were part of the Shahidka movement, the Islamist Chechen female suicide bombers, according to Kristal L. Alfonso. This assertion ignores the primary motivation of men and women, the cultural importance of personal honor, and the desire for retribution for the sake of honor against the Russian occupiers. Men and women were fighting for their people and culture. The wives of the martyred mujahideen find their homes and honor threatened. They refuse to accept the humiliation and occupation. The erroneous reports "highlight the infatuation with terrorists' religious views [and make] no mention of other underlying causes," according to Alfonso.[42]

The cultural norm of taking revenge upon the offender is strengthened if the attacker has had overpowering personal trauma, Kurz and Bartles stated. The taking revenge norm is often accompanied with an ideology. Islamic radicalism and/or Wahabbism support killing innocent people to satisfy revenge. Kurz and Bartles believed that separatism was the primary motivation for the Chechens, and that Wahabbism provided mental and spiritual support for committing the act of bombing.[43]

The U.S. Army's assessment of the Beslan attack focuses on two cultural traditions, *adat* and *teip*, to understand, in part, the regional terrorist threat behind the Beslan attack. "*Adat* is a traditional concept of retribution or revenge. *Teip* is the tradition of clan or tribe and the allegiance required to an extended family and its ancestral lands. Such concepts compel groups with a sense of separatism or independence from external influences, and expect guidance from group elders, as well as protection of their culture by their young men."[44] The concepts of *adat* and *teip* demonstrate the individual does not operate in a vacuum, but has a direct relationship to other groups, familial, community, and military. Whether it is religion, revenge, or separatism motivation, no one profile fits the terrorists at Beslan, according to the *Handbook*. Some rebels were expecting to survive and were not on a suicidal mission. Female terrorists wore suicide belt-vests.

Pape and Feldman found that of 42 foreigners, 38 were from the Caucasus. These results indicate that the resistance was regional rather than being a global jihad waged to create an Islamic fundamentalist state. Almost suicide attackers are ethnically Chechen and overwhelmingly from the Caucasus region, Pape and Feldman concluded.[45]

Jim Nichol reports that increasing violence and acquiring more recruits have resulted from the increasing extent of public dissatisfaction with zachistki, a special operation without sanction, such as soldiers searching houses and detaining inhabitants; profound economic and social distress; and interethnic and religious tensions.[46] The Chechen society does not approve of suicide bombing, so unlike those societies—the Palestinian for example, who reward bombers and their families—there is no motivation to be a suicide attacker to reap societal rewards, as is the case for the Palestinian bomber.[47]

OUTCOMES

By 2011, President Ramzan A. Kadyrov, who was appointed by Vladimir Putin in 2007, succeeded in suppressing the insurgency, but only at the expense of widespread human rights violations, according to the *New York Times*. Kadyrov had mandated Islamic standards, including a ban on alcohol and gambling and pressure on women to assume Islamic dress. Moscow spent billions of rubles on a postwar Chechnya, resulting in the emergence of a bright new Grozny. The violence shifted to Dagestan, where violence still occurs at a reduced rate. In the first 9 months of 2011, 315 people were killed and 224 wounded. In Chechnya, 81 were killed and 103 wounded.[48]

Chechen officials justify the mandated Islamic dress code on traditional grounds. Human Rights Watch has spoken out against the dress code stating that it is contrary to Russian law, discriminatory, and leads to abuses. Human Rights Watch does not take a position on Sharia-inspired norms or cultural dress practices, but opposes all laws or policies that encroach on basic rights, including government-mandated public dress codes.[49]

The U.S. National Counterterrorism Center reported that, in May 2011, the U.S. State Department designated Imarat Kavkaz (or Caucasus Emirate, IK) as a specially designated terrorist group. In 2007, Chechen extremist Doku Umarov founded the Imarat Kavkaz, an Islamist militant organization based in Russia's North Caucasus. He remains at large. The organization's goal is the liberation of what it believes to be Muslim lands from Moscow. It regularly conducts attacks against Russian security forces in the North Caucasus. In 2010–2011, it carried out high-profile suicide bombings against civilian targets in Moscow. In addition to the Imarat Kavkaz, two extremist groups based in Pakistan's federally administered tribal areas are dedicated to the overthrow of the government in Uzbekistan: the Islamic Movement of Uzbekistan (IMU) and its splintered group, the Islamic Jihad Union. In 2000, the state department designated the IMU as a terrorist organization.[50]

CONCLUSION

The Chechen separatists continue their struggle to be independent from Russia and continue to conduct suicide attacks as part of that struggle. The likelihood of their prevailing in their quest remains small, but, as long as they have weapons, including individuals who are willing to be weapons, the struggle will go on.

CHAPTER 10

Al Qaeda

September 11, 2001 and May 2, 2011 are two dates most closely associated with Osama bin Laden and al Qaeda. September 11, 2001 was a tragic day for the United States and the world. It was the day of celebration and victory for Osama bin Laden and al Qaeda. The suicide attacks that destroyed the twin towers of the World Trade Center and killed 3,000 and damaged severely the Pentagon succeeded beyond bin Laden's expectations. They triggered a massive response from nations around the world to combat al Qaeda and its leader. Nearly a decade later, on May 2, 2011, Osama bin Laden was killed in a Navy SEAL attack on his home in Abbottabad, Pakistan. His death marked the intensification of the efforts to destroy al Qaeda and its ability to affect the world.

THE FOUNDING AND ORGANIZATION OF AL QAEDA

Osama bin Laden founded al Qaeda in1988, and in Arabic, the name means "the base." Although it was an outgrowth of the Services Office, a clearinghouse for the international Muslim brigade opposed to the 1979 Soviet invasion of Afghanistan, its goal is to rid Muslim countries of influence of the West and replace their governments with fundamentalist Islamic regimes.[1] The al Qaeda organization is a network of small independent groups that supports the ideology. It can form locally and operate with little or no reference to the core leadership. Abdel Bari Atwan wrote that in the horizontal expansion, al Qaeda became stronger while the Internet made its ideology and strategy easily available to any of its branches or groups any place or any time with no need for license of approval.[2]

Al Qaeda's overall strategic objective is to establish a worldwide Islamic caliphate where Shar'ia or Islamic law is the sole law (see Chapter 4). The organization has a global reach and appeal, and has inspired the formation and function of other extremist groups.[3] Yet, at the time of Osama bin Laden's death in May 2011, al Qaeda had not pulled off an attack in the United States in 10 years, and his death brought only minor protests in the Muslim world, observed Peter Bergen. Bin Laden died knowing his ideas and organization had largely faded, and that he had become irrelevant.[4] Brian Michael Jenkins and John Paul Godges reached a somewhat different conclusion: "While the killing of bin Laden led to a brief display of national euphoria, few analysts—and none of the authors in this volume—believe that his death spells the end of al Qaeda or its terrorist campaign. His demise is a semicolon in the ongoing contest, not a period."[5] Max L. Gross, a former defense intelligence analyst, spoke to the "semicolon," when he stated, "Al Qaeda is significantly degraded. That's at the core of the uprisings that have been taking place in a lot of Muslim countries, which have sort of sidelined al Qaeda. A lot of the membership that has traditionally been associated with al Qaeda has moved on. They are more interested in the revolutionary changes that are taking place in Tunisia, Egypt, Bahrain, Jordan, Yemen, Libya, and Syria."[6] Reportedly, the unrest known as the Arab Spring occurred in these countries without being led by any terror group,[7] but Gross's review of bin Laden's history indicates al Qaeda's influence was already in these countries. In an interview, Gross said,

On October 7, 2001, bin Laden gave a message where he called upon Muslims for an uprising against invaders, the Americans, who were attacking Afghanistan, and that Muslims had a duty to respond to it.[8] Then in April of the following year, he gave another speech where he expressed disillusionment that they had not done that. He was still calling for action, but it was a speech that expressed disappointment that the Americans had attacked and were occupying Afghanistan, and no one was doing anything about it. My analysis is that he himself favored attacking the far enemy, attacking the snake at its head, the United States. But the real aim of al Qaeda was to achieve regime change in Muslim countries and to get rid of the authoritarian, corrupt, and, as he called them, Godless regimes. Of course, the other half was the formation of Islamic governments. Bin Laden's ultimate message was embodied in these revolutions. He was calling for events like them. Of course, he wanted the aim to be an Islamic state. He would favor the Muslim Brotherhood coming to power in Egypt, but it would be a militant Muslim Brotherhood. One that would make certain that no Americans, no Brits, no foreigners had any role to play in Egypt.[9]

CULTURE

Suicide warfare occurs within the context of a society, whether that society is one country such as Chechnya, a geographical area such as the Southeast Asian group Jemaah Islamiyah, or an across the globe group such as al Qaeda. In the case of al Qaeda, religion plays an important role. One of the multiple causes of an individual becoming a bomber is the interrelationship of society and religion. "The role of religion symbolically embodies society itself. Religion's power is through representations. God, for example, is societally transfigured and symbolically expressed.[10] Society is the source of the sacred and it is society that defines what is sacred and what profane."[11] In 2011, al Qaeda in the Arabian Peninsula (AQAP) in Yemen changed its name to Ansar al-Sharia to refocus on its religious legitimacy.[12]

While some authors focus on al Qaeda as Islamic terrorism with the emphasis on the religious dimension, Jeroen Gunning and Richard Jackson caution against labeling groups that have both religious and secular characteristics. Al Qaeda is "often viewed as the quintessential 'religious terrorist' group,"[13] but it also displays secular characteristics ranging from its strategic aims that include overthrowing regimes, ending occupation, freeing Palestine, and the caliphate goal to its targets such as embassies, warships, the Pentagon, transport infrastructure, and its secular professional personnel, to its Pan-Islamic rhetoric.

Brian M. Drinkwine wrote that al Qaeda's tactic of suicide bombers or martyrdom is fundamental in their strategy. They contend the Koran justifies the symbolism of a bomber as a martyr in the context of a religious jihad or holy war. Martyrs receive the rewards of heaven. Al Qaeda exploits the religious, social, cultural, and political symbols of martyrdom to appeal to the wider Muslim audience beyond the core loyalists.[14] This strategic cool and rational thinking aims to recruit individuals to be bombers.

THE MILITARY

Al Qaeda has groups who believe in the near or far enemy. Murad Ismayilov noted that Faisal Devji believed the main cause of jihad was a deterritorialized anti-imperialist effort to realize a caliphate. Struggles in specific states were only important so long as they upheld the metaphysical goals of Islam as global entity.[15] Ismayilov stated that the rationality of terrorist violence is supported by the view that al Qaeda's backing of suicide terrorism led the way in a new form of networked militancy, and represented one of the strategies of the fourth generation warfare. Closely related to my own philosophy is the strategic logic within Thomas Hammes's idea is that it "uses all available networks—political, economic, social, and military—to convince the enemy's political decision makers that their strategic goals are either unachievable or too costly for the perceived benefit."[16] According to Ismayilov, Charles Tilly and the U.S. State Department hold similar views.[17]

The al Qaeda manual details the mission and structure of its military component. The military must have a commander, advisory council, soldiers, and a clearly defined strategy. The military organization requirements include forged documents and counterfeit currency, apartments and hiding places, communication means, transportation means, information, arms and ammunition, and transport. The primary military mission is to overthrow godless regimes and replace them with Islamic regimes. Other missions include the following:

1. Gathering information about the enemy, the land, the installations, and the neighbors
2. Kidnapping enemy personnel, documents, secrets, and arms
3. Assassinating enemy personnel as well as foreign tourists
4. Freeing the brothers who are captured by the enemy
5. Spreading rumors and writing statements that instigate people against the enemy
6. Blasting and destroying the places of amusement, immorality, and sin; not a vital target
7. Blasting and destroying the embassies and attacking vital economic centers
8. Blasting and destroying bridges leading into and out of the cities[18]

Al Qaeda military attacks function to exploit "enemy vulnerabilities, inspire others, awaken the masses, and attract recruits. Al Qaeda's strategy is not based upon military superiority. Rather, al Qaeda's spiritual superiority will ultimately triumph over its enemy's technological superiority. . . . Strategy does not drive operations—operations are the strategy. In order to scatter and exhaust its enemies, al Qaeda must launch attacks on all fronts. It is a global war. The battlefield is everywhere. There are no front lines, no home fronts, no distinction between combatants and non-combatants," stated Jenkins.[19] Since it has become more difficult to get followers to training sites in Pakistan and Afghanistan, al Qaeda places more emphasis on do-it-yourself attacks, encouraging local would-be warriors to do whatever they can, wherever they are, Jenkins concluded.

Drinkwine believed that the organization benefits because a suicide attacker is the greatest smart bomb that is inexpensive and efficient. These attacks also enhance the organizational and the individual's image. Bombers are nearly impossible to stop or defend against, and an attack almost always reaches a larger audience and results in greater effects.[20]

Insights from the Abbottabad Letters

Letter, May 2010—The last document in Don Rassler et al.'s collection, *Letters from Abbottabad,* is a May 2010 lengthy letter to Shaykh Mahmud (Atiyaa) from bin Laden. Written after the death of Sheikh Sa'id (Mustafa Abu'l-Yazid), bin Laden designated Atiyaa as Sa'id's successor. In this letter, we not only see how the al Qaeda military operates, but also the relationship of the military to the societies in which the operations are carried out. Bin Laden is concerned with mistakes that the regional jihadi groups have made that caused unnecessary deaths of Muslim civilians. To address these mistakes, bin Laden writes, "We are now in a new phase of assessing Jihad activities and developing them beyond what they were in the past in two areas, military activity and media releases" (See Appendix F).[21]

As bin Laden assessed the military operations, he raised the issue of the "barricade argument," that is, whether it is acceptable to kill Muslims who are used as human shields by the enemy. This tactic had resulted in the killing of Muslims. No Muslims should fall victim except when it is absolutely essential, wrote bin Laden. Killing Muslims is the first mistake bin Laden outlined. Other mistakes included carrying out several attacks without exercising caution. These attacks had an effect on the sympathy of the nation's crowds toward the mujahideen. In essence, he wrote, "It would lead us to winning several battles while losing the war at the end." The two main reasons to avoid implementing attacks in Islamic countries were first, it would increase the number of victims among the Muslims, and second, the attacks could cause a person loss or damage to the "brothers in the region" and therefore to the jihad.[22]

Bin Laden sought advice on the jihad's capability when he asked whether attacks should be carried out inside America and in open fronts, for example targeting American interests in non-Islamic countries such as South Korea. This approach would avoid carrying out attacks in Islamic countries except in cases where countries had been invaded and directly occupied. Bin Laden outlined the disadvantages of an attack in Islamic countries other than loss of life. He considered it a waste of time to involve themselves in a situation where removal of the ruler where Americans were not reluctant to accuse an Islamic country of failing, because the regime would have an enormous reaction toward the mujahideen that would lead to defending themselves and avenging the regime. Bin Laden reasoned, "The brothers and the regime would then engage in a war which we did not begin against it, because the power of the brothers is not ready for it, as such it would be one result."[23] The brothers should respond to a direct attack upon them thereby gaining the people's hatred toward the rulers who, for example, did not defend, and actually fought, in Palestine, Iraq, and Afghanistan. In the May 2010 letter, bin Laden wrote that because of impact, every effort should be spent on attacks in America rather than outside of it.

Letter April 26, 2011—One week before his death, bin Laden wrote to Shaykh Mahmud (Atiyya) outlining two strategies in response to Arab Spring. The initial strategy was "inciting the people who have not revolted yet, and encouraging them to get against the rulers."[24] The second strategy addresses the continuation of the obligation of jihad as

a duty to establish the rule of Allah (Shari'a) in it, and it is the path toward conducting the larger duty, which is liberating the one-and-half billion-person nation and regain its holies. So while we are conducting jihad in Afghanistan and bleeding down the head of the international apostasy, until it reaches such weakness that the Muslim people have regained some self confidence and daring, and removed some of the oppressive pressure that was exhausting and failing anyone who thought of crossing Americas agents, the pressure of the supreme power that threatened to keep whom it desires and remove whom it desires, and with the gradual deterioration of that pressure, the comprehensive revolutions launched at the hands of the people whose extreme majority are Islam loving.[25]

THE INDIVIDUAL AS A WEAPON

Individual Motivation for Becoming a Suicide Attacker

Much is expected of the individual in al Qaeda's military. The manual lists 14 qualifications. Among them are a member must be Muslim, commit to the organization's ideology, and have a certain level of maturity not usually found in a minor. Most important is "Sacrifice: He has to be willing to do the work and undergo martyrdom for the purpose of achieving the goal and establishing the religion of majestic Allah on earth."[26]

In 2006, I wrote, "Bombers do not perform as individuals but as parts of organizations. These organizations and their roles in the bombing must be understood. Rarely do suicide attackers work on their own. Some experts believe that instead of thinking of suicide bombers as driven to kill themselves and others out of a spontaneous surge of emotion, we should view them as a guided missile, carefully prepared and launched by some larger, organized group."[27] Religious reasons and honor often motivate would-be bombers.

The attack on the London subway on July 7, 2005 killed 56 people, including 4 suicide bombers. Mark Kukis reported the itineraries of two of the bombers. One had attended a Pakistani madrassa, an Islamic religious school. The other had attended an orientation session at a fundamentalist madrassa as well as at militant training camps operated by the Pakistani army. One training camp located in the town of Mansehra had an introductory course three weeks long. Each day started before dawn with about 100 trainees saying prayers and recitations from the Koran, followed by a two-hour exercise period. Classes in small arms and ambush tactics took place after breakfast. If volunteers were not good enough for the Kashmir conflict, they had to enroll in other training camps with more difficult curriculum or be content to serve in less difficult situations such as with Taliban that was facing a withering Northern Alliance in the spring of 2002. Pervez Musharraf closed many of the camps, but others remained open.[28]

Newsweek reported on al Qaeda training of recruits in Afghanistan in 2002. One recruit was a 36-year-old Kabul business man, Mohammad Rasul. He was one of 28 new Afghan recruits at a jihadist training camp. The camp was run by two seasoned fighters, a Yemeni and a Chechen. The Yemeni informed the recruits that their target was Americans and America's servants. Rasul had experience fighting against the Soviets in the 1980s. Two days into the two-week training session, he became an assistant trainer. He helped teach the other recruits to launch BM-12 rockets from simple, jury-rigged stands; fire RPG-7s; antiaircraft guns; planted antitank and antipersonnel mines; and made bombs using diesel fuel and chemical fertilizer, and small-unit combat and ambush tactics. When the course was completed, they had a name of their own, the Avenging Martyrs Brigade, and spread out over Afghanistan to apply their training.[29]

Another story of a recruit involved a young boy, Hanif, who since the age of 7, when America invaded Afghanistan, had grown up wanting to join the jihad. His purpose in life always was to become a martyr. He said, "I want to attack infidels who insult Muslim women, who occupy Palestine, Iraq, and Afghanistan. There is nothing more to be strived for in this life except joining the jihad and becoming a shahid."[30]

When he was 15 years old at a café in Karachi, he met an elder tribesman, who was a recruiter. The recruiter told him many stories. Hanif expressed his desire to become a suicide bomber, and, in a few days, the recruiter telephoned him to join and to go to a training camp. He never arrived at the camp, because he decided to stay at an al Qaeda base near Datta Khel on the Afghan border. His three-month training course included running; exercises; prayers at a mosque five times a day; learning to ride a motorbike; drive a car, a pickup, and a truck; defend himself in a one-on-one fight; use a knife and an AK-47; handle explosives; and make improvised explosive devices and suicide vests. Hanif also learned how to operate the vest and how to avoid appearing nervous while approaching a target. It is important to get as close as possible to the target, and not set off the vest when the target first appears in the distance. He signed his last will and testament that is required of all bombers.

In *Newsweek*, Hanif describes of the result of drone attacks on al Qaeda targets:

They eventually found [the] attack that killed a Qaeda commander known as Abu Suleiman. They eventually found his head. After another drone attack, they dug for eight to nine hours in the debris of a collapsed house to try to find a Qaeda fighter, his wife, and his kids who had been killed. "We finally found parts of them," Hanif recalls, "but not all of them." "In the past year," he estimates, "drones have killed some 80 Qaeda members, many of them senior commanders."[31]

These stories reflect young men reacting in a disintegrated society. Conditions existed that fostered their decisions to turn as suicide bombers to answer a societal problem. Most compelling are Hanif's reasons for becoming a martyr to avenge the occupiers and those who insult their country's women.

THE WAR WITH AL QAEDA

Gross's analysis that al Qaeda philosophy operated where it appeared the organization was not present makes it difficult to say how much al Qaeda's influence abated after bin Laden's death. It is plausible that the organization slowed, especially because of the number of al Qaeda leaders killed since his death in May 2011 alone. Among those killed are the following: Anwar al-Awlaki, AQAP leader, killed in Khashef, Yemen, September 30, 2011. He was tied to the failed Christmas Day underwear bomber Umar Faruq Abdulmuttalab, the Fort Hood shooter Nidal Hasan of November 2009, and the failed Times Square bomber Faisal Shahzad of May 2010. Ilyas Kashmiri, one of al Qaeda's most dangerous commanders, was killed in Pakistan, June 3, 2011. Senior leader Fazul Abdullah Mohammed was also known as Harun Fazul, al Qaeda in East Africa. Fazul helped orchestrate the attacks on the U.S. embassies in Nairobi, Kenya and Dar es Salaam, Tanzania, in 1998. He was killed in Mogadishu, Somalia, June 7, 2011. All 2011 operatives mentioned except for bin Laden and Fazul Abdullah Mohammed were killed by drone attacks. U.S. Navy SEALs squadron from Team Six helicopter assault killed bin Laden, and Somalia security forces killed Mohammed as he attempted to speed through a checkpoint. In addition, nearly two dozen top operatives were killed in 2009 and 2010 (see Table 10.1).[32] From April to May 29, 2012, drone strikes numbered 14 in Yemen and 6 in Pakistan.[33] Of the top leaders, only Ayman al-Zawahiri has survived, according to Peter Bergen.[34]

The events surrounding the killing of bin Laden exemplify the interrelationship of suicide warfare (see Appendix E). In this trajectory, we see President Obama as head of state with a powerful military announcing to the American society that a military operation killed Osama bin Laden. The American society had suffered the blows of al Qaeda, a less powerful nonstate actor, who 10 years earlier hijacked 4 commercial jet airplanes and crashed them into the World Trade Center in New York City, the Pentagon in Washington, D.C., and a field in Shanksville, Pennsylvania. In the aftermath, America lost more lives than did al Qaeda and expended much more in funds and person power.

Table 10.1
Top al Qaeda Leaders Killed, 2009–June 5, 2012.[1]

Name and Association	Selected Act(s)	Date/Location/Method
2009		
Baitullah Mahsud, Tehrik e-Taliban Pakistan leader	Alleged assassination of former prime minister, Benazir Bhutto, and numerous suicide bombings, including Marriott Hotel, Islamabad, killing over 50 people in September 2008.	August 5. South Waziristan, Pakistan. Drone missile strike.
Noordin Muhammad Top, Jemayah Islamiya operational planner	Marriott in Jakarta, 2003; suicide bombings, Australian Embassy, 2004; and Bali bombings, 2005.	August 10. Beji village, Indonesia. Police gun battle.
Saleh Ali Saleh Nabhan, al Qaeda of East Africa planner	Al Qaeda cell leader in Kenya, suicide bombing of Israeli hotel on the coast, Paradise, in Mombasa 2002, suspected participant in attacks on two American embassies, East Africa, 1998.	September 14. Near Merka in southern Somalia. American commandos, helicopter raid.
Saleh al-Somali, al Qaeda operational commander outside Afghanistan and Pakistan	External operations chief.	December 9. Pakistan. Drone strike.
Abdallah Sa'id, al Qaeda operational leader and commander of the Lashkar al-Zil, or the elite paramilitary Shadow Army	Fought conventional battles against the Northern Alliance and U.S. forces in Afghanistan.	December 9. Pakistan. Drone strike.

(Continued)

Table 10.1
(Continued)

Name and Association	Selected Act(s)	Date/Location/Method
2010		
Ayed al-Shabwani	On the government's list of most-wanted al Qaeda-linked militants.	July 19. Zinjibar, Yemen. Fight. Also thought to have died in January 15, Yemen airstrike.
Qassem al-Rimi, al Qaeda in the Arabian Peninsula (AQAP) military senior official	Escaped from a state security prison in Sanaa in February 2006 that left the Yemeni government embarrassed. AQAP claimed responsibility for failed bomb attack on U.S.-bound airliner on December 25, 2009.	January 15. Yemen airstrike.
Ammar al-Waili	AQAP claimed responsibility for failed bomb attack on U.S.-bound airliner on December 25, 2009.	January 15. Yemen airstrike.
Saleh al-Tais	AQAP claimed responsibility for failed bomb attack on U.S.-bound airliner on December 25, 2009.	January 15. Yemen airstrike.
Ibrahim Mohammed Saleh al-Banna, Egyptian, a.k.a. Abu Aymen al-Masri	Thought to be an ideologist. AQAP claimed responsibility for failed bomb attack on U.S.-bound airliner on December 25, 2009.	January 15. Yemen airstrike.
Muhammad Haqqani, Haqqani network commander with 4,000–12,000 Taliban fighters under his command; technically a member of the Afghan Taliban leadership in Quetta, capital of Baluchistan Province in Pakistan.	Haqqani network blamed for helping plan the suicide bombing against the CIA base in Afghanistan in December. C.I.A. operatives and a Jordanian intelligence officer were killed.	February 16. Pakistan. Drone missile hit white station wagon in Dande Darpakhel, a village in North Waziristan, bordering Afghanistan.

Name	Description	Action
Qari Zafar, Lashkar-e Jhangvi, Sunni Muslim extremist group, leader	Wanted by United States and Pakistani for March 2006 attack on U.S. consulate in Karachi.	February 24. North Waziristan, Pakistan. U.S. drone airstrike.
Hussein al-Yemeni, al Qaeda operative, planner, and explosive experts	Key role in bombing of CIA post, Afghanistan, December 2009.	March 17. Miram Shah, the main town in North Waziristan, Pakistan. Missile strike.
Dulmatin, senior Jemayah Islamiya operative	Alleged mastermind behind the 2002 Bali bombings.	March 8. Jakarta, Indonesia. Raid.
Abu Ayyub al-Masri, Egyptian, assumed command of al Qaeda in Mesopotamia after death of Abu Musab al-Zarqawi	Supplied suicide bombers and car bombs, and was responsible for all operations in southern Iraq.	April 18. Near Tikrit. Joint raid between Iraqi and U.S. forces.
Abu Omar al-Baghdadi, al Qaeda in Iraq leader	Head of the Islamic State of Iraq.	April 18. Near Tikrit. Joint raid between Iraqi and U.S. forces.
Sheik Saeed al-Masri, al Qaeda's number three commander	Link between Osama bin Laden and Ayman al-Zawahiri and the remainder of the organization.	May 21. Tribal areas, Pakistan. Missile strike.
Hamza al-Jawfi, al Qaeda commander from Egypt	Led Jundallah, Pakistani terror group based in Karachi, and has close ties with al Qaeda.	June 29. Karikot, Pakistan. Unmanned predator.
2011		
Osama bin Laden, al Qaeda leader	Formed al Qaeda network, carried out global strikes against Western interests, culminating with 9/11 attacks on U.S. World Trade Center and Pentagon.	May 1. Compound. Abbottabad, Pakistan. U.S. Navy Seals squadron from Team Six helicopter assault.
Anwar al-Awlaki, AQAP leader	Tied to failed Christmas day underwear bomber Umar Faruq Abdulmuttalab, Fort Hood shooter Nidal Hasan of November 2009, and failed Times Square bomber Faisal Shahzad of May 2010.	September 30. Five miles from Khashef, Yemen. Type of predator drone.

(*Continued*)

Table 10.1
(Continued)

Name and Association	Selected Act(s)	Date/Location/Method
Abu Hafs al-Shahri, al Qaeda chief of Pakistan operations	Key operational and administrative role and worked closely with Taliban to carry out attacks in Pakistan.	September 11. Waziristan, Pakistan. Unmanned U.S. predators and reapers.
Atiyah Abd al-Rahman, deputy leader of al Qaeda	Al Qaeda number two figure under Ayman al-Zawahri, top operational planner.	August 22. Pakistan's tribal areas. Drone strike.
Ilyas Kashmiri, one of the most dangerous commanders	Responsible for the March 2006 car bomb attack on the U.S. Consulate in Karachi, Pakistan that killed diplomat David Foy and three others.	June 3. Ghawa Khawa, Pakistan. Drone strike.
Fazul Abdullah Mohammed, senior leader, also known as Harun Fazul	Helped orchestrate the attacks on the U.S. embassies in Nairobi, Kenya and Dar es Salaam, Tanzania, in 1998.	June 7. Mogadishu, Somalia. Somalia security forces killed him as he attempted to speed through a checkpoint.
2012		
Badr Mansoor	Instigator behind many suicide attacks in Pakistan.	February 9. Miran Shah, Pakistan's North Waziristan. Drone strike.
Fahd al-Quso	Indicted in the United States for role in the 2000 bombing of USS *Cole* in the harbor of Aden, Yemen.	May 6. Rafd, a remote mountain valley in Shabwa, Yemen. Drone strike.
Abu Yahya al-Libi, al Qaeda number two in command	Libyan citizen late 1940s, and thought dead in 2009. Captured in	June 4. Hesokhel, near Miranshah, capital of North Waziristan, Pakistan. Drone strike,

2002 in Afghanistan, and escaped in 2005.

third group of missiles destroyed his vehicle and a militant compound.

¹Jake Tapper, "The Terrorist Notches on Obama's Belt," *ABC News Blogs*, September 30, 2011, http://abcnews.go.com/blogs/politics/2011/09/the-terrorist-notches-on-obamas-belt/.; Declan Walsh, "Air Strike Kills Taliban Leader Baitullah Mehsud," *The Guardian*, August 7, 2009, http://www.guardian.co.uk/world/2009/aug/07/baitullah-mehsud-dead-taliban-pakistan; "Senior Leader of Yemeni Qaeda Branch Is Said to Be Dead," *The New York Times*, July 21, 2011, http://www.nytimes.com/2011/07/22/world/middleeast/22yemen.html; Richard Shears, "Terrorist Mastermind Noordin Mohammed Top Shot Dead after a 17-Hour Siege," *Mail Online*, August 10, 2009, http://www.dailymail.co.uk/news/article-1205164/Terrorist-mastermind-Noordin-Mohammed-Top-shot-dead-17-hour-seige.html; Jeffrey Gettleman and Eric Schmitt, "U.S. Kills Top Qaeda Militant in Southern Somalia," *The New York Times*, September 14, 2009, http://www.nytimes.com/2009/09/15/world/africa/15raid.html; "Al Qaeda Figure Hussein al-Yemeni Believed to Have Been Killed in U.S. Missile Strike," *The New York Times*, March 18, 2010, http://www.nydailynews.com/news/world/al-qaeda-figure-hussein-al-yemeni-believed-killed-u-s-missile-strike-article-1.173124; "Yemen Confirms Qaeda Chiefs' Deaths," *Daleje.com*, January 16 2010, http://dalje.com/en-world/yemen-confirms-qaeda-chiefs-deaths/290351; Pir Zubair Shah, "Missile Kills Militant's Brother in Pakistan," *The New York Times*, February 19, 2010, http://www.nytimes.com/2010/02/20/world/asia/20pstan.html; "Abu Ayyub al-Masri," *The New York Times*, April 19, 2010, http://topics.nytimes.com/top/reference/timestopics/people/m/abu_ayyub_almasri/index.html; Bill Roggio, "Al Qaeda Commander Killed in US Strike on Safehouse in South Waziristan," *The Long War Journal*, June 29, 2010, http://www.longwarjournal.org/archives/2010/06/us_strikes_al_qaeda_1.php; Bill Roggio, "Abu Hafs al Shahri Confirmed Killed in Predator Strike in Pakistan," *The Long War Journal*, September 17, 2011, http://www.longwarjournal.org/archives/2011/09/abu_hafs_al_shahri_c.php, November 18, 2011; Terry Moran, Martha Raddatz, Nick Schifrin, Brian Ross, and Jake Tapper, "Target: Bin Laden—The Death and Life of Public Enemy Number One," *ABC News*, June 9, 2011, Jake Tapper, Chapter Six: The President Takes Aim, http://abcnews.go.com/Politics/target-bin-laden-death-life-osama-bin-laden/story?id=13786598; "Officials Thought They Might Kill Awlaki on 9/11 Anniversary," *ABC News*, September 30, 2011, http://abcnews.go.com/blogs/politics/2011/09/officials-thought-they-might-kill-awlaki-on-911-anniversary/; Bill Roggio, "Al Qaeda's Shadow Army Commander Outlines Afghan Strategy," *The Long War Journal*, April 13, 2009, http://www.longwarjournal.org/archives/2009/04/al_qaedas_shadow_arm.php; Nick Schifrin, Pierre Thomas, and Jake Tapper, "Al Qaeda No. 2 Atiyah Abd al-Rahman Killed in Pakistan," *ABC News*, August 27, 2011, http://abcnews.go.com/International/al-qaeda-atiyah-abd-al-rahman-killed-pakistan/story?id=14394690; "Ilyas Kashmiri Killed in Drone Attack," *Sydney Morning Herald*, June 5, 2011, http://www.smh.com.au/world/ilyas-kashmiri-killed-in-drone-attack-20110605-1fmv6.html; "Al Qaeda's Fazul Abdullah Mohammed Killed, but Who Will Be Next Is't Godane, Shangole or Mansuur?," *Somalia Online*, June 14, 2011, http://www.somaliaonline.com/community/showthread.php/57919-Al-Qaeda%E2%80%99s-Fazul-Abdullah-Mohammed-Killed-but-who-will-be-next-is-t-Godane-shangole-OR-Mansuur; Mark Mazzetti, "C.I.A. Drone Is Said to Kill Al Qaeda's No. 2," *The New York Times*, August 27, 2011, http://www.nytimes.com/2011/08/28/world/asia/28qaeda.html; "US Air Strike Kills Top al-Qaida Leader in Yemen," *The Guardian*, May 7, 2012, http://www.guardian.co.uk/world/2012/may/07/us-airstrike-kills-al-qaida-leader-yemen; Rob Crilly and Nazar Ul Islam, "Al-Qaeda Leader Abu Yahya al-Libi Killed in US Drone Dtrike," *The Telegraph*, June 5, 2012, http://www.telegraph.co.uk/news/worldnews/al-qaeda/9312536/Al-Qaeda-leader-Abu-Yahya-al-Libi-killed-in-US-drone-strike.html.

A reason al Qaeda's influence may not totally abate is that new leadership appears to have emerged. According to *BBC*, Ayman al-Zawahiri, an Egyptian eye surgeon, helped found the Egyptian militant group Islamic Jihad. Following bin Laden's death, Zawahiri was named the new leader on June 16, 2011. The United States has indicted Zawahiri for his role in the 1998 U.S. Embassy bombings in Africa. Egypt has sentenced him to death in absentia for his 1990 activities with Islamic Jihad. Other new leaders identified include Abu Yahya al-Libi (a.k.a. Hasan Qayid); Yunis al-Sahrawi, former Libyan Islamic Fighting Group member, now a field commander in Afghanistan; Adnan Gulshair el Shukrijumah, chief al Qaeda external operations council, lived for over 15 years in the United States, named in a U.S. federal indictment as a conspirator in the case against three men accused of plotting the 2009 suicide bomb attacks on New York's subway system, and suspected of having played a role in plotting al Qaeda attacks in Panama, Norway, and the United Kingdom; Saif al-Adel, once bin Laden's security chief; Fahd Mohammed Ahmed al-Quso, 2000 bomb attack on the USS *Cole* in Aden, killed in 2012; Nasser Abdul Karim al-Wuhayshi, former aide to bin Laden, and the leader of AQAP; and Abou Mossab Abdelwadoud, bomb maker and the leader of al Qaeda in the Islamic Maghreb (AQIM).[35]

The leadership that emerges will have to address the undesirable consequences that may result from the large amount of sensitive information the U.S. forces recovered from bin Laden's home when he was killed. "That information is likely to prove damaging to al-Qaeda operations," stated Peter Bergen.[36]

Information collected during the raid suggests that bin Laden had continued to play a strong role in planning and directing attacks by al Qaeda and its affiliates in Yemen and Somalia. *MSNBC* and *AP* reported that the material demonstrated that top al Qaeda commanders and other key insurgents were spread throughout Pakistan, and were supported and given sanctuary by Pakistanis.[37] The al Qaeda organization issued a statement following bin Laden's death: "to continue on the path of jihad that our leaders, led by Sheikh Osama chose."[38]

Murad Batal al-Shishani indicated the form of the organization has changed since bin Laden's death. Ideology of remaining leaders of core al Qaeda (based along the Afghanistan–Pakistan border) will decide its direction. These figures include Egyptian jihadist Dr. Ayman al-Zawahiri. Al-Shishani noted that al Qaeda ideologue, Abdul Majid, remarked on the change of the organization's form, "Al-Qaeda is no longer just a hierarchal organization [built] on specific names, but has become a jihadi mission held [in common] by all mujahedeen of the umma [Islamic community]."[39]

The Council on Foreign Relations stated that estimated numbers of al Qaeda members range from several hundred to several thousand members.[40] But it is the strength of the organization that is its influence throughout the network that "makes the core operatives so difficult to identify, even though the leadership in different countries may be known by name," according to James Veitch and John Martin. In addition, members are prepared to die for its cause.[41] John Rollins stated, "Al Qaeda . . . has evolved into a significantly different terrorist organization than the one that perpetrated the September 11, 2001, attacks."[42] In 2001, al Qaeda consisted primarily of a core cadre of veterans of the Afghan insurgency against the Soviet Union. Egyptians made up the centralized leadership structure. Organizational operations either came from or were approved by leadership. Rollins concludes that some believe that the al Qaeda of that period no longer exists.

Most analysts adopted the concepts of core, branch, and franchise. Veitch and Martin note the writing of Leah Farrall, "The composition of each element remains elusive. There is doubt about whom or what the core consists of—especially with the demise of bin Laden. The branch 'offices' are identifiable but the 'franchisees' become more complex comprising those who have an affiliation approved by the core command and those who have 'adopted the brand.'"[43] Farrell stated that the recent accounts that al Qaeda's organization is on the decline are not taking into consideration how the central al Qaeda organization is separate from its subsidiaries, thus overlooking its power and influence through them. Farrell believes conceptions of the organization need to be updated. Their organization is comparable to a pyramid rather than a hierarchy. Communication and coordination among al Qaeda's core, branch, and franchises largely takes place through respective information committees. The committees have access to senior leaders, distribution networks, and close ties to operations in each group. Branch and franchise messages go through the second-tier leadership that in turn briefs Zawahiri or bin Laden, when alive. Because second-tier leadership manages the interaction, Farrell believes that the elimination of either Zawahiri or bin Laden would not overly affect the unity or communication among the organization's core, branch, and franchises. Most importantly, these groups carry out the attacks. Farrell concludes, "It is important that the strategic picture of al Qaeda accurately reflect the organization's broad operating dynamics instead of wishful thinking about the central organization's degraded capacity."[44] Citing the Yemen-based Arabian Peninsula's active attacks on the United States and the Somalian al-Shabaab's branching out for the first time to strike in Uganda, Bernard I. Finel stated, "Osama bin Laden's death may be occurring just as al Qaeda is beginning to really walk without his leadership."[45] In spite of the organization's ability to demonstrate durability through replacing its losses, drone attacks have presented a leadership challenge, wrote Finel (see Table 10.1).

Thus, in spite of the recent leadership deaths, the Arab Spring, and lack of hierarchical command structure, al Qaeda finds some of its organizational strength in its autonomous underground or sleeper cells, branch offices, and franchises, according to Veitch and Martin. Underground cells exist in approximately 100 countries, according to the Council on Foreign Relations. For example, law enforcement has weakened al Qaeda cells in the United Kingdom, the United States, Italy, France, Spain, Germany, Albania, and Uganda. The Council on Foreign Relations stated that less than a dozen groups share al Qaeda's Sunni Muslim fundamentalist views (see Table 10.2).

Many of these groups formed for domestic reasons, usually discontent over and resistance to government actions. The focus of some became transnational as well. For example, the Iraq War was a factor for al Qaeda in the Islamic Maghreb in Algeria, and U.S. interests in the disputed region of Kashmir was a factor for the Lashkar-e-Taiba and Jaish-e-Muhaamad. Whether operating on the domestic or transnational level, the societal elements that were present influenced the individual terrorists to reflect. In some cases, the military played a key role such as in Algeria. In any case, the groups demonstrate ideological clashes whether they be religious, ethnic, or political of individuals who have formed because of their collective inclination to oppose the larger society (see Chapter 1).

Part of al Qaeda's metamorphosis may be in name changes of some of these groups. For example, a website sponsored by USCENTCOM, *Al-Shorfa.com*, reported that AQAP in Yemen changed its name to Ansar al-Sharia. The Yemen groups portray themselves as local organizations with religious legitimacy, but execute al Qaeda's agenda and methods. *Al-Shorfa* reported that a July 18 report in *Inspire*, al Qaeda's online magazine, verified the link between Ansar al-Sharia and al Qaeda. Reported also was that a letter bin Laden wrote on his personal computer, found from the Abbottabad raid, indicated that he wanted a name change.[46] In one of the *Letters from Abbottabad*, whose authorship is unclear, discusses the need to change the name because the name al Qaeda "reduces the feeling of Muslims that we belong to them."[47] This document is also concerned that the name al Qaeda lacks a religious connotation, and therefore has allowed the United States to launch a war on al Qaeda without offending Muslims. The document states that the name al Qaeda

allows the enemies to claim deceptively that they are not at war with Islam and Muslims, but they are at war with the organization of al-Qa'ida, which is an outside entity from the teachings of Islam and this is what was raised repeatedly in the past as indicated by Obama, that our war is not on Islam or on the Muslim people but rather our war is on the al-Qa'ida organization, so if the word al-Qa'ida was derived from or had strong ties to the word Islam or Muslims; or if it had the name Islamic party, it would be difficult for Obama to say that.[48]

Thus, the possibility of name change may indicate that the groups represented in Table 10.2 may be but a guide for a capsule in time.

Regardless, Yemen, for example, has emerged one of the central fronts in the struggle against terrorism because of the activities of AQAP, according to W. Andrew Terrill. Two examples are when on December 25, 2009,

Table 10.2
Groups Associated with al Qaeda, 2011.[1]

Group	Societal Elements	Current Activity
Abu Sayyaf Group (Philippines, Islamist separatists); formed 1990; and international 2000	Separate Islamic state for Muslim minority; founding of a commission to improve the plight of ethnic Filipinos in Malaysia; and release of incarcerated World Trade Center bomber Ramsey Yousef.	Although armed strength decreased from about 1,000 in 2002 to between 200 and 400 in 2006, growth has occurred to between 200 and 500 in 2008.
Al Qaeda in the Arabian Peninsula (Yemen, militant jihadists); formed 1990s; and Saudi and Yemeni merged 2009	Advocate of Yemeni discontent with the political status quo.	Membership, a few hundred. Ideologically closest to the al Qaeda core; Umar Farouk Abdulmutallab, 2009 Christmas day bomber; 2010 several attacks; 2000 bombing of U.S. *Cole*.
Al Qaeda in China (government discontent); training in Afghanistan 1979–1989; formed 2008	Muslim Uighurs dislike strict rules restricting religion, Han migration, and policies that favor Han Chinese.	China's successful efforts to prevent the global jihad from spreading has been a challenge of al Qaeda.
Al Qaeda in Iraq; also known as al Qaeda in Mesopotamia; originally Jama'at al-Tawhid wal-Jihad (jihadists); formed 2003	Rose to prominence after the U.S.-led invasion of Iraq; Sunni Muslim extremist group seeks to spread civil unrest in Iraq, to establish a calip hate—a single, transnational Islamic state.	Weakened, but attacks remain consistent, and target civilians.

(Continued)

Table 10.2
(Continued)

Group	Societal Elements	Current Activity
Al Qaeda in the Islamic Maghreb (Algeria); formerly Salafist Group for Call and Combat; also known as GIA, Groupe Islamique Armé, or al-Jama'ah al-Islamiyah al-Musallaha; training in Afghanistan 1979–1989; formed 1992	Began as Islamist resistance movement to the secular military Algerian government when it canceled the second round of parliamentary elections, and it appeared that the Islamic Salvation Front, a coalition of Islamist militants and moderates, might win and take power. No longer a local insurgency against a military government but now intends to attack Western targets, and had sent a squad of jihadis to Iraq.	Has a significant presence in Iraq. On the decline. Algerian police forces launched a widespread crackdown in 2004 on all local terrorist groups. Over 400 members of GIA and the Salafists were arrested causing the demise of the groups.
Egyptian Islamic Jihad or Jamaat al-Islamiyya; also known as Gama'a al-Islamiyya, al-Gama'at, Egyptian al-Gama'at al-Islamiyya, Islamic Gama'at, Islamic Group, or Jama'a Islamia; formed 1970s	Overthrow the secular Egyptian government and replace it with an Islamic regime.	For the most part, honors the March 1999 cease-fire with government.
Islamic Movement of Uzbekistan; formed 1991	Unrest as result of the major's refusal to give young Muslims land to build a mosque.	Often are bodyguards for top Pakistani Taliban and al Qaeda leaders. Fights alongside the Taliban in Pakistan and Afghanistan, and has increased attacks in Central Asian countries.
Jemaah Islamiyah;also known as Jemaah Islamiah Southeast Asia; formed 1970s or 1980s	During early years, renounced violence, but shifted tactics in the late 1990s because of suspected links with al Qaeda in Afghanistan.	Cells operate in Southeast Asia, including Indonesia, Malaysia, Singapore, and possibly the Philippines, Cambodia, and Thailand. Membership varies 500–1,000.

| Lashkar-e-Taiba, formed 1993; and Jaish-e-Muhammad (Kashmir), formed 2000 | Disputed region of Kashmir between India and Pakistan. Seeks to incorporate Kashmir into the Pakistan, and has openly declared war on the United States. | Formed as the military wing of Pakistani Islamist organization Markaz-ud-Dawa-wal-Irshad. One of the largest and most proficient of the Kashmir-based terrorist groups. Several hundred armed supporters and tens of thousands of followers. Pakistan outlawed these groups, and attacks in Kashmir and Pakistan have been carried out under other guises, such as charity groups, to avoid detection. Militant attacks continue harming the peace process. |
| Libyan Islamic Fighting Group; formed 1990s | Anti-Kaddafi group. | When United States improved relations, group suspected of allying with al Qaeda, and funneled fighters to Iraq against United States. |

[1]Jayshree Bajoria and Greg Bruno, "al-Qaeda (a.k.a. al-Qaida, al-Qa'ida)," *Council on Foreign Relations*, August 29, 2011, http://www.cfr.org/terrorist-organizations/al-qaeda-k-al-qaida-al-qaida/p9126; Mark Burgess, "Current List of Foreign Terrorist Organizations and Other Terrorist Organizations," *Center for Defense Information*, August 12, 2005, http://www.cdi.org/program/document.cfm?DocumentID=384&StartRow=1&ListRows=10&appendURL=&Orderby=D.DateLastUpdated&ProgramID=39&from_page=index.cfm; Mark Burgess, "In the Spotlight: Islamic Movement of Uzbekistan (IMU)," *Center of Defense Information*, March 25, 2002, http://www.cdi.org/terrorism/imu.cfm; Lee Ferran and Rym Momtaz, "From Terror Group Founder to Libyan Rebel Military Commander," *ABC News*, August 29, 2011, http://abcnews.go.com/Blotter/terror-group-founder-libyan-rebel-military-commander/story?id=14405319; Bill Roggio, "Islamic Movement of Uzbekistan Claims Panjshir Suicide Attack," *The Long War Journal*, October 17, 2011, http://www.longwarjournal.org/archives/2011/10/islamic_movement_of_6.php; John Rollins, "Al Qaeda and Affiliates: Historical Perspective, Global Presence, and Implications for U.S. Policy," *Congressional Research Service Report*, February 5, 2010, 25, http://fpc.state.gov/documents/organization/137015.pdf; James Veitch and John Martin, *The Death of Osama bin Laden and the Future of al-Qaeda* (Dhaka: Bangladesh Institute of Peace and Security Studies, 2011), 37–43, http://www.bipss.org.bd/pdf/BIPSS%20Paper.pdf.

a Yemen trained operative attempted to blow up a Northwest Airline passenger jet with 280 people aboard; and in 2010, AQAP failed attacks involving two parcel bombs that were to be sent to Jewish organizations in Chicago. Perhaps more critical is AQAP's progress in challenging the government within Yemen itself. It may be moving from a terrorist group to an insurgency. An example of this move is seen in the August 2010 combat operations in the southern town of Loder. Yemen expelled al Qaeda from Loder at that time. But AQAP and its allies seized the town of Zinjibar in southern Yemen in May 2011, and remain there. As of May 2011, the Yemeni government has been unable to drive it out.[49]

SCOPE

Al Qaeda and associated groups that I identified in the *Chicago Project on Security and Terrorism (CPOST)* database from Table 10.2 represented 6,563 deaths and 21,046 wounded. The 169 attacks ranged from isolated attacks by the Egyptian Islamic Jihad on August 15, 1993 to violence by al Qaeda versus the United States and its allies in Yemen on November 26, 2010 (see Table 10.3). Included is al Qaeda's 9/11 targeting the Pentagon and World Trade Center that killed 2,955 and attack in the United States wounded totaled 6,291.[50]

These attacks took place in seven campaigns (see Table 10.4). The Iraqi rebels versus United States and its allies conducted by far the most attacks,

Table 10.3
Suicide Attacks and Casualties by Groups Associated with al Qaeda, as of 2011.

Group	Attacks	Killed	Wounded
Al Qaeda	89	4,725	15,647
Al Qaeda in Iraq	33	948	2,963
Al Qaeda in Islamic North Africa	6	34	84
Al Qaeda in Mesopotamia	8	90	122
Al Qaeda in the Arabian Peninsula	4	37	26
Al Qaeda in the Islamic Maghreb	8	223	628
Egyptian Islamic Jihad	1	5	18
Jaish-e-Muhammad	5	58	95
Jama'at al-Tawhid Wa'al-Jihad	9	161	631
Jemaah Islamiya	4	242	691
Lashkar-e-Taiba	2	40	141
Total	169	6,563	21,046

Source: Suicide Attack Search Database, *Chicago Project on Security and Terrorism (CPOST)*, October 14, 2011, http://cpost.uchicago.edu/search.php.

Table 10.4
Suicide Attacks and Casualties by Campaign by Groups Associated with al Qaeda, as of 2011.

Campaign	Attacks	Killed	Wounded
Iraqi rebels versus United States and its allies	111	2,372	6,234
Al Qaeda versus United States and its allies	30	3,774	13,536
Isolated attacks	12	228	779
Pakistani militants versus Pakistan (U.S. ally)	6	55	243
Kashmiri rebels versus India	4	40	43
Afghani rebels versus United States and its allies	3	66	183
Al Qaeda in Islamic North Africa	2	26	28
Total	168	6,561	21,046

Source: Suicide Attack Search Database, *Chicago Project on Security and Terrorism (CPOST)*, October 14, 2011, http://cpost.uchicago.edu/search.php.

111 compared to 30 by al Qaeda versus United States and its allies who ranked second. However, in the numbers killed and wounded, al Qaeda ranked higher at 3,774 and 13,536 to the Iraqi rebels, 2,372 and 6,234, respectively. Al Qaeda's 9/11 attack again accounts for its disproportionate numbers representing the small number of attacks. The Iraq War is a reason for the high number of attacks. Strikingly, the numbers killed for each group, 2,372 and 3,774, clearly demonstrate al Qaeda's higher lethality rate, 125.8 and 21.4 (not shown on Table 10.4).[51]

When these attacks took place present a similar pattern in that the numbers killed, 2,987, and wounded, 6,291, by the al Qaeda 2001 attack on the United States dwarf all other casualty figures. Only the 1998 attacks on the embassies in Kenya and Tanzania that resulted in 224 killed and 4,487 wounded come anywhere near the killed and wounded in the 9/11 attacks (see Table 10.5). When the location of the attack is considered, Iraq has the greatest number, 111, the number killed and wounded fall well below that of the attack of 9/11 (see Table 10.6).[52]

Table 10.5
Suicide Attacks and Casualties by Year by Groups Associated with al Qaeda, 1993–2011.

Year	Attacks	Killed	Wounded
1993	1	5	18
1994	0	0	0
1995	2	22	60

(*Continued*)

Table 10.5
(*Continued*)

Year	Attacks	Killed	Wounded
1996	1	0	0
1997	0	0	0
1998	1	224	4,877
1999	0	0	0
2000	1	17	40
2001	3	2,987	6,291
2002	3	219	380
2003	8	185	1,604
2004	39	689	2,297
2005	47	908	1,965
2006	6	46	92
2007	17	540	1,110
2008	14	208	438
2009	12	314	1,511
2010	13	197	363
2011	0	0	0
Total	168	6,561	21,046

Source: Suicide Attack Search Database, *Chicago Project on Security and Terrorism (CPOST)*, October 14, 2011, http://cpost.uchicago.edu/search.php.

The airplane proved the most lethal when attack by weapon was considered, killing 2,955 on 9/11; the 116 car bombs closely followed, killing 2,785. When attacks were evaluated by target, the most attacks were on security, 95. Although attacks on political targets ranked third, 37 and the number killed was 3,952 Civilian targets ranked second in number of attacks 47, killing 4,592 (see Table 10.7).[53]

Table 10.6
Suicide Attacks and Casualties by Location by Groups Associated with al Qaeda, as of 2011.

Country	Attacks	Killed	Wounded
Iraq	111	2,317	6,174
Algeria	12	257	708
Yemen	9	95	112
Pakistan	6	55	243

(*Continued*)

Table 10.6
(Continued)

Country	Attacks	Killed	Wounded
Saudi Arabia	6	80	391
India	4	40	43
Afghanistan	3	66	183
Egypt	3	35	182
Indonesia	3	225	631
Turkey	3	86	1,007
Morocco	2	1	1
Jordan	1	57	120
Kenya	1	160	3,305
Mauritania	1	0	3
Tanzania	1	112	2,439
United Kingdom	1	52	0
United States	1	2,955	6,291
Total	168	6,593	21,833

Source: Suicide Attack Search Database, *Chicago Project on Security and Terrorism (CPOST)*, October 14, 2011, http://cpost.uchicago.edu/search.php.

Table 10.7
Suicide Attacks and Casualties by Weapon and Target Type by Groups Associated with al Qaeda, as of 2011.

	Attacks	Killed	Wounded
Weapon			
Airplane	1	2,955	6,291
Belt Bomb	34	744	1,267
Car Bomb	116	2,785	12,920
Other	15	187	571
Unknown	10	419	1,087
Total	176	7,090	22,136
Target Type			
Security	95	1,515	4,108
Political	37	3,952	14,564
Civilian	47	4,592	11,198
Other	0	0	0
Unknown	2	41	139
Total	181	10,100	30,009

Source: Suicide Attack Search Database, *Chicago Project on Security and Terrorism (CPOST)*, October 14, 2011, http://cpost.uchicago.edu/search.php.

AL QAEDA SUICIDE ATTACKS
IN THE UNITED STATES

Almost all suicide bombers in the United States were self-radicalized rather than recruited, stated Jenkins. Most began their radicalization on the Internet where they discovered resonance and reinforcement of their own dissatisfactions and middlemen who legitimized and directed their anger. The would-be terroristic bombers identified in Jenkins testimony possessed earnest intent. "Their ideological commitment was manifest. They were ready to be terrorists."[54]

A large number of the characteristics of the individuals who bomb fall into the unknown category, whether measurement was for gender, religion, occupation, or education, reveals the *CPOST* database. The demographics do not reveal motivation, but an examination of each demographic can reveal what reason might be common. Excluding the unknown factor, in the groups associated with al Qaeda (see Table 10.2), more were male attackers, 176 (61.5%) compared to 6 (2.1%) females. Women had a higher proportion of attacks, 5 of 6 compared to the males 114 of 176. Male attacks killed more individuals, 5,148 (77.9%) than either unknowns, 1,333 (20.2%), or females, 124 (1.9%). The predominant known religion was Muslim (NA). Most attackers had either a professional or skilled occupation at 6 each, and student followed at 4. Unskilled followed with 3, and unemployed was 1. Of the attackers whose occupation was known, most of them had a postsecondary education, which probably explains why more were in a professional or skilled occupation. But for the bulk of attackers, 266, their occupations were unknown (see Table 10.8).

Robert A. Pape believed that that early strategy on the war on terrorism was based on a faulty premise, that suicide terrorism and al Qaeda suicide terrorism in particular is mainly driven by an evil ideology Islamic fundamentalism independent of other circumstances. From 1980 to 2005, over half of suicide terrorist attacks were secular. Pape estimated that over 95 percent of suicide attacks were not about religion, but were for a specific strategic purpose: to force democracies to withdraw military forces from the territory that the terrorists view as their homeland or prize greatly. "This is in fact a centerpiece of al Qaeda's strategic logic, which is to compel the United States and Western countries to abandon military commitments on the Arabian Peninsula."[55]

Most suicide attackers are socially integrated, productive members of their community, are working class and middle class, are walk-in volunteers, are not long-time members of the militant organization, and join the group just a few months or weeks before their very first act of violence and their own suicide attack. Pape said, most are "deeply angered by military policies, especially foreign combat troops on territory that they prize and that they believe they have no other means to change those policies"[56]

Table 10.8

Suicide Attackers, Attacks, and Casualties by Gender, Religion, Occupation, and Education by Groups Associated with al Qaeda, as of 2011.

	Attackers (Percent)	Attacks (Percent)	Killed (Percent)	Wounded (Percent)
Gender				
Male	176 (61.5)	114 (64.4)	5,148 (77.9)	17,578 (83.4)
Female	6 (2.1)	5 (2.8)	124 (1.9)	267 (1.3)
Unknown	104 (36.4)	58 (32.8)	1,333 (20.2)	3,215 (15.3)
Total	286 (100)	177 (100)	6,605 (100)	21,060 (100)
Religion				
Muslim (NA)	43 (15.0)	21 (12.0)	3,633 (55.0)	13,195 (62.7)
Muslim (Sunni)	2 (0.7)	2 (1.1)	2 (0)	14 (0)
None	1 (0.3)	1 (0.6)	8 (0.1)	25 (0.1)
Unknown	240 (84.0)	151 (86.3)	2,962 (44.9)	7,827 (37.2)
Total	286 (100)	175 (100)	6,605 (100)	21,061 (100)
Occupation				
Professional	6 (2.1)	5 (2.8)	354 (5.4)	791 (3.8)
Skilled	6 (2.1)	4 (2.3)	495 (7.5)	1,022 (4.8)
Student	4 (1.4)	2 (1.1)	497 (7.5)	1,053 (5.0)
Unemployed	1 (0.4)	1 (0.6)	156 (2.4)	331 (1.6)
Unknown	266 (93.0)	161 (91.5)	5,071 (76.7)	17,665 (83.9)
Unskilled	3 (1.0)	3 (1.7)	33 (0.5)	197 (0.9)
Total	286 (100)	176 (100)	6,606 (100)	21,059 (100)
Education				
None	2 (0)	2 (1.2)	81 (1.3)	217 (0.1)
Postsecondary	23 (8.0)	9 (5.2)	2,281 (34.5)	5,006 (24.8)
Secondary	5 (2.0)	4 (2.3)	206 (3.1)	620 (2.9)
Unknown	256 (90.0)	158 (91.3)	4,037 (61.1)	15,206 (72.2)
Total	286 (100)	173 (100)	6,605 (100)	21,049 (100)

Source: Suicide Attack Search Database, *Chicago Project on Security and Terrorism (CPOST)*, October 14, 2011, http://cpost.uchicago.edu/search.php.

CPOST Note: "Please note, the results include all attacks in which attackers of the selected gender were involved—attacks committed by multiple attackers of both genders (or 'unknown') will result in multiple genders being reported, not just those that have been selected."

Ousting the Taliban and Safehavens

In 2001, Al Qaeda leadership failed to foresee the quick collapse of the Taliban regime in Afghanistan. Up to that point, Afghanistan had been a training ground for about 60,000 jihadists. Although Bruce Riedel wrote that al Qaeda leaders welcomed the U.S. and allied invasion thinking they would follow the Soviets pattern 20 years earlier and get caught up in conflict, the U.S. military supremacy sent al Qaeda senior leaders and the Taliban into hiding in the badlands along the Pakistani–Afghan border. Here al Qaeda formed a new base of operations around Quetta, in the Baluchistan region of Pakistan.[57]

Death of Osama bin Laden

Few terrorist groups have encountered the military supremacy in their opposition, as al Qaeda has with the United States and its allies. Not until after the atrocity of 9/11, did bin Laden experience such wrath until the United States and its allies went to war in Afghanistan on October 7, 2001. Nor would he again experience the U.S. military's superiority after he was killed on May 1, 2011 by a small team of U.S. Navy special forces during a 40-minute operation at a compound in Abbottabad, Pakistan (see Appendix E).

Al Qaeda in 2012

The National Counterterrorism Center stated that al-Zawahiri was quickly named bin Laden's successor, and that "Al-Qaida remains a cohesive organization and al-Qaida core's leadership continues to be important to the global movement."[58] Even though the organization suffered leadership losses, it remains committed to carrying out attacks in the United States and against American interests abroad. Al Qaeda's ability to continue attacks while under sustained counterterrorism pressure suggests it may be planning more attacks.

Al Qaeda in Iraq and Other Groups

High-profile attacks in 2009 and 2010 established the relevance of al Qaeda in Iraq (AQI) after the coalition withdrawal from Iraq in 2009. Two top leaders, Ibrahim Mohammed Saleh al-Banna, (Egyptian, a.k.a. Abu Aymen al-Masri) and Abu Omar al-Baghdadi, were killed, yet the group continues. For example, on August15, 2011, AQI carried out attacks in 17 cities.[59]

There are many active affiliated al Qaeda groups, but the activities of a few serve as an example that al Qaeda remains operative. AQIM, an

Algeria-based Sunni Muslim jihadist group, remains active. In 2011, the organization killed two French hostages during an attempted rescue operation. AQIM still holds four French hostages and an Italian tourist kidnapped in Algeria. AQAP has increased its operations since 2008. For example, in 2012, due to local unrest, the group is attempting to seize control of parts of Yemen's Abyan governorate. The senior leadership of al-Shabaab in Somalia is affiliated with al Qaeda. The group is known for employing suicide bombing. In 2011, they blocked delivery of aid from some Western relief agencies during a famine. The Afghan Taliban are responsible for many attacks in Afghanistan. In 2011, they and the Haqqani Network assaulted the Intercontinental Hotel in Kabul. Also in 2011, they assassinated Ahmed Wali Karzai, chief of the Kandahar Provincial Council and the half-brother of Afghan President Hamid Karzai. The Tehrik-e Taliban Pakistan number of attacks in Pakistan after bin Laden's death indicates a great deal of activity, according to the U.S. National Counterterrorism Center.[60]

Leaders at Large

Several al Qaeda leaders remain at large and are wanted by the United States, according to the U.S. National Counterterrorism Center. The following list serves as example that al Qaeda leadership, though reduced, is not absent. The listing is not exhaustive. At large, leaders include Ayman al-Zawahiri, Egyptian Islamic Jihad; Ali Sayyid Muhamed Mustafa al-Bakri, al Qaeda Shura Council; Mullah Omar, his Taliban Afghan regime sheltered bin Laden and his al Qaeda network before 9/11; Abdul Rahman Yasin, 1993 World Trade Center bombing; Husayn Muhammed al-Umari, 1982 bombing of Pan American World Airways flight 830; Qari Mohammad Zafar, connection with the 2002 bombing of the U.S. Consulate in Karachi, Pakistan; Abu Du'a, senior leader AQI; and Sirajuddin Haqqani, senior leader of the Haqqani. Jamal Mohammad al-Badawi and Abdullah al-Rimi are wanted for their role in the October 2000 bombing of the USS *Cole*, and Anas al-Liby, Ahmed Mohamed Hamed, and Abdullah Ahmed Abdullah for their roles in the 1998 embassy bombings in Tanzania and Nairobi.[61]

Intelligence Gathered from Abbottabad Letters

One of Osama bin Laden's communications retrieved from the Abbottabad letters told of bin Laden's command to his network to organize special cells in Afghanistan and Pakistan to attack the aircraft of President Obama and General David H. Petraeus, commander in Afghanistan. Bin Laden explained why to his top lieutenant, "The reason for concentrating

on them is that Obama is the head of infidelity and killing him automatically will make [Vice President] Biden take over the presidency. . . . Biden
is totally unprepared for that post, which will lead the U.S. into a crisis.
As for Petraeus, he is the man of the hour . . . and killing him would alter
the war's path" in Afghanistan.[62] David Ignatius reported that it is doubtful that bin Laden and his network had the capability to attack the president's aircraft.

The U.S. government declassified and released to the Combating Terrorism Center (CTC) at West Point documents captured during the Abbottabad raid. CTC's report studies 17 electronic or draft letters totaling
175 pages in Arabic and 197 in English. Bin Laden as well as others authored the communications and the dates range from September 2006 to
April 2011. Although al Qaeda's public statements focused on injustice,
bin Laden's private letters centered on Muslims' suffering caused by jihadi brothers. Bin Laden "is at pain advising them to abort domestic attacks that cause Muslim civilian casualties and focus on the United States,
'our desired goal.' Bin Laden's frustration with regional jihadi groups and
his seeming inability to exercise control over their actions and public statements is the most compelling story to be told on the basis of the 17 declassified documents," wrote Don Rassler et al.[63]

These 17 documents were part of a total of more than 6,000 documents
that were recovered. The U.S. government permitted Peter Bergin to review hundreds of pages of declassified, but unpublished memos from
the Abbottabad. The documents demonstrated several insights: that although bin Laden micromanaged a lot of details, he believed that al Qaeda
could reverse the larger picture, U.S. policy. The memos reveal some of
the schemes to attack the United States. The memos show many elements
about the al Qaeda organization. For example, the organization understood the American drone strikes in Pakistan's tribal regions had put it in
danger and that the attacks had been killing its leadership since summer
2008, that al Qaeda's brand name was in trouble because the organization
had killed so many people, and that a set of self-inflicted mistakes by al
Qaeda's affiliate in Iraq were of concern to bin Laden and his top advisers.
They complained internally that attacks against Iraqi Christians had not
been authorized by bin Laden.[64]

The CIA thwarted the al Qaeda plot to blow up civilian aircraft using
an advanced explosive device designed by the terrorist network's affiliate
in Yemen. The plot was stopped before any aircraft or passengers could
be put in harms way. The timing of the plot happened at the same time of
the United States' major escalation of the clandestine drone campaign in
Yemen. The explosive was improved and would likely avoid detection.

Even though the May 2012 al Qaeda plot to blow up an airplane with
an underwear bomb was stopped, predictions of al Qaeda's defeat appear
premature, according to Andrew Liepman, who stepped down on May 18,
2012 as deputy director of the National Counterterrorism Center. During

his tenure, he had monitored repeated threats. Strategically, al Qaeda has not been defeated, and bin Laden's global jihadist ideology still has effect, he contends.[65] The threat of AQAP is still growing because of its territorial gains that allow it to set up more training camps and make it more dangerous to the United States and its Western allies.[66] The United States increased intelligence capabilities, and counterterrorist actions including the drone offensive may reverse these gains and lead to the ultimate defeat of al Qaeda.

CONCLUSION

Suicide as a Weapon in War

Suicide has been a phenomenon in human societies for thousands of years. Each society responds to suicide in its own way. Whether a society accepts it or rejects it depends on how the society values life. If the societal belief is that life should be affirmed and should continue no matter what the circumstances, then suicide is rejected. If the societal belief is that the individual is to subjugate self to the will of the society, then there may be circumstances in which suicide is accepted as honorable and is rewarded. The 9/11 suicide bombers were given assurances that their sacrifice would receive rich rewards in the afterlife. A dilemma faces societies that believe in a positive afterlife and at the same time believe that life should be lived to its natural end. In Christian societies, the religious institutions teach about the perfect life after death, but admonish the faithful that they should not commit suicide to get there. Some even teach that a person who commits suicide will not receive rewards in the afterlife and, instead, will be eternally punished.

No matter what the societal beliefs are, suicide is a phenomenon that exists in all societies and must be understood to maintain or modify its existence in a society. Suicide in the context of war has three dimensions: as an attack weapon, as a method of defense, and as an effect. In World War II, the Japanese military used suicide attackers as part of its strategy to prevent the U.S. Navy from reaching the shores of Japan. Suicide attackers have been used by Germany, Russia, Hezbollah, Hamas, al Qaeda, Chechen rebels, and Tamil Tigers, among others.

SUICIDE AS WEAPON OF DEFENSE

Suicide as a defense has long been an instrument of individuals and groups in wars. Suicide as a defense occurs when a person kills herself or himself without attempting to kill or injure others. Weapons include swords, firearms, poisons, fire, and bombs. The common motivations for committing defensive suicide are to protest injustice, to avoid dishonor, to prevent being captured, and to avoid being tortured. The mass suicide of the 960 Zealot defenders of Masada in the first century was defensive suicide.[1] When Tunisian Mohamed Bouazizi set himself on fire to protest being denied a way to earn his living, his self-immolation sparked worldwide protest, which was the beginning of the "Arab Spring."[2]

In the aftermath of the Iraq and Afghanistan wars, a disturbing number of American military personnel have committed suicide. Since the start of the wars, more than 1,100 soldiers have taken their own lives, and the numbers are escalating. From 1977 to 2003, suicide rates in the army closely matched those in civilian population and were on a downward trend. After 2004, the army suicide rates began to climb rapidly. In 2007 and 2008, 255 active duty soldiers committed suicide, and in 2010, the number was 301. Since 2004, men committed suicide by a large majority; 69 percent of them had seen active combat duty. Nearly half were between ages 18 and 24. Fifty-four percent of those who committed suicide were lower-rank enlisted personnel. Suicide rates were higher among soldiers who had been diagnosed with a mental illness in the year before their death. Soldiers with major depression disorder were more than 11 times as likely to commit suicide, and those with anxiety are 10 times more likely. Posttraumatic stress disorder (PTSD) is receiving more attention and is being studied, in part, because of the increased likelihood that those diagnosed with PTSD will commit suicide.

SUICIDE AS A WEAPON OF ATTACK

In World War II, Japan deployed thousands of kamikaze (divine wind) pilots as it fought to keep the U.S. military from advancing to its shores. Japan's military was able to use suicide attackers as a tactic in its overall strategy to defeat the United States because the culture and individuals within the culture were willing to support the strategy. In this case, the culture, the military, and the individual were aligned. In other instances, in which suicide attackers have been used, the support of the culture, the military, or the individual was not there. When al Qaeda attacked the United States on 9/11, they did so in a country that does not support suicide as a choice for the individual or for society.

CULTURE

The culture in which suicide as a weapon of attack is used significantly affects whether the state or group that uses this weapon is successful.

When Al Qaeda attacked the United States, the American people—who reject suicide—supported the government's and the military's powerful response against al Qaeda and its ally, the Taliban, in Afghanistan. The war, begun one month after the 9/11 attacks, drove the Taliban from power within weeks.

The Japanese culture supported the use of suicide as a weapon, in part, because the name kamikaze means divine wind and reminded the Japanese people of the winds that blew the ships of Kubla Khan away from their shores and prevented an invasion in 1281AD. The culture was strong in nationalism and its allegiance to the emperor who was cloaked in divinity. It also had honor suicide by the Samurai. The cultures in Sri Lanka, Chechnya, Afghanistan, and Palestine did not historically support the use of suicide attackers. Support came from the nonstate groups that used them and from their followers, not from the dominant culture. In most cases where suicide attackers were used, it met stiff resistance from the general populace.

THE MILITARY

Why do the military use suicide attackers? Whether against the opposition's military or the civilian population, they are used because a single attacker can get closer to the target. Suicide attack is used as a tactic to supplement other means of waging the war as did al Qaeda. In Iraq and Afghanistan, al Qaeda has used suicide attackers against the U.S.-led forces, but they relied more on improvised explosive devices, car bombs, and conventional weapons. The Tamil Tigers used male and female attackers to assassinate high-profile targets like the Prime Minister of India and the President of Sri Lanka, but they also used other methods of combat. The Japanese did not begin the use of kamikaze pilots in the Battle of Leyte Gulf until October 1944, almost three years after Pearl Harbor. They used them in an effort to slow the U.S. Navy's steady march toward the Japanese mainland. Kamikaze planes did not have to return so they could be programmed to carry greater firepower. Not all Japanese attack planes were kamikaze. The Japanese military had other kamikaze units (submarines, torpedoes, and frogmen) ready if the U.S. forces got close to the mainland, but the dropping of atomic bombs on Hiroshima and Nagasaki ended the war before they could be fully used.

A major problem with using suicide attackers is attrition. A successful attacker can only be sent once. There is a concern about drop in the number and quality of the combat force. The early kamikaze pilots were better trained and had better equipment than did the pilots later in the war. Recruitment requires constant effort and the ability to motivate individuals to be a suicide attacker. Al Qaeda recruits that were involved in the 9/11 attacks in the United States were better trained and successful than those who came later: the shoe bomber, the underwear bomber, and the Times

Square bomber. The later attackers failed, in part, because they were not trained as a combatant would be and they did not have reliable equipment. They also failed because the methods of surveillance and detection had improved.

THE INDIVIDUAL AS A WEAPON

Why an individual is motivated to become a suicide attacker varies greatly with the conflict and the groups engaged in it. In the Palestinian–Israeli conflict, hatred for Israel's occupation of the Palestinian territories and its treatment of Palestinians since the 1967 war are powerful motivators. In Japan, nationalism and subservience to the will of the state were dominant motivators. The motivating reasons are sometimes personal: avenging the death of a relative, securing funds for relatives upon one's death, and promise of a rewarding afterlife. In any case, the motivation has to be tied to cause and be strong enough if the individual is to attach explosives to her or his body and blow oneself up.

OUTCOMES

No state or group that has used suicide attackers has reached its goal in the conflict. The kamikaze did not keep Japan from defeat in World War II. The Chechen rebels did not achieve independence from Russia. The Tamil Tigers did not gain a separate state. The Palestinians have not secured an agreement that gives them full control over their territory. Al Qaeda has not established bin Laden's Islamic caliphate. And yet, each state or group has inflicted immense damage on their targets. Al Qaeda on 9/11 destroyed the World Trade Center and over 3,000 lives. It inflicted damage on the Pentagon and destroyed the faith of the American public in the country's invincibility from attack. In its response, the United States has spent over $1 trillion on homeland security and other antiterrorism efforts, and $1 trillion and over 7,000 military lives on the wars in Afghanistan and Iraq. And that is only the easily identified damage. Japan inflicted severe damage on the U.S. Navy and its personnel. The Tamil Tigers were overcome when the Sri Lankan government conducted bloody attacks that took hundreds of Tamil lives.

SUICIDE ATTACKERS IN THE FUTURE

Suicide attacks continue. The number of groups that use them is increasing. Will they succeed in enabling a group to secure victory in its conflict? Probably not. Will they continue to be used in today's asymmetrical warfare? Yes.

APPENDIX

Documents

A. PRESIDENT GEORGE W. BUSH, THE NATIONAL SECURITY STRATEGY, PREEMPTIVE SELF-DEFENSE, "THE BUSH DOCTRINE"—EXCERPT

We will disrupt and destroy terrorist organizations by . . . defending the United States, the American people, and our interests at home and abroad by identifying and destroying the threat before it reaches our borders. While the United States will constantly strive to enlist the support of the international community, we will not hesitate to act alone, if necessary, to exercise our right of self-defense by acting pre-emptively against such terrorists, to prevent them from doing harm against our people and our country. . . . Given the goals of rogue states and terrorists, the United States can no longer solely rely on a reactive posture as we have in the past. The inability to deter a potential attacker, the immediacy of today's threats, and the magnitude of potential harm that could be caused by our adversaries' choice of weapons, do not permit that option. We cannot let our enemies strike first. . . . For centuries, international law recognized that nations need not suffer an attack before they can lawfully take action to defend themselves against forces that present an imminent danger of attack. Legal scholars and international jurists often conditioned the legitimacy of pre-emption on the existence of an imminent threat—most often a visible mobilization of armies, navies, and air forces preparing to attack. We must adapt the concept of imminent threat to the capabilities and objectives of today's adversaries. . . . The United States has long maintained the option of pre-emptive actions to counter a sufficient threat to our national security. The greater the threat, the greater is the risk of inaction—and the more compelling the case for taking anticipatory action to defend ourselves, even if uncertainty remains as to the time and place of the enemy's attack. To forestall or prevent such hostile acts by our adversaries, the United States will, if necessary, act pre-emptively.

Source: *The National Security Strategy of the United States of America* (Washington, D.C.: Government Printing Office, September 2002), http://georgewbush-white house.archives.gov/nsc/nss/2002/index.html.

B. PRESIDENT BARACK OBAMA'S ACCEPTANCE OF THE NOBEL PEACE PRIZE, OSLO, NORWAY, DECEMBER 10, 2009, JUST WAR—EXCERPT

I do not bring with me today a definitive solution to the problems of war. What I do know is that meeting these challenges will require the same vision, hard work, and persistence of those men and women who acted so boldly decades ago. And it will require us to think in new ways about the notions of just war and the imperatives of a just peace.

We must begin by acknowledging the hard truth: We will not eradicate violent conflict in our lifetimes. There will be times when nations—acting individually or in concert—will find the use of force not only necessary but morally justified.

I make this statement mindful of what Martin Luther King Jr. said in this same ceremony years ago: "Violence never brings permanent peace. It solves no social problem: it merely creates new and more complicated ones." As someone who stands here as a direct consequence of Dr. King's life work, I am living testimony to the moral force of non-violence. I know there's nothing weak—nothing passive—nothing naïve—in the creed and lives of Gandhi and King.

But as a head of state sworn to protect and defend my nation, I cannot be guided by their examples alone. I face the world as it is, and cannot stand idle in the face of threats to the American people. For make no mistake: Evil does exist in the world. A non-violent movement could not have halted Hitler's armies. Negotiations cannot convince al Qaeda's leaders to lay down their arms. To say that force may sometimes be necessary is not a call to cynicism—it is a recognition of history; the imperfections of man and the limits of reason.

I raise this point, I begin with this point because in many countries there is a deep ambivalence about military action today, no matter what the cause. And at times, this is joined by a reflexive suspicion of America, the world's sole military superpower.

But the world must remember that it was not simply international institutions—not just treaties and declarations—that brought stability to a post-World War II world. Whatever mistakes we have made, the plain fact is this: The United States of America has helped underwrite global security for more than six decades with the blood of our citizens and the strength of our arms. The service and sacrifice of our men and women in uniform has promoted peace and prosperity from Germany to Korea, and enabled democracy to take hold in places like the Balkans. We have borne this burden not because we seek to impose our will. We have done so out of enlightened self-interest—because we seek a better future for our children and grandchildren, and we believe that their lives will be better if others' children and grandchildren can live in freedom and prosperity.

So yes, the instruments of war do have a role to play in preserving the peace. And yet this truth must coexist with another—that no matter how justified, war promises human tragedy. The soldier's courage and sacrifice is full of glory, expressing devotion to country, to cause, to comrades in arms. But war itself is never glorious, and we must never trumpet it as such.

So part of our challenge is reconciling these two seemingly irreconcilable truths—that war is sometimes necessary, and war at some level is an expression of human folly. Concretely, we must direct our effort to the task that President Kennedy called for long ago. "Let us focus," he said, "on a more practical, more attainable peace, based not on a sudden revolution in human nature but on a gradual evolution in human institutions." A gradual evolution of human institutions.

What might this evolution look like? What might these practical steps be?

To begin with, I believe that all nations—strong and weak alike—must adhere to standards that govern the use of force. I—like any head of state—reserve the right to act unilaterally if necessary to defend my nation. Nevertheless, I am convinced that adhering to standards, international standards, strengthens those who do, and isolates and weakens those who don't.

The world rallied around America after the 9/11 attacks, and continues to support our efforts in Afghanistan, because of the horror of those senseless attacks and the recognized principle of self-defense. Likewise, the world recognized the need to confront Saddam Hussein when he invaded Kuwait—a consensus that sent a clear message to all about the cost of aggression.

Furthermore, America—in fact, no nation—can insist that others follow the rules of the road if we refuse to follow them ourselves. For when we don't, our actions appear arbitrary and undercut the legitimacy of future interventions, no matter how justified.

And this becomes particularly important when the purpose of military action extends beyond self-defense or the defense of one nation against an aggressor. More and more, we all confront difficult questions about how to prevent the slaughter of civilians by their own government, or to stop a civil war whose violence and suffering can engulf an entire region.

I believe that force can be justified on humanitarian grounds, as it was in the Balkans, or in other places that have been scarred by war. Inaction tears at our conscience and can lead to more costly intervention later. That's why all responsible nations must embrace the role that militaries with a clear mandate can play to keep the peace.

America's commitment to global security will never waver. But in a world in which threats are more diffuse, and missions more complex, America cannot act alone. America alone cannot secure the peace. This is true in Afghanistan. This is true in failed states like Somalia, where terrorism and piracy is joined by famine and human suffering. And sadly, it will continue to be true in unstable regions for years to come.

The leaders and soldiers of NATO countries, and other friends and allies, demonstrate this truth through the capacity and courage they've shown in Afghanistan. But in many countries, there is a disconnect between the efforts of those who serve and the ambivalence of the broader public. I understand why war is not popular, but I also know this: The belief that peace is desirable is rarely enough to achieve it. Peace requires responsibility. Peace entails sacrifice. That's why NATO continues to be indispensable. That's why we must strengthen U.N. and regional peacekeeping, and not leave the task to a few countries. That's why we honor those who return home from peacekeeping and training abroad to Oslo and Rome; to Ottawa and Sydney; to Dhaka and Kigali—we honor them not as makers of war, but of wagers—but as wagers of peace.

Let me make one final point about the use of force. Even as we make difficult decisions about going to war, we must also think clearly about how we fight it. The Nobel Committee recognized this truth in awarding its first prize for peace to Henry Dunant—the founder of the Red Cross, and a driving force behind the Geneva Conventions.

Where force is necessary, we have a moral and strategic interest in binding ourselves to certain rules of conduct. And even as we confront a vicious adversary that abides by no rules, I believe the United States of America must remain a standard bearer in the conduct of war. That is what makes us different from those whom we fight. That is a source of our strength. That is why I prohibited torture. That is why I ordered the prison at Guantanamo Bay closed. And that is why I have reaffirmed America's commitment to abide by the Geneva Conventions. We lose ourselves when we compromise the very ideals that we fight to defend. (Applause.) And we honor—we honor those ideals by upholding them not when it's easy, but when it is hard.

I have spoken at some length to the question that must weigh on our minds and our hearts as we choose to wage war. But let me now turn to our effort to avoid such tragic choices, and speak of three ways that we can build a just and lasting peace.

First, in dealing with those nations that break rules and laws, I believe that we must develop alternatives to violence that are tough enough to actually change behavior—for if we want a lasting peace, then the words of the international community must mean something. Those regimes that break the rules must be held accountable. Sanctions must exact a real price. Intransigence must be met with increased pressure—and such pressure exists only when the world stands together as one.

One urgent example is the effort to prevent the spread of nuclear weapons, and to seek a world without them. In the middle of the last century, nations agreed to be bound by a treaty whose bargain is clear: All will have access to peaceful nuclear power; those without nuclear weapons will forsake them; and those with nuclear weapons will work towards disarmament. I am committed to upholding this treaty. It is a centerpiece of my foreign policy. And I'm working with President Medvedev to reduce America and Russia's nuclear stockpiles.

But it is also incumbent upon all of us to insist that nations like Iran and North Korea do not game the system. Those who claim to respect international law cannot avert their eyes when those laws are flouted. Those who care for their own security cannot ignore the danger of an arms race in the Middle East or East Asia. Those who seek peace cannot stand idly by as nations arm themselves for nuclear war.

The same principle applies to those who violate international laws by brutalizing their own people. When there is genocide in Darfur, systematic rape in Congo, repression in Burma—there must be consequences. Yes, there will be engagement; yes, there will be diplomacy—but there must be consequences when those things fail. And the closer we stand together, the less likely we will be faced with the choice between armed intervention and complicity in oppression.

This brings me to a second point—the nature of the peace that we seek. For peace is not merely the absence of visible conflict. Only a just peace based on the inherent rights and dignity of every individual can truly be lasting.

It was this insight that drove drafters of the Universal Declaration of Human Rights after the Second World War. In the wake of devastation, they recognized that if human rights are not protected, peace is a hollow promise.

And yet too often, these words are ignored. For some countries, the failure to uphold human rights is excused by the false suggestion that these are somehow Western principles, foreign to local cultures or stages of a nation's development. And within America, there has long been a tension between those who describe themselves as realists or idealists—a tension that suggests a stark choice between the narrow pursuit of interests or an endless campaign to impose our values around the world.

I reject these choices. I believe that peace is unstable where citizens are denied the right to speak freely or worship as they please; choose their own leaders or assemble without fear. Pent-up grievances fester, and the suppression of tribal and religious identity can lead to violence. We also know that the opposite is true. Only when Europe became free did it finally find peace. America has never fought a war against a democracy, and our closest friends are governments that protect the rights of their citizens. No matter how callously defined, neither America's interests—nor the world's—are served by the denial of human aspirations.

So even as we respect the unique culture and traditions of different countries, America will always be a voice for those aspirations that are universal. We will bear witness to the quiet dignity of reformers like Aung Sang Suu Kyi; to the bravery of Zimbabweans who cast their ballots in the face of beatings; to the hundreds of thousands who have marched silently through the streets of Iran. It is telling that the leaders of these governments fear the aspirations of their own people more than the power of any other nation. And it is the responsibility of all free people and free nations to make clear that these movements—these movements of hope and history—they have us on their side.

Let me also say this: The promotion of human rights cannot be about exhortation alone. At times, it must be coupled with painstaking diplomacy. I know that engagement with repressive regimes lacks the satisfying purity of indignation. But I also know that sanctions without outreach—condemnation without discussion—can carry forward only a crippling status quo. No repressive regime can move down a new path unless it has the choice of an open door.

In light of the Cultural Revolution's horrors, Nixon's meeting with Mao appeared inexcusable—and yet it surely helped set China on a path where millions of its citizens have been lifted from poverty and connected to open societies. Pope John Paul's engagement with Poland created space not just for the Catholic Church, but for labor leaders like Lech Walesa. Ronald Reagan's efforts on arms control and embrace of perestroika not only improved relations with the Soviet Union, but empowered dissidents throughout Eastern Europe. There's no simple formula here. But we must try as best we can to balance isolation and engagement, pressure and incentives, so that human rights and dignity are advanced over time.

Third, a just peace includes not only civil and political rights—it must encompass economic security and opportunity. For true peace is not just freedom from fear, but freedom from want.

It is undoubtedly true that development rarely takes root without security; it is also true that security does not exist where human beings do not have access to enough food, or clean water, or the medicine and shelter they need to survive. It does not exist where children can't aspire to a decent education or a job that supports a family. The absence of hope can rot a society from within.

And that's why helping farmers feed their own people—or nations educate their children and care for the sick—is not mere charity. It's also why the world must come together to confront climate change. There is little scientific dispute that if we do nothing, we will face more drought, more famine, more mass displacement—all of which will fuel more conflict for decades. For this reason, it is not merely scientists and environmental activists who call for swift and forceful action—it's military leaders in my own country and others who understand our common security hangs in the balance.

Agreements among nations. Strong institutions. Support for human rights. Investments in development. All these are vital ingredients in bringing about the evolution that President Kennedy spoke about. And yet, I do not believe that we will have the will, the determination, the staying power, to complete this work without something more—and that's the continued expansion of our moral imagination; an insistence that there's something irreducible that we all share.

As the world grows smaller, you might think it would be easier for human beings to recognize how similar we are; to understand that we're all basically seeking the same things; that we all hope for the chance to live out our lives with some measure of happiness and fulfillment for ourselves and our families.

And yet somehow, given the dizzying pace of globalization, the cultural leveling of modernity, it perhaps comes as no surprise that people fear the loss of what they cherish in their particular identities—their race, their tribe, and perhaps most powerfully their religion. In some places, this fear has led to conflict. At times, it even feels like we're moving backwards. We see it in the Middle East, as the conflict between Arabs and Jews seems to harden. We see it in nations that are torn asunder by tribal lines.

And most dangerously, we see it in the way that religion is used to justify the murder of innocents by those who have distorted and defiled the great religion of Islam, and who attacked my country from Afghanistan. These extremists are not the first to kill in the name of God; the cruelties of the Crusades are amply recorded. But they remind us that no Holy War can ever be a just war. For if you truly believe that you are carrying out divine will, then there is no need for restraint—no need to spare the pregnant mother, or the medic, or the Red Cross worker, or even a person of one's own faith. Such a warped view of religion is not just incompatible with the concept of peace, but I believe it's incompatible with the very purpose of faith—for the one rule that lies at the heart of every major religion is that we do unto others as we would have them do unto us.

Adhering to this law of love has always been the core struggle of human nature. For we are fallible. We make mistakes, and fall victim to the temptations of pride, and power, and sometimes evil. Even those of us with the best of intentions will at times fail to right the wrongs before us.

But we do not have to think that human nature is perfect for us to still believe that the human condition can be perfected. We do not have to live in an idealized world to still reach for those ideals that will make it a better place. The non-violence practiced by men like Gandhi and King may not have been practical or possible in every circumstance, but the

love that they preached—their fundamental faith in human progress—
that must always be the North Star that guides us on our journey. For if
we lose that faith—if we dismiss it as silly or naïve; if we divorce it from
the decisions that we make on issues of war and peace—then we lose
what's best about humanity. We lose our sense of possibility. We lose
our moral compass. Like generations have before us, we must reject that
future. As Dr. King said at this occasion so many years ago, "I refuse to
accept despair as the final response to the ambiguities of history. I refuse
to accept the idea that the 'isness' of man's present condition makes him
morally incapable of reaching up for the eternal 'oughtness' that forever
confronts him." Let us reach for the world that ought to be—that spark
of the divine that still stirs within each of our souls. (Applause.)

Somewhere today, in the here and now, in the world as it is, a soldier
sees he's outgunned, but stands firm to keep the peace. Somewhere today,
in this world, a young protestor awaits the brutality of her government,
but has the courage to march on. Somewhere today, a mother facing punishing poverty still takes the time to teach her child, scrapes together what
few coins she has to send that child to school—because she believes that a
cruel world still has a place for that child's dreams.

Let us live by their example. We can acknowledge that oppression will
always be with us, and still strive for justice. We can admit the intractabil-
ity of depravation, and still strive for dignity. Clear-eyed, we can understand that there will be war, and still strive for peace. We can do that—for
that is the story of human progress; that's the hope of all the world; and at
this moment of challenge, that must be our work here on Earth.

Source: Barack Obama, "Remarks by the President at the Acceptance of the Nobel
Peace Prize," *The White House*, December 10, 2009, http://www.whitehouse.gov/
the-press-office/remarks-president-acceptance-nobel-peace-prize.

C. AL QAEDA'S SEVEN STAGES PLAN*

1. The Awakening from 2000 to 2003: the planning of the 9/11 attacks to the
American entrance into the Iraq war. Qaeda's strategic experts reported that
the Americans were obliged to leave their traditional bases making Americans
and their allies closer and easier targets.

2. The Eye-Opening from 2003 to 2006. This phase realizes direct confrontations
with Israel, burning Arab oil to deprive the West and its allies; electronic jihad;
preparation of the second generation leadership; using Iraq as a base to build
an army; and preparation of Islamic law studies so that Muslims can provide
the mujahidin financial and material support, and to dry up American financial
resources.

3. Arising and Standing on Our Own Two Feet from 2007–2010. The Jihadi operations shift from Iraq to Syria, Lebanon, Jordan, and Israel as well as the Jewish
population in Turkey. In this stage, al Qaeda will earn the support of educated
youth to carry out Stage Four.

4. Healing and Gathering Strength for Change from 2010 to 2013. Burning Arab oil continues to cause the economies of the U.S. and other enemy regimes to fail. A mature effort for an electronic war will be utilized to weaken the United States' economy. Springer et al. report that Hasnin maintained that al Qaeda recruited economists and researchers to refute the theory that American and Jewish economies can print money without needing to support it with precious metals. Al Qaeda would emphasize the importance of backing currency with gold and world markets would go back to a gold standard, devaluing the dollar. This devaluation, lack of access to Arab oil, and exhaustion from constant war causes a currency crisis. Countries will withdraw investments from the U.S. American and Jewish economists who introduced the printing of money theory actually purchased precious metals as a safety measure against economic depression. But the American people will view it as a deception, a major transition will take place and American support for Israel will decrease.

5. Proclaiming the State from 2013 to 2016. The control of United States' on the Arab regions will have been weakened. Israel will no longer be able to execute assassinations. China and India will become new powers. The European Union will discontinue. The Jihad will establish an Islamic caliphate.

6. The Total Confrontation Stage from 2016 to 2020. The world will be divided into the camp of the faith and the camp of the infidels.

7. The Final Victory in 2020. More than one and a half billion Jihadists will terrorize their enemies, particularly Israel as the Islamic caliphate leads the human race.

Source Note: Based on the International Institute for Counter-Terrorism (ICT); Springer et al. contribute to Stage Four.

Sources: "Al-Qaeda's Operational Strategies—The Attempt to Revive the Debate Surrounding the Seven Stages Plan," *International Institute for Counter-Terrorism,* July 2009, http://www.ict.org.il/Portals/0/Internet%20Monitoring%20Group/ JWMG_Al-Qaeda_Operational_Strategies.pdf and Devin R. Springer, James L. Regens, and David N. Edger, *Islamic Radicalism and Global Jihad* (Washington, D.C.: Georgetown University Press, 2009), 77.

D. CHECHEN SEPARATIST NOTE OF DEMANDS TO PRESIDENT PUTIN, AUGUST 30, 2004

Vladimir Putin, you were not the one to start the war, but you could be the one to end it, that is if you find the courage and resolve to act like de Gaulle. We are offering you peace on a mutually beneficial basis in line with the principle "independence for security." We can guarantee that if you withdraw the [Russian] troops and recognize Chechen independence, then: we will not strike any political, military or economic deals with anyone against Russia; we will not have any foreign military bases even temporary ones; we will not support or finance groups fighting the Russian Federation; we will join the Commonwealth of Independent States; we will stay in the ruble zone; we could sign the Collective Security Treaty, although we would prefer the status of a neutral state; we can guarantee that all of Russia's Muslims will refrain from armed methods of struggle against the Russian Federation, at least for 10–15 years, on condition that freedom of religion is respected. . . . The Chechen nation is involved in the national liberation struggle for its Freedom and Independence and for its preservation. It is not fighting to humiliate Russia or destroy it. As a free nation, we are interested in a strong neighbor.

We are offering peace and the choice is yours.

Source: *Terror Operations: Case Studies in Terrorism*, TRADOC G2 Handbook No. 1.01 (Fort Leavenworth, KS: U.S. Army Training and Doctrine Command, July 25, 2007), 6–23, http://www.fas.org/irp/threat/terrorism/sup1.pdf.

E. THE KILLING OF OSAMA BIN LADEN

Part 1

May 1 2011, 1:10 A.M. local Pakistan time.(Monday in Pakistan, Sunday afternoon, 4:00 EDT, in Washington D.C.) Osama bin Laden is killed by a bullet fired by a United States Navy SEAL during a 40 minute helicopter assault on bin Laden's compound in Abbottabad, Pakistan. (Location is about 100 miles from the Afghanistan border on the far eastern side of Pakistan (about 20 miles from India). The compound is 0.8 miles southwest of the Pakistan Military Academy.). Two helicopters with forty members of SEAL Team Six, the Naval Special Warfare Development Group aboard, land inside the compound. Helicopter pilots are from the 160th Special Ops Air Regiment, part of the Joint Special Operations Command. The CIA is the operational commander of the mission, but it is tasked to Special Forces.[1] In the ensuing firefight, two Bin Laden couriers, one of Osama Bin Laden's sons, Khaled, and a woman used as a shield by one of the men are killed. Other women and children present are not harmed. *ABC News* reports that, according to U.S. officials, bin Laden fired his weapon, was asked to surrender but did not. A CH47 Chinook helicopter is damaged during the landing. U.S. forces destroy it. The compound is searched to secure intelligence material. Bin Laden's body is taken to Afghanistan to verify his identity.[2] U.S. officials match bin Laden's DNA with DNA sample taken from his late sister's brain. At 1:00 A.M. EDT, Monday (10:10 A.M., Monday, Pakistan time) bin Laden's body taken to the aircraft carrier USS *Carl Vinson* and buried in the northern part of the Arabian Sea. Traditional Islamic rites are performed.[3]

May 1, 2011, afternoon, Situation Room, Obama meets with senior officials. At 3:50 p.m. EDT Obama learns bin Laden is tentatively identified.[4]

May 1, 2011, 11.35 P.M. Sunday President Obama tells the nation in a speech from the White House: "Good evening. Tonight, I can report to the American people and to the world that the United States has conducted an operation that killed Osama bin Laden, the leader of al Qaeda, and a terrorist who's responsible for the murder of thousands of innocent men, women, and children."[5]

May 3, 2011 White House Press Secretary Jay Carney gives the official statement.

On orders of the president, a small U.S. team assaulted a secure compound in an affluent suburb of Islamabad to capture or kill Osama bin Laden.

The raid was conducted with U.S. military personnel assaulting on two helicopters. The team methodically cleared the compound moving from room to room in an operation lasting nearly 40 minutes. They were engaged in a firefight throughout the operation and Osama Bin Laden was killed by the assaulting force.

In addition to the bin Laden family, two other families resided in the compound: one family on the first floor of the bin Laden building and one family in a second building. One team began the operation on the first floor of the bin Laden house and worked their way to the third floor; a second team cleared the separate building.

On the first floor of bin Laden's building, two Al Qaeda couriers were killed along with a woman who was killed in cross-fire. Bin Laden and his family were found on the second and third floor of the building. There was concern that bin Laden would oppose the capture operation and indeed he resisted.

In the room with bin Laden, a woman—bin Laden's wife—rushed the U.S. assaulter and was shot in the leg but not killed. Bin Laden was then shot and killed. He was not armed.

Following the firefight, the non-combatants were moved to a safe location as the damaged helicopter was detonated.

The team departed the scene via helicopter to the USS *Carl Vinson* in the North Arabian Sea.

Aboard the USS *Carl Vinson*, the burial of bin Laden was done in conformance with Islamic precepts and practices. The deceased's body was washed and then placed in a white sheet. The body was placed in a weighted bag; a military officer read prepared religious remarks, which were translated into Arabic by a native speaker. After the words were complete, the body was placed on a prepared flat board, tipped up, and the deceased body eased into the sea.[6]

Part 2 Events Leading up to the Assault on bin Laden's Compound

April 30, 2011, Friday, afternoon. National security adviser Thomas E. Donilon prepares the formal orders for the operation. He arranges a meeting with senior national security officials to plan for the operation

April 30, 2011, Friday, 8:20 a.m. Diplomatic Room with senior officials present, Obama gives the order for the action that ends in bin Laden's death.[7]

February 2011, midway Obama decides there is a sound intelligence for pursuing bin Laden and develops courses of action in case it proved correct.[8]

March 2011, second half Obama holds five National Security meetings to discuss possible action.[9]

September 2010 CIA works with Obama on a set of intelligence assessment that leads him to believe bin Laden is located in the compound.[10]

September 2010 Eight months before Osama bin Laden's death, the original tip-off to the CIA is made.[11]

2009 After years of searching for the courier, U.S. officials narrow down the region in Pakistan where he works.[12]

August 2009 U.S. officials find bin Laden's compound.[13]

2002–2003 Time uncertain during Guantanamo Detainees Interrogation. Khalid Sheikh Mohammed (KSM) is reported to have been repeatedly subjected to methods of torture including waterboarding" and stress positions. He provides the CIA with the name of bin Laden's personal courier that does not appear in his file, but rather in file of detainee Abu Faraj al-Libi, the name, Maulawi Abd al-Khaliq, appears.[14]

Part 3 Selected Events of al Qaeda Causing the 10-Year Hunt of bin Laden

September 11, 2001 Hijackings of U.S. aircraft.[15]

August 7, 1998 Bombing attacks on the U.S. Embassies in Nairobi, Kenya and Dar es Salaam, Tanzania.[16]

1988 Bin Laden and other radicals found al Qaeda.[17]

F. OSAMA BIN LADEN'S LAST LETTER, LATE MAY 2010, TO SHAYKH MAHMUD ('ATIYYA)—EXCERPT

Page 3

Regarding military activities:

The conditions that grew more serious after the attacks on New York and Washington and the Crusader campaign against Afghanistan filled Muslims with sympathy toward their fellow Mujahidin, as it became patently clear that the Mujahidin are the vanguard and standard-bearers of the Islamic community in fighting the Crusader-Zionist alliance that has caused the people to endure various forms of pain and degradation. One indication of that is the wide-scale spread of Jihadist ideology, especially on the Internet, and the tremendous number of young people who frequent the Jihadist websites—a major achievement for Jihad, through the grace of God, despite our enemies and their efforts.

On the other hand, after the war expanded and the Mujahidin spread out into many regions, some of the brothers became totally absorbed in fighting our local enemies, and more mistakes have

Page 4

been made due to miscalculations by the brothers planning the operations or something that arises before it is carried out, in addition to some who have expanded the "barricade argument" (TN: on whether it is acceptable to kill Muslims being used as human shields by the enemy) which has resulted in the killing of Muslims (we ask God to have mercy on them and forgive them, and compensate their families). I reckon that the barricade argument was been debated centuries ago amid circumstances different from those of today, and it needs to be revisited based on the modern-day context and clear boundaries established for all the brothers, so that no Muslims fall victim except when it is absolutely essential.

Amongst the mistakes made were the killing of some, the Muslims did not understand the justification behind allowing their killing. As you may know, one of the principles of Shari'ah is to bring in the interests and repulse evil. This is what the Messenger of Allah, Peace and Prayers be upon him had done with the head of hypocrisy 'Abdallah Bin Abi; not to underestimate the fact that these issues, amongst others, led to the loss of the Muslims sympathetic approach towards the Mujahidin. What also led to the loss of the Mujahidin was exploitation of the foes to several of their mistakes and tainting their picture before the crowds of the nation; the purpose was to split them from their popular bases, and needless to say that this issue involving the loss of the nation's audience paralyzed the Jihadist movements.

Here is an important issue that we should pay attention to; carrying out several attacks without exercising caution, which impacted the sympathy of the nation's crowds towards the Mujahidin. It would lead us to winning several battles while losing the war at the end. It requires an accurate criteria for the ramifications of any attack prior to carrying it out; also weighing the advantages and disadvantages, to then determine what would be the most likely to carry out.

Page 5

There is the need to collect anything within the capacity to collect—such as information, especially the Afghanistan commando operations carried out by the Mujahidin or others, the Palestinian Liberation Organization; also to study the advantages and disadvantages as the study would include two aspects:

The aspect of the operational steps required to ensure the success of the operation, or the hindrances leading to its failure, as well as the impact on the foe.

The other aspect involves the impact on the nation's impression towards the Mujahidin and being sympathetic towards them. The operations that bear extreme negative impact on the partisans of the Jihad include targeting the apostates in mosques or nearby—such as the assassination attempt of Dustum during the holiday worship location, and the assassination of General Muhammad Yusuf in one of the Pakistani mosques. It is extremely sad for an individual to fall into the same mistake more than once.

I would also like to seek your advice on an opinion as follows: whatever exceeds our capability or what we are unable to disburse on attacks inside America, as well as on the Jihad in open fronts, would be disbursed targeting American interests in non-Islamic countries first, such as South Korea. We shall avoid carrying out attacks in Islamic countries except for the countries that fell under invasion and direct occupation.

There are two major reasons to avoid carrying out attacks in Islamic countries as follows: the first involves attacks amongst the Muslims which would increase the possibility of victims amongst them; even though the brothers were previously warned not to expand the shield issue (TN: possibly killing Muslims who are being used as human shields by the enemy), that was not made clear to them. The operational fact continues to expand in terms of the shield.

Page 6

Firstly, it holds us responsible before Allah, praise and glory be to him, while in reality it holds us responsible for the losses and damages in the call to Jihad.

The second reason is the extremely great damage that impacts the brothers in the region where the work begins, following the alert of the state against the youths who are engaged in the Jihad work or even the preaching work. Tens of thousands are being arrested, similar to what happened in Egypt, and the arrest of thousands such as in the country of the two holy sanctuaries (TN: Saudi Arabia), while the issue is one involving time. The fact requires that we maintain the attrition of the head of disbelief (TN: Kufar) and the life artery of these apostate organizations on open fronts without bearing additional losses on the Jihad; by that, eliminating the ruler's despotism with these large numbers of devoted youths and Muslim prisoners.

When the global disbelief reaches the level of attrition, it would lead to its collapse; we would then engage in a conflict with the rulers, after they have been weakened following its weakness. We would then find the brothers there with their entire strength and energy.

Some of the disadvantages in carrying out attacks against the Americans in Islamic countries, where the components for success had not been prepared and the removal of the ruler is in an effort for the Americans not to accuse it of failing, the regime shall have a huge reaction towards the Mujahidin; this would lead to defending themselves and avenging the regime. The brothers and the regime would then engage in a war which we did not begin against it, because the power of the brothers is not ready for it, as such it would be one result.

The disadvantages in engaging as previously mentioned would change the general line—meaning to avoid wasting our energy with these regimes at this stage; that, in addition to losing the sympathy of the Muslims towards us.

Page 7

This is when we lose the perception of the Muslims towards us, which is that we are the ones defending the Muslims and fighting their biggest enemy, the Crusader Zionist alliance—without killing those that the general public consider Muslims.

So, if we fight the rulers while being in this situation, and we do not respond other than with direct defense during their offense against us, and this issue is being repeated several times, it would appear that we are wronged and the rulers are the tyrants; it would increase the hatred of the people towards them and make them feel that the rulers did not defend our brothers in Palestine, Iraq and Afghanistan. They were not content with that, but they fought the Mujahidin that defend our people there.

However, if we engage in a fight against the rulers outside the direct defense, we would have eliminated the damage the rulers would have carried out in their fight against us; the reason is that it would reveal the truth, and the media shall demonstrate to the people that we are the ones fighting the government and killing the Muslims. Between the roar of the killing and the fight, the people shall forget who began the fight against the other—as such we shall lose the people and strengthen the stance of the government without cutting its hostility against us.

What aids the success of our fight against the Americans in non-Islamic countries and reducing its cost, is for limited groups, distanced from the Muslim and devout circles, to launch from countries with the Mujahidin presence without announcing their launching location; this is to avoid the reaction against the Mujahidin in that country. Given the potential for the foes to reveal that issue, it would be better for the training to be carried out and launched from the open fronts where naturally the foes would be exerting their utmost efforts.

Page 8

Amongst the opportunities to be exploited in targeting the Americans is the state of security laxity found in countries where we had not carried out any attacks.

Given that the difference of the impact of attacks against the foes inside or outside of America is substantial, we need to confirm to the brothers that every effort that could be spent on attacks in America would not be spent outside of it.

The overflow of the work (TN: meaning attacks) outside of America and the work in non-Islamic countries could be spent in targeting the U.S. interests in the Islamic countries where we have no bases or partisans or Jihadist Islamic groups that could be threatened by danger. The Islamic groups there would express their stance against us and renounce us—a fact that would prevent the regime from retaliating against them following our attacks. The condition is to be extremely cautious and take necessary measures to avoid misleading the Muslims in these operations.

Source: Don Rassler, Gabriel Koehler-Derrick, Liam Collins, Muhammad al-Obaidi, and Nelly Lahoud, "Letters from Abbottabad: Bin Ladin Sidelined?" *Combating Terrorism Center at West Point,* May 03, 2012, Osama bin Laden letter to Shaykh Mahmud (Atiyaa), File SOCOM-2012-0000019, 3–8, http://www.ctc.usma.edu/posts/letters-from-abbottabad-bin-ladin-sidelined.

Notes

PREFACE

1. Peter Baker, Helene Cooper, and Mark Mazzetti, "Bin Laden Is Dead, Obama Says," *The New York Times*, May 1, 2011, http://www.nytimes.com/2011/05/02/world/asia/osama-bin-laden-is-killed.html.

2. Suicide Attack Search Database, *Chicago Project on Security and Terrorism (CPOST)*, October 14, 2011, http://cpost.uchicago.edu/search.php; "Georgia Cities Ranked by Population (Based on 2010 U.S. Census)," *GeorgiaInfo*, http://georgiainfo.galileo.usg.edu/citypopulationrank.htm; and "Selected Cities in the World with 30,000 to 35,000 Inhabitants in 2005," *Mongabay.com*, 2007, http://www.mongabay.com/igapo/2005_world_city_populations/2005_city_population_24.html.

3. Emile Durkheim, *Suicide: A Study in Sociology*, trans. John A. Spaulding and George Simpson, ed. George Simpson (New York: Free Press, 1951), 299.

4. Jörg Rössel and Randall Collin, "Conflict Theory and Interaction Rituals: The Microfoundations of Conflict Theory," in *Handbook of Sociological Theory*, ed. Jonathan H. Turner (New York: Kluwer Academic/Plenum, 2001), 528.

PART I

1. Mills, C. Wright, *The Sociological Imagination* (New York: Oxford University Press, 1959), 5, 7.

2. Peter Berger, *Invitation to Sociology: A Humanistic Perspective* (Garden City, NY: Doubleday, 1963), 67.

3. Dr. Zaki Badawi, Chair, Council of Imams and Mosques, London, interview, April 11, 2005, quoted in Abdel Bari Atwan, *The Secret History of al Qaeda*,

2nd ed. (Berkeley, CA: University of California Press, 2008), 90, 91. See also *Bible,* Judges 16: 25–30.

4. Richard Jackson, Department of International Politics, Aberystwyth University, Aberystwyth, interview by Rosemarie Skaine, e-mail, June 14, 2011. See also Jacob Bercovitch and Richard Jackson, *Conflict Resolution in the 21st Century: Principles, Methods, and Approaches* (Ann Arbor, MI: University of Michigan Press, 2009).

5. "America and Its Profession of Arms, Is the Relationship Healthy?" presented at U.S. Army War College's American Society and Its Profession of Arms XXII Annual Strategy Conference, Carlisle, PA, April 5–7, 2011, https://www.strategicstudiesinstitute.army.mil/.

6. John Sterling, closing keynote on April 7, 2011 at U.S. Army War College's American Society and Its Profession of Arms XXII Annual Strategy Conference, Carlisle, PA, April 5–7, 2011, http://www.youtube.com/watch?v=om1kYJHthRU&feature=mfu_in_order&list=UL. See also Bob Woodward, *Obama's Wars* (New York: Simon & Schuster, 2010); Daniel Bates and Mark Duell, "'Death Squad': Full Horror Emerges of How Rogue U.S. Brigade Murdered and Mutilated Innocent Afghan Civilians—and Kept Their Body Parts as Trophies," *Mail Online,* September 23, 2011, http://www.dailymail.co.uk/news/article-1370758/Shocking-video-shows-U-S-troops-cheering-airstrike-blows-Afghan-civilians.html; and Kristina Wong, "Rising Suicides Stump Military Leaders," *ABC Good Morning America,* September 27, 2011, http://abcnews.go.com/US/rising-suicides-stump-military-leaders/story?id=14578134.

7. Sterling, XXII Annual Strategy Conference.

8. Ibid.

9. Rhonda Cornum, "Comprehensive Soldier Fitness: Strong Minds, Strong Bodies," keynote address, power point presentation at WREI Women in the Military Conference, Arlington, VA, September 25, 2009, http://www.4militarywomen.org/WIM09Presentations/Cornum.pdf, quoted in Skaine, *Women in Combat: A Reference Handbook* (Santa Barbara, CA: ABC-CLIO/Greenwood, 2011), 54.

10. Aqil Shah, "Getting the Military Out of Pakistani Politics," *Foreign Affairs* 90, no. 3 (2011): 69–82.

11. Bryan R. Early, "Larger Than a Party, yet Smaller Than a State: Locating Hezbollah's Place within Lebanon's State and Society," *World Affairs* 168, no. 3 (2006): 115–28.

12. Jeremy Lind and Jude Howell, "Counter-terrorism and the Politics of Aid: Civil Society Responses in Kenya," *Development and Change* 41, no. 2 (2010): 335, 351, http://onlinelibrary.wiley.com/doi/10.1111/j.1467-7660.2010.01637.x/abstract;jsessionid=4A7838AAB3A9F9E338376A63BCA8E328.d03t04.

13. David B. Muhlhausen and Jena Baker McNeill, *Terror Trends: 40 Years' Data on International and Domestic Terrorism* (Washington, D.C.: The Heritage Foundation, May 20, 2011), http://report.heritage.org/sr0093.

14. National Counterterrorism Center, *2010 Report on Terrorism* (Washington, D.C.: U.S. Office of the Director of National Intelligence, April 30, 2011), 8, http://nctc.gov/.

15. Scott Helfstein, Nassir Abdullah, and Muhammad al-Obaidi, *Deadly Vanguards: A Study of al-Qa'ida's Violence against Muslims* (West Point, NY: Combating Terrorism Center, December 2009), 2, http://www.ctc.usma.edu/wp-content/uploads/2010/10/deadly-vanguards_complete_l.pdf.

CHAPTER 1

1. Ronald M. Holmes and Stephen T. Holmes, *Suicide: Theory, Practice, and Investigation* (Thousand Oaks, CA: Sage Publications, 2005), 2.

2. Lee A. Headley, *Suicide in Asia and the Near East* (Berkeley, CA: University of California Press, 1982), 350.

3. Holmes and Holmes, *Suicide*, 3, 27–32 and Robert A. Pape, *Dying to Win: The Strategic Logic of Suicide Terrorism* (New York: Random House, 2005), 186, 187, 197, 198, 200, 201, 211.

4. Emile Durkheim, *Suicide: A Study in Sociology*, trans. John A. Spaulding and George Simpson, ed. George Simpson (New York: Free Press, 1951), 15.

5. Ibid., 15, 276 note 25.

6. Ibid, 16.

7. Ibid., 22, 23, 25, 26, 37 quoted in Rosemarie Skaine, *Female Suicide Bombers* (Jefferson, NC: McFarland, 2006), 1, 2.

8. Ibid, 299.

9. Randall Collins, *Conflict Sociology: Towards an Explanatory Science* (New York: Academic Press, 1975), quoted in Jörg Rössel and Randall Collins, "Conflict Theory and Interaction Rituals: The Microfoundations of Conflict Theory," in *Handbook of Sociological Theory*, ed. Jonathan H. Turner (New York: Kluwer Academic/Plenum, 2001), 528.

10. Ibid.

11. John Carpenter, "Conflict, War, and Terrorism," *Sociology B2: Problems of a Modern Society*, Power Point Presentation No. 15 (Bakersfield, CA: Bakersfield College, Spring 2011), Slides 15, 25, 26, 31, 32, www2.bakersfieldcollege.edu/jcarpenter/PowerPoint/B2/chap%2015a.ppt.

12. Ibid., Slides 35–38.

13. U.S. Air Force, Secretary of the Air Force, *Irregular Warfare*, Air Force Doctrine Document 2–3, August 1, 2007, 2, http://www.fas.org/irp/doddir/usaf/afdd2-3.pdf.

14. Rosemarie Skaine, *Women in Combat: A Reference Handbook* (Santa Barbara, CA: ABC-CLIO/Greenwood, 2011), 307.

15. John Kelsay, *Islam and War* (Louisville, KY: John Knox Press, 1993), 106, 107, quoted in Youssef H Aboul-Enein and Sherifa Zuhu, *Islamic Rulings on Warfare* (Carlisle, PA: Strategic Studies Institute, U.S. Army War College, October 2004), http://insct.syr.edu/uploadedFiles/insct/uploadedfiles/PDFs/Aboul-Enein.Zuhur.Islamic%20Rulings%20on%20Warfare(1).pdf.

16. Aboul-Enein and Zuhur, *Islamic Rulings*, 28.

17. M. Zajam, "Suicide Missions: Nothing Islamic about It," *TwoCircles.net*, February 20, 2011, http://twocircles.net/2011feb20/suicide_missions_nothing_islamic_about_it.html; Gabriella Gamini, "Argentine Pilots Claim They Had to Adopt Kamikaze Tactics," *The London Times*, April 1, 1992, 13.

18. Joseph S. Tuman, *Communicating Terror: The Rhetorical Dimensions of Terrorism*, 2nd ed. (Thousand Oaks, CA: Sage Publications, Inc., 2010), 2, 3.

19. Ibid., 4–7.

20. Ibid., 8.

21. Alex P. Schmidt et al., *Political Terrorism* (Amsterdam: Transaction Books, 1988), 5, quoted in Boaz Ganor, "Defining Terrorism—Is One Man's Terrorist Another Man's Freedom Fighter?" *International Institute for Counter-Terrorism*,

http://www.ict.org.il/ResearchPublications/tabid/64/Articlsid/432/Default. aspx#Defining_Terrorism:_The_Present_Situation.

22. Ganor, "Defining Terrorism."

23. Ibid.

24. Jaideep Saikia and Ekaterina Stepanova, eds., *Terrorism: Patterns of Internationalization* (Thousand Oaks, CA: Sage Publications Ltd., 2009), xv.

25. Gus Martin, *Understanding Terrorism: Challenges, Perspectives, and Issues,* 3rd ed. (Thousand Oaks, CA: Sage Publications, Inc., 2010), 42, 43.

26. H.H.A. Cooper, "Terrorism: The Problem of Definition Revisited," in *Terrorism in Perspective,* eds. Sue G. Mahan and Pamala L. Griset, 2nd ed. (Thousand Oaks, CA: Sage, 2007), 16.

27. Ibid., 15.

28. Ibid., 22.

29. Cindy C. Combs and Martin Slann, "Introduction," in *Encyclopedia of Terrorism,* eds. Cindy C. Combs and Martin Slann, rev. ed. (New York: Facts on File, Inc., 2007), xiii.

30. George P. Fletcher, "The Indefinable Concept of Terrorism," *Journal of International Criminal Justice* 4, no. 5 (November 1, 2006): 894.

31. Rohan Gunaratna, "Suicide Terrorism: A Global Threat," *FRONTLINE/ World,* October 2000, http://www.pbs.org/frontlineworld/stories/srilanka/ globalthreat.html, cited in R. Ramasubramanian, "Suicide Terrorism in Sri Lanka," *IPCS Research Papers* 5 (August 2004): 3, quoted in U.S. Department of Defense, Deputy Chief of Staff for Intelligence (DCSINT), *Suicide Bombing in the COE (Common Operating Environment),* Handbook No. 1.03 (Fort Leavenworth, KS: U.S. Army Training and Doctrine Command, August 10, 2006), I-2, http://www.fas. org/irp/threat/terrorism/sup3.pdf.

32. DCSINT, *Suicide Bombing,* I-2.

33. Jessica Berry, "Fury over Hijacker's Visit to Britain," *Telegraph Network,* May 27, 2002, http://www.telegraph.co.uk/news/uknews/1395466/Fury-over-hijackers-visit-to-Britain.html, quoted in Skaine, *Female Suicide Bombers,* 58.

34. Ibid.

35. Ashley M. Heher, "Female Suicide Bombers an Extension of an Old Tradition," *Cox News Service,* April 28, 2002, quoted in Skaine, *Female Suicide Bombers,* 68.

36. Rear Admiral (RADM) D.M. Williams, Jr., USN (Retd.), former commander, Naval Investigative Service (NIS) Command, interview, May 16, 2005, quoted in Skaine, *Female Suicide Bombers,* 68–70.

37. Antonio Cassese, "The Multifaceted Criminal Notion of Terrorism in International Law," *Journal of International Criminal Justice* 4, no. 5 (November 1, 2006): 933.

38. Ibid.

39. Marco Sassòli, "Terrorism and War," *Journal of International Criminal Justice* 4, no. 5 (November 1, 2006): 959.

40. Williams, interview, quoted in Skaine, *Female Suicide Bombers,* 70.

41. Haroon Siddiqui, "How Many Civilians Have Died?" *Star.com,* September 20, 2007, http://www.thestar.com/columnists/article/258511.

42. Joint Staff, Joint Education and Doctrine Division, J-7, *DoD Dictionary of Military Terms,* December 31, 2010, http://www.dtic.mil/doctrine/dod_dictionary/.

43. Ibid.

44. Mette Eilstrup-Sangiovanni and Calvert Jones, "Assessing the Dangers of Illicit Networks: Why al-Qaida May Be Less Threatening Than Many Think," *International Security* 33, no. 2 (Fall 2008): 7.

45. Thomas M. Sanderson, "Transnational Terror and Organized Crime: Blurring the Lines," *SAIS Review* 24, no. 1 (2004): 49.

46. Ron Chepesiuk, "Dangerous Alliance: Terrorism and Organized Crime," *Global Politician*, September 11, 2007, http://www.globalpolitician.com/23435-crime.

47. Daniel Byman, "The Changing Nature of State Sponsorship of Terrorism," *National Interest* 96 (July/August 2008): 52–59.

48. Ibid.

49. Ibid.

50. Henry A. Giroux, "Dirty Democracy and State Terrorism: The Politics of the New Authoritarianism in the United States," *Comparative Studies of South Asia, Africa and the Middle East* 26, no. 2 (2006): 164.

51. Giorgio Agamben, "On Security and Terror," *Frankfurter Allgemeine Zeitung*, trans. Soenke Zehle, September 20, 2001, www.egs.edu/faculty/agamben/agamben-on-security-and-terror.html, quoted in Giroux, "Dirty Democracy and State Terrorism," 164.

52. Ibid., 164.

53. Adam Lankford, "Do Past U.S. Acts Constitute Terrorism? Implications for Counterterrorism Policy," *International Criminal Justice Review* 20, no. 4 (December 2010): 421, http://icj.sagepub.com/content/20/4/417.

54. Scott Shane, "Wars Fought and Wars Googled," *The New York Times,* June 26, 2010, http://www.nytimes.com/2010/06/27/weekinreview/27shane.html?_r=1.

55. Lankford, "Do Past U.S. Acts Constitute Terrorism?" 422.

56. Paul R. Pillar, "The Diffusion of Terrorism," *Mediterranean Quarterly* 21, no. 1 (Winter 2010): 4.

57. U.S. Department of State, Office of the Coordinator for Counterterrorism, *State Sponsors of Terrorism,* 2011, http://www.state.gov/j/ct/c14151.htm.

58. Rosemarie Skaine, *Women of Afghanistan under the Taliban* (Jefferson, NC: McFarland, 2002), 41. See also Rosemarie Skaine, "Neither Afghan nor Islam," *Ethnicities* 2, no. 2 (June 2002): 142 and David Aaron, *In Their Own Words: Voices of Jihad—Compilation and Commentary* (Santa Monica, CA: RAND Corporation, 2008), iii, http://www.rand.org/pubs/monographs/MG602.html.

59. Aboul-Enein and Zuhur, *Islamic Rulings,* iii, v.

60. Skaine, *Female Suicide Bombers,* 3, 4.

61. C. Wright Mills, *The Sociological Imagination* (New York: Oxford University Press, 1959), 11.

62. Talip Kucukcan, "Sociology of Terrorism: A Key to Understanding Social Origins?" *International Relations* 6, no. 24 (Winter 2010): 33.

63. Durkheim, *Suicide,* 16, quoted in Skaine, *Female Suicide Bombers,* 1.

64. Skaine, *Female Suicide Bombers,* 3.

65. Kucukcan, "Sociology of Terrorism," 33.

66. Anthony Oberschall, "Theories of Social Conflict," *Annual Review of Sociology* 4 (August 1978): 291, http://www.annualreviews.org/doi/abs/10.1146/annurev.so.04.080178.001451?journalCode=soc. See also Lewis A. Coser, *The Functions of Social Conflict* (Glencoe, IL: The Free Press, 1956), 8.

67. Kucukcan, "Sociology of Terrorism," 55.

68. Durkheim, *Suicide*, 52, quoted in Skaine, *Female Suicide Bombers*, 3.

69. George Ritzer and Douglas J. Goodman, *Sociological Theory*, 6th ed. (Boston, MA: McGraw-Hill, 2004), 73, 107, quoted in Skaine, *Female Suicide Bombers*, 3.

70. Chris Lang, *A Brief History of Literary Theory VI: The Philosophy of Ludwig Wittgenstein* (Columbus, OH: Xenos Christian Fellowship, 2011), http://www.xenos.org/essays/litthry7.htm.

71. Richard Jackson, Department of International Politics, Aberystwyth University, Aberystwyth, interview by Rosemarie Skaine, e-mail, June 14, 2011.

72. Karunya Jayasena, "Defining Suicide Terrorism," *IUP Journal of International Relations* 5, no. 3 (July 2011): 20–34, http://www.iupindia.in/1107/International%20Relations/Defining_Suicide_Terrorism.html.

73. Marie Breen-Smyth, "A Critical Research Agenda for the Study of Political Terror," *European Political Science* 6, no. 3 (September 2007): 260.

74. Marie Breen-Smyth, Chair in International Politics, Codirector, Centre for International Intervention, Director of Research, School of Politics, University of Surrey, Guildford, interview by Rosemarie Skaine, telephone, March 18, 2012.

CHAPTER 2

1. Josh Sanburn, "A Brief History of Self-Immolation," *Time*, January 20, 2011, http://www.time.com/time/world/article/0,8599,2043123,00.html.

2. "China Detains Hundreds in Tibet over Self-Immolation Protests," *The Telegraph*, May 31, 2012, http://www.telegraph.co.uk/news/worldnews/asia/tibet/9301849/China-detains-hundreds-in-Tibet-over-self-immolation-protests.html and "Self-Immolation Fact Sheet," *Campaign for Tibet*, June 4, 2012, http://www.savetibet.org/resource-center/maps-data-fact-sheets/self-immolation-fact-sheet.

3. "Seppuku," *Wikipedia*, June 11, 2012, http://en.wikipedia.org/wiki/Seppuku; "Torture," *Wikipedia*, July 8, 2012, http://en.wikipedia.org/wiki/Torture; "Capital Punishment," *Wikipedia*, July 13, 2012, http://en.wikipedia.org/wiki/Capital_punishment; and "Shame Society," *Wikipedia*, June 18, 2012, http://en.wikipedia.org/wiki/Shame_society.

4. "Masada," *Jewish Virtual Library*, 2012, http://www.jewishvirtuallibrary.org/jsource/Judaism/masada.html.

5. Robert Hal, "Allied 'bandits' Behind Enemy Lines," *BBC News*, June 5, 2009, http://news.bbc.co.uk/2/hi/uk_news/8085383.stm, quoted in "Suicide Pill," *Wikipedia*, June 1, 2012, http://en.wikipedia.org/wiki/Suicide_pill.

6. U.S. Senate, Select Committee to Study Governmental Operations with Respect to Intelligence Activities, *Unauthorized Storage of Toxic Agents*, 94th Cong., 1st Sess., Vol. 1, Hearing, September 16–18, 1975, 7, quoted in *Assassination Archives and Research Center*, http://www.aarclibrary.org/publib/church/reports/vol1/html/ChurchV1_0006b.htm, quoted in "Suicide Pill," *Wikipedia*, June 1, 2012, http://en.wikipedia.org/wiki/Suicide_pill.

7. Don Oberdorfer, ed., *The Two Koreas: Revised and Updated a Contemporary History* (New York: Basic Books, 1997), 184, http://books.google.co.in/books?id=yJZKpYXh2SAC&pg=PA184&redir_esc=y, quoted in "Suicide Pill," *Wikipedia*, June 1, 2012, http://en.wikipedia.org/wiki/Suicide_pill.

8. Rosemarie Skaine, *Female Suicide Bombers* (Jefferson, NC: McFarland, 2006), 21, 50, 88.

9.   Ibid., 107.

10.   "Essential Military Terms You Should Know," *MilitaryDictionery.com*, 2011, http://www.dtic.mil/doctrine/dod_dictionary/.

11.   "Second Chechen War," *Wikipedia*, August 1, 2005, updated, http://en.wikipedia.org/wiki/Second_Chechen_War, quoted in Skaine, *Female Suicide Bombers*, 98.

12.   Viv Groskop, "Chechnya's Deadly 'Black Widows,'" *New Statesman* 133, no. 4704 (September 6, 2004): 32(2) and "Factbox: Major Terrorist Incidents Tied to Russian-Chechen War," *Radio Free Europe/Radio Liberty*, September 6, 2004, http://www.rferl.org/content/article/1054699.html, quoted in Skaine, *Female Suicide Bombers*, 108.

13.   Luca Ricolfi and Paolo Campana, *Suicide Missions in the Palestinian Area: A New Database* (2004), 2, 3, http://www.prio.no/upload/suicide_missions.pdf.

14.   S. Azmat Hassan, *Countering Violent Extremism: The Fate of the Tamil Tigers* (New York: EastWest Institute, 2009), 15, http://docs.ewi.info/Tigers.pdf.

15.   Niel A. Smith, "Understanding Sri Lanka's Defeat of the Tamil Tigers," *Joint Force Quarterly* 59 (October 2010): 40, 42, http://www.ndu.edu/press/understanding-sri-lanka.html.

16.   Skaine, *Female Suicide Bombers*, 111.

17.   Peter Brownfeld, "The Afghanisation of Chechnya," *The International Spectator* 38, no. 3 (March 2003): 137, 145, http://www.iai.it/pdf/articles/brownfeld.pdf.

18.   U.S. Department of Homeland Security, *Underlying Reasons for Success and Failure of Terrorist Attacks: Selected Case Studies* (Arlington, VA: Homeland Security Institute, June 4, 2007), 85–91, http://www.dtic.mil/dtic/tr/fulltext/u2/a494447.pdf.

19.   Ibid., 40.

20.   Department of Defense, *Dictionary of Military and Associated Terms*, Joint Publication 1-02, April 12, 2001 (as amended through October 7, 2004), quoted in U.S. Department of Defense, Deputy Chief of Staff for Intelligence (DCSINT), *Suicide Bombing in the COE (Common Operating Environment)*, Handbook No. 1.03 (Fort Leavenworth, KS: U.S. Army Training and Doctrine Command, August 10, 2006), 5, http://www.fas.org/irp/threat/terrorism/sup3.pdf.

21.   Bruce Hoffman, "The Logic of Suicide Terrorism," in *Terrorism and Counterterrorism: Understanding the New Security Environment*, eds. Russell D. Howard and Reid L. Sawyer (Guilford: McGraw-Hill/Dushkin, 2004), 268 and U.S. Department of State, Office of the Coordinator for Counterterrorism, *Patterns of Global Terrorism 2003* (Washington, D.C., April 2004, revised 22 June 2004), 176, quoted in DCSINT, *Suicide Bombing in the COE*, 2.

22.   DCSINT, *Suicide Bombing in the COE*, 17.

23.   "Essential Military Terms," *MilitaryDictionery.com*.

24.   "Terrorist Bombing of the Marine Barracks, Beirut, Lebanon," *Arlington National Cemetery Website*, October 23, 2008, http://www.arlingtoncemetery.net/terror.htm.

25.   *Law-Glossary.com*, 2011, http://www.law-glossary.com.

26.   Yoram Schweitzer, "Suicide Bombings—The Ultimate Weapon?" *International Institute of Counter-Terrorism*, July 8, 2001, http://www.ict.org.il/Articles/tabid/66/Articlsid/68/Default.aspx, quoted in Skaine, *Female Suicide Bombers*, 87.

27.   Jason Fisher, "Targeted Killing, Norms, and International Law," *Columbia Journal of Transnational Law* 45, no. 3 (2007): 711.

28. "Is Osama bin Laden Killing Legal? International Law Experts Divided," *International Business Times,* May 7, 2011, http://www.ibtimes.com/articles/142448/20110507/osama-bin-laden-killing-legal-violate-international-law-experts-lawyers-divided.htm.

29. Eric Holder in U.S. Congress, House Committee Judiciary, "Justice Department Oversight, Part 1," *C-SPAN Video Library,* 112th Cong., 1st Sess., Hearing, May 4, 2011, http://www.c-spanvideo.org/program/JusticeDepartmentOve.

30. Joshua Raines, "Student Note: Osama, Augustine, and Assassination: The Just War Doctrine and Targeted Killings," *Transnational Law and Contemporary Problems* 12, no. 1 (Spring, 2002): 218.

31. "Authorization for Use of Military Force," *Find Law,* Public Law 107-40 [S.J. RES. 23], 107th Cong., September 18, 2001, http://news.findlaw.com/hdocs/docs/terrorism/sjres23.es.html.

32. "Is Osama bin Laden Killing Legal?" *International Business Times.*

33. "Essential Military Terms," *MilitaryDictionery.com.*

34. Ibid.

35. Jason D. Söderblom, *The Historical Pedigree and Relevance of Suicide 'Martyr' Bio-Terrorism* (Canberra: Terrorism Intelligence Centre, July 19, 2004), 2, http://world-ice.com/Articles/Martyr.pdf.

36. Ibid., 7, 10.

37. Carlos E. Sluzki, "Psychosocial Scenarios Following a Bioterrorist Attack," Advanced draft, Web Archive of Carlos E. Sluzki, MD, September 9–21, 2002, 102a, http://sluzki.com/?articles&id=102a.

38. "Cult: On Anniversary of Japanese Subway Attack, Many Fear Cult Resurgence," *CNN World,* March 20, 1999, http://articles.cnn.com/1999-03-20/world/9903_20_japan.cult_1_gas-attack-aum-shinri-kyo-tokyo-subway-system?_s=PM:WORLD and "Sarin Gas Attack on the Tokyo Subway," *Japan-101: Information Resource,* http://www.japan-101.com/culture/sarin_gas_attack_on_ the_ tokyo_su.htm.

39. "Archbishop's Appeal: Individual Will and Action; Guarding Personality," *The Times* (London), December 28, 1937, 9, quoted in W. Seth Carus, *Defining "Weapons of Mass Destruction,"* Occasional Paper 4 (Washington, D.C.: Center for the Study of Weapons of Mass Destruction, National Defense University Press, February 2006), 2, 3, http://www.ndu.edu/WMDCenter/docUploaded//OP4Carus.pdf.

40. Joint declaration signed by President Harry Truman, Prime Minister Clement Attlee of the United Kingdom, and Prime Minister Mackenzie King of Canada. See U.S. Department of State, Historical Office, *Documents on Disarmament 1945–1969, Volume I: 1945–1956,* Publication 7008, August 1960, 1–3, quoted in Carus, *Defining "Weapons of Mass Destruction,"* 2, 3.

41. U.N. Assembly Resolution 1(I), "Establishment of a Commission to Deal with the Problem Raised by the Discovery of Atomic Energy," January 24, 1946, http://daccess-dds-ny.un.org/doc/RESOLUTION/GEN/NR0/032/52/IMG/NR003252.pdf?OpenElement, quoted in Carus, *Defining "Weapons of Mass Destruction,"* 3.

42. Commission for Conventional Armaments, U.N. Document S/C.3/32/Rev.1, August 1948, as quoted in U.N. Office of Public Information, *The United Nations and Disarmament, 1945–1965,* U.N. Publication 67.I.8, 28, quoted in Carus, *Defining "Weapons of Mass Destruction,"* 3.

43. "What Are Weapons of Mass Destruction?" *FBI*, http://www.fbi.gov/about-us/investigate/terrorism/wmd/wmd_faqs.

44. Ibid.

45. James C. McKinley, Jr. and Sarah Wheaton, "Agents Say Saudi Man Was Acting Alone in Bomb Plot," *The New York Times*, February 26, 2011, A14(L).

46. Logan G. Carver, "Terror Suspect Aldawsari's Trial Moved to Amarillo, Set for June," *Lubbock Avalanche-Journal*, April 18, 2012, http://lubbockonline.com/crime-and-courts/2012-04-17/terror-suspect-aldawsaris-trial-moved-amarillo-set-june#.UDTAbqkgfow.

47. Donna Leinwand, "Colo. Man Pleads Guilty to Terror Plot," *USA Today*, February 23, 2010.

48. Jeralyn E. Merritt, "Najibullah Zazi Testifies for Government in Terrorism Trial," *Talk Left: The Politics of Crime*, April 17, 2012, http://www.talkleft.com/story/2012/4/17/172034/285.

49. Paul I. Bernstein, John P. Caves, Jr., and W. Seth Carus, *Countering Weapons of Mass Destruction: Looking Back, Looking Ahead*, Occasional Paper 7 (Washington, D.C.: Center for the Study of Weapons of Mass Destruction, National Defense University Press, October 2009), 4, http://permanent.access.gpo.gov/lps116426/op7cswmd.pdf.

50. U.S. Senate, Select Committee on Intelligence, *Report on the U.S. Intelligence Community's Prewar Intelligence Assessments on Iraq: Ordered Report*, 108th Cong., 2nd Sess., July 7, 2004, 14, http://web.mit.edu/simsong/www/iraqreport2-textunder.pdf.

51. "Timeline of Hezbollah Violence," *Committee for Accuracy in Middle East Reporting in America*, July 17, 2006, http://www.camera.org/index.asp?x_context=2&x_outlet=118&x_article=1148.

52. "Chronology of Suicide Bomb Attacks by LTTE Tamil Tiger Terrorists in Sri Lanka," *Sri Lanka News Online*, July 5, 1987–April 20, 2009, http://www.slnewsonline.net/chronology_of_suicide_bomb_attacks_by_Tamil_Tigers_in_sri_Lanka.htm.

53. Combs and Slann, *Encyclopedia of Terrorism*, 313.

54. "Timeline Turkey 1961–2008," *Timelines of History*, http://timelines.ws/countries/TURKEY_B.HTML.

55. "Timeline: Al-Qaeda," *BBC News*, August 7, 2008, http://news.bbc.co.uk/2/hi/in_depth/7546355.stm (accessed March 25, 2011) and "Terrorism: Questions and Answers: Is Suicide Terrorism Becoming More Common?" *Council on Foreign Relations*, http://www.cfr.org/terrorist-organizations/al-qaeda-k-al-qaida-al-qaida/p9126?co=C005001 (accessed March 25, 2011), quoted in Skaine, *Female Suicide Bombers*, 9.

56. Shaul Kimhi and Shemuel Even, "Who are the Palestinian Suicide Bombers," *Terrorism and Political Violence* 16, no. 4 (Winter 2004): 816, quoted in Skaine, *Female Suicide Bombers*, 9.

57. Paul Thompson, "Day of 9/11 Timeline," *Amazon S3*, http://s3.amazonaws.com/911timeline/main/dayof911.html.

58. "1994 to 2011—Terror Attacks against Russia . . . ," *Windows to Russia*, http://windowstorussia.com/1994-to-2011-terror-attacks-against-russia.html#.UDTGOKkgfow.

59. Robert J. Bunker and John P. Sullivan, *Suicide Bombings in Operation Iraqi Freedom* (Arlington, VA: Institute of Land Warfare, Association of the United States

Army, 2004), 70, quoted in Philip E. Kapusta, *Suicide Bombers in CONUS* (Fort Leavenworth, KS: School of Advanced Military Studies, May 7, 2007), 22, http://www.dtic.mil/cgi-bin/GetTRDoc?AD=ADA470697.

60. U.S. National Counterterrorism Center, *2009 NCTC Report on Terrorism* (Washington, D.C.: National Counterterrorism Center, Office of the Director of National Intelligence, April 30, 2010), 10, 11, http://www.nctc.gov/.

61. U.S. National Counterterrorism Center, "Worldwide Incident Tracking System (WITS): 2010 Suicide Attacks by Region," *2012 Counterterrorism Calendar,* 139, http://www.nctc.gov/site/pdfs/ct_calendar_2012_141.pdf.

62. U.S. National Counterterrorism Center, *2009 NCTC Report on Terrorism,* 11.

63. "Worldwide Incidents Tracking System (WITS)," *National Counterterrorism Center,* http://www.nctc.gov/site/other/wits.html.

64. "The Terrorist Attack Cycle: Selecting the Target," *Stratfor Global Intelligence,* September 30, 2005, http://www.stratfor.com/.

65. Deb Riechmann, "Taliban Show Resolve to Fight on After Bin Laden," *The Washington Times,* May 13, 2011, http://www.washingtontimes.com/news/2011/may/13/taliban-show-resolve-fight-after-bin-laden/.

66. "Attacks on Iraqi Pipelines, Oil Installations, and Oil Personnel: 2003–2008," *Iraq Pipeline Watch,* March 27, 2008, http://www.iags.org/iraqpipelinewatch.htm.

67. Assaf Moghadam, "Palestinian Suicide Terrorism in the Second Intifada: Motivations and Organizational Aspects." *Studies in Conflict and Terrorism* 26 (2003): 85, http://werzit.com/intel/classes/amu/classes/lc514/LC514_Week_05_Motivations_and_Organizational_Aspects_of_Palestinian_Suicide_Bombers.pdf.

68. U.S. Department of Homeland Security, *A Military Guide to Terrorism in the Twenty-First Century,* Appendix A, Terrorist Planning Cycle, August 15, 2007, A-1.

69. Ibid., A-3.

70. DCSINT, *Suicide Bombing in the COE,* V-1.

71. Bruce Hoffman, *Lessons of 9/11: Testimony* (Arlington, VA: RAND, October 2002), 11, http://www.rand.org/pubs/testimonies/2005/CT201.pdf.

72. Clay Wilson, "Improvised Explosive Devices in Iraq: Effects and Countermeasures," *CRS Report for Congress,* November 23, 2005, 2, http://fpc.state.gov/documents/organization/57512.pdf; Mark D. Klingelhoefer, *Captured Enemy Ammunition in Operation Iraqi Freedom and Its Strategic Importance in Post-Conflict Operations* (Carlisle, PA: Strategic Studies Institute, U.S. Army War College, March 18, 2005), 1, 2, http://www.strategicstudiesinstitute.army.mil/pdffiles/ksil72.pdf.

73. Richard G. Priem, Dennis M. Hunter, and Joseph M. Polisar, "Terrorists and Suicide Tactics: Preparing for the Challenge," *Police Chief,* April 2011, http://www.policechiefmagazine.org/magazine/index.cfm?fuseaction=display_arch&article_id=1265&issue_id=92007 and DCSINT, *Suicide Bombing in the COE,* V-1, V-2.

74. DCSINT, *Suicide Bombing in the COE,* V-3.

75. Jill Dougherty, " 'Bribe' Got Bomber on Russian Jet," *CNN World,* September 15, 2004, http://www.cnn.com/2004/WORLD/europe/09/15/russia.planecrash/index.html and Mariya Rasner, " 'Black Widow' Fears Surround a Russian Verdict," *Women's eNews,* February 6, 2005, http://www.womensenews.org/article.cfm/dyn/aid/2175/context/cover/, quoted in Skaine, *Female Suicide Bombers,* 107.

76. U.S. Department of Justice, "Al Qaeda Associates Charged in Attack on USS *Cole,* Attempted Attack on Another U.S. Naval Vessel," *USDOJ,* Press Release, May 15, 2003, http://www.justice.gov/opa/pr/2003/May/03_crm_298.htm.

77. U.S. Department of Homeland Security, *A Military Guide to Terrorism*, A-3.

78. Ibid., A-4.

79. DCSINT, *Suicide Bombing in the COE*, V-2.

80. Robert A. Pape, *Dying to Win: The Strategic Logic of Suicide Terrorism* (New York: Random House, 2005), 229.

81. Bruce Riedel, "Al Qaeda Strikes Back: Terrorism and al Qaeda, Afghanistan," *Brookings*, May/June 2007, http://www.brookings.edu/articles/2007/05terrorism_riedel.aspx. This article was originally published in the May/June 2007 issue of *Foreign Affairs*.

82. U.S. Department of Homeland Security, *A Military Guide to Terrorism*, A-5.

83. "Suicide Bombers," *The Infantry Rifle Company*, Field Manual No. 3-21.10 (Washington, D.C.: U.S. Department of the Army, July 2006), Appendix G, Section 2, https://rdl.train.army.mil/soldierPortal/atia/adlsc/view/public/23168–1/FM/3–21.10/toc.htm#toc.

84. Wilson, "Improvised Explosive Devices in Iraq," 3.

85. U.S. Department of Homeland Security, "Potential Threat to Homeland Using Heavy Transport Vehicles," *Information Bulletin*, July 30, 2004, https://www.hsdl.org/?view&did=461034.

86. "The Execution," *USA Today*, June 20, 2001, http://www.usatoday.com/news/nation/mcveighindex.htm.

87. Moghadam, "Palestinian Suicide Terrorism," 85.

88. DCSINT, *Suicide Bombing in the COE*, V-2.

89. Wilson, "Improvised Explosive Devices in Iraq," 3.

90. "Improvised Explosive Devices (IEDs)/Booby Traps: IED Overview," *Global Security.org*, http://www.globalsecurity.org/military/intro/ied.htm and John W. Anderson, Steve Fainaru, and Jonathan Finer, "Bigger, Stronger Homemade Bombs Now to Blame for Half of U.S. Deaths," *The Washington Post*, October 26, 2005, A1, http://www.washingtonpost.com/wp-dyn/content/article/2005/10/25/AR2005102501987.html, quoted in Wilson, "Improvised Explosive Devices in Iraq," 2, 3.

91. DCSINT, *Suicide Bombing in the COE*, VI-3.

92. "The Beslan Attack & Qaeda Link," *Diplomat News Service* 61, no. 11 (September 13, 2004); John Kampfner, "A President Craves Understanding," *New Statesman* 133, no. 4705 (September 13, 2004): 10(4); "Suspect Retells Beslan's Horror; Leader Blew up Female Bombers after They Balked at Taking Children Hostage, Court Told," *The Record*, June 1, 2005, final ed., Sec. Front, A7, quoted in Skaine, *Female Suicide Bombers*, 108.

93. "Russian Extremists Remotely Detonate Suicide Bombs," *Homeland Security News Wire*, February 8, 2011, http://homelandsecuritynewswire.com/russian-extremists-remotely-detonate-suicide-bombs.

94. *The Infantry Rifle Company*, Appendix G, Section 2.

95. U.S. Department of Homeland Security, *A Military Guide to Terrorism*, A-5.

96. Ibid., A-6.

97. U.N. Assistance Mission in Afghanistan (UNAMA), "Suicide Attacks in Afghanistan (2001–2007)," *ReliefWeb*, September 9, 2007, 3, http://reliefweb.int/report/afghanistan/suicide-attacks-afghanistan-2001-2007.

98. U.S. Department of State, "Types of Attacks," *National Counterterrorism Center: Annex of Statistical Information*, August 5, 2010, http://www.state.gov/j/ct/rls/crt/2009/140902.htm.

99. Monica Czwarno and Ana Marte, "Profiling Discord: Suicide Bombings in the Insurgent Campaign," *Defense Monitor* 36, no. 5 (September–October 2007): 6.

100. Laura Rozen, "Researcher: Suicide Terrorism Linked to Military Occupation," *Politico*, October 11, 2010, http://www.politico.com/blogs/laura rozen/1010/Researcher_Suicide_terrorism_linked_to_military_occupation.html; Matt Loffman, "For First Time, More US Troops in Afghanistan than Iraq," *ABC News*, May 24, 2010, http://blogs.abcnews.com/politicalpunch/2010/05/for-first-time-more-us-troops-in-afghanistan-than-iraq.html; and "Obama's Afghan Speech: Full Text," *BBC News*, December 2, 2009, http://news.bbc.co.uk/go/pr/fr/-/2/hi/americas/8389849.stm.

101. Tom Vanden Brook, "Afghan Insurgents Match Surge with More IEDs," *USA Today*, January 10, 2011.

102. Afghan Mission NY, "Afghan Civilian Death Toll Jumps 31 Percent due to Insurgent Attacks," *Permanent Mission of Afghanistan to the United States in New York*, August 10, 2010, http://www.afghanistan-un.org/2010/08/afghan-civilian-death-toll-jumps-31-per-cent-due-to-insurgent-attacks-%E2%80%93-un/.

103. U.N. Assistance Mission in Afghanistan (UNAMA), *Afghanistan Annual Report 2011 Protection of Civilians in Armed Conflict* (Kabul: UNAMA, February 2012), 3, 4, http://unama.unmissions.org/Portals/UNAMA/Documents/UNAMA%20POC%202011%20Report_Final_Feb%202012.pdf.

104. Monica Czwarno and Ana Marte, "Profiling Discord: Suicide Bombings in the Insurgent Campaign," *Defense Monitor* 36, no. 5 (September–October 2007): 7.

105. George W. Bush, "Full Text: George Bush's Address on the Start of War," *The Guardian*, March 20, 2003, http://www.guardian.co.uk/world/2003/mar/20/iraq.georgebush.

106. Barack Obama, "Remarks by the President in Address to the Nation on the End of Combat Operations in Iraq," *The White House*, August 31, 2010,http://www.whitehouse.gov/the-press-office/2010/08/31/remarks-president-address-nation-end-combat-operations-iraq.

107. "Guide: Armed Groups in Iraq," *BBC News*, August 15, 2006, http://news.bbc.co.uk/2/hi/middle_east/4268904.stm.

108. U.S. National Counterterrorism Center, "Worldwide Incident Tracking System (WITS)," 30.

109. Sabrina Tavernise, "U.S. Quietly Issues Estimate of Iraqi Civilian Casualties," *The New York Times*, October 30, 2005, http://www.nytimes.com/2005/10/30/international/middleeast/30civilians.html?pagewanted=1&_r=1.

110. "Iraqi Deaths from Violence in 2010: Analysis of the Year's Civilian Death Toll from Iraq Body Count—Everyday Terrorists," *Iraq Body Count*, first published December 30, 2010, http://www.iraqbodycount.org/analysis/numbers/2010/.

111. Ibid., "WikiLeaks Recap and Update" and "Interactive Graph."

112. Russell Goldman and Luis Martinez, "WikiLeaks Documents Reveal Death Count, Torture," *ABC News*, October 23, 2010, http://abcnews.go.com/Politics/wikileaks-iraqi-civilian-deaths-higher-reported/story?id=11953723#.UDW7FMEgfow.

113. Anne Gearan and Robert Burns, "WikiLeaks Releases 400,000 Files on Iraq: Leaked Files Show Iraqi Deaths Higher Than U.S. Count," *Army Times*, October 23, 2010, http://www.armytimes.com/news/2010/10/ap-Iraqi-deaths-higher-than-US-count-102310/.

114. Iraq Body Count, *A Dossier of Civilian Casualties 2003–2005* (Oxford: IBC, July 2005), 11, 14, 15, http://reports.iraqbodycount.org/a_dossier_of_civilian_casualties_2003-2005.pdf.

115. Priem et al., "Terrorists and Suicide Tactics."

116. Merle Miyasato, "Suicide Bombers: Profiles, Methods and Techniques," *Foreign Military Studies Office,* March 16, 2007, http://fmso.leavenworth.army.mil/documents/Suicide-Bombers.pdf.

117. Brian Michael Jenkins, *Would-Be Warriors: Incidents of Jihadist Terrorist Radicalization in the United States since September 11, 2001* (Santa Monica, CA: RAND Corporation, 2010), 7, http://www.rand.org/pubs/occasional_papers/OP292.

118. "Afghanistan: Suicide Bomber 'Aged 12' Kills Four," *BBC News,* May 1, 2011, http://www.bbc.co.uk/news/world-south-asia-13252786.

119. Skaine, *Female Suicide Bombers,* 36, 38, 48. John P. Sullivan, "Child Soldiers: Despair, Barbarization, and Conflict," *Air and Space Power Journal* (2008),

120. Nasra Hassan, "An Arsenal of Believers," *The New Yorker,* November 19, 2001, 36–41 and Avishai Margalit, "The Suicide Bombers," *The New York Review of Books,* January 16, 2003, quoted in Mario Ferrero, "Martyrdom Contracts," *Journal of Conflict Resolution* 50, no. 6 (December 2006): 856.

121. Audrey Kurth Cronin, "Sources of Contemporary Terrorism," in *Attacking Terrorism: Elements of a Grand Strategy,* eds. Audrey Kurth Cronin and James M. Ludes (Washington, D.C.: Georgetown University Press, 2004), 20–27 and Jerrold Post, "The Radical Group in Context 1: An Integrated Framework for the Analysis of Group Risk for Terrorism," *Studies in Conflict and Terrorism* 25, no. 2 (April 2002), 90, quoted in Marta Sparago, *Terrorist Recruitment: The Crucial Case of Al Qaeda's Global Jihad Terror Network* (New York: Center for Global Affairs, New York University, Spring 2007), 11, 17, http://www.scps.nyu.edu/export/sites/scps/pdf/global-affairs/marta-sparago.pdf.

122. Marie Breen-Smyth, Chair in International Politics, Codirector, Centre for International Intervention, Director of Research, School of Politics, University of Surrey, Guildford, interview by Rosemarie Skaine, telephone, March 18, 2012.

123. Ibid.

124. Julian Madsen, "Suicide Terrorism: Rationalizing the Irrational," *Strategic Insights* 3 no. 8 (August 2004): 3, http://www.au.af.mil/au/awc/awcgate/nps/madsen_aug04.pdf.

125. Laura Rozen, "Suicide Attacks Linked to Military Occupation: Report," *Huffington Post,* October 11, 2010, http://www.huffingtonpost.com/2010/10/11/suicide-attacks-military-occupation-pape_n_758759.html.

126. Jenkins, *Would-Be Warriors,* 4.

CHAPTER 3

1. U.S. Constitution, Article II, § 2, cl. 1 and "Constitution of the United States: Amendments," *U.S. Senate,* http://www.senate.gov/civics/constitution_item/constitution.htm.

2. U.S. Constitution, Article II, § 1.

3. U.S. Constitution, Article I, § [11].

4. James P. Terry, "The President as Commander in Chief," *Ave Maria Law Review* 7, no. 2 (Spring 2009): 405.

5. Ray Raphael, "Washington's 5 Rules for Honorable War," *HistoryNet*, December 11, 2009, http://www.historynet.com/washingtons-5-rules-for-honorable-war.htm.

6. Richard B. Jackson, "Stick to the High Ground," *The Army Lawyer* (July 2005): 2, http://www.au.af.mil/au/awc/awcgate/law/high_ground.pdf.

7. Philip Babcock Gove, "hors de combat," *Webster's Third New International Dictionary of the English Language, Unabridged* (Springfield, MA: Merriam-Webster, 2002), http://unabridged.merriam-webster.com.

8. Jean-Marie Henckaerts and Louise Doswald-Beck, "Rule 47," in *Customary International Humanitarian Law, Volume I: Rules* (Cambridge: Cambridge University Press, 2005), 164, 166–68. See also "Rule 47. Attacks against Persons Hors de Combat," *ICRC*, http://www.icrc.org/customary-ihl/eng/docs/v1_rul_rule47.

9. "Washington's Farewell Address," A Century of Lawmaking for a New Nation: U.S. Congressional Documents and Debates, 1774–1875, *Annals of Congress*, 4th Cong., 2878, http://memory.loc.gov/cgi-bin/ampage?collId=llac&fileName=006/llac006.db&recNum=677.

10. Terry, "The President as Commander in Chief," 469.

11. Melvyn P. Leffler, "9/11 and the Past and Future of American Foreign Policy," *International Affairs* 79, no. 5 (2003): 1053.

12. Paul Wolfowitz, Testimony, U.S. Senate, Select Committee on Intelligence and the House Permanent Select Committee on Intelligence, *Joint Inquiry Hearing on Counterterrorist Center*, 107th Cong., 2nd Sess., September 19, 2002, http://www.dtic.mil/dtic/, quoted in Melvyn P. Leffler, "9/11 and the Past and Future," 1053.

13. "Threats to International Peace and Security Caused by Terrorist Acts," U.N. Security Council Resolution 1368, September 12, 2001 and "Threats to International Peace and Security Caused by Terrorist Acts," U.N. Security Council Resolution 1373, September 28, 2001, http://www.un.org/Docs/scres/2001/sc2001.htm, quoted in Mary Ellen O'Connel, *The Myth of Preemptive Self-Defense* (Washington, D.C.: American Society of International Law, August 2002), Note 48, http://www.asil.org/taskforce/oconnell.pdf.

14. U.N. Charter, Article 2, para. 4, signed June 26, 1945, in force October 24, 1945, quoted in O'Connel, *The Myth of Preemptive Self-Defense*, Note 12.

15. O'Connel, *The Myth of Preemptive Self-Defense*, 21.

16. James A. Green, "Docking the Caroline: Understanding the Relevance of the Formula in Contemporary Customary International Law Concerning Self-Defense," *Cardozo Journal of International and Comparative Law* 14, no.2 (Fall 2006): 430.

17. "Woodrow Wilson—The Treaty Fight in the United States 1919–1920," *Profiles of U.S. Presidents*, April 2002, http://www.presidentprofiles.com/Grant-Eisenhower/Woodrow-Wilson-The-treaty-fight-in-the-united-states-1919-1920.html#b.

18. Jonathan Zasloff, "Law and the Shaping of American Foreign Policy: From the Gilded Age to the New Era," *New York University Law Review* 78 (April 2003): 241.

19. Aaron Xavier Fellmeth, "A Divorce Waiting to Happen: Franklin Roosevelt and the Law of Neutrality, 1935–1941," *Buffalo Journal of International Law* 3, no. 2 (Winter 1996–1997): 417.

20. Ibid., 418.

21. Mary L. Dudziak, "Desegregation as a Cold War Imperative," *Stanford Law Review* 41, no. 1 (November 1988): 74.

22. Terry, "The President as Commander in Chief," 446–48.

23. "Bay of Pigs," *John F. Kennedy Presidential Library and Museum*, http://www.jfklibrary.org/JFK/JFK-in-History/The-Bay-of-Pigs.aspx.

24. David B. Rivkin, Jr., Lee A. Casey, and Mark Wendell DeLaquil, "War, International Law, and Sovereignty: Reevaluating the Rules of The Game in A New Century: Preemption and Law in the Twenty-First Century," *Chicago Journal of International Law* 5, no. 2 (Winter 2005): 481 and "Cuban Missile Crisis," *John F. Kennedy Presidential Library and Museum*, http://www.jfklibrary.org/JFK/JFK-in-History/Cuban-Missile-Crisis.aspx.

25. D. J. Lecce, "International Law Regarding Pro-Democratic Intervention: A Study of the Dominican Republic and Haiti," *Naval Law Review* 45 (1998): 261.

26. Terry, "The President as Commander in Chief," 447.

27. Ibid., 479.

28. "American President: A Reference Resource—Ronald Wilson Reagan," *Miller Center*, 2011, http://millercenter.org/president/reagan/essays/biography/print.

29. "General Article: The Invasion of Grenada," *American Experience*, 1998, http://www.pbs.org/wgbh/americanexperience/features/general-article/reagan-grenada/.

30. Terry, "The President as Commander in Chief," 471.

31. "General Article: The Iran-Contra Affair," *American Experience*, 1998, http://www.pbs.org/wgbh/americanexperience/features/general-article/reagan-iran/.

32. "Operation Desert Shield/Desert Storm Timeline," *U.S. War Dogs Association*, July 20, 2011, http://www.uswardogs.org/id105.html.

33. Terry, "The President as Commander in Chief," 415, 450, 456.

34. Ibid., 412, 488, 494, notes 346 and 581 and Michael Isikoff, "U.S. Failure to Retaliate for USS *Cole* Attack Rankled Then—and Now," *NBCNews*, October 12, 2010, http://www.msnbc.msn.com/id/39622062/ns/us_news-security/t/us-failure-retaliate-uss-cole-attack-rankled-then-now/.

35. Marc A. Thiessen ed., *A Charge Kept: The Record of the Bush Presidency 2001–2009* (Washington, D.C.: Executive Office of the President, 2009), 4, http://georgewbush-whitehouse.archives.gov/infocus/bushrecord/documents/charge-kept.pdf.

36. Jorge Alberto Ramirez, "Iraq War: Anticipatory Self-Defense or Unlawful Unilateralism?" *California Western International Law Journal* 34, no. 1 (Fall 2003): 3, 5.

37. George W. Bush in Rachel S. Taylor, "The United Nations, International Law, and the War in Iraq," *World Press Review Online*, September 17, 2002, http://www.worldpress.org/specials/iraq/.

38. Eric Schmitt and Thom Shanker, "Washington Recasts Terror War as 'Struggle,'" *The New York Times*, July 27, 2005, http://www.nytimes.com/2005/07/26/world/americas/26iht-terror.html.

39. "Observer: A War of the Words in Washington," *Financial Times*, August 4, 2005, http://www.ft.com/intl/cms/s/0/5aceb7e8-0483-11da-a775-00000e2511c8.html#axzz24Lnu5vJ2.

40. Terry, "The President as Commander in Chief," 392, 419.

41. Kenneth Jost and the CQ Researcher Staff, "The Obama Presidency: Can Barack Obama Deliver the Change He Promises?" *CQ Researcher* 19, no. 4 (January 30, 2009), http://www.sagepub.com/upm-data/31933_12.pdf.

42. "Foreign Policy," *The White House,* http://www.whitehouse.gov/issues/foreign-policy, quoted in Danica Curavic, "Compensating Victims of Terrorism or Frustrating Cultural Diplomacy? The Unintended Consequences of the Foreign Sovereign Immunities Act's Terrorism Provisions," *Cornell International Law Journal* 43 (Spring 2010): 404, http://www.lawschool.cornell.edu/research/ilj/upload/curavic.pdf.

43. Barack Obama, "Text: Obama's Speech in Cairo," *The New York Times,* June 4, 2009, http://www.nytimes.com/2009/06/04/us/politics/04obama.text.html?pagewanted=1, quoted in Curavic, "Compensating Victims of Terrorism."

44. "Barack Obama and Joe Biden: Champions for Arts and Culture," *Obama for America,* http://www.artsdel.org/advocacy/Obama_Arts.pdf.

45. Scott Shane, Mark Mazzetti, and Robert F. Worth, "Secret Assault on Terrorism Widens on Two Continents," *The New York Times,* August 14, 2010, http://www.nytimes.com/2010/08/15/world/15shadowwar.html.

46. Thomas C. Wingfield, "The Convergence of Traditional Theory and Modern Reality: Just War Doctrine and Tyrannical Regimes," *Ave Maria Law Review* 2, no. 1 (Spring 2004): 94.

47. Michael N. Schmitt, "The Confluence of Law and Morality: Thoughts on Just War," *USAFA Journal of Legal Studies* 3 (1992): 103 (quoting Archbishop J. Ryan, *Pastoral Letter in Time of War (1991)*), quoted in Wingfield, "The Convergence of Traditional Theory and Modern Reality," 94.

48. Wingfield, "The Convergence of Traditional Theory and Modern Reality," 122.

49. Barack Obama, "Remarks by the President at the Acceptance of the Nobel Peace Prize," *The White House,* December 10, 2009, http://www.whitehouse.gov/the-press-office/remarks-president-acceptance-nobel-peace-prize.

50. Richard C. Anderson, *Redefining Just War Criteria in the Post 9/11 World and the Moral Consequences of Preemptive Strikes* (West Point, NY: United States Military Academy, January 24, 2003), http://isme.tamu.edu/JSCOPE03/Anderson03.html.

51. Michael Walzer, *Just and Unjust Wars,* 3rd ed. (New York: Basic Books, 2000), 62, quoted in Anderson, *Redefining Just War Criteria.*

52. Carsten Stahn, "Jus Post Bellum: Mapping the Discipline(s)," *American University International Law Review* 23 (2008): 311, 312.

53. Obama, "Remarks by the President," *The White House.*

54. Ibid.

55. Dominic Casciani, "Q&A: Sharia Law Explained," *BBC News,* http://news.bbc.co.uk/2/hi/uk_news/7234870.stm.

56. John Kelsay, "Suicide Bombers: The 'Just War' Debate, Islamic Style," *The Christian Century,* August 14–27, 2002, 22–25, http://www.religion-online.org/showarticle.asp?title=2616.

57. Ibid.

58. Youssef H. Aboul-Enein and Sherifa Zuhur, *Islamic Rulings on Warfare* (Carlisle, PA: Strategic Studies Institute, U.S. Army War College, October 2004), 7, http://insct.syr.edu/uploadedFiles/insct/uploadedfiles/PDFs/Aboul-Enein.Zuhur.Islamic%20Rulings%20on%20Warfare(1).pdf.

59. "Bin Laden's Fatwa," *PBS News Hour,* August 1996, http://www.pbs.org/newshour/terrorism/international/fatwa_1996.html.

60. John L. Esposito, "Jihad: Holy or Unholy War?" *United Nations Alliance of Civilians,* 6, http://www.unaoc.org/repository/Esposito_Jihad_Holy_Unholy.pdf. This article was drawn from John L. Esposito, *Unholy War: Terror in the Name of Islam and What Everyone Needs to Know about Islam* (New York: Oxford University Press, 2002).

61. Rosemarie Skaine, *Female Suicide Bombers* (Jefferson, NC: McFarland, 2006), 80, 81, 85, 97, 99.

62. Edward Marks, "Terrorism in Context: From Tactical to Strategic," *Mediterranean Quarterly* 17, no. 4 (2006): 46.

63. Ibid.

64. Edward T. Canuel, "Nationalism, Self-Determination, and Nationalist Movements: Exploring the Palestinian and Quebec Drives for Independence," *Boston College International and Comparative Law Review* 20, no. 1 (Winter 1997): 85.

65. Robert A. Pape, "Nationalism Motivates Suicide Terrorists," in *What Motivates Suicide Bombers?* ed. Lauri S. Friedman (San Diego, CA: Greenhaven Press, 2005): 44.

66. Robert A. Pape in Patricia Wilson, "Religion, Suicide Terrorism Link Disputed in Book," *Reuters,* June 3, 2005, http://www.democraticunderground.com/discuss/duboard.php?az=view_all&address=124x92979, quoted in Skaine, *Female Suicide Bombers,* 14.

67. Ganesh Sitaraman, "Counterinsurgency, the War on Terror, and the Laws of War," *Virginia Law Review* 95, no. 7 (2009): 1747, http://www.virginialawreview.org/content/pdfs/95/1745.pdf.

68. Ibid., 1745.

69. "Definitions [Terrorism]," *US Code,* Title 22, Ch. 38, § 2656f(d), http://www.law.cornell.edu/uscode/text/22/2656f.

70. Colin S. Gray, *Irregular Enemies and the Essence of Strategy: Can the American Way of War Adapt?* (Carlisle, PA: Strategic Studies Institute, U.S. Army War College, March 2006), 15, http://www.strategicstudiesinstitute.army.mil/pdffiles/pub650.pdf.

71. Claudia Brunner, "Occidentalism Meets the Female Suicide Bomber: A Critical Reflection on Recent Terrorism Debates: A Review Essay," *Signs: Journal of Women in Culture and Society* 32, no. 4 (2007): 957–71.

72. Ibid.

73. Richard Jackson, Marie Breen Smyth, and Jeroen Gunning, *Critical Terrorism Studies: A New Research Agenda* (London: Routledge, 2009), 218, quoted in Amentahru Wahlrab, "Transforming Research and Debate on Terrorism," *Amazon,* Customer Reviews, June 30, 2009, http://www.amazon.com/Critical-Terrorism-Studies-Research-Agenda/product-reviews/0415574153/ref=sr_1_1_cm_cr_acr_txt?ie=UTF8&showViewpoints=1.

74. Alex P. Schmid, "Critical Terrorism Studies: A New Research Agenda," *Perspectives on Terrorism* 3, no 4 (2009), http://www.terrorismanalysts.com/pt/index.php/pot/article/view/83/html, quoted by Richard Jackson, Department of International Politics, Aberystwyth University, Aberystwyth, interview by Rosemarie Skaine, e-mail, June 14, 2011.

75. Jackson, interview.

76. Richard B. Jackson, "Unknown Knowns: The Subjugated Knowledge of Terrorism Studies," *Critical Studies on Terrorism* 5, no. 1 (April 2012): 11–29.

77. Ivan Eland, "Does U.S. Intervention Overseas Breed Terrorism? The Historical Record," *CATO Institute,* Foreign Policy Brief No. 50, December 17, 1998, http://www.cato.org/pubs/fpbriefs/fpb-050es.html, quoted in Jackson, interview.

78. Jackson, interview.

79. Jacquelyn L. Williams-Bridgers, *Combating Terrorism: U.S. Government Strategies and Efforts to Deny Terrorists Safe Haven* (Washington, D.C.: GAO, June 3, 2011), 4, http://homeland.house.gov/sites/homeland.house.gov/files/Testimony%20Williams-Bridgers.pdf.

80. Ibid., 1.

81. "[Geneva] Convention (III) Relative to the Treatment of Prisoners of War. Geneva, 12 August 1949," *International Humanitarian Law—Treaties & Documents,* http://www.icrc.org/ihl.nsf/FULL/375.

82. "Protocol Additional to the Geneva Conventions of August 12, 1949, and Relating to the Protection of Victims of International Armed Conflicts (Protocol I), 8 June 1977," *International Humanitarian Law—Treaties & Documents,* http://www.icrc.org/ihl.nsf/WebART/470–750054?OpenDocument.

83. "Torture," *US Code,* Title 18, Part I, Ch. 113c.

84. *US Code,* Title 18, §§ 2340–2340A.

85. Charles Doyle, "Terrorism: Section by Section Analysis of the USA Patriot Act," *CRS Report for Congress,* December 10, 2001, Title VIII, § 811, 51, http://www.au.af.mil/au/awc/awcgate/crs/rl31200.pdf

86. "Convention against Torture and Other Cruel, Inhuman or Degrading Treatment or Punishment: Adopted and Opened for Signature, Ratification and Accession by General Assembly Resolution 39/46 of 10 December 1984, Entry into Force 26 June 1987, in Accordance with Article 27 (1)," *Office of the United Nations High Commissioner for Human Rights,* Part 1, Article 1(1), http://www2.ohchr.org/english/law/pdf/cat.pdfs.

87. "A Court Covers Up," *The New York Times,* May 24, 2012, http://www.nytimes.com/2012/05/25/opinion/a-court-covers-up.html?nl=todaysheadlines&emc=edit_th_20120525. See also "U.S. Court of Appeals for the Second Circuit: American Civil Liberties Union v. Department of Justice," *FindLaw,* March 9, 2012–May 21, 2012, http://caselaw.findlaw.com/us-2nd-circuit/1601185.html.

88. Harrold J. McCracken, *Unprivileged Belligerents: "You Can't Tell the Players without a Scorecard"* (Carlisle, PA: Strategic Studies Institute, U.S. Army War College, March 25, 2010), 2, www.hsdl.org/?view&did=706227.

89. James R. Schlesinger, *Final Report of Independent Panel to Review the Department of Defense Detention Operations* (Arlington, VA: Independent Panel to Review the DoD Detention Operations, August 24, 2004), 82, http://fl1.findlaw.com/news.findlaw.com/wp/docs/dod/abughraibrpt.pdf.

90. McCracken, *Unprivileged Belligerents,* 1, 2.

91. Ibid., 3.

92. Robert Chesney, Testimony, U.S. Congress, House Armed Services Committee, *Ten Years after the Authorization for Use of Military Force: Current Status of Legal Authorities, Detention, and Prosecution in the War on Terror,* 111th Cong., 1st Sess., Hearing, July 26, 2011, 3, http://armedservices.house.gov/index.cfm/files/serve?File_id=dd0064b1–7416–44ab-bb0c-233d20cee4ef.

93. Michael B. Mukasey, Testimony, U.S. Congress, House Armed Services Committee, Subcommittee on Emerging Threats and Capabilities, *Ten Years On: The Evolution of the Terrorist Threat Since 9/11*, 111th Cong., 1st Sess., Hearing, June 22, 2011, 3–5, http://armedservices.house.gov/index.cfm/.

94. Chesney, *Ten Years after the Authorization*, 1, 17, 18.

95. Steven A. Engel, Testimony, U.S. Congress, House Armed Services Committee, *Ten Years after the Authorization for Use of Military Force: Current Status of Legal Authorities, Detention, and Prosecution in the War on Terror*, 111th Cong., 1st Sess., July 26, 2011, 2, http://armedservices.house.gov/index.cfm/.

96. "Detainee Treatment Act of 2005 [White House]," *Jurist Legal News and Research*, December 31, 2005, http://jurist.law.pitt.edu/gazette/2005/12/detainee-treatment-act-of-2005-white.php.

97. U.S. Congress, Senate and House of Representatives, *Military Commissions Act 2006*, Public Law 109-366, 109th Cong., 2nd sess., October 17, 2006, S. 3930, http://www.loc.gov/rr/frd/Military_Law/pdf/PL-109-366.pdf.

98. Joanne Mariner, "A First Look at the Military Commissions Act of 2009, Part One," *FindLaw*, November 4, 2009, http://writ.news.findlaw.com/mariner/20091104.html?pagewanted=all.

99. Vienna Colucci, "Congress Blocks Prosecution of Gitmo Detainees in Federal Courts," *Human Rights Now*, December 22, 2010, http://blog.amnestyusa.org/us/congress-blocks-prosecution-of-gitmo-detainees-in-federal-courts/.

100. Mukasey, *Ten Years On*, 5–7.

101. Ibid., 6.

102. "Affirmation of Armed Conflict with Al-Qaeda, the Taliban, and Associated Forces—Detention in the War on Terror," *National Defense Authorization Act of Fiscal Year 2012*, § 1034(3), quoted in Engel, *Ten Years after the Authorization*, 3.

103. Engel, *Ten Years after the Authorization*, 14, 15.

104. Schlesinger, *Final Report of Independent Panel*, 5.

105. George W. Bush, memorandum, "Humane Treatment of al Qaeda and Taliban Detainees," February 7, 2002, quoted in Schlesinger, *Final Report of Independent Panel*, Appendix C.

106. Schlesinger, *Final Report of Independent Panel*, 81.

107. John Hagan, Gabrielle Ferrales, and Guillermina Jasso, "Collaboration and Resistance in the Punishment of Torture in Iraq: A Judicial Sentencing Experiment," *Wisconsin International Law Journal* 28, no. 1 (Spring 2010): 5.

108. Scott Shane and Charlie Savage, "Bin Laden Raid Revives Debate on Value of Torture," *The New York Times*, May 3, 2011, http://www.nytimes.com/2011/05/04/us/politics/04torture.html?_r=1.

109. Carrie Dann and Reuters, "CIA Chief: Waterboarding Aided bin Laden Raid," *NBCNews*, May 3, 2011, http://today.msnbc.msn.com/id/42880435/ns/today-today_news/t/cia-chief-waterboarding-aided-bin-laden-raid.

110. *Ensuring Lawful Interrogations*, Executive Order No. 13491, Title 3, § 2(f), January 22, 2009, http://edocket.access.gpo.gov/2009/pdf/E9–1885.pdf.

111. *Review and Disposition of Individuals Detained at the Guantanamo Bay Naval Base and Closure of Detention Facilities*, Executive Order No. 13492, Title 3, § 2(b), January 22, 2009, http://edocket.access.gpo.gov/2009/pdf/E9–1893.pdf.

112. *Review of Detention Policy Options*, Executive Order No. 13493, Title 3, § 1(a) (e), January 22, 2009, http://edocket.access.gpo.gov/2009/pdf/E9–1895.pdf.

113. Donna Cassata, "Gates: Prospect Very Low that Guantanamo Closes," *San Diego Union-Tribune*, February 17, 2011, http://www.utsandiego.com/news/2011/feb/17/gates-prospect-very-low-that-guantanamo-closes/.

114. David Johnston, "U.S. Says Rendition to Continue, but with More Oversight," *The New York Times*, August 24, 2009, http://www.nytimes.com/2009/08/25/us/politics/25rendition.html.

115. V. Noah Gimbel, "Has the Rendition Program Disappeared?" *Foreign Policy in Focus*, June 16, 2011, http://www.fpif.org/articles/has_the_rendition_program_disappeared.

116. Colin S. Gray, *Irregular Enemies and the Essence of Strategy: Can the American Way of War Adapt?* (Carlisle, PA: Strategic Studies Institute, U.S. Army War College, March 2006), 51, 54, 55, http://www.strategicstudiesinstitute.army.mil/pdf-files/pub650.pdf.

117. Steven Metz and Phillip Cuccia, "Defining War for the 21st Century," in *2010 Strategic Studies Institute Annual Strategy Conference Report* (Carlisle, PA: Strategic Studies Institute, U.S. Army War College, February 2011), 1, http://www.strategicstudiesinstitute.army.mil/pdffiles/PUB1036.pdf.

118. Ibid., 23.

119. Dr. Albert Pierce quoted in Metz and Cuccia, "Defining War for the 21st Century," 25.

120. Ibid., 26.

121. Ibid., 27.

122. Ibid., 27, 28. See also "US Envoy: Afghanistan, Pakistan Say bin Laden's Killing Is 'Shared Achievement,'" *Voice of America*, May 3, 2011, http://www.voanews.com/english/news/asia/US-Envoy-Afghanistan-Pakistan-Say-bin-Ladens-Killing-Is-Shared-Achievement-121166614.html and "Photos Show Some Killed in Bin Laden Raid," *CBS News*, May 4, 2011, http://www.cbsnews.com/8301-503543_162-20059828-503543.html.

123. Charlie Savage, "Secret U.S. Memo Made Legal Case to Kill a Citizen," *The New York Times*, October 8, 2011, http://www.nytimes.com/2011/10/09/world/middleeast/secret-us-memo-made-legal-case-to-kill-a-citizen.html?_r=1&pagewanted=all.

124. Ibid.

125. Frank G. Hoffman, *Conflict in the 21st Century: The Rise of Hybrid Wars* (Arlington, VA: Potomac Institute for Policy Studies, December 2007), 7, 8, http://www.potomacinstitute.org/images/stories/publications/potomac_hybrid-war_0108.pdf.

126. *The Joint Operating Environment* (Suffolk, VA: Joint Forces Command, 2010), 6, quoted in Metz and Cuccia, "Defining War for the 21st Century," 42.

127. Gregory P. Noone, Christian P. Fleming, Robert P. Morean, John V. Danner, Jr., Philip N. Fluhr, Jr., Jonathan I. Shapiro, Sandra L. Hodgkinson, Edward J. Cook, and Dillon L. Ross, IV, "Prisoners of War in the 21st Century: Issues in Modern Warfare," *Naval Law Review* 50 (2004), http://www.dtic.mil/dtic/tr/fulltext/u2/a477125.pdf. See also "Instructions for the Government of Armies of the United States in the Field (Lieber Code). 24 April 1863," *International Humanitarian Law—Treaties & Documents*, http://www.icrc.org/ihl.nsf/FULL/110?OpenDocument.

128. David P. Cavaleri, *The Law of War: Can 20th-Century Standards Apply to the Global War on Terrorism?* (Fort Leavenworth, KS: Combat Studies Institute Press, 2005), 1, http://www.dtic.mil/dtic/tr/fulltext/u2/a446304.pdf.

129. "[Geneva] Convention (III)," *International Humanitarian Law—Treaties & Documents,* 1, 2.

130. "Geneva Conventions of 1949 and Their Additional Protocols," *International Committee of the Red Cross,* July 7, 2011, http://www.icrc.org/eng/war-and-law/treaties-customary-law/geneva-conventions/index.jsp.

131. Ibid.

132. Ibid.

133. "Geneva Convention (III)," *International Humanitarian Law—Treaties & Documents.*

134. Cavaleri, *The Law of War,* 22.

135. McCracken, *Unprivileged Belligerents,* Abstract.

136. Ibid., 21.

137. Dann and Reuters, *NBCNews.*

138. "Terrorism Law and Policy: World Anti-terrorism Laws," *Jurist,* 2003, http://jurist.law.pitt.edu/terrorism/terrorism3a.htm.

139. United Nations, *Charter of the United Nations,* Art. 2, Para. 4, signed June 26, 1945, in force October 24, 1945, http://www.un.org/en/documents/charter/index.shtml.

140. U.N. General Assembly, "Resolution 2625: Declaration on Principles of International Law Concerning Friendly Relations and Cooperation among States in Accordance with the Charter of the United Nations," *Resolutions Adopted by the General Assembly during Its Twenty-fifth Session,* October 24, 1970, 122, http://www.un.org/documents/ga/res/25/ares25.htm.

141. U.N. General Assembly, "Resolution 3314: Definition of Aggression," *Resolutions Adopted by the General Assembly during Its Twenty-ninth Session,* December 14, 1974, 143, http://www.un.org/documents/ga/res/29/ares29.htm.

142. Cavaleri, *The Law of War,* 98.

CHAPTER 4

1. Charles Tilly, "Terror as Strategy and Relational Process," *International Journal of Comparative Sociology* 46, nos. 1–2 (February–April 2005): 21.

2. Ibid., 19, 22.

3. Jessica Stern, "Mind over Martyr: How to Deradicalize Islamist Extremists," *Foreign Affairs* 89, no. 1 (January–February 2010): 95.

4. Tilly, "Terror as Strategy and Relational Process," 27.

5. Lauri S. Friedman, ed., *What Motivates Suicide Bombers?* (San Diego, CA: Greenhaven Press, 2005), 7, 8, quoted in Rosemarie Skaine, *Female Suicide Bombers* (Jefferson, NC: McFarland, 2006), 58, see also 38, 39.

6. Ronald Meinardus, "Terrorism as Political Ideology," *Friedrich Naumann Foundation for Liberty,* http://www.fnf.org.ph/liberallibrary/terrorism-as-political-ideology.htm.

7. Department of Defense, *Dictionary of Military and Associated Terms,* Joint Publication 1-02, November 8, 2010 (as amended through December 31, 2010), http://www.dtic.mil/doctrine/dod_dictionary.

8. Eli Berman and David Laitin, *Hard Targets: Theory and Evidence on Suicide Attacks* (Cambridge, MA: National Bureau of Economic Research, 2006), 3, http://dss.ucsd.edu/~elib/Hardtargets.pdf.

9. Nicholas Corbett, *Comparative Insurgencies: The Role of Suicide Tactics in Iraq and Afghanistan* (Ottawa: Conference of Defense Associations, 2009), 2, http://www.cda-cdai.ca/cdai/uploads/cdai/2009/04/corbett08.pdf.

10. Ibid., 12, 17.

11. Ibid., 5.

12. Skaine, *Female Suicide Bombers*, 31, 32, 35, 36, 41.

13. Raphael Israeli, "The Promise of an Afterlife Motivates Suicide Bombers," in *What Motivates Suicide Bombers?* ed. Lauri S. Friedman (San Diego, CA: Greenhaven Press, 2005), 38, quoted in Skaine, *Female Suicide Bombers*, 15.

14. Corbett, *Comparative Insurgencies*, 6.

15. Raphael Israeli, "Palestinian Women: The Quest for A Voice in the Public Square through 'Islamikaze Martyrdom,'" *Terrorism and Political Violence* 16, no. 1 (Spring 2004): 38, quoted in Skaine, *Female Suicide Bombers*, 15.

16. Gabriel Ben-Dor and Ami Pedahzur, "The Uniqueness of Islamic Fundamentalism and the Fourth Wave of International Terrorism," *Totalitarian Movements and Political Religions* 4, no. 3 (Winter 2003): 85.

17. Ibid., 86.

18. Devin R. Springer, James L. Regens, and David N. Edger, *Islamic Radicalism and Global Jihad* (Washington, D.C.: Georgetown University Press, 2009), 57–59, 273.

19. Bruce Riedel, *Search for Al Qaeda: Its Leadership, Ideology, and Future* (Washington, D.C.: Brookings Institution Press, 2008), 121, 122, 125.

20. Springer et al., *Islamic Radicalism*, 59, 60, 67, 70, 71, 73, 75.

21. "Al-Qaeda's Operational Strategies—The Attempt to Revive the Debate Surrounding the Seven Stages Plan," *International Institute for Counter-Terrorism*, July 2009, http://www.ict.org.il/Portals/0/Internet%20Monitoring%20Group/JWMG_Al-Qaeda_Operational_Strategies.pdf and Springer et al., *Islamic Radicalism*, 77.

22. Abu-Ubayd al-Qurashi, "The 11 September Raid: The Impossible Becomes Possible," *Why War?* August 5, 1999, www.why-war.com/files/alqaida_statements.pdf, quoted in Springer et al., *Islamic Radicalism*, 168, 179, 180.

23. Peter Knoope and Anno Bunnik, "Why the People of Tunisia and Egypt Confirm the Bankruptcy of Al Qaeda's Tactics," *International Institute for Counter-Terrorism*, June 3, 2011, http://www.ict.org.il/NewsCommentaries/Commentaries/tabid/69/Articlsid/905/currentpage/2/Default.aspx.

24. Moshe Covo and Gilad Zahavi, "Will Al-Qaeda Adjust Its Strategy to Accommodate the Changes in the Regional System?" *International Institute for Counter-Terrorism*, July 31, 2011, http://www.ict.org.il/NewsCommentaries/Commentaries/tabid/69/Articlsid/964/currentpage/1/Default.aspx.

25. "Announcement of Ayman al Zawahiri's Appointment [in Arabic]," al Qaeda General Leadership, June 16, 2011, http://www.hanein.info/vb/showthread.php?t=246183; "Al-Qaeda Messages [in Arabic]," the first tape, published by Ayman Al-Zawahiri after his appointment as Al-Qaeda's leader; and "Uprising in Syria [in Arabic]," 7 minute video, Jihadi Forums, July 28, 2011, http://as-ansar.com/vb/showthread.php?t=44649, quoted in Covo and Zahavi, "Will Al-Qaeda Adjust Its Strategy."

26. Jihadi Websites Monitoring Group, "Osama Bin Laden's Elimination through the Prism of Al-Qaeda's Affiliates and Global Jihad Supporters—Follow-Up Report," *ICT Special Reports: The Death of Osama bin Laden*, 8, http://www.ict.org.il/LinkClick.aspx?fileticket=_wciKVnJUs0%3d&tabid=428 and http://gate.

ahram.org.eg/News/37172.aspx [Arabic], quoted in Covo and Zahavi, "Will Al-Qaeda Adjust Its Strategy."

27. Michael W.S. Ryan, "After Bin Laden: Al-Qaeda Strategy in Yemen," *Terrorism Monitor* 9, no. 20 (May 20, 2011), http://www.jamestown.org/programs/gta/single/?tx_ttnews%5Btt_news%5D=37949&cHash=1de1f787ecd2d22a697e3e acf3451d12.

28. Boaz Ganor, "How Will Al-Qaida Plan Attacks without bin Laden?" *Jerusalem Post*, May 3, 2011, http://www.jpost.com/International/Article.aspx?id=219006.

29. Murad Batal al-Shishani, "Understanding Strategic Change in al-Qaeda's Central Leadership after Bin Laden," *Terrorism Monitor* 9, no. 23 (June 9, 2011), http://www.jamestown.org/single/?no_cache=1&tx_ttnews%5Btt_news%5D=38037.

30. Steven Metz and Raymond Millen, *Insurgency in Iraq and Afghanistan: Change and Continuity* (Carlisle, PA: Strategic Studies Institute, U.S. Army War College, August 19, 2004), 1, 2, 4, 8, http://www.au.af.mil/au/awc/awcgate/cia/nic2020/insurgency.pdf.

31. Springer et al., *Islamic Radicalism*, 89.

32. "Bin Laden's Fatwa," *PBS News Hour*, August 1996, http://www.pbs.org/newshour/terrorism/international/fatwa_1996.html.

33. Patrick Porter, "Review Essay: Shadow Wars: Asymmetric Warfare in the Past and Future," *Security Dialogue* 37 (2006): 556, http://sdi.sagepub.com/content/37/4/551.

34. Springer et al., *Islamic Radicalism*, 90, 92.

35. Mohammed M. Hafez, *Suicide Bombers in Iraq: The Strategy and Ideology of Martyrdom* (Washington, D.C.: United States Institute of Peace, 2007), 211–14, 224–26, quoted in Brian M. Drinkwine, *The Serpent in Our Garden: Al-Qa'ida and the Long War* (Carlisle, PA: Strategic Studies Institute, U.S. Army War College, January 2009), 23, http://www.strategicstudiesinstitute.army.mil/pdffiles/PUB877.pdf.

36. Ibid., 211–20, quoted in Drinkwine, *The Serpent in Our Garden*, 21, 22.

37. Ibid., 218–21, quoted in Drinkwine, *The Serpent in Our Garden*, 21, 22.

38. Metz and Millen, *Insurgency in Iraq and Afghanistan*, 9.

39. Nicole Stracke, "Iraq: Suicide Bombing as Tactical Means of Asymmetric Warfare," *Insights* 5 (March 2007): 10.

40. Metz and Millen, *Insurgency in Iraq and Afghanistan*, 19.

41. Ahmed Rashid, "The Taliban: Exporting Extremism," *Foreign Affairs* (November/December 1999): 22, 35, quoted in Rosemarie Skaine, *The Women of Afghanistan under the Taliban* (Jefferson, NC: McFarland, 2002), 52.

42. Skaine, *The Women of Afghanistan*, 6, 7, 57 and "Terrorist Group Profile: The Taliban," *Terroristplanet*, July 7, 2011, http://www.terroristplanet.com/2010/02/terrorist-group-profile-the-taliban/ (accessed July 7, 2011).

43. Stanley A. McChrystal, "Becoming the Enemy," *Foreign Policy* 185 (2011): 10, 66–70, http:// proquest.com.

44. Haroun Mir and Vahid Mojdeh quoted in Roy Gutman, "Afghanistan War: How Taliban Tactics Are Evolving," *Christian Science Monitor*, March 15, 2010, http://www.csmonitor.com/World/2010/0315/Afghanistan-war-How-Taliban-tactics-are-evolving.

45. Ibid.

46. Mullah Omar, "Key Quotes from New Taliban Book," *Al Jazeera*, July 27, 2009, http://english.aljazeera.net/news/asia/2009/07/200972775236982270.html.

47. Alissa J. Rubin, "Taliban Overhaul Image to Win Allies," *The New York Times,* January 20, 2010, http://www.nytimes.com/2010/01/21/world/asia/21taliban. html?pagewanted=all.

48. Sanjeev Miglani and Hamid Shalizi, "Fear in Kabul after 20-Hour Taliban Siege," *Reuters,* September 14, 2011, http://mobile.reuters.com/article/topNews/ idUSTRE78D0NC20110914.

49. Thomson Reuters, "Air Strike Kills Taliban Militants Responsible for Fatal Helicopter Crash: NATO," *National Post,* August 10, 2011, http://news.national post.com/2011/08/10/air-strike-kills-taliban-leader-responsible-for-fatal-heli copter-crash-nato/#more-86515.

50. Gilles Dorronsoro, *The Taliban's Winning Strategy in Afghanistan* (Washington, D.C.: Carnegie Endowment for International Peace, 2009), 7, 21–24, http:// carnegieendowment.org/files/taliban_winning_strategy.pdf.

51. Ahmed Rashid, "What the Taliban Want," *New York Review Blog,* August 29, 2011, http://www.nybooks.com/blogs/nyrblog/2011/aug/29/what-taliban-wants.

52. Brendan Trembath, "Reports Qatar to Host Taliban Office," *ABC News,* September 13, 2011, http://www.abc.net.au/news/2011–09–13/reports-qatar-to-host-taliban-office/2897864?section=world.

53. Amir Shah, "Suicide Attacks at Afghan Hotel; Hostages Taken," *Yahoo News,* June 21, 2012, http://news.yahoo.com/suicide-attacks-afghan-hotel-hostages-taken-013108640.html.

54. Alissa J. Rubin, "Taliban Using Modern Means to Add to Sway," *The New York Times,* October 4, 2011, http://www.nytimes.com/2011/10/05/world/asia/ taliban-using-modern-means-to-add-to-sway.html?_r=1&nl=todaysheadlines& emc=tha22.

55. "Afghan Aide Burhanuddin Rabbani's Killer 'Pakistani,'" *BBC News,* October 2, 2011, http://www.bbc.co.uk/news/world-south-asia-15141985.

56. Robert Mackey, "Suicide Attack Follow Obama's Afghanistan Visit," *The New York Times,* May 2, 2012, http://thelede.blogs.nytimes.com/2012/05/02/ suicide-bomb-attacks-hours-after-president-obamas-visit-to-afghanistan/.

57. Chris Blake and Rahim Faiez, "Gunman Kills Afghan Peace Council Member," *Yahoo News,* May 13, 2012, http://news.yahoo.com/gunman-kills-afghan-peace-council-member-kabul-081424155.html.

58. AEIVideos, "Peter Bergen: Pakistan Will Remain Important," *You Tube,* March 15, 2012, http://www.youtube.com/watch?v=-kWsBCtGY0w.

59. Haron Amin, Afghan Diplomat, First Secretary, Islamic State of Afghanistan, United Nations, interview by Rosemarie Skaine, telephone, February 3, 2000, quoted in Rosemarie Skaine, *The Women of Afghanistan,* 47, 48.

60. Ashley J. Tellis, *Pakistan and the War on Terror: Conflicted Goals, Compromised Performance* (Washington, D.C.: Carnegie Endowment for International Peace, 2008), 1, http://www.carnegieendowment.org/files/tellis_pakistan_final.pdf.

61. Jayshree Bajoria, "Pakistan's New Generation of Terrorists," *Council on Foreign Relations,* December 9, 2011, http://www.cfr.org/pakistan/pakistans-new-generation-terrorists/p15422#p2.

62. Robert A. Pape and James K. Feldman, *Cutting the Fuse: The Explosion of Global Suicide Terrorism and How to Stop It* (Chicago, IL: University of Chicago, 2010), 138, 144.

63. Ibid.

64. "Pakistan Assessment 2012," *South Asian Terrorism Portal,* http://www. satp.org/satporgtp/countries/pakistan/.

65. Naveed Ahmad Shinwari, *Understanding FATA: Attitudes towards Governance, Religion and Society in Pakistan's Federally Administrated Tribal Areas*, Vol. IV (Peshawar: CAMP, 2010), quoted in *Reviewing the Decade Long Counter-Terrorism Struggle* (Islamabad: Individualland, February 2011), 13, 27, http://www.individ ualland.com/index.php?option=com_rokdownloads&view=file&Itemid=160.

66. Melissa Finn, "Terrorists, Female," in *Encyclopedia of Women in Today's World*, eds. Mary Zeiss Stange, Carol K. Oyster, and Jane E. Sloan (Thousand Oaks, CA: Sage Publications, 2011), http://www.sage-ereference.com/womentoday/Article_n836.html.

67. Emile Durkheim, *Suicide: A Study in Sociology*, trans. John A. Spaulding and George Simpson, ed. George Simpson (New York: Free Press, 1951), 14.

68. Skaine, *Female Suicide Bombers*, 3.

69. Karunya M. Jayasena, "Female Suicide Bombers and Sociological Analysis" (Master's thesis, California State University, Northridge, 2009), 20.

70. *Threat Assessment: Female Suicide Bombers* (Washington, D.C.: U.S. Customs and Border Protection, Office of Intelligence and Operations Coordination, March 2010), 12, http://info.publicintelligence.net/femalesuicidebombers.pdf, quoted in Rosemarie Skaine *Women in Combat* (Santa Barbara, CA: ABC-CLIO, 2011), 112.

71. Farhana Ali and Jennie Dow, "Women and Al Qaeda: Examining the Role and Contribution of Muslim Women to the Global Jihadi Movement," power point presentation at International Institute for Strategic Studies's Counter-Terrorism Series Conference: Female Suicide Bombing and Europe, London, March 6, 2006, Slides 13–15, http://www.iiss.org/conferences/counter-terrorism-series/female-suicide-bombing-and-europe/, quoted in Skaine, *Women in Combat*, 112.

72. Yoni Fighel, "Palestinian Islamic Jihad and Female Suicide Bombers," *ICT Journal* 167 (2003): 3, http://www.ict.org.il/Articles/tabid/66/Articlsid/167/Default.aspx, quoted in Jayasena, "Female Suicide Bombers and Sociological Analysis," 39.

73. *Threat Assessment*, 11.

74. Lindsey A. O'Rourke, "What's Special about Female Suicide Terrorism?" *Security Studies* 18, no. 4 (2009): 689, http://dx.doi.org/10.1080/09636410903369084.

75. Ibid., 692.

76. Skaine, *Female Suicide Bombers*, 88, 95.

77. Robert A. Pape, *Dying to Win: The Strategic Logic of Suicide Terrorism* (New York: Random House, 2005): 229, quoted in Skaine, *Female Suicide Bombers*, 95.

78. Yoram Schweitzer, "Suicide Bombing—The Ultimate Weapon?" *International Institute for Counter-Terrorism*, July 8, 2001, http://www.ict.org.il/Articles/tabid/66/Articlsid/68/Default.aspx, quoted in Skaine, *Female Suicide Bombers*, 87 and K.T. Rajasingham, "Sri Lanka: The Untold Story—Rajiv Gandhi's Assassination," *Asia Times*, 1995–2005, http://www.lankalibrary.com/pol/rajiv.htm, quoted in Skaine, *Female Suicide Bombers*, 93.

79. Skaine, *Female Suicide Bombers*, 100, 108.

80. "Growing Threat from Female Suicide Bombers," *Investigative Project on Terrorism News*, March 29, 2010, http://www.investigativeproject.org/1882/the-growing-threat-from-female-suicide-bombers.

81. Skaine, *Female Suicide Bombers*, 26.

82. O'Rourke, "What's Special about Female Suicide Terrorism?" 699.

83. Jason Lewis, "Now Al Qaeda Sends Women Suicide Bombers to Target West," *Mail Online*, January 24, 2010, http://www.dailymail.co.uk/news/article-1245600/Now-Al-Qaeda-sends-women-suicide-bombers-target-West.html.

84. Bobby Ghosh, "The Mind of a Female Suicide Bomber," *Time*, June 22, 2008, http://www.time.com/time/world/article/0,8599,1817158,00.html.

85. Reuters, "Pakistan: Female Suicide Bomber Carries out Attack Near Police Checkpost," *The Guardian*, August 11, 2011, http://www.guardian.co.uk/world/2011/aug/11/pakistan-female-suicide-bomber.

86. "Growing Threat from Female Suicide Bombers," *Investigative Project on Terrorism News*.

87. Rear Admiral D. M. Williams, Jr., USN (Retd.), Former Commander, Naval Investigative Service (NIS) Command, interview by Rosemarie Skaine, e-mail, July 6, 2011.

88. Joint Chiefs of Staff, *Department of Defense Dictionary of Military and Associated Terms*, Joint Publication 1-02 (Washington, D.C.: U.S. Government Printing Office, June 10,1998), quoted in Timothy L. Thomas, "Deciphering Asymmetry's Word Game," *Military Review* (July–August 2001): 32, http://www.au.af.mil/au/awc/awcgate/milreview/thomas_asym.pdf.

89. Joint Chiefs of Staff, *Joint Doctrine for Multinational Operations*, Joint Publication 3-16 (Washington, D.C.: U.S. Government Printing Office, April 5, 2000), I-4, http://smallwarsjournal.com/.

90. Clinton J. Ancker, III, and Michael D. Burke, "Doctrine for Asymmetric Warfare," *Military Review* (July–August 2003): 18, http://www.au.af.mil/au/awc/awcgate/milreview/ancker.pdf.

91. *Operations*, Field Manual No. 3-0 (Washington, D.C.: U.S. Department of the Army, February 27, 2008), viii, http://www.dtic.mil/doctrine/jel/service_pubs/fm3_0a.pdf.

92. William B. Caldwell, IV, cited in John Harlow, "Army Unveils New Field Manual for Operations," *U.S. Army: The Official Homepage*, February 27, 2008, http://www.army.mil/article/7644/Army_Unveils_New_Field_Manual_for_Operations/.

93. *Operations*, 1–4.

94. Ibid., 1–20.

95. Ibid., 1–4.

96. Ibid., 3–5.

97. Joint Chiefs of Staff, *Joint Operations*, Joint Publication 3-0 (Washington, D.C.: U.S. Government Printing Office, March 22, 2010), I-6, http://www.dtic.mil/doctrine/new_pubs/jp3_0.pdf.

98. Ibid., I-7.

99. Domenico Tosini, "Al-Qaeda's Strategic Gamble: The Sociology of Suicide Bombings in Iraq," *Canadian Journal of Sociology* 35, no. 2 (2010): 272.

100. Metz and Millen, *Insurgency in Iraq and Afghanistan*, 5, 9

101. Tosini, "Al-Qaeda's Strategic Gamble," 290.

102. Colin S. Gray, *Irregular Enemies and the Essence of Strategy: Can the American Way of War Adapt?* (Carlisle, PA: Strategic Studies Institute, U.S. Army War College, March 2006), 25, http://www.strategicstudiesinstitute.army.mil/pdffiles/pub650.pdf.

103. John W. Jandora, "Center of Gravity and Asymmetric Conflict: Factoring in Culture," *Joint Force Quarterly* 39 (October 2005): 78, http://www.au.af.mil/au/awc/awcgate/jfq/1439.pdf.

104. William R. Polk, *Neighbors and Strangers: The Fundamentals of Foreign Affairs* (Chicago, IL: University of Chicago Press, 1997), 30, 218, cited in Jandora, "Center of Gravity and Asymmetric Conflict," 79.

105. Ibid.

106. Jandora, "Center of Gravity and Asymmetric Conflict," 81–83.

107. Gray, *Irregular Enemies and the Essence of Strategy,* 13.

108. Marie Breen-Smyth, Chair in International Politics, Codirector, Centre for International Intervention, Director of Research, School of Politics, University of Surrey, Guildford, interview by Rosemarie Skaine, telephone, March 18, 2012.

109. Donald H. Rumsfeld, "Rumsfeld on Creating a 'Modular Army' for the 21st Century," *Wall Street Journal,* February 4, 2004, Op-ed, cited in Skaine, *Women in Combat,* 10, 11.

110. Aidan Kirby, "The London Bombers as 'Self-Starters,'" *Studies in Conflict and Terrorism* 30 no. 5 (2007): 415–28, quoted in Domenico Tosini, "Al-Qaeda's Strategic Gamble," 291.

111. Donald J. Reed, "Beyond the War on Terror: Into the Fifth Generation War and Conflict," *Studies in Conflict and Terrorism* 31, no. 8 (2008): 716, quoted in Domenico Tosini, "Al-Qaeda's Strategic Gamble," 291.

112. "Appendix C: The Army Modular Force," *Operations,* C1, C2.

113. Joint Chiefs of Staff, *Irregular Warfare: Countering Irregular Threats Joint Operating Concept,* Version 2.0 (Washington, D.C.: U.S. Department of Defense, May17, 2010), 42, http://www.dtic.mil/futurejointwarfare/concepts/iw_joc2_0.pdf.

114. Thomas, "Deciphering Asymmetry's Word Game," 33.

115. Ibid., 34.

116. "Dossier: Suicide Bombing as a Problem in Asymmetric Warfare," *The Estimate* 15, no. 8 (April 19, 2002), http://www.theestimate.com/public/041902.html.

117. Paul Allan Schott, *Reference Guide to Anti-Money Laundering and Combating the Financing of Terrorism: Second Edition and Supplement on Special Recommendation IX* (Washington, D.C.: World Bank, January 2006), I-1, http://zunia.org/uploads/media/knowledge/Reference_Guide_AMLCFT_2ndSupplement1.pdf.

118. Ibid., I-3.

119. CIA, intelligence reporting, April 12, 2001, quoted in John Roth, Douglas Greenburg, and Serena B. Wille, *Monograph on Terrorist Financing: Staff Report to the Commission* (Washington, D.C.: National Commission on Terrorist Attacks upon the United States, 2004), 18, http://govinfo.library.unt.edu/911/staff_statements/911_TerrFin_Monograph.pdf.

120. U.N. General Assembly, "International Convention for the Suppression of the Financing of Terrorism," Resolution 54/109, December 9, 1999, http://www.un.org/law/cod/finterr.htm.

121. U.N. Secretary General, "International Convention for the Suppression of the Financing of Terrorism," adopted December 9, 1999, entered into force April 10, 2002, Obligations, http://www.nti.org/.

122. "Terrorist Finance Tracking Program (TFTP)," *U.S. Department of the Treasury,* site updated as of August 8, 2011, but program conceived within days post-9/11, http://www.treasury.gov/resource-center/terrorist-illicit-finance/Terrorist-Finance-Tracking/Pages/tftp.aspx.

123. "Terrorist Finance Tracking Program (TFTP): Questions and Answers," *U.S. Department of the Treasury,* August 5, 2011, Q: 1, http://www.treasury.gov/resource-center/terrorist-illicit-finance/Terrorist-Finance-Tracking/Documents/Final%20Updated%20TFTP%20Brochure%20(8-5-11).pdf.

124. Roth et al., *Monograph on Terrorist Financing,* 4.

125. Ibid., 17.

126. Ibid., 67, 68.

127. Ibid.

128. Adam Entous, "U.S. Balks at Pakistani Bills," *Wall Street Journal*, May 16, 2011, http://online.wsj.com/article/SB1000142405274870373080457632157090261 7838.html, quoted in Susan B. Epstein and Alan Kronstadt, "Pakistan: U.S. Foreign Assistance," *Congressional Research Service Report*, July 28, 2011, 13, note 33, http://www.fas.org/sgp/crs/row/R41856.pdf.

129. Ibid.

130. "Terrorism and Illicit Finance: Executive Orders," *U.S. Department of the Treasury*, August 8, 2011, http://www.treasury.gov/resource-center/terrorist-illicit-finance/Pages/protecting-charities_exec-orders.aspx.

131. *Typologies and Open Source Reporting on Terrorist Abuse of Charitable Operations in Post-Earthquake Pakistan and India* (Washington, D.C.: U.S. Department of the Treasury, 2005), 2, http://www.treasury.gov/resource-center/terrorist-illicit-finance/Documents/charities_post-earthquake.pdf.

132. Joshua Partlow and Kamran Khan, "Charity Funds Said to Provide Clues to Alleged Terrorist Plot," *The Washington Post*, August 15, 2006, http://www.washingtonpost.com/wp-dyn/content/article/2006/08/14/AR2006081401196.html.

133. Omar Waraich, "Terrorism-Linked Charity Finds New Life amid Pakistan Refugee Crisis," *Time*, May 13, 2009, http://www.time.com/time/world/article/0,8599,1898127,00.html.

134. Matthew Levitt, *Hamas: Politics, Charity, and Terrorism in the Service of Jihad* (Washington, D.C.: Washington Institute for Near East Policy, 2006), 58, 109, 123.

135. Christopher Heffelfinger, "Mission Not Accomplished," *Foreign Policy*, August 5, 2011, http://www.foreignpolicy.com/articles/2011/08/05/mission_not_accomplished.

136. National Intelligence Council, "Global Trends 2015: A Dialogue about the Future with Nongovernment Experts," *CIA*, December 2000, 50, https://www.cia.gov/news-information/cia-the-war-on-terrorism/terrorism-related-excerpts-from-global-trends-2015-a-dialogue-about-the-future-with-nongovernment-experts.html.

137. Robert A. Pape, "Introduction: What is New about Research on Terrorism," *Security Studies* 18 no. 4 (2009): 646, http://dx.doi.org/10.1080/09636410903369100.

138. Ibid., 649.

139. Lorenzo Vidino, *Radicalization, Linkage, and Diversity: Current Trends in Terrorism in Europe* (Arlington, VA.: RAND Corporation, 2011), ix, x, http://www.rand.org/content/dam/rand/pubs/occasional_papers/2011/RAND_OP333.pdf.

140. Ian O. Lesser, Bruce Hoffman, John Arquilla, David Ronfeldt, and Michele Zanini, *Countering the New Terrorism* (Santa Monica, CA: RAND, 1999), 9, 35–38, http://www.rand.org/pubs/monograph_reports/2009/MR989.pdf.

141. National Counterterrorism Center, *2010 Report on Terrorism* (Washington, D.C.: U.S. Office of the Director of National Intelligence, April 30, 2011), 5, http://eib.edu.pl/wp-content/uploads/2012/04/2010_report_on_terrorism.pdf.

142. Ibid., 6.

143. Ibid., 7.

144. Yochi J. Dreazen, "Allyn: Use of Children in Suicide Attacks Part of 'Ruthless' Escalation for Taliban," *National Journal*, June 20, 2011, http://www.

nationaljournal.com/nationalsecurity/taliban-s-use-of-children-in-suicide-at tacks-marks-a-ruthless-escalation-allyn-says-20110620.

145. U.S. State Department, Office of the Coordinator for Counterterrorism, "Chapter 1: Strategic Assessment," *Country Reports on Terrorism 2010*, August 18, 2011, http://www.state.gov/j/ct/rls/crt/2010/170253.htm.

CHAPTER 5

1. ngccommunitymoderator, "Remembering 9/11: New Insights 10 Years Later," *Inside NGC Blog*, July 27, 2011, http://tvblogs.nationalgeographic. com/2011/07/27/remembering-911-new-insights-10-years-later/.

2. Rachel Maddow and Richard Engel, *Day of Destruction, Decade of War*, msnbc Documentary, September 1, 2011, http://maddowblog.msnbc.msn.com/_ news/2011/08/18/7410051-day-of-destruction-decade-of-war-to-air-91-at-9-pm-et.

3. National Counterterrorism Center, *2010 Report on Terrorism* (Washington, D.C.: U.S. Office of the Director of National Intelligence, April 30, 2011), 8, http:// eib.edu.pl/wp-content/uploads/2012/04/2010_report_on_terrorism.pdf.

4. National Commission on Terrorist Attacks upon the United States, *The 9/11 Commission Report: Final Report of the National Commission on Terrorist Attacks upon the United States* (New York: W. W. Norton and Co., Inc., 2004), 1, http://govinfo. library.unt.edu/911/report/911Report_Exec.pdf and Paul Thompson, "Abridged 9/11 Timeline," *Amazon S3*, http://s3.amazonaws.com/911timeline/main/time- lineshort.html, quoted in Rosemarie Skaine, *Female Suicide Bombers* (Jefferson, NC: McFarland, 2006), 7.

5. Brian Michael Jenkins and John Paul Godges, eds., *The Long Shadow of 9/11: America's Response to Terrorism* (Santa Monica, CA: RAND, August 9, 2011), 2, http://www.rand.org/content/dam/rand/pubs/monographs/2011/RAND_ MG1107.pdf.

6. Brian Michael Jenkins, "The Land of the Fearful, or the Home of the Brave?" in Jenkins and Godges, *The Long Shadow of 9/11*, 204, 205.

7. Maddow and Engel, *Day of Destruction.*

8. Amy Belasco, "The Cost of Iraq, Afghanistan, and Other Global War on Terror Operations since 9/11," *Congressional Research Service Report*, March 29, 2011, 1, http://www.fas.org/sgp/crs/natsec/RL33110.pdf.

9. Eisenhower Study Group, *The Costs of War since 2001: Iraq, Afghanistan, and Pakistan—Executive Summary* (Providence, RI: Watson Institute, Brown University, June 2011), 9, http://costsofwar.org/sites/default/files/Costs%20of%20War%20 Executive%20Summary.pdf.

10. Ibid., 1–5, 9.

11. Scott Helfstein, Nassir Abdullah, and Muhammad al-Obaidi, *Deadly Van- guards: A Study of al-Qa'ida's Violence against Muslims* (West Point, NY: Combat- ing Terrorism Center, December 2009), 2, http://www.ctc.usma.edu/wp-content/ uploads/2010/10/deadly-vanguards_complete_l.pdf.

12. Stephen M. Walt, "Why They Hate Us (II): How Many Muslims Has the U.S. Killed in the Past 30 Years?" *Foreign Policy*, November 30, 2009, http://walt. foreignpolicy.com/posts/2009/11/30/why_they_hate_us_ii_how_many_mus lims_has_the_us_killed_in_the_past_30_years.

13. Jenkins, "The Land of the Fearful," 203, 204.

14. David B. Muhlhausen and Jena Baker McNeill, *Terror Trends: 40 Years' Data on International and Domestic Terrorism* (Washington, D.C.: The Heritage Foundation, May 20, 2011), http://report.heritage.org/sr0093.

15. Jenkins, "The Land of the Fearful," 204.

16. Christopher Torchia, "The Private Worry of US Marines in Afghanistan," *Yahoo News,* September 21, 2011, http://news.yahoo.com/private-worry-us-marines-afghanistan-065944218.html.

17. Elizabeth C. Borja, *Brief Documentary History of the Department of Homeland Security, 2001–2008* (Washington, D.C.: Homeland Security, History Office, 2008), 4, http://www.dhs.gov/.

18. Ibid., 7.

19. *U.S. Department of Homeland Security,* "Mission," 2012, http://www.dhs.gov/mission.

20. "United States Department of Homeland Security," *Wikipedia,* June 25, 2012, http://en.wikipedia.org/wiki/United_States_Department_of_Homeland_Security.

21. Kurt Andersen, "Beyond 9/11: September 11 Did Not Change Everything," *Time,* September 19, 2011, 64.

22. Jenkins, "The Land of the Fearful," 196, 197.

23. "Our History: How We Began," *Transportation Security Administration,* http://www.tsa.gov/research/tribute/history.shtm.

24. Maddow and Engel, *Day of Destruction.*

25. Jenkins, "The Land of the Fearful," 22.

26. James Risen and Eric Lichtblau, "Bush Lets U.S. Spy on Callers without Courts," *The New York Times,* December 16, 2005, http://www.nytimes.com/2005/12/16/politics/16program.html?pagewanted=all.

27. Eisenhower Study Group, *The Costs of War since 2001,* 9.

28. Rachel L. Swarns, "Special Registration for Arab Immigrants Will Reportedly Stop," *The New York Times,* November 22, 2003, http://www.nytimes.com/2003/11/22/us/special-registration-for-arab-immigrants-will-reportedly-stop.html; American-Arab Anti-Discrimination Committee and Penn State University Dickinson School of Law Center for Immigrants' Rights, *NSEERS: The Consequences of America's Efforts to Secure Its Borders,* March 31, 2009, 6, http://www.adc.org/PDF/nseerspaper.pdf; and Sam Dolnick, "A Post-9/11 Registration Effort Ends, but Not Its Effects," *The New York Times,* May 30, 2011, quoted in Jenkins, "The Land of the Fearful," 199, notes 2–5.

29. Maddow and Engel, *Day of Destruction.*

30. Cherif Bassiouni, *Perspectives on Terrorism* (Wilmington, DE: Scholarly Resources Inc., 1985), 181, cited in Clara Beyler, "Messengers of Death—Female Suicide Bombers," *International Institute for Counter-Terrorism,* December 2, 2003, 12, http://www.ict.org.il/Articles/tabid/66/Articlsid/94/%20currentpage/20/Default.aspx.

31. Ibid.

32. James Castonguay, "Conglomeration, New Media, and the Cultural Production of the 'War on Terror,'" *Cinema Journal* 43, no. 4 (Summer 2004): 103.

33. "Acquiescent Media after 9/11: Transcript," *On [The Media],* September 9, 2011, http://www.onthemedia.org/2011/sep/09/complaisant-media-after-911/transcript/.

34. Tom Farer, "Un-Just War against Terrorism and the Struggle to Appropriate Human Rights," *Human Rights Quarterly* 30, no. 2 (May 2008): 362.

35. Dick Cheney, quoted in "War and the Media Press Freedom vs. Military Censorship," *Constitutional Rights Foundation*, 2011, http://www.crf-usa.org/war-in-iraq/press-freedom.html.

36. David A. Frenznick, "The First Amendment on the Battlefield," *Pacific Law Journal* 23 (1992): 315, http://www.wilkefleury.com/userfiles/articles/THE-FIRST-AMENDMENT-ON-THE-BATTLEFIELD.pdf.

37. *Editor & Publisher*, quoted in Naomi Spencer, "Military Censorship of the War in Iraq," *World Socialist Web Site*, July 31, 2008, http://www.wsws.org/articles/2008/jul2008/cens-j31.shtml.

38. Ibid.

39. Jenkins, "The Land of the Fearful," 207.

40. C. Busby, M. Hamdan, and E. Ariabi, "Cancer, Infant Mortality and Birth Sex-Ratio in Fallujah, Iraq 2005–2009," *International Journal of Environmental Research and Public Health* 7(2010): 2828–37, quoted in Eisenhower Study Group, *The Costs of War since 2001*, 11, 12.

41. "America's Image in the World: Findings from the Pew Global Attitudes Project," *Pew Research Center*, March 14, 2007, http://www.pewglobal.org/2007/03/14/americas-image-in-the-world-findings-from-the-pew-global-attitudes-project.

42. Rohan Gunaratna and Karunya Jayasena, "Global Support for al Qaeda and Osama Bin Laden: An Increase or Decrease?" *UNISCI Discussion Papers* 25 (January/Enero 2011): 199.

43. Ibid., 214.

44. "On Anniversary of bin Laden's Death, Little Backing of al Qaeda," *Pew Research Center*, April 30, 2012, http://www.pewglobal.org/2012/04/30/on-anniversary-of-bin-ladens-death-little-backing-of-al-qaeda.

45. Ibid.

46. U.S. Federal Bureau of Investigation, "2003 Significant Events: January 30, 2003—Richard C. Reid Sentenced," *Terrorism 2002–2005*, http://www.fbi.gov/.

47. Ed O'Keefe and Ashley Halsey, III, "Shoe Removal Requirement at Airports to be Phased out," *The Washington Post*, September 6, 2011, http://www.washingtonpost.com/local/shoe-removal-requirement-at-airports-to-be-phased-out/2011/09/06/gIQAknLD7J_story.html; Lee Moran, "Shoe Bomber in Supermax: Richard Reid Pictured for First Time inside High Security Prison," *Mail Online*, October 10, 2011, http://www.dailymail.co.uk/news/article-2047093/Shoe-bomber-Richard-Reid-pictured-inside-US-Supermax-jail.html.

48. "TSA Shares Tips to Streamline Summer Travel," *Transportation and Security Administration*, May 25, 2012, http://www.tsa.gov/press/releases/2012/0525.shtm.

49. "Umar Farouk Abdulmutallab," *The New York Times*, October 12, 2011, http://topics.nytimes.com/top/reference/timestopics/people/a/umar_farouk_abdulmutallab/index.html?inline=nyt-per.

50. "Underwear Bomber Gets 4 Life Sentences," *San Francisco Chronicle*, February 17, 2012, A5, http://www.sfgate.com/crime/article/Underwear-bomber-gets-4-life-sentences-3338151.php.

51. "Terrorist Organizational Models," *A Military Guide to Terrorism in the Twenty-First Century*, Handbook No. 1 (Fort Leavenworth, KS: U.S. Army Training

and Doctrine Command, August 15, 2007), Chapter 3, 3.1–3.14, http://www.au.af.
mil/au/awc/awcgate/army/guidterr/ch03.pdf.

52. "Terrorist Groups," *Terrorism Research,* http://www.terrorism-research.
com/groups/.

53. Skaine, *Female Suicide Bombers,* Chapters 5 and 6.

54. Bruce Hoffman, "Bin Ladin's Killing and Its Effect on Al-Qa'ida: What
Comes Next?" *Combating Terrorism Center at West Point,* May 1, 2011, http://
www.ctc.usma.edu/posts/bin-ladin%E2%80%99s-killing-and-its-effect-on-
al-qaida-what-comes-next.

55. "Full Statement from al Qaeda on Osama bin Laden's Death," *CNN News
Blog,* May 6, 2011, http://news.blogs.cnn.com/2011/05/06/full-statement-from-
al-qaeda-on-osama-bin-ladens-death/.

56. Hoffman, "Bin Ladin's Killing and Its Effect on Al-Qa'ida."

57. R. Kim Cragin and Sara A. Daly, *The Dynamic Terrorist Threat: An Assessment of Group Motivations and Capabilities in a Changing World* (Santa Monica, CA:
RAND, 2003), xv, 61–84, http://www.rand.org/content/dam/rand/pubs/mono
graph_reports/2005/MR1782.pdf.

58. Ibid.

59. Mark Hamm, "Prisoner Radicalization: Assessing the Threat in U.S. Correctional Institutions," *National Institute of Justice Journal* 261 (2010): 18, https://
www.ncjrs.gov/pdffiles1/nij/224085.pdf.

60. Greg Hannah, Lindsay Clutterbuck, and Jennifer Rubin, *Radicalization
or Rehabilitation: Understanding the Challenge of Extremist and Radicalized Prisoners*
(Santa Monica, CA: RAND, 2008), x, http://www.rand.org/content/dam/rand/
pubs/technical_reports/2008/RAND_TR571.pdf.

61. "Iraq: Abu Ghraib's Legacy," *CNN,* December 19, 2011, http://www.cnn.
com/video/#/video/world/2011/12/19/nat-abu-ghraib-legacy.cnn.

62. "Prisoner Abuse at Abu Ghraib," *C-SPAN Video Library,* July 22, 2004,
http://www.c-spanvideo.org/program/182821–1.

63. Diane Marie Amann, "Abu Ghraib," *University of Pennsylvania Law Review*
153 (2005): 2139.

64. Ibid., 2140.

65. Richard Jackson, Department of International Politics, Aberystwyth University, Aberystwyth, interview by Rosemarie Skaine, e-mail, June 14, 2011. See
also Jacob Bercovitch and Richard Jackson, *Conflict Resolution in the 21st Century:
Principles, Methods, and Approaches* (Ann Arbor, MI: University of Michigan Press,
2009).

66. Jackson, interview.

67. Ibid.

68. Ibid.

69. "Measuring Systemic Peace," *Global Conflict Trends,* March 19, 2012, http://
www.systemicpeace.org/conflict.htm.

PART II

1. William Gerald Beasley, *The Perry Mission to Japan, 1853–1854* (New
York: Routledge, 2002), 140–146 and Amir Butler, "An Enduring Freedom for
the Moros," *The Wisdom Fund,* February 15, 2002, http://www.twf.org/News/

Y2002/0215-Moros.html, cited in Brian M. Drinkwine, *The Serpent in Our Garden: Al-Qa'ida and the Long War* (Carlisle, PA: Strategic Studies Institute, U.S. Army War College, January 2009), 20, http://www.strategicstudiesinstitute.army.mil/pdf files/PUB877.pdf.

2. Adel Beshara, "Antun Sa'adeh and the Struggle for Syrian National Independence (1904–1949)," *Syrian Social Nationalist Party*, April 1, 2001, http://web.archive.org/web/20010410195803/http://www.geocities.com/CapitolHill/Lobby/3577/adel_bechara2.html, in Rosemarie Skaine, *Female Suicide Bombers* (Jefferson, NC: McFarland, 2006), 75.

3. Clara Beyler, "Messengers of Death—Female Suicide Bombers," *International Institute for Counter-Terrorism*, December 2, 2003, http://www.ict.org.il/Articles/tabid/66/Articlsid/94/%20currentpage/20/Default.aspx.

4. "Kongra-Gel (KGK)," *National Counterterrorism Center*, http://www.nctc.gov/site/groups/kgk.html.

5. "Al Shabaab," *National Counterterrorism Center*, http://www.nctc.gov/site/groups/al_shabaab.html.

6. Ibid.

7. Sentinel Staff, "Recent Highlights in Terrorist Activity," *Combating Terrorism Center at West Point*, May 22, 2012, http://www.ctc.usma.edu/posts/recent-highlights-in-terrorist-activity-30.

8. David Cook, "Boko Haram Escalates Attacks on Christians in Northern Nigeria," *Combating Terrorism Center at West Point*, April 23, 2012, http://www.ctc.usma.edu/posts/boko-haram-escalates-attacks-on-christians-in-northern-nigeria.

9. Murad Ismayilov, "Conceptualizing Terrorist Violence," *Journal of Strategic Security* 3, no. 3 (2010): 15.

10. Paul Gil, "Suicide Bomber Pathways among Islamic Militants," *Policing: A Journal of Policy and Practice* 2, no. 4 (2008): 412, 413.

11. Marie Breen-Smyth, "A Critical Research Agenda for the Study of Political Terror," *European Political Science* 6, no. 3 (September 2007): 260.

12. Ibid.

CHAPTER 6

1. M. Zajam, "Suicide Missions: Nothing Islamic about It," *TwoCircles.net*, February 20, 2011, http://twocircles.net/2011feb20/suicide_missions_nothing_islamic_about_it.html and Gabriella Gamini, "Argentine Pilots Claim They Had to Adopt Kamikaze Tactics," *The London Time*, April 1, 1992, 13.

2. Roger Pineau, "Preface," in *Divine Wind: Japan's Kamikaze Force in World War II*, eds. Rikihei Inoguchi, Tadashi Nakajima, Roger Pineau (Annapolis, MD: U.S. Naval Institute Press, 1994), xi.

3. "Religion in Japan," *Wikipedia*, June 17, 2012, http://en.wikipedia.org/wiki/Religion_in_Japan.

4. "Japanese Religion," *Patheos Library*, http://www.patheos.com/Library/Japanese-Religion.html.

5. Nicolai Timenes, Jr., *Defense against Kamikaze Attacks in World War II and Its Relevance to Anti-Ship Missile Defense; Volume I: An Analytical History of Kamikaze Attacks against Ships of the United States Navy during World War II* (Arlington, VA: Center for Naval Analyses, Operations Evaluation Group, November 1970), 2.

6. Ibid.

7. Ibid., 15.

8. Ibid., 27.

9. Ibid., 41.

10. Ibid., 45, 47.

11. Ibid., 54, 55.

12. Max Gadney, "Kamikazes, Deconstructed," *World War II* 23, no. 1 (April/May 2008): 46, 47.

13. Ibid.

14. Gerald W. Thomas, "Suicide Tactics: The Kamikaze during WWII," *Air Group 4 "Casablanca to Tokyo,"* 2011, http://www.airgroup4.com/kamikaze.htm.

15. Albert Axell and Hideaki Kase, *Kamikaze: Japan's Suicide Gods* (New York: Longman, 2002), 180, 181, 183.

16. U.S. Department of the Navy, Naval History and Heritage Command, *Anti-Suicide Action Summary,* Secret (Declassified), COMINCH P-0011, August 31, 1945, 1, http://www.history.navy.mil/library/online/Anti_Suicide_Action_Summary.htm#I.

17. Ibid., 2.

18. Ibid.

19. "Kamikaze Attack, 1944," *EyeWitness to History,* 2005, http://www.eyewitnesstohistory.com/kamikaze.htm.

20. G. Miki Hayden, "What Motivated the Kamikazes?" *Naval History* 19, no. 2 (April 2006): 22–24.

21. Peggy Warner and Denis Warner, *The Sacred Warriors: Japan's Suicide Legions* (New York: Avon Books, 1984), 160, 161, 166.

22. Kenneth J. Dale, "Cultural and Linguistic Barriers to Communicating the Christian Religion in Japan," *Intercultural Communication Studies* 8, no. 1 (1998–1999): 151, 153.

23. John Orbell and Tomonori Morikawa, "An Evolutionary Account of Suicide Attacks: The Kamikaze Case," *Political Psychology* 32, no. 2 (January 9, 2011): 297–322.

24. Emiko Ohnuki-Tierney, "Betrayal by Idealism and Aesthetics: Special Attack Force (Kamikaze) Pilots and Their Intellectual Trajectories (Part 1)," *Anthropology Today* 20, no. 2 (April 2004): 15, 18.

25. Inoguchi et al., *Divine Wind,* 187.

26. Axell and Kase, *Kamikaze,* 77, note 1, 83.

27. For example, "Notes from a Suicide Manual," *USS Yorktown and US Navy Targets,* http://www.yorktownsailor.com/yorktown/kamikaze.htm.

28. Ohnuki-Tierney, "Betrayal by Idealism and Aesthetics," 18.

29. Ibid., 19.

30. Ibid., 15, 19.

31. Warner and Warner, *The Sacred Warriors,* 147.

32. Ibid., 148.

33. William L. Worden, "Kamikaze: Aerial Banzai Charge," *Saturday Evening Post* 217, no. 152 (June 23, 1945): 17.

34. Orbell and Morikawa, "An Evolutionary Account of Suicide Attacks," 297–322.

35. Albert Axell, "The Kamikaze Mindset," *History Today* 52, no. 9 (September 2002): 3–5.

36. Worden, "Kamikaze," 17.

37. Mario Ferrero, "Martyrdom Contracts," *Journal of Conflict Resolution* 50 (2006): 867, 868.

38. Hayashi Ichizo, "Letters to His Mother from the Kanoya Base (1945)," first letter, quoted in Emiko Ohnuki-Tierney, *Kamikaze Diaries: Reflections of Japanese Student Soldiers* (Chicago, IL: University of Chicago Press, 2010), 182, 183.

39. Inoguchi et al., *Divine Wind,* 208.

40. Timenes, Jr., *Defense against Kamikaze Attacks,* 83.

41. Inoguchi et al., *Divine Wind,* 188–94.

42. Warner and Warner, *The Sacred Warriors,* 146.

43. Ohnuki-Tierney, "Betrayal by Idealism and Aesthetics," 20.

44. Shimoshizu Air Unit in Chiba Prefecture, *Basic Instructions for To-Go Flyers* (1945), 88pp., quoted in Axell and Kase, *Kamikaze,* xi, xii.

CHAPTER 7

1. Alan Richards, *Socio-economic Roots of Radicalism? Towards Explaining the Appeal of Islamic Radicals* (Carlisle, PA: Strategic Studies Institute, U.S. Army War College, 2003), v, http://www.strategicstudiesinstitute.army.mil/pdffiles/pub105.pdf.

2. Ibid., 23, 25.

3. "Lebanon Profile," *BBC News,* January 11, 2012, http://www.bbc.co.uk/news/world-middle-east-14647308.

4. "The World Factbook: Lebanon," *CIA,* https://www.cia.gov/library/publications/the-world-factbook/geos/le.html.

5. Faten Ghosn and Amal Khoury, "Lebanon after the Civil War: Peace or the Illusion of Peace?" *Middle East Journal* 65, no. 3 (Summer 2011): 382, 383.

6. Rosemarie Skaine, *Female Suicide Bombers* (Jefferson, NC: McFarland, 2006), 73.

7. Jad Chaaban, Hala Ghattas, Rima Habib, Sari Hanafi, Nadine Sahyoun, Nisreen Salti, Karin Seyfert, and Nadia Naamani, *Socio-Economic Survey of Palestinian Refugees in Lebanon* (Beirut: American University of Beirut, December 31, 2010), x, http://www.unrwa.org/userfiles/2011012074253.pdf.

8. David B. Doroquez, "The Israeli-Lebanon Conflict: Past and Present," *Doroquez.com,* 2003, 1, http://www.doroquez.com/arts/documents/rsoc03.pdf, in Skaine, *Female Suicide Bombers,* 73, 74 and "Lebanon Profile: A Chronology of Key Events," *BBC News,* January 11, 2012, http://www.bbc.co.uk/news/world-middle-east-14649284.

9. Kathryn Westcott, "Who Are Hezbollah?" *BBC News,* April, 4, 2002, http://news.bbc.co.uk/2/hi/1908671.stm.

10. Max L. Gross, former Senior Research Fellow, Islam in Southeast Asia Project, Center for Strategic Intelligence Research, Joint Military Intelligence College, Washington, D.C. and former Dean, School of Intelligence Studies, Joint Military Intelligence College, interview by Rosemarie Skaine, telephone, February 23, 2011.

11. Fawwaz Traboulsi, interview by Paul Jay, *Real News Network,* July 15, 2010, http://therealnews.com/t2/index.php?option=com_content&task=view&id=31&Itemid=74&jumival=5322.

12. "Press Briefing by Secretary of State Condoleezza Rice," *The White House,* July 16, 2006, http://georgewbush-whitehouse.archives.gov/news/relea ses/2006/07/20060716-2.html.

13. "Week of 7.21.06—Timeline: Israel-Lebanon Crisis," *Now,* http://www. pbs.org/now/shows/229/middle-east-history.html.

14. Paul McGeough and Ed O'Loughlin, "Israeli Tanks Crash Border into Lebanon," *The Age,* July 23, 2006, http://www.theage.com.au/news/national/israeli-tanks-crash-border-into-lebanon/2006/07/23/1153166638729.html.

15. Gross, interview.

16. Westcott, "Who are Hezbollah?"

17. Brian A. Jackson et al., *Aptitude for Destruction: Case Studies of Organizational Learning in Five Terrorist Groups,* Vol. 2 (Arlington, VA: RAND, 2005), 49, 53, 54, http://www.rand.org/pubs/monographs/MG332.html.

18. Ibid., 41.

19. "Hezbollah Terrorism Incidents Database Search," *RAND Database of Worldwide Terrorism Incidents,* January 1, 1968–December 31, 2010, http://smapp. rand.org/rwtid/search_form.php and Peter Wehner, "The Unintended Consequences of a Retreat," *Commentary,* June 21, 2011, http://www.commentarymaga zine.com/2011/06/21/the-unintended-consequences-of-a-retreat/.

20. Daniel Helmer, "Hezbollah's Employment of Suicide Bombing during the 1980s: The Theological, Political, and Operational Development of a New Tactic," *Military Review* 86, no. 4 (July–August 2006): 72, http://usacac.army.mil/CAC2/ MilitaryReview/Archives/English/MilitaryReview_20060831_art012.pdf.

21. Ibid., 74–76.

22. Ibid., 76, 77.

23. Ibid., 78.

24. Ibid., 79.

25. Westcott, "Who are Hezbollah?"

26. Robert A. Pape, interview by Kerry O'Brien, "US 'Misread Motivation' of Suicide Bombers," *The 7:30 Reports,* July 20, 2005, http://www.abc.net.au/7.30/ content/2005/s1418817.htm.

27. William M. Arkin and Matthew G. McKinzie, "Imaging Destruction in Lebanon," *Imaging Notes* 22, no 3 (Fall 2007), http://www.imagingnotes.com/go/ article_free.php?mp_id=111.

28. Paul Gill, "A Multi-Dimensional Approach to Suicide Bombing," *International Journal of Conflict and Violence* 1, no. 2 (2007): 156, http://ijcv.org/index.php/ ijcv/article/viewFile/12/12.

29. Nicola Pratt, "On *Suicide Terrorism* by Ami Pedahzur, Polity, 2005, 240 pp," *Democratiya* 6 (Autumn 2006): 85, http://dissentmagazine.org/democratiya/ article_pdfs/d6Pratt.pdf.

30. Gill, "A Multi-Dimensional Approach," 146.

31. Gross, interview.

32. Jackson et al., *Aptitude for Destruction,* 48.

33. Gill, "A Multi-Dimensional Approach," 147.

34. Ibid., 156.

35. Gross, interview.

36. U.S. National Counterterrorism Center, "Worldwide Incident Tracking System (WITS): Hizballah," *2012 Counterterrorism Calendar,* 50, http://www.nctc. gov/site/pdfs/ct_calendar_2012_141.pdf.

37. Zeina Karam, "Hezbollah Rise in Lebanon Gives Syria, Iran Sway," *The Huffington Post*, June 13, 2011, http://www.huffingtonpost.com/2011/06/13/hezbollah-syria-iran-influence_n_876329.html.

38. Mona Alami, "Hezbollah's Muted Response to Syria Uprising Divides Arabs," *USA Today*, February 2, 2012, http://www.usatoday.com/news/world/story/2012-02-01/hezbollah-arab-spring/52919250/1.

39. U.S. National Counterterrorism Center, "WITS: Hizballah."

40. "The World Factbook: Gaza Strip," *CIA*, April 11, 2012, https://www.cia.gov/library/publications/the-world-factbook/geos/gz.html and "The World Factbook: West Bank," *CIA*, April 11, 2012, https://www.cia.gov/library/publications/the-world-factbook/geos/we.html.

41. "A History of Conflict: Israel and the Palestinians," *BBC News*, Introduction and 1250BC–638AD, http://news.bbc.co.uk/2/shared/spl/hi/middle_east/03/v3_ip_timeline/html/.

42. Charles K. Rowley and Jennis Taylor, "The Israel and Palestine Land Settlement Problem, 1948–2005: An Analytical History," *Public Choice* 128 (2006): 77.

43. Sari Bashi and Kenneth Mann, *Disengaged Occupiers: The Legal Status of Gaza* (Tel-Aviv: Gisha, Legal Center for Freedom of Movement, January 2007), 9, http://www.gisha.org/userfiles/file/report%20for%20the%20website.pdf.

44. Angel Rabasa et al., *Beyond al-Qaeda: Part 2, The Outer Rings of the Terrorist Universe* (Santa Monica, CA: RAND Corporation, 2006), xiv, xv, 20, http://www.rand.org/content/dam/rand/pubs/monographs/2006/RAND_MG430.pdf.

45. Ibid., xiv, xv, 21, 22.

46. "Terrorist Organization Profile: Hamas," *National Consortium for the Study of Terrorism and Responses to Terrorism (START)*, http://www.start.umd.edu/start/data_collections/tops/terrorist_organization_profile.asp?id=49.

47. Rabasa et al., *Beyond al-Qaeda*, 15, 16, Notes 3235 pp. 15–16.

48. Ahmad Yassin, ed., *The Hamas Charter (1988)* (Gelilot: Intelligence and Terrorism Information Center at the Center for Special Studies, March 21, 2006), http://www.terrorism-info.org.il/malam_multimedia/English/eng_n/pdf/hamas_charter.pdf.

49. "Terrorist Organization Profile: Hamas," *National Consortium for the Study of Terrorism and Responses to Terrorism (START)*.

50. Rabasa et al., *Beyond al-Qaeda*, 16, 17.

51. Suicide Attack Search Database, *Chicago Project on Security and Terrorism (CPOST)*, October 14, 2011, http://cpost.uchicago.edu/search.php.

52. Robert A. Pape and James K. Feldman, *Cutting the Fuse: The Explosion of Global Suicide Terrorism and How to Stop It* (Chicago, IL: University of Chicago, 2010), 209.

53. Jackson et al., *Breaching the Fortress Wall: Understanding Terrorist Efforts to Overcome Defensive Technologies* (Santa Monica, CA: RAND Corporation, 2007), 18, 21, http://www.rand.org/pubs/monographs/2007/RAND_MG481.pdf.

54. *CPOST*.

55. Pape and Feldman, *Cutting the Fuse*, 218.

56. Ibid., 207.

57. Charles K. Rowley and Jennis Taylor, "The Israel and Palestine Land Settlement Problem, 1948–2005: An Analytical History," *Public Choice* 128 (2006): 89.

58. "Israel-Palestine Liberation Organization Agreement: 1993," *The Avalon Project: Documents in Law, History and Diplomacy*, http://avalon.law.yale.

edu/20th_century/isrplo.asp and Daoud Kuttab, "The Two Intifadas: Differing Shades of Resistance," *The Jerusalem Fund,* Information Brief No. 66, February 8, 2001, http://www.thejerusalemfund.org/ht/display/ContentDetails/i/2120, quoted in Skaine, *Female Suicide Bombers,* 121.

59. "Declaration of Principles—Main Points," *Israel Ministry of Foreign Affairs,* September 13, 1993, http://www.mfa.gov.il/MFA/Peace+Process/Guide+to+ the+Peace+Process/Declaration+of+Principles+-+Main+Points.htm.

60. Jonathan Schachter, "The End of the Second Intifada," *Canada Free Press,* November 22, 2010, http://www.canadafreepress.com/index.php/article/30258.

61. Pape and Feldman, *Cutting the Fuse,* 218, 221.

62. Robert J. Brym and Bader Arajthe, "Suicide Bombing as Strategy and Interaction: The Case of the Second Intifada," *Social Forces* 84, no. 4 (June 2006): Analyses.

63. Pape and Feldman, *Cutting the Fuse,* Table 8.1 at 220.

64. Ibid., 221, 222.

65. Ibid., 222.

66. "Israeli–Palestinian Conflict," *Wikipedia,* February 14, 2012, http://en.wikipedia.org/wiki/Israeli-Palestinian_conflict, cited in Skaine, *Female Suicide Bombers,* 121.

67. Pape and Feldman, *Cutting the Fuse,* 222.

68. Rabasa et al., *Beyond al-Qaeda,* 19, 20.

69. Robert J. Brym and Bader Araj, "Palestinian Suicide Bombing Revisited: A Critique of the Outbidding Thesis," *Political Science Quarterly* 123, no. 3 (2008): 491.

70. Ibid., 491, 492.

71. Ibid.

72. Ibid., 493.

73. Clyde R. Mark, "Israel's Proposal to Withdraw from Gaza," *Congressional Research Service Report,* February 2, 2005, http://fpc.state.gov/documents/organization/43994.pdf.

74. Pape and Feldman, *Cutting the Fuse,* 207.

75. Ibid., 207, 224.

76. Mia Bloom, "Palestinian Suicide Bombing: Public Support, Market Share, and Outbidding," *Political Science Quarterly* 119, no. 1 (Spring, 2004): 61, 62.

77. Rabasa et al., *Beyond al-Qaeda,* 8.

78. CPOST.

79. Bloom, "Palestinian Suicide Bombing," 86.

80. Pape and Feldman, *Cutting the Fuse,* 207.

81. Andrew H. Kydd and Barbara F. Walter, "The Strategies of Terrorism," *International Security* 31, no. 1 (Summer 2006): 60.

82. CPOST.

83. Lori Allen, "There Are Many Reasons Why: Suicide Bombers and Martyrs in Palestine," *Middle East Report* 223 (Summer, 2002): 37.

84. Amira Hass, "Confessions of a Dangerous Mind," *Ha'aretz,* April 3, 2003, quoted in I. W. Charny, *Fighting Suicide Bombing: A Worldwide Campaign for Life* (Westport, CT: Praeger Security International, 2007), 74, ebooksclub.org__Fighting_Suicide_Bombing__A_Worldwide_Campaign_for_Life.

85. Brym and Arajthe, "Suicide Bombing as Strategy and Interaction," 1969.

86. Anat Berko and Edna Erez, "'Ordinary People' and 'Death Work': Palestinian Suicide Bombers as Victimizers and Victims," *Violence and Victims* 20, no. 6 (December 2005): 610, 611.

87. Allen, "There Are Many Reasons Why," 34.

88. Manuela Dviri, "My Dream Was to Be a Suicide Bomber. I Wanted to Kill 20, 50 Jews. Yes, Even Babies," *The Telegraph News*, June 26, 2005, http://www.telegraph.co.uk/news/worldnews/middleeast/israel/1492836/My-dream-was-to-be-a-suicide-bomber.-I-wanted-to-kill-20–50-Jews.-Yes-even-babies.html, quoted in Skaine, *Female Suicide Bombers*, 148.

89. "Women on the Edge of Destruction," *Cageprisoners*, July 2, 2005, http://old.cageprisoners.com/articles.php?id=5186 (first printed in the *Guardian*), cited in Skaine, *Female Suicide Bombers*, 148, 149.

90. Marie Breen-Smyth, Chair in International Politics, Codirector, Centre for International Intervention, Director of Research, School of Politics, University of Surrey, Guildford, interview by Rosemarie Skaine, telephone, March 18, 2012.

91. "Terrorist Organization Profile: Hamas," *National Consortium for the Study of Terrorism and Responses to Terrorism (START)*.

92. "Palestinian Parliamentary Elections 2006," *GlobalSecurity.org*, http://www.globalsecurity.org/military/world/palestine/pa-elections2006.htm.

93. Marc Lynch, *Rhetoric and Reality: Countering Terrorism in the Age of Obama* (Washington, D.C.: Center for a New American Security, 2010), 14, http://www.cnas.org/files/documents/publications/CNAS_Rhetoric%20and%20Reality_Lynch.pdf.

94. Karin Laub and Mohammed Daraghmeh, "Palestinian Fatah Looks Ill-Prepared for Election," *Yahoo News*, January 20, 2012, http://news.yahoo.com/palestinian-fatah-looks-ill-prepared-election-064258667.html.

95. Hugh Naylor, "Palestinian Elections Delayed by Hamas-Fatah Bickering," *The National*, March 9, 2012, http://www.americantaskforce.org/daily_ news_article/2012/03/09/1331269200_8.

96. Jodi Rudoren and Fares Akram, "Palestinians Sign Deal to Set up Elections," *The New York Times*, May 20, 2012, http://www.nytimes.com/2012/05/21/world/middleeast/hamas-and-fatah-agree-in-cairo-to-begin-work-on-elections.html.

97. Ali Abunimah, "Full Text 'State of Palestine' UN Application and Documents," *The Electronic Intifada*, September 24, 2011, http://electronicintifada.net/blog/ali-abunimah/full-text-state-palestine-un-application-letter-and-documents.

98. Reuters, "Palestinian Leader Asks UN for Statehood," *NBCNews*, September 23, 2011, http://www.msnbc.msn.com/id/44638003/ns/world_news-mideast_n_africa/t/palestinian-leader-asks-un-statehood/.

99. Helene Cooper, "Obama Says Palestinians Are Using Wrong Forum," *The New York Times*, September 21, 2011, http://www.nytimes.com/2011/09/22/world/obama-united-nations-speech.html.

CHAPTER 8

1. "Sri Lanka Profile," *BBC News*, May 20, 2012, http://www.bbc.co.uk/news/world-south-asia-11999611.

2. Christopher Moore, "Tamils Will Present United Front/Peace Talks with Sri Lankan Government," *The Guardian*, July 31, 1985.

3. "The World Factbook: Sri Lanka," *CIA*, March 6, 2012, https://www.cia.gov/library/publications/the-world-factbook/geos/ce.html.

4. Bruce Vaughn, "Sri Lanka: Background and U.S. Relations," *Congressional Research Service Report*, June 16, 2011, 1, http://www.fas.org/sgp/crs/row/RL31707.pdf.

5. Azmat S. Hassan, *Countering Violent Extremism: The Fate of the Tamil Tigers* (New York: East West Institute, 2009), 1, http://docs.ewi.info/Tigers.pdf.

6. "About Liberation Tigers of Tamil Eelam," *Tamil Eelam*, http://www.eelam.com/ltte and Rosemarie Skaine, *Female Suicide Bombers* (Jefferson, NC: McFarland, 2006), 85, 86.

7. Karunya M. Jayasena, *Motivations of Female Suicide Bombers from a Sociological Perspective* (Northridge, CA: California State University, 2009), Case Study 1, LTTE, http://books.google.co.in/books/about/Motivations_of_Female_Suicide_Bombers_fr.html?id=w4qkYgEACAAJ&redir_esc=y.

8. "Liberation Tigers of Tamil Eelam (LTTE)," *South Asia Terrorism Portal*, http://www.satp.org/satporgtp/countries/shrilanka/terroristoutfits/LTTE.HTM.

9. Robert I. Rothberg, ed., *Creating Peace in Sri Lanka: Civil War and Reconciliation* (Washington, D.C.: Brookings Institution Press, 1999), 6, quoted in Matthew P. Dearing, "Understanding Female Suicide Terrorism in Sri Lanka through a Constructivist Lens," *Strategic Insights* 9, no. 1 (Spring/Summer 2010): 72, http://www.nps.edu/Academics/Centers/CCC/Research-Publications/Strategic Insights/2010/Jul/SI_V9_I1_2010_Dearing_65.pdf.

10. Niel A. Smith, "Understanding Sri Lanka's Defeat of the Tamil Tigers," *Joint Force Quarterly* 59 (4th quarter, 2010): 41, http://www.ndu.edu/press/understanding-sri-lanka.html.

11. "Sri Lanka Profile: Timeline," *BBC News*, May 20, 2012, http://www.bbc.co.uk/news/world-south-asia-12004081.

12. Suicide Attack Search Database, *Chicago Project on Security and Terrorism (CPOST)*, October 14, 2011, http://cpost.uchicago.edu/search.php.

13. "History," *Background Notes on Countries of the World: Democratic Socialist Republic of Sri Lanka* (April 2011): 4.

14. Rohan Gunaratna, "Suicide Terrorism in Sri Lanka," in *Countering Suicide Terrorism* (Herzliya: International Policy Institute for Counter-Terrorism, The Interdisciplinary Center, 2006), 70, http://www.ict.org.il/Portals/0/51563-Countering%20Suicide%20Terrorism.pdf.

15. Ibid., 71.

16. "Sri Lanka Profile: Timeline," *BBC News*.

17. "History," 4.

18. Amantha Perera, "Sri Lanka: Blood over Water," *South Asia Intelligence Review*, Weekly Assessments and Briefings 5, no. 4 (August 7, 2006), http://satp.org/satporgtp/sair/Archives/5_4.htm#assessment1.

19. Ajit Kumar Singh, "Eelam War IV: Imminent End," *South Asian Outlook* 8, no. 9 (March 2009), http://www.southasianoutlook.com/issues/2009/march/sri_lanka_eelam_war_IV_imminent_end.html.

20. *CPOST*.

21. Robert A. Pape and James K. Feldman, *Cutting the Fuse: The Explosion of Global Suicide Terrorism and How to Stop It* (Chicago, IL: University of Chicago, 2010), 342.

22. *CPOST*.

23. Ibid.

24. Skaine, *Female Suicide Bombers*, 51, 87, 88 and "Sri Lanka Assessment 2012," *South Asia Terrorism Portal*, http://www.satp.org/satporgtp/countries/shrilanka/index.html.

25. Skaine, *Female Suicide Bombers*, 85; "Timeline of the Tamil Conflict: Early Years," *BBC News*, September, 4, 2000, http://news.bbc.co.uk/2/hi/south_asia/51435.stm; "Government Takes Policy Decision to Abrogate Failed CFA [Updated]," *Ministry of Defence and Urban Development, Democratic Socialist Republic of Sri Lanka*, December 30, 2010, http://www.defence.lk/new.asp?fname=20080102_12; and "Sri Lanka Timeline—1931–2012," *South Asia Terrorism Portal*, http://www.satp.org/satporgtp/countries/shrilanka/timeline/index.html.

26. Matthew P. Dearing, "Understanding Female Suicide Terrorism in Sri Lanka through a Constructivist Lens," *Strategic Insights* 9, no. 1 (Spring/Summer 2010), 70, 71, http://www.nps.edu/Academics/Centers/CCC/Research-Publications/StrategicInsights/2010/Jul/SI_V9_I1_2010_Dearing_65.pdf.

27. Gunaratna, "Suicide Terrorism in Sri Lanka," 69 and "Timeline of the Tamil Conflict," *BBC News*.

28. Jonathan Fine, "Contrasting Secular and Religious Terrorism," *Middle East Quarterly* 15, no. 1 (Winter 2008): 59–69, http://www.meforum.org/1826/contrasting-secular-and-religious-terrorism#_ftnref37.

29. *CPOST*, Attack ID 1782123892; Clara Beyler, "Messengers of Death—Female Suicide Bombers," *International Institute for Counter-Terrorism*, December 2, 2003, http://www.ict.org.il/Articles/tabid/66/Articlsid/94/Default.aspx; and K. T. Rajasingham, "Sri Lanka: The Untold Story—Rajiv Gandhi's Assassination, *Asia Times*, 1995–2005, http://www.lankalibrary.com/pol/rajiv.htm, quoted in Skaine, *Female Suicide Bombers*, 88, 89.

30. *CPOST*, Attack ID-1823289960.

31. Gunaratna, "Suicide Terrorism in Sri Lanka," 71.

32. "History," 4.

33. Bureau of South and Central Asian Affairs, "Background Note: Sri Lanka," *U.S. Department of State*, April 6, 2011, http://www.state.gov/r/pa/ei/bgn/5249.htm.

34. Hassan, *Countering Violent Extremism*, 2.

35. Jayasena, *Motivations of Female Suicide Bombers*, Introduction.

36. Pape and Feldman, *Cutting the Fuse*, 342.

37. Adele Balasingham, *Women Fighters of Liberation Tigers* (Jaffna: LTTE, 1993), quoted in Jayasena, *Motivations of Female Suicide Bombers*, Case Study 1, LTTE.

38. Robert A. Pape, *Dying to Win: The Strategic Logic of Suicide Terrorism* (New York: Random House, 2005), 226, 227, in Skaine, *Female Suicide Bombers*, 89.

39. Lisa Kruger, "Gender and Terrorism: Motivations of Female Terrorists" (M.Sc. thesis, Joint Military Intelligence College, July 2005), 67.

40. Hector N. Qirko, "Altruism in Suicide Terror Organizations," *Zygon* 44, no. 2 (June 2009): 289, 308, 314, 315.

41. Ibid., 315.

42. Tim Coles, "How Britain Armed the Sri Lanka Massacre," *Peace Review: A Journal of Social Justice* 23, no. 1 (2011): 77.

43. "Fears of Mass Suicide as Tamil Tigers Face Final Defeat," *Sunday Times*, May 17, 2009, 26, 27.

44. Matt Wade, "After Decades of Fighting, Tamils Lay Down Their Guns," *The Age*, May 18, 2009, http://www.theage.com.au/news/world/after-decades-of-fighting-tamils-lay-down-guns/2009/05/17/1242498638549.html.

45. "History," 4.

46. U.N. Secretary General, *Report of the Secretary-General's Panel of Experts on Accountability in Sri Lanka* (Geneva: United Nations, March 31, 2011), ii–v, 115 (Sec. 421), http://www.un.org/News/dh/infocus/Sri_Lanka/POE_Report_Full. pdf.

47. Jim McDonald, "UN: Investigate Sri Lanka War Crimes," *Human Rights Now Blog,* April 27, 2011, http://blog.amnestyusa.org/justice/un-investigate-sri-lanka-war-crimes/.

48. "Sri Lanka Warns UN Not to Release War Crimes Report," *The Guardian,* April 21, 2011, http://www.guardian.co.uk/world/2011/apr/21/sri-lanka-un-war-crimes-report.

49. Jayshree Bajoria, "The Sri Lankan Conflict," *Council on Foreign Relations,* May 18, 2009, http://www.cfr.org/terrorist-organizations/sri-lankan-conflict/p11407.

50. Charles Haviland, "Sri Lanka Government Publishes War Death Toll Statistics," *BBC News,* February 24, 2012, http://www.bbc.co.uk/news/world-asia-17156686.

51. "History," 4.

52. Claudia Brunner, "Occidentalism Meets the Female Suicide Bomber: A Critical Reflection on Recent Terrorism Debates; A Review Essay," *Journal of Women in Culture and Society* 32, no. 4 (2007): 969, quoted in Matthew P. Dearing, "Understanding Female Suicide Terrorism in Sri Lanka through a Constructivist Lens," *Strategic Insights* 9, no. 1 (Spring/Summer 2010): 69, http://www.nps.edu/Academics/Centers/CCC/Research-Publications/StrategicInsights/2010/Jul/SI_V9_I1_2010_Dearing_65.pdf.

53. "Sri Lanka Assessment 2012," *South Asia Terrorism Portal.*

CHAPTER 9

1. "Chechnya," *Encyclopedia Britannica Online,* http://www.britannica.com/EBchecked/topic/108244/Chechnya.

2. Angel Rabasa et al., *Beyond al-Qaeda: Part 1, The Global Jihadist Movement* (Santa Monica, CA: RAND Corporation, 2006), 105, http://www.rand.org/pubs/monographs/MG429.html.

3. Rosemarie Skaine, *Female Suicide Bombers* (Jefferson, N.C.: McFarland, 2005), 97, 98.

4. Mark Kramer, "The Perils of Counterinsurgency: Russia's War in Chechnya," *International Security* 29, no. 3 (Winter 2004–2005): 5.

5. "Q&A: The Chechen Conflict," *BBC News,* July 10, 2006, http://news.bbc.co.uk/2/hi/europe/3293441.stm.

6. James Hughes, *From Nationalism to Jihad* (Philadelphia, PA: University of Pennsylvania, 2007), 65, 87.

7. Kramer, "The Perils of Counterinsurgency," 7.

8. Emma Gilligan, *Terror in Chechnya: Russia and the Tragedy of Civilians in War* (Princeton, NJ: Princeton University, 2010), 15, quoted in Lara J. Nettelfield, "Terror in Chechnya: Russia and the Tragedy of Civilians in War (Review),"*Human Rights Quarterly* 33, no. 3 (August 2011): 887.

9. Robert A. Pape and James K. Feldman, *Cutting the Fuse: The Explosion of Global Suicide Terrorism and How to Stop It* (Chicago, IL: University of Chicago, 2010), 237.

10. Preeti Bhattacharji, "Backgrounder: Chechen Terrorism (Russia, Chechnya, Separatist)," *Council on Foreign Relations,* April 8, 2010, http://www.cfr.org/terrorism/chechen-terrorism-russia-chechnya-separatist/p9181.

11. Ekkehard Maass, *Chechnya—War and History: 400 Years of Colonial Conquest—400 Years of Resistance,* trans. Kate Vanovitch (Berlin: German-Caucasian Society, 2003), 25, 42, 43, http://www.d-k-g.de/downloads/Tschetschenien_Broschuere_en.pdf.

12. Raven Healing, "Chechnya: After Aslan Maskhadov," *World War 4 Report,* April 10, 2005, http://ww4report.com/chechnyamaskhadov.

13. Mark Galeotti, "Umarov's Volte-Face Opens Split in the Chechen Rebel 'Caucasus Emirate,'" *Analysis and Assessment of Russian Crime and Security: In Moscow's Shadows,* August 14, 2010, http://inmoscowsshadows.wordpress.com/2010/08/14/umarovs-volte-face-opens-split-in-the-chechen-rebel-caucasus-emirate/ and "Obituary: Aslan Maskhadov," *BBC News,* March 8, 2005, http://news.bbc.co.uk/2/hi/europe/459302.stm.

14. Jeff Collins, "Explaining Chechnya's 'Black Widows': An Organisational Analysis," *The Globalized World Post,* March 22, 2012, http://thegwpost.com/2012/03/22/explaining-chechnyas-black-widows-an-organisational-analysis/.

15. Ibid.

16. Robert W. Kurz, and Charles K. Bartles, "Chechen Suicide Bombers," *Journal of Slavic Military Studies* 20 (2007): 540, 541.

17. Ibid, 540 and Attack ID-1391550085, *Chicago Project on Security and Terrorism (CPOST),* December 17, 2002, http://cpost.uchicago.edu/search_results.php.

18. David Johnson, "Doku Umarov Vows 'Year of Tears,'" *Johnson's Russia List,* February 7, 2011, http://www.cdi.org/russia/johnson/russia-chechnya-militancy-umarov-feb-308.cfm (accessed April 9, 2012).

19. Kurz and Bartles, "Chechen Suicide Bombers," 541, 542.

20. James DeFronzo, *Revolutionary Movements in World History: From 1750 to Present* (Santa Barbara, CA: ABC-CLIO, 2006), 104, 105.

21. Andrew Osborn, "Moscow Bombing: Who Are the Black Widows?" *The Telegraph,* March 29, 2010, http://www.telegraph.co.uk/news/worldnews/europe/russia/7534464/Moscow-bombing-who-are-the-Black-Widows.html; Bill Gillespie, "The Avenging Black Widows," *CBC News,* March 31, 2010, http://www.cbc.ca/news/world/story/2010/03/30/f-russia-black-widow.html; "Suspect Retells Beslan's Horror; Leader Blew up Female Bombers after They Balked at Taking Children Hostage, Court Told," *The Record,* June 1, 2005, A7, quoted in Skaine, *Female Suicide Bombers,* 108; and Clara Beyler, "Female Suicide Bombers: An Update," *International Institute for Counter-Terrorism,* July 3, 2004, http://www.ict.org.il/Articles/tabid/66/Articlsid/558/currentpage/21/Default.aspx.

22. "Chechnya," *The New York Times,* March 25, 2012, http://topics.nytimes.com/top/news/international/countriesandterritories/russiaandtheformersovietunion/chechnya/index.html.

23. "A Timeline of Major Terror Attacks in Russia," *New Zealand Herald,* January 25, 2011.

24. Gilligan, *Terror in Chechnya,* 4, quoted in Nettelfield, "Terror in Chechnya," 886.

25. Maass, *Chechnya—War and History,* 46.

26. Kramer, "The Perils of Counterinsurgency," 12.

27. *CPOST.*

28. Ibid.

29. Kramer, "The Perils of Counterinsurgency," 7, 12, 19–21, 26–29, 32.

30. Ibid., 47.

31. Kurz and Bartles, "Chechen Suicide Bombers," 532.

32. *Terror Operations: Case Studies in Terrorism,* TRADOC G2 Handbook No. 1.01 (Fort Leavenworth, KS: U.S. Army Training and Doctrine Command, July 25, 2007), 6–20, http://www.fas.org/irp/threat/terrorism/sup1.pdf.

33. Charles Gurin, "Ingush Ex-Cop Reportedly among Hostage-Takers," *Eurasia Daily Monitor* 1, no. 80 (September 8, 2004), http://www.jamestown. org/single/?no_cache=1&tx_ttnews%5Btt_news%5D=26823; "The Beslan Attack & Qaeda Link," *Diplomat News Service* 61, no. 11 (September 13, 2004); John Kampfner, "A President Craves Understanding," *New Statesman* 133, no. 4705 (September 13, 2004): 10; "Suspect Retells Beslan's Horror," quoted in Skaine, *Female Suicide Bombers,* 108.

34. *Terror Operations,* 6–33.

35. Anne Speckhard, Nadejda Tarabrina, Valery Krasnov, and Khapta Akmedova, "Research Note: Observations of Suicidal Terrorists in Action," *Terrorism and Political Violence* 16, no. 2 (Summer 2004): 305, 306, 308, quoted in Skaine, *Female Suicide Bombers,* 111.

36. "Factbox: Major Terrorist Incidents Tied To Russian-Chechen War," *Radio Free Europe/Radio Liberty,* September 6, 2004, http://www.rferl.org/content/arti cle/1054699.html, quoted in Skaine, *Female Suicide Bombers,* 111.

37. Speckhard et al., "Research Note," 317, quoted in Skaine, *Female Suicide Bombers,* 113.

38. *Terror Operations,* 6–12.

39. Osborn, "Moscow Bombing."

40. "Chechnya," *The New York Times.*

41. *CPOST.*

42. Kristal L. Alfonso, "Femme Fatale 2010," *Air and Space Power Journal* 24, no. 3 (Fall 2010): 65.

43. Kurz and Bartles, "Chechen Suicide Bombers," 534.

44. *Terror Operations,* 6–10.

45. Pape and Feldman, *Cutting the Fuse,* 245.

46. Jim Nichol, "Stability in Russia's Chechnya and Other Regions of the North Caucasus: Recent Developments," *Congressional Research Service Report,* December 13, 2010, Summary, http://www.fas.org/sgp/crs/row/RL34613.pdf.

47. Kurz and Bartles, "Chechen Suicide Bombers," 535.

48. "Chechnya," *The New York Times.*

49. *"You Dress According to Their Rules": Enforcement of an Islamic Dress Code for Women in Chechnya* (New York: Human Rights Watch, 2011), 3, http://www.hrw. org/sites/default/files/reports/chechnya0311webwcover.pdf.

50. "Central Eurasian and Central Asian Terrorism," *National Counterterrorism Center,* http://www.nctc.gov/site/groups/cent_eurasian.html.

CHAPTER 10

1. Jayshree Bajoria and Greg Bruno, "Al-Qaeda (a.k.a. al-Qaida, al-Qa'ida),"
Council on Foreign Relations, August 29, 2011, http://www.cfr.org/terrorist-
organizations/al-qaeda-k-al-qaida-al-qaida/p9126. See also U.S. District Court,
Southern District of New York, *Indictment,* SC101, 98 Cr., 1023 (LBS) vs. Usamma
bin Laden et al., November 5, 1998, http://fl1.findlaw.com/news.findlaw.com/
hdocs/docs/binladen/usbinladen-1a.pdf and U.S. District Judge Lewis A. Kaplan
in New York ordered that the entire case be voided against bin, June 17, 2011, see
Patricia Hurtado and Chris Dolmetsch, "U.S. Dismisses Terror Indictment against
Osama Bin Laden," *Bloomberg Businessweek,* June 17, 2011, http://www.business
week.com/news/2011-06-17/u-s-dismisses-terror-indictment-against-osama-
bin-laden.html.

2. Abdel Bari Atwan, *The Secret History of al Qaeda,* 2nd ed. (Berkeley, CA:
University of California Press, 2008), 10.

3. Brian M. Drinkwine, *The Serpent in Our Garden: Al-Qa'ida and the Long War*
(Carlisle, PA: Strategic Studies Institute, U.S. Army War College, January 2009, 1,
http://www.strategicstudiesinstitute.army.mil/pdffiles/PUB877.pdf.

4. Peter Bergen and Erik Thompson, "The Last Days Osama bin Laden," *Nat-
geotv.com,* November 6, 2011.

5. Brian Michael Jenkins and John Paul Godges, eds., *The Long Shadow of 9/11:
America's Response to Terrorism* (Santa Monica, CA: RAND Corporation, August
9, 2011), 1, http://www.rand.org/content/dam/rand/pubs/monographs/2011/
RAND_MG1107.pdf.

6. Max L. Gross, former Senior Research Fellow, Islam in Southeast Asia Proj-
ect, Center for Strategic Intelligence Research, Joint Military Intelligence College,
Washington, D.C. and former Dean, School of Intelligence Studies, Joint Military
Intelligence College, interview by Rosemarie Skaine, telephone, October 29, 2011.

7. Pam Benson, "Unreleased bin Laden Audio Message Called 'Puzzling,'"
CNN U.S., May 13, 2011, http://www.cnn.com/2011/US/05/13/pakistan.bin.
laden.message/index.html?hpt=T2.

8. "Bin Laden's Warning: Full Text," *BBC News,* October 7, 2001, http://news.
bbc.co.uk/2/hi/south_asia/1585636.stm.

9. Gross, interview.

10. Emile Durkheim, *Suicide: A Study in Sociology,* trans. John A. Spaulding and
George Simpson, ed. George Simpson (New York: Free Press, 1951), 52, quoted in
Rosemarie Skaine, *Female Suicide Bombers* (Jefferson, NC: McFarland, 2006), 3.

11. George Ritzer and Douglas J. Goodman, *Sociological Theory,* 6th ed. (Boston, MA: McGraw-Hill, 2004), 93, 107, cited in Skaine, *Female Suicide Bombers,* 3.

12. Jeremy Scahill, "Washington's War in Yemen Backfires," *The Nation,* March
5–12, 2012, http://www.thenation.com/article/166265/washingtons-war-yemen-
backfires and Buck Sexton, "Yemen's Al Qaeda Branch Renaming Itself for Public
Relations Makeover," *The Blaze,* December 14, 2011, http://www.theblaze.com/
stories/yemens-al-qaeda-branch-renaming-itself-for-public-relations-makeover/.

13. Jeroen Gunning and Richard Jackson, "What's so 'Religious' about 'Religious Terrorism'?" *Critical Studies on Terrorism* 4 no. 3 (2011): 377, http://dx.doi.
org/10.1080/17539153.2011.623405.

14. Drinkwine, *The Serpent in Our Garden,* 20.

15. Oliver Roy, *Globalised Islam: The search for a New Ummah* (New York: Columbia University Press, 2006), quoted in Murad Ismayilov, "Conceptualizing Terrorist Violence," *Journal of Strategic Security* 3, no. 3 (2010): 20.

16. Thomas Hammes, *The Sling and the Stone* (St. Paul, MN: Zenith Press, 2006), quoted in Ismayilov, "Conceptualizing Terrorist Violence," 20.

17. U.S. Department of State, *The Terrorist Enemy,* 2010, http://www.state.gov/j/ct/enemy/index.htm and Charles Tilly, "Terror, Terrorism, Terrorists," *Sociological Theory* 22, no. 1 (2004): 5–13, quoted in Ismayilov, "Conceptualizing Terrorist Violence," 20.

18. "UK/BM-12 Translation," *Al Qaeda Manual* (Washington, D.C.: Department of Justice), 13, http://www.thewednesdayreport.com/twr/al%20quaeda/manualpart1_1.pdf.

19. Brian Michael Jenkins, *The al Qaeda-Inspired Terrorist Threat: An Appreciation of the Current Situation,* CT-353 (Santa Monica, CA: RAND, December 6, 2010), 5, http://www.rand.org/content/dam/rand/pubs/testimonies/2010/RAND_CT353.pdf.

20. Drinkwine, *The Serpent in Our Garden,* 20.

21. Don Rassler, Gabriel Koehler-Derrick, Liam Collins, Muhammad al-Obaidi, and Nelly Lahoud, "Letters from Abbottabad: Bin Ladin Sidelined?" *Combating Terrorism Center at West Point,* May 03, 2012, Osama bin Laden Letter to Shaykh Mahmud (Atiyaa), File SOCOM-2012-0000019, 3, http://www.ctc.usma.edu/posts/letters-from-abbottabad-bin-ladin-sidelined.

22. Ibid., 4, 6.

23. Ibid., 6.

24. Ibid., File SOCOM-2012-0000010-HT, 3.

25. Ibid., 2.

26. "UK/BM-15 Translation," *Al Qaeda Manual,* 16.

27. Skaine, *Female Suicide Bombers,* 3.

28. Mark Kukis, "With Friends Like These . . . Camp Fire," *The New Republic,* February 20, 2006, http://www.tnr.com/article/friends-these.

29. Sami Yousafzai, Ron Moreau, John Barry, Faisal Enayat Khan, Babak Dehghanpisheh, and Rod Nordland, "Back in Business," *Newsweek,* November 25, 2002, 26.

30. Sami Yousafzai and Ron Moreau, "Inside al Qaeda," *Newsweek,* September 13, 2010, 30–37.

31. Ibid.

32. See Tables 10.1 and 10.2 sources.

33. Jo Becker and Scott Shane, "Secret 'Kill List' Proves a Test of Obama's Principles and Will," *The New York Times,* May 29, 2012, http://www.nytimes.com/2012/05/29/world/obamas-leadership-in-war-on-al-qaeda.html?_r=1&nl=todaysheadlines&emc=edit_th_20120529.

34. Peter Bergen, "And Now, Only One Senior Al Qaeda Leader Left," *Peter Bergen,* June 6, 2012, http://peterbergen.com/and-now-only-one-senior-al-qaeda-leader-left/.

35. "Al-Qaeda's Remaining Leaders," *BBC News,* September 30, 2011, http://www.bbc.co.uk/news/world-south-asia-11489337.

36. Peter Bergen, Testimony, U.S. Senate Committee on Foreign Relations, *Al-Qaeda, the Taliban, and Other Extremist Groups in Afghanistan and Pakistan,* 111th

Cong., 1st Sess., Hearing, May 24, 2011, 7, http://foreign.senate.gov/hearings/hearing/?id=805120d6–5056-a032–5247–313a14503d33.

37. "US to Release bin Laden Home Videos, Propaganda Tapes, Officials Say," *NBCNews*, May 7, 2011, http://www.msnbc.msn.com/id/42941138/ns/world_news-death_of_bin_laden/.

38. "Full Statement from al Qaeda on Osama bin Laden's Death," *CNN*, May 6, 2011, http://news.blogs.cnn.com/2011/05/06/full-statement-from-al-qa eda-on-osama-bin-ladens-death/?iref=allsearch. The statement was issued by the al-Qaeda organization—General Command on Tuesday May 3, 2011.

39. Abdul Majid full interview [in Arabic] at http://www.tawhed.ws/r?i=19061015, quoted in Murad Batal al-Shishani, "Understanding Strategic Change in al-Qaeda's Central Leadership after bin Laden," *Terrorism Monitor* 9, no. 23 (June 9, 2011): 7, http://www.jamestown.org/uploads/media/TM_009_56.pdf.

40. Bajoria and Bruno, "al-Qaeda (a.k.a. al-Qaida, al-Qa'ida)."

41. James Veitch and John Martin, *The Death of Osama bin Laden and the Future of al-Qaeda* (Dhaka: Bangladesh Institute of Peace and Security Studies, 2011), 14, http://www.bipss.org.bd/pdf/BIPSS%20Paper.pdf.

42. John Rollins, "Al Qaeda and Affiliates: Historical Perspective, Global Presence, and Implications for U.S. Policy," *Congressional Research Service Report*, January 25, 2011, http://fpc.state.gov/documents/organization/156542.pdf.

43. Leah Farrall, "How al Qaeda Works: What the Organization's Subsidiaries Say about Its Strength," *Foreign Affairs*, March/April 2011, http://www.foreignaf fairs.com/articles/67467/leah-farrall/how-al-qaeda-works, quoted in Veitch and Martin, "The Death of Osama bin Laden," 36, 37.

44. Ibid.

45. Bernard I. Finel, "Are We Winning? Measuring Progress in the Struggle against al Qaeda and Associated Movements: 10 Report," *American Security Project*, May 1, 2010, 3, http://americansecurityproject.org/media/AWW%202010%20 Final.pdf.

46. Faisal Darem, "Yemeni Terrorism Experts: Ansar al-Sharia is Re-branded al-Qaeda," *Al-Shorfa*, August 3, 2011, http://al-shorfa.com/cocoon/meii/xhtml/en_GB/features/meii/features/main/2011/08/03/feature-01. See also "Complete Inspire Al-Qaeda in the Arabian Peninsula (AQAP) Magazine," *Public Intelligence*, October 11, 2010–September 27, 2011, http://publicintelligence.net/complete-inspire-al-qaeda-in-the-arabian-peninsula-aqap-magazine/.

47. Rassler et al., "Letters from Abbottabad," File SOCOM-2012-0000009-HT, 1.

48. Ibid.

49. "Fighting Turns Southern Yemen into 'Hell,'" *Khaleej Times*, May 9, 2011, quoted in W. Andrew Terrill, "The Arab Upheavals and the Future of the U.S. Military Policies and Presence in the Middle East and the Gulf," *Strategic Studies Institute*, June 27, 2011, http://www.strategicstudiesinstitute.army.mil/index.cfm/articles/Arab-Upheavals-and-the-Future-of-the-US-Military-Policies-and-Presence-in-the-Middle-East-and-the-Gulf/2011/6/27#_ednref28.

50. Suicide Attack Search Database, *Chicago Project on Security and Terrorism (CPOST)*, October 14, 2011, http://cpost.uchicago.edu/search.php.

51. Ibid.

52. Ibid.

53. Ibid.

54. Jenkins, *The al Qaeda-Inspired Terrorist Threat*, 8.

55. Robert A. Pape, interview by Kerry O'Brien, "US 'Misread Motivation' of Suicide Bombers," *The 7.30 Report*, July 20, 2005, http://www.abc.net.au/7.30/content/2005/s1418817.htm.

56. Ibid.

57. Bruce Riedel, "Al Qaeda Strikes Back: Terrorism and al Qaeda, Afghanistan," *Brookings*, May/June 2007, http://www.brookings.edu/articles/2007/05terrorism_riedel.aspx. This article was originally published in the May/June 2007 issue of *Foreign Affairs*.

58. U.S. National Counterterrorism Center, "Al-Qa'ida (AQ)," *2012 Counterterrorism Calendar*, 4, http://www.nctc.gov/site/pdfs/ct_calendar_2012_141.pdf.

59. Ibid, 30.

60. Ibid., 96, 98, 100, 116.

61. Ibid. 6, 8, 14, 17, 28, 32, 36, 38, 42, 43, 48, 118.

62. David Ignatius, "The bin Laden Plot to Kill President Obama," *The Washington Post*, March 16, 2012, http://www.washingtonpost.com/opinions/the-bin-laden-plot-to-kill-president-obama/2012/03/16/gIQAwN5RGS_story.html.

63. Rassler et al, "Letters from Abbottabad."

64. Peter Bergen, "Bin Laden: Seized Documents Show Delusional Leader and Micromanager," *CNN Opinion*, May 1, 2012, http://www.cnn.com/2012/04/30/opinion/bergen-bin-laden-document-trove/index.html?iref=allsearch.

65. Greg Miller, "Counterterrorism Expert Sees Much to Be Done," *The Washington Post*, May 17, 2012, http://www.washingtonpost.com/world/national-security/counterterrorism-expert-sees-much-to-be-done/2012/05/17/gIQAtPcFXU_story.html?wpisrc=nl_headlines.

66. Greg Miller and Karen DeYoung, "Al-Qaeda Airline Bomb Plot Disrupted, U.S. Says," *The Washington Post*, May 7, 2012, http://www.washingtonpost.com/world/national-security/cia-disrupts-airline-bomb-plot/2012/05/07/gIQA9qE08T_story.html.

CHAPTER 11

1. "Masada," *Jewish Virtual Library*, 2012, http://www.jewishvirtuallibrary.org/jsource/Judaism/masada.html.

2. Josh Sanburn, "A Brief History of Self-Immolation," *Time*, January 20, 2011, http://www.time.com/time/world/article/0,8599,2043123,00.html.

APPENDIX: DOCUMENT E

1. Michael Murray, "Osama Bin Laden Dead: The Navy SEALs Who Hunted and Killed Al Qaeda Leader," *ABC News*, May 2, 2011, http://abcnews.go.com/US/osama-bin-laden-dead-navy-seal-team-responsible/story?id=13509739 and James Veitch and John Martin, *The Death of Osama bin Laden and the Future of al-Qaeda* (Dhaka: Bangladesh Institute of Peace and Security Studies, 2011), 15, http://www.bipss.org.bd/pdf/BIPSS%20Paper.pdf.

2. Brian Ross et al., "Osama Bin Laden Killed by Navy SEALs in Firefight," *ABC News The Blotter*, May 2, 2011, http://abcnews.go.com/Blotter/osama-bin-laden-killed-navy-seals-firefight/story?id=13505792.

3. "Navy SEALs Complete bin Laden Mission," *Military Channel*, http://military.discovery.com/history/middle-east/navy-seals-bin-laden-mission.html.

4. Scott Wilson, Craig Whitlock, and William Branigin, "Osama bin Laden Killed in U.S. Raid, Buried at Sea," *The Washington Post*, May 2, 2011, http://www.washingtonpost.com/national/osama-bin-laden-killed-in-us-raid-buried-at-sea/2011/05/02/AFx0yAZF_story.html.

5. Barack Obama, "Text of President Obama's Statement to U.S. People," *Reuters*, May 2, 2011, http://www.reuters.com/article/2011/05/02/us-obama-binladen-text-idUSTRE7410ZG20110502.

6. Jay Carney, "Press Briefing by Press Secretary Jay Carney," *The White House*, May 3, 2011, http://www.whitehouse.gov/the-press-office/2011/05/03/press-briefing-press-secretary-jay-carney-532011.

7. Wilson et al., "Osama bin Laden Killed in U.S. Raid."

8. Ibid.

9. Ibid.

10. Ibid.

11. "Navy SEALs Complete bin Laden Mission," *Military Channel.*

12. Ibid.

13. Ibid.

14. Mark Tran, "CIA Admit 'Waterboarding' al-Qaida Suspects," *The Guardian*, February 5, 2008, http://www.guardian.co.uk/world/2008/feb/05/india.terrorism and Tim Ross, "WikiLeaks: Osama bin Laden Killed after Tip-offs from Guantanamo," *The Telegraph*, May 2, 2011, http://www.telegraph.co.uk/news/worldnews/asia/pakistan/8488436/WikiLeaks-Osama-bin-Laden-killed-after-tip-offs-from-Guantanamo.html.

15. Wilson et al., "Osama bin Laden Killed in U.S. Raid."

16. Ibid.

17. Ibid.

Bibliography

ARTICLES AND BOOK CHAPTERS

"About Liberation Tigers of Tamil Eelam." *Tamil Eelam,* http://www.eelam.com/ltte.

"Acquiescent Media after 9/11: Transcript." *On [The Media],* September 9, 2011, http://www.onthemedia.org/2011/sep/09/complaisant-media-after-911/transcript/.

"Afghan Aide Burhanuddin Rabbani's Killer 'Pakistani.'" *BBC News,* October 2, 2011, http://www.bbc.co.uk/news/world-south-asia-15141985.

"Afghanistan: Suicide Bomber 'Aged 12' Kills Four." *BBC News,* May 1, 2011, http://www.bbc.co.uk/news/world-south-asia-13252786.

"Al Qaeda's Fazul Abdullah Mohammed Killed, but Who Will Be Next Is't Godane, Shangole or Mansuur?" *Somalia Online,* June 14, 2011, http://www.somalia online.com/community/showthread.php/57919-Al-Qaeda%E2%80%99s-Fazul-Abdullah-Mohammed-Killed-but-who-will-be-next-is-t-Godane-shangole-OR-Mansuur.

"Al-Qaeda's Operational Strategies—The Attempt to Revive the Debate Surrounding the Seven Stages Plan." *International Institute for Counter-Terrorism,* July 2009, http://www.ict.org.il/Portals/0/Internet%20Monitoring%20Group/JWMG_Al-Qaeda_Operational_Strategies.pdf.

"Al-Qaeda's Remaining Leaders." *BBC News,* September 30, 2011, http://www.bbc.co.uk/news/world-south-asia-11489337.

"Al Qaeda Training Camps Go Local, Mobile." *CBS News,* November 10, 2009, http://www.cbsnews.com/2100-202_162-5584584.html.

Al-Shishani, Murad Batal. "Understanding Strategic Change in al-Qaeda's Central Leadership after Bin Laden." *Terrorism Monitor* 9, no. 23 (June 9, 2011), http://www.jamestown.org/single/?no_cache=1&tx_ttnews%5Btt_news%5D=38037.

Alami, Mona. "Hezbollah's Muted Response to Syria Uprising Divides Arabs." *USA Today*, February 2, 2012, http://www.usatoday.com/news/world/story/2012–02–01/hezbollah-arab-spring/52919250/1.

Alfonso, Kristal L. "Femme Fatale 2010." *Air and Space Power Journal* 24, no. 3 (Fall 2010): 59–73.

Amann, Diane Marie. "Abu Ghraib." *University of Pennsylvania Law Review* 153 (2005): 2085–141.

Ancker, Clinton J., III, and Michael D. Burke. "Doctrine for Asymmetric Warfare." *Military Review* (July–August 2003): 18–25, http://www.au.af.mil/au/awc/awcgate/milreview/ancker.pdf.

Andersen, Kurt. "Beyond 9/11: September 11 Did Not Change Everything." *Time*, September 19, 2011, 64.

Anderson, Richard C. *Redefining Just War Criteria in the Post 9/11 World and the Moral Consequences of Preemptive Strikes* (West Point, NY: United States Military Academy, January 24, 2003), http://isme.tamu.edu/JSCOPE03/Anderson03.html.

AP. "Suicide Bomber Is al-Qaida's Deadliest Weapon." *NBCNews*, 2008, http://www.msnbc.msn.com/id/23651109/ns/world_news/.

AP. "US Air Strike Kills Top Al-Qaida Leader in Yemen." *The Guardian*, May 7, 2012, http://www.guardian.co.uk/world/2012/may/07/us-airstrike-kills-al-qaida-leader-yemen.

Arkin, William M., and Matthew G. McKinzie. "Imaging Destruction in Lebanon." *Imaging Notes* 22, no 3 (Fall 2007), http://www.imagingnotes.com/go/article_free.php?mp_id=111.

"Attacks on Iraqi Pipelines, Oil Installations, and Oil Personnel: 2003–2008." *Iraq Pipeline Watch*, March 27, 2008, http://www.iags.org/iraqpipelinewatch.htm.

Avishai, Bernard. "A Plan for Peace That Still Could Be." *The New York Times*, February 7, 2011, http://www.nytimes.com/2011/02/13/magazine/13Israel-t.html?pagewanted=1&_r=1.

"Awakening Movement in Iraq." *The New York Times*, October 19, 2010, http://topics.nytimes.com/top/news/international/countriesandterritories/iraq/awakening_movement/index.html?inline=nyt-classifier.

Axell, Albert. "The Kamikaze Mindset." *History Today* 52, no. 9 (September 2002): 3–5.

Baker, Peter, Helene Cooper, and Mark Mazzetti. "Bin Laden Is Dead, Obama Says." *The New York Times*, May 1, 2011, http://www.nytimes.com/2011/05/02/world/asia/osama-bin-laden-is-killed.html.

Bajoria, Jayshree. "Pakistan's New Generation of Terrorists." *Council on Foreign Relations*, December 9, 2011, http://www.cfr.org/pakistan/pakistans-new-generation-terrorists/p15422#p2.

Bajoria, Jayshree. "The Sri Lankan Conflict." *Council on Foreign Relations*, May 18, 2009, http://www.cfr.org/terrorist-organizations/sri-lankan-conflict/p11407.

Bajoria, Jayshree, and Greg Bruno. "Al-Qaeda (a.k.a. al-Qaida, al-Qa'ida)." *Council on Foreign Relations*, August 29, 2011, http://www.cfr.org/terrorist-organizations/al-qaeda-k-al-qaida-al-qaida/p9126.

Bashir, Mohammad. "More Violence Rattles Afghanistan after U.N. Killings." *Reuters*, April 2, 2011, http://www.reuters.com/article/2011/04/02/us-afghanistan-violence-un-idUSTRE7310GZ20110402.

Bates, Daniel, and Mark Duell. "'Death Squad': Full Horror Emerges of How Rogue U.S. Brigade Murdered and Mutilated Innocent Afghan Civilians—and Kept Their Body Parts as Trophies." *Mail Online*, September 23, 2011, http://www.dailymail.co.uk/news/article-1370758/Shocking-video-shows-U-S-troops-cheering-airstrike-blows-Afghan-civilians.html.

Becker, Jo, and Scott Shane. "Secret 'Kill List' Proves a Test of Obama's Principles and Will." *The New York Times*, May 29, 2012, http://www.nytimes.com/2012/05/29/world/obamas-leadership-in-war-on-al-qaeda.html?_r=1&nl=todaysheadlines&emc=edit_th_20120529.

Ben-Dor, Gabriel, and Ami Pedahzur. "The Uniqueness of Islamic Fundamentalism and the Fourth Wave of International Terrorism." *Totalitarian Movements and Political Religions* 4, no.3 (Winter 2003): 71–90.

Benson, Pam. "Unreleased bin Laden Audio Message Called 'Puzzling.'" *CNN U.S.*, May 13, 2011, http://www.cnn.com/2011/US/05/13/pakistan.bin.laden.message/index.html?hpt=T2.

Bergen, Peter. "Bin Laden: Seized Documents Show Delusional Leader and Micromanager." *CNN Opinion*, May 1, 2012, http://www.cnn.com/2012/04/30/opinion/bergen-bin-laden-document-trove/index.html?iref=allsearch.

Bergen, Peter. "And Now, Only One Senior Al Qaeda Leader Left." *Peter Bergen*, June 6, 2012, http://peterbergen.com/and-now-only-one-senior-al-qaeda-leader-left/.

Berko, Anat, and Edna Erez. "'Ordinary People' and 'Death Work': Palestinian Suicide Bombers as Victimizers and Victims." *Violence and Victims* 20, no. 6 (December 2005): 603–23.

Berman, Eli, and David Laitin. *Hard Targets: Theory and Evidence on Suicide Attacks* (Cambridge, MA: National Bureau of Economic Research, 2006), http://dss.ucsd.edu/~elib/Hardtargets.pdf.

Berry, Jessica. "Fury over Hijacker's Visit to Britain." *Telegraph Network*, May 27, 2002, http://www.telegraph.co.uk/news/uknews/1395466/Fury-over-hijackers-visit-to-Britain.html.

Beyler, Clara. "Messengers of Death—Female Suicide Bombers." *International Institute for Counter Terrorism*, December 2, 2003, http://www.ict.org.il/Articles/tabid/66/Articlsid/94/%20currentpage/20/Default.aspx.

Beyler, Clara. "Female Suicide Bombers: An Update." *International Institute for Counterterrorism*, July 3, 2004, http://www.ict.org.il/Articles/tabid/66/Articlsid/558/currentpage/21/Default.aspx.

Bhattacharji, Preeti. "Backgrounder: Chechen Terrorism (Russia, Chechnya, Separatist)." *Council on Foreign Relations*, April 8, 2010, http://www.cfr.org/terrorism/chechen-terrorism-russia-chechnya-separatist/p9181.

"Bin Laden's Fatwa," *PBS News Hour*, August 1996, http://www.pbs.org/newshour/terrorism/international/fatwa_1996.html.

"Bin Laden's Warning: Full text." *BBC News*, October 7, 2001, http://news.bbc.co.uk/2/hi/south_asia/1585636.stm.

Blake, Chris, and Rahim Faiez. "Gunman Kills Afghan Peace Council Member." *Yahoo News*, May 13, 2012, http://news.yahoo.com/gunman-kills-afghan-peace-council-member-kabul-081424155.html.

Breen-Smyth, Marie. "A Critical Research Agenda for the Study of Political Terror." *European Political Science* 6, no. 3 (September 2007): 260.

Brownfeld, Peter. "The Afghanisation of Chechnya." *The International Spectator* 38, no. 3 (March 2003): 137–45, http://www.iai.it/pdf/articles/brownfeld.pdf.

Brunner, Claudia. "Occidentalism Meets the Female Suicide Bomber: A Critical Reflection on Recent Terrorism Debates: A Review Essay." *Signs: Journal of Women in Culture and Society* 32, no. 4 (2007): 957–71.

Brym, Robert J., and Bader Araj. "Palestinian Suicide Bombing Revisited: A Critique of the Outbidding Thesis." *Political Science Quarterly* 123, no. 3 (2008): 485–500.

Brym, Robert J., and Bader Araj. "Suicide Bombing as Strategy and Interaction: The Case of the Second Intifada." *Social Forces* 84, no. 4 (June 2006): 1969–86.

Burgess, Mark. "Current List of Foreign Terrorist Organizations and Other Terrorist Organizations." *Center for Defense Information*, August 12, 2005, http://www.cdi.org/program/document.cfm?DocumentID=384&StartRow=1&ListRows=10&appendURL=&Orderby=D.DateLastUpdated&ProgramID=39&from_page=index.cfm.

Burgess, Mark. "In the Spotlight: Islamic Movement of Uzbekistan (IMU)." *Center of Defense Information*, March 25, 2002, http://www.cdi.org/terrorism/imu.cfm.

Bush, George W. "Full Text: George Bush's Address on the Start of War." *The Guardian*, March 20, 2003, http://www.guardian.co.uk/world/2003/mar/20/iraq.georgebush.

Byman, Daniel. "The Changing Nature of State Sponsorship of Terrorism." *National Interest* 96 (July/August 2008): 52–59.

Canuel, Edward T. "Nationalism, Self-Determination, and Nationalist Movements: Exploring the Palestinian and Quebec Drives for Independence." *Boston College International and Comparative Law Review* 20, no. 1 (Winter 1997): 85–123.

Carver, Logan G. "Terror Suspect Aldawsari's Trial Moved to Amarillo, Set for June." *Lubbock Avalanche-Journal*, April 18, 2012, http://lubbockonline.com/crime-and-courts/2012-04-17/terror-suspect-aldawsaris-trial-moved-amarillo-set-june#.UDTAbqkgfow.

Casciani, Dominic. "Q&A: Sharia Law Explained." *BBC News*, http://news.bbc.co.uk/2/hi/uk_news/7234870.stm.

Cassata, Donna. "Gates: Prospect Very Low that Guantanamo Closes." *San Diego Union-Tribune*, February 17, 2011, http://www.utsandiego.com/news/2011/feb/17/gates-prospect-very-low-that-guantanamo-closes/.

Cassese, Antonio. "The Multifaceted Criminal Notion of Terrorism in International Law." *Journal of International Criminal Justice* 4, no. 5 (November 1, 2006): 933.

Castonguay, James. "Conglomeration, New Media, and the Cultural Production of the 'War on Terror.'" *Cinema Journal* 43, no. 4 (Summer 2004): 102–8.

"Chechnya." *Encyclopedia Britannica Online*, http://www.britannica.com/EBchecked/topic/108244/Chechnya.

"Chechnya." *The New York Times*, March 25, 2012, http://topics.nytimes.com/top/news/international/countriesandterritories/russiaandtheformersoviet union/chechnya/index.html.

Cheney, Dick. Quoted in "War and the Media Press Freedom vs. Military Censorship." *Constitutional Rights Foundation*, 2011, http://www.crf-usa.org/war-in-iraq/press-freedom.html.

Chepesiuk, Ron. "Dangerous Alliance: Terrorism and Organized Crime." *Global Politician*, September 11, 2007, http://www.globalpolitician.com/23435-crime.

"China Detains Hundreds in Tibet over Self-Immolation Protests." *The Telegraph,* May 31, 2012, http://www.telegraph.co.uk/news/worldnews/asia/tibet/9301849/China-detains-hundreds-in-Tibet-over-self-immolation-protests.html.

CNN Wire Staff. "Al Qaeda Threats, Terror Plans Surface." *CNN World,* May 6, 2011, http://www.cnn.com/2011/WORLD/asiapcf/05/06/pakistan.bin.laden/index.html?hpt=P1&iref=NS1.

CNN Wire Staff. "Taliban and Pakistan Reject Speculation Mullah Omar Is Dead." *CNN World,* May 23, 2011, http://www.cnn.com/2011/WORLD/asiapcf/05/23/afghanistan.omar/index.html?iref=allsearch.

Coles, Tim. "How Britain Armed the Sri Lanka Massacre." *Peace Review: A Journal of Social Justice* 23, no. 1 (2011): 77–85.

Collins, Jeff. "Explaining Chechnya's 'Black Widows': An Organisational Analysis." *The Globalized World Post,* March 22, 2012, http://thegwpost.com/2012/03/22/explaining-chechnyas-black-widows-an-organisational-analysis/.

Colucci, Vienna. "Congress Blocks Prosecution of Gitmo Detainees in Federal Courts." *Human Rights Now,* December 22, 2010, http://blog.amnestyusa.org/us/congress-blocks-prosecution-of-gitmo-detainees-in-federal-courts/.

Combs, Cindy C., and Martin Slann. "Introduction." In *Encyclopedia of Terrorism,* edited by Cindy C. Combs and Martin Slann, rev. ed. (New York: Facts on File, Inc., 2007), xi–xiv.

"Convention against Torture and Other Cruel, Inhuman or Degrading Treatment or Punishment: Adopted and Opened for Signature, Ratification and Accession by General Assembly Resolution 39/46 of December 10, 1984, Entry into Force June 26, 1987, in Accordance with Article 27 (1)." *Office of the United Nations High Commissioner for Human Rights,* Part 1, Article 1(1), http://www2.ohchr.org/english/law/pdf/cat.pdfs.

Cook, David. "Boko Haram Escalates Attacks on Christians in Northern Nigeria." *Combating Terrorism Center at West Point,* April 23, 2012, http://www.ctc.usma.edu/posts/boko-haram-escalates-attacks-on-christians-in-northern-nigeria.

Cooper, H.H.A. "Terrorism: The Problem of Definition Revisited." In *Terrorism in Perspective,* edited by Sue G. Mahan and Pamala L. Griset, 2nd ed. (Thousand Oaks, CA: Sage, 2007), 15–23.

Cooper, Helene. "Obama Says Palestinians Are Using Wrong Forum." *The New York Times,* September 21, 2011, http://www.nytimes.com/2011/09/22/world/obama-united-nations-speech.html.

Corbett, Nicholas. *Comparative Insurgencies: The Role of Suicide Tactics in Iraq and Afghanistan* (Ottawa: Conference of Defense Associations, 2009), http://www.cda-cdai.ca/cdai/uploads/cdai/2009/04/corbett08.pdf.

Cornum, Rhonda. "Comprehensive Soldier Fitness: Strong Minds, Strong Bodies." Keynote address. Power point presentation at WREI Women in the Military Conference, Arlington, VA, September 25, 2009, http://www.4militarywomen.org/WIM09Presentations/Cornum.pdf.

"A Court Covers Up." *The New York Times,* May 24, 2012, http://www.nytimes.com/2012/05/25/opinion/a-court-covers-up.html?nl=todaysheadlines&emc=edit_th_20120525.

Covo, Moshe, and Gilad Zahavi. "Will Al-Qaeda Adjust Its Strategy to Accommodate the Changes in the Regional System?" *International Institute for*

Counter-Terrorism, July 31, 2011, http://www.ict.org.il/NewsCommentaries/Commentaries/tabid/69/Articlsid/964/currentpage/1/Default.aspx.

Culter, David. "Timeline: Deadliest Attacks in Iraq in 2012." *Chicago Tribune,* June 16, 2012, http://articles.chicagotribune.com/2012-06-16/news/sns-rt-iraq-violenceblasts-timelinel5e8hg327-20120616_1_shi-ite-pilgrims-suicide-car-people-and-wounds.

Curavic, Danica. "Note: Compensating Victims of Terrorism or Frustrating Cultural Diplomacy? The Unintended Consequences of the Foreign Sovereign Immunities Act's Terrorism Provision." *Cornell International Law Journal* 43 (Spring 2010): 381–405, http://www.lawschool.cornell.edu/research/ilj/upload/curavic.pdf.

Czwarno, Monica, and Ana Marte. "Profiling Discord: Suicide Bombings in the Insurgent Campaign." *Defense Monitor* 36, no. 5 (September–October 2007): 6, 7.

Dale, Kenneth J. "Cultural and Linguistic Barriers to Communicating the Christian Religion in Japan." *Intercultural Communication Studies* 8, no. 1 (1998–1999): 149–54.

Dann, Carrie, and Reuters. "CIA Chief: Waterboarding Aided bin Laden Raid." *NBCNews,* May 3, 2011, http://today.msnbc.msn.com/id/42880435/ns/today-today_news/t/cia-chief-waterboarding-aided-bin-laden-raid.

Darem, Faisal. "Yemeni Terrorism Experts: Ansar al-Sharia is Re-branded al-Qaeda." *Al-Shorfa,* August 3, 2011, http://al-shorfa.com/cocoon/meii/xhtml/en_GB/features/meii/features/main/2011/08/03/feature-01.

Dearing, Matthew P. "Understanding Female Suicide Terrorism in Sri Lanka through a Constructivist Lens." *Strategic Insights* 9, no. 1 (Spring/Summer 2010), http://www.nps.edu/Academics/Centers/CCC/Research-Publications/StrategicInsights/2010/Jul/SI_V9_I1_2010_Dearing_65.pdf.

Desmond, Joan Frawley. " 'Justice Has Been Done,' States President Obama, and Just-War Scholars Agree." *National Catholic Register,* May, 4, 2011, http://www.ncregister.com/daily-news/justice-for-bin-laden/.

"Dossier: Suicide Bombing as a Problem in Asymmetric Warfare." *The Estimate* 15, no. 8 (April 19, 2002), http://www.theestimate.com/public/041902.html.

Douse, Diana. "Select Bibliography of Terrorism Resources." *House of Commons Library,* Standard Note: SN/HA/5866, June 29, 2012, http://www.parliament.uk/briefing-papers/SN05866.

Dreazen, Yochi J. "Allyn: Use of Children in Suicide Attacks Part of 'Ruthless' Escalation for Taliban." *National Journal,* June 20, 2011, http://www.nationaljournal.com/nationalsecurity/taliban-s-use-of-children-in-suicide-attacks-marks-a-ruthless-escalation-allyn-says-20110620.

Dudziak, Mary L. "Desegregation as a Cold War Imperative." *Stanford Law Review* 41, no. 1 (November 1988): 61–120.

Dumitriu, Eugenia. "The E.U.'s Definition of Terrorism: The Council Frame-work Decision on Combating Terrorism, Part 1 of 2." *German Law Journal* 5, no. 5 (May 1, 2004): 585–602, http://www.germanlawjournal.com/pdfs/Vol05No05/PDF_Vol_05_No_05_585–602_special_issue_Dumitriu.pdf.

Early, Bryan R. "Larger Than a Party, yet Smaller Than a State: Locating Hezbollah's Place within Lebanon's State and Society." *World Affairs* 168, no. 3 (2006): 115–28, http://callisto10.ggimg.com/doc/UBER1/RangeFetch=contentSet=UBER1=prefix=PI-2393–2006-WNT00-IDSI-=startPage=15=suffix==npages=14.pdf.

Eilstrup-Sangiovanni, Mette, and Calvert Jones. "Assessing the Dangers of Illicit Networks: Why al-Qaida May Be Less Threatening Than Many Think." *International Security* 33, no. 2 (Fall 2008): 7–44.

El Assimi, Abu Baçir. Quoted in Tom Newton Dunn. "Al-Qaeda in Gay Rape Horror." *The Sun*, February 4, 2009, http://www.thesun.co.uk/sol/homepage/news/2203190/Al-Qaeda-in-gay-rape-horror.html.

Ensuring Lawful Interrogations. Executive Order No. 13491, Title 3, § 2(f), January 22, 2009, http://edocket.access.gpo.gov/2009/pdf/E9–1885.pdf.

Entous, Adam. "U.S. Balks at Pakistani Bills."*Wall Street Journal*, May 16, 2011, http://online.wsj.com/article/SB10001424052748703730804576321570902617838.html.

Esposito, John L. "Jihad: Holy or Unholy War?" *United Nations Alliance of Civilians*, 6, http://www.unaoc.org/repository/Esposito_Jihad_Holy_Unholy.pdf. [Based on Esposito, John L. *Unholy War: Terror in the Name of Islam and What Everyone Needs to Know about Islam* (New York: Oxford University Press, 2002).]

"The Execution." *USA Today*, June 20, 2001, http://www.usatoday.com/news/nation/mcveighindex.htm.

"Factbox-Afghanistan: Who Are the Insurgents?" *Reuters*, March 27, 2009, http://www.reuters.com/article/2009/03/27/idUSISL427398.

Farer, Tom. "Un-Just War against Terrorism and the Struggle to Appropriate Human Rights." *Human Rights Quarterly* 30, no. 2 (May 2008): 356–403.

Farrall, Leah. "How al Qaeda Works: What the Organization's Subsidiaries Say about Its Strength." *Foreign Affairs*, March/April 2011, http://www.foreignaffairs.com/articles/67467/leah-farrall/how-al-qaeda-works.

"Fears of Mass Suicide as Tamil Tigers Face Final Defeat." *Sunday Times*, May 17, 2009, 26, 27.

Fellmeth, Aaron Xavier. "A Divorce Waiting to Happen: Franklin Roosevelt and the Law of Neutrality, 1935–1941." *Buffalo Journal of International Law* 3, no. 2 (Winter 1996–1997): 413–517.

Ferran, Lee, and Rym Momtaz. "From Terror Group Founder to Libyan Rebel Military Commander." *ABC News*, August 29, 2011, http://abcnews.go.com/Blotter/terror-group-founder-libyan-rebel-military-commander/story?id=14405319.

Ferrero, Mario. "Martyrdom Contracts." *Journal of Conflict Resolution* 50, no. 6 (December 2006): 855–77.

Fine, Jonathan. "Contrasting Secular and Religious Terrorism." *Middle East Quarterly* 15, no. 1 (Winter 2008): 59–69, http://www.meforum.org/1826/contrasting-secular-and-religious-terrorism#_ftnref37.

Finn, Melissa. "Terrorists, Female." In *Encyclopedia of Women in Today's World*, edited by Mary Zeiss Stange, Carol K. Oyster, and Jane E. Sloan (Thousand Oaks, CA: Sage Publications, 2011), http://www.sage-ereference.com/womentoday/Article_n836.html.

Fisher, Jason. "Targeted Killing, Norms, and International Law." *Columbia Journal of Transnational Law* 45, no. 3 (2007): 711.

Fishman, Brian. "The Political Impact of Suicide Attacks in Iraq." In *Suicide as a Weapon*, edited by Center of Excellence Defence Against Terrorism (Washington, D.C.: IOS Press, 2007), 64–75, http://www.booksonline.iospress.nl/Content/View.aspx?piid=7801.

Fletcher, George P. "The Indefinable Concept of Terrorism." *Journal of International Criminal Justice* 4, no. 5 (November 1, 2006): 894.

Forsloff, Carol. "Al Qaeda Accused of Using Male Rape to Recruit Suicide Bombers." *Digital Journal*, July 1, 2009, http://www.digitaljournal.com/article/275122.

Frenznick, David A. "The First Amendment on the Battlefield." *Pacific Law Journal* 23 (1992): 315, http://www.wilkefleury.com/userfiles/articles/THE-FIRST-AMENDMENT-ON-THE-BATTLEFIELD.pdf.

"Full Statement from al Qaeda on Osama bin Laden's Death." *CNN News Blog*, May 6, 2011, http://news.blogs.cnn.com/2011/05/06/full-statement-from-al-qaeda-on-osama-bin-ladens-death/.

Gadney, Max. "Kamikazes, Deconstructed." *World War II* 23, no. 1 (April/May 2008): 46, 47.

Galeotti, Mark. "Umarov's Volte-Face Opens Split in the Chechen Rebel 'Caucasus Emirate.'" *Analysis and Assessment of Russian Crime and Security: In Moscow's Shadows*, August 14, 2010, http://inmoscowsshadows.wordpress.com/2010/08/14/umarovs-volte-face-opens-split-in-the-chechen-rebel-caucasus-emirate/.

Gamini, Gabriella. "Argentine Pilots Claim They Had to Adopt Kamikaze Tactics." *The London Times*, April 1, 1992, 13.

Ganor, Boaz. "Defining Terrorism—Is One Man's Terrorist Another Man's Freedom Fighter?" *International Institute for Counter-Terrorism*, http://www.ict.org.il/ResearchPublications/tabid/64/Articlsid/432/Default.aspx#Defining_Terrorism:_The_Present_Situation.

Ganor, Boaz. "The First Iraqi Suicide Bombing: A Hint of Things to Come?" *International Institute for Counter-Terrorism*, March 30, 2003, http://www.ict.org.il/Articles/tabid/66/Articlsid/595/currentpage/21/Default.aspx.

Ganor, Boaz. "How Will Al-Qaida Plan Attacks without bin Laden?" *Jerusalem Post*, May 3, 2011, http://www.jpost.com/International/Article.aspx?id=219006.

"Gas Attack: On Anniversary of Japanese Subway Attack, Many Fear Cult Resurgence." *CNN World*, March 20, 1999, http://articles.cnn.com/1999-03-20/world/9903_20_japan.cult_1_gas-attack-aum-shinri-kyo-tokyo-subway-system?_s=PM:WORLD.

Gearan, Anne, and Robert Burns. "WikiLeaks Releases 400,000 Files on Iraq: Leaked Files Show Iraqi Deaths Higher Than U.S. Count." *Army Times*, October 23, 2010, http://www.armytimes.com/news/2010/10/ap-Iraqi-deaths-higher-than-US-count-102310/.

"General Article: The Invasion of Grenada." *American Experience*, 1998, http://www.pbs.org/wgbh/americanexperience/features/general-article/reagan-grenada/.

"General Article: The Iran-Contra Affair." *American Experience*, 1998, http://www.pbs.org/wgbh/americanexperience/features/general-article/reagan-iran/.

"[Geneva] Convention (III) Relative to the Treatment of Prisoners of War. Geneva, 12 August 1949." *International Humanitarian Law—Treaties & Documents*, Part I, Article 3, http://www.icrc.org/ihl.nsf/FULL/375.

"Geneva Conventions of 1949 and Their Additional Protocols." *International Committee of the Red Cross*, July 7, 2011, http://www.icrc.org/eng/war-and-law/treaties-customary-law/geneva-conventions/index.jsp.

"Georgia Cities Ranked by Population (Based on 2010 U.S. Census)." *GeorgiaInfo,* http://georgiainfo.galileo.usg.edu/citypopulationrank.htm.

Georgy, Michael, and Mirwais Harooni. "Suicide Bombers Kill 7 after Obama Leaves Afghan Capital." *Chicago Tribune,* May 2, 2012, http://articles.chi cagotribune.com/2012-05-02/business/sns-rt-us-afghanistan-kabul-blast-bre841025-20120501_1_haqqani-network-afghan-capital-suicide-bombers.

Gettleman, Jeffrey, and Eric Schmitt. "U.S. Kills Top Qaeda Militant in Southern Somalia." *The New York Times,* September 14, 2009, http://www.nytimes. com/2009/09/15/world/africa/15raid.html.

Ghosh, Bobby. "The Mind of a Female Suicide Bomber." *Time,* June 22, 2008, http://www.time.com/time/world/article/0,8599,1817158,00.html.

Ghosn, Faten, and Amal Khoury. "Lebanon after the Civil War: Peace or the Illusion of Peace?" *Middle East Journal* 65, no. 3 (Summer 2011): 382–97.

Gill, Paul. "A Multi-Dimensional Approach to Suicide Bombing." *International Journal of Conflict and Violence* 1, no. 2 (2007): 142–59, http://ijcv.org/index. php/ijcv/article/viewFile/12/12.

Gill, Paul. "Suicide Bomber Pathways among Islamic Militants." *Policing: A Journal of Policy and Practice* 2, no. 4 (2008): 412–22.

Gillespie, Bill. "The Avenging Black Widows." *CBC News,* March 31, 2010, http://www.cbc.ca/news/world/story/2010/03/30/f-russia-black-widow.html.

Gimbel, V. Noah. "Has the Rendition Program Disappeared?" *Foreign Policy in Focus,* June 16, 2011, http://www.fpif.org/articles/has_the_rendition_program_disappeared.

Giroux, Henry A. "Dirty Democracy and State Terrorism: The Politics of the New Authoritarianism in the United States." *Comparative Studies of South Asia, Africa and the Middle East* 26, no. 2 (2006): 163–77.

Goldman, Russell, and Luis Martinez. "WikiLeaks Documents Reveal Death Count, Torture." *ABC News,* October 23, 2010, http://abcnews.go.com/Pol itics/wikileaks-iraqi-civilian-deaths-higher-reported/story?id=11953723#. UDW7FMEgfow.

Green, James A. "Docking the Caroline: Understanding the Relevance of the Formula in Contemporary Customary International Law Concerning Self-Defense." *Cardozo Journal of International and Comparative Law* 14, no.2 (Fall 2006): 429–80.

Grimland, Maytal, Alan Apter, and Ad Kerhof. "The Phenomenon of Suicide Bombings: A Review of Psychological and Nonpsychological Factors." *Crisis* 27, no. 3 (2006):107–18, http://my.ilstu.edu/~dfgrayb/Personal/Phe nomenon%20of%20Suicide %20Bombing.pdf.

"Growing Threat from Female Suicide Bombers." *Investigative Project on Terrorism News,* March 29, 2010, http://www.investigativeproject.org/1882/ the-growing-threat-from-female-suicide-bombers.

"Guide: Armed Groups in Iraq," *BBC News,* August 15, 2006, http://news.bbc. co.uk/2/hi/middle_east/4268904.stm.

Gunaratna, Rohan. "Suicide Terrorism: A Global Threat." *FRONTLINE/World,* October 2000, http://www.pbs.org/frontlineworld/stories/srilanka/global threat.html. In R. Ramasubramanian. "Suicide Terrorism in Sri Lanka." *IPCS Research Papers* 5 (August 2004): 3. Quoted in U.S. Department of Defense, Deputy Chief of Staff for Intelligence (DCSINT). *Suicide Bombing in the COE (Common Operating Environment),* Handbook No. 1.03

(Fort Leavenworth, KS: U.S. Army Training and Doctrine Command, August 10, 2006), I-2, http://www.fas.org/irp/threat/terrorism/sup3.pdf.

Gunaratna, Rohan. "Suicide Terrorism in Sri Lanka." In *Countering Suicide Terrorism* (Herzliya: International Policy Institute for Counter-Terrorism, The Interdisciplinary Center, 2006), 68–72, http://www.ict.org.il/Portals/0/51563-Countering%20Suicide%20Terrorism.pdf.

Gunaratna, Rohan, and Karunya Jayasena. "Global Support for al Qaeda and Osama Bin Laden: An Increase or Decrease?" *UNISCI Discussion Papers* 25 (January/Enero 2011): 199–214.

Gunning, Jeroen, and Richard Jackson. "What's So 'Religious' about 'Religious Terrorism'?" *Critical Studies on Terrorism* 4, no. 3 (2011): 369–88, http://dx.doi.org/10.1080/17539153.2011.623405.

Gurin, Charles. "Ingush Ex-Cop Reportedly among Hostage-Takers." *Eurasia Daily Monitor* 1, no. 80 (September 8, 2004), http://www.jamestown.org/single/?no_cache=1&tx_ttnews%5Btt_news%5D=26823.

Gutman, Roy. "Afghanistan War: How Taliban Tactics Are Evolving." *Christian Science Monitor*, March 15, 2010, http://www.csmonitor.com/World/2010/0315/Afghanistan-war-How-Taliban-tactics-are-evolving.

Hafez, Mohammed M. "Rationality, Culture, and Structure in the Making of Suicide Bombers: A Preliminary Theoretical Synthesis and Illustrative Case Study." *Studies in Conflict and Terrorism* 29, no. 2 (March 2006): 165–85.

Hagan, John, Gabrielle Ferrales, and Guillermina Jasso. "Collaboration and Resistance in the Punishment of Torture in Iraq: A Judicial Sentencing Experiment." *Wisconsin International Law Journal* 28, no. 1 (Spring 2010): 1–38.

Hamm, Mark. "Prisoner Radicalization: Assessing the Threat in U.S. Correctional Institutions." *National Institute of Justice Journal* 261 (2010): 14–18, https://www.ncjrs.gov/pdffiles1/nij/224085.pdf.

Hassan, Azmat S. *Countering Violent Extremism: The Fate of the Tamil Tigers* (New York: East West Institute, 2009), http://docs.ewi.info/Tigers.pdf.

Haviland, Charles. "Sri Lanka Government Publishes War Death Toll Statistic." *BBC News*, February 24, 2012, http://www.bbc.co.uk/news/world-asia-17156686.

Hayden, G. Miki. "What Motivated the Kamikazes?" *Naval History* 19, no. 2 (April 2006): 22–24.

Healing, Raven. "Chechnya: After Aslan Maskhadov." *World War 4 Report*, April 10, 2005, http://ww4report.com/chechnyamaskhadov.

Heffelfinger, Christopher. "Mission Not Accomplished." *Foreign Policy*, August 5, 2011, http://www.foreignpolicy.com/articles/2011/08/05/mission_not_accomplished.

Heher, Ashley M. "Female Suicide Bombers an Extension of an Old Tradition." *Cox News Service*, April 28, 2002. Quoted in Rosemarie Skaine, *Female Suicide Bombers* (Jefferson, NC: McFarland, 2006), 68.

Helmer, Daniel. "Hezbollah's Employment of Suicide Bombing during the 1980s: The Theological, Political, and Operational Development of a New Tactic." *Military Review* 86, no. 4 (July–August 2006): 71–82, http://usacac.army.mil/CAC2/MilitaryReview/Archives/English/MilitaryReview_20060831_art012.pdf.

Henckaerts, Jean-Marie, and Louise Doswald-Beck. *Customary International Humanitarian Law* (Cambridge: Cambridge University Press, 2005), Vols. I, II,

689 pp, http://www.icrc.org/eng/assets/files/other/customary-interna
tional-humanitarian-law-i-icrc-eng.pdf.

"History." *Background Notes on Countries of the World: Democratic Socialist Republic of Sri Lanka* (April 2011): 4.

"A History of Conflict: Israel and the Palestinians." *BBC News,* Introduction and 1250BC–638AD, http://news.bbc.co.uk/2/shared/spl/hi/middle_east/03/v3_ip_timeline/html/.

Hoffman, Bruce. "Bin Laden's Killing and its Effect on Al-Qa'ida: What Comes Next?" *Combating Terrorism Center at West Point,* May 1, 2011, http://www.ctc.usma.edu/posts/bin-ladin%E2%80%99s-killing-and-its-effect-on-al-qaida-what-comes-next.

Holder, Eric. In U.S. Congress, House Committee Judiciary. "Justice Department Oversight Hearing, Part 1." *C-SPAN Video Library,* 112th Cong., 1st Sess., Hearing, May 4, 2011, http://www.c-spanvideo.org/program/JusticeDepartmentOve.

Hurtado, Patricia, and Chris Dolmetsch. "U.S. Dismisses Terror Indictment against Osama Bin Laden." *Bloomberg Businessweek,* June 17, 2011, http://www.businessweek.com/news/2011-06-17/u-s-dismisses-terror-indictment-against-osama-bin-laden.html.

Ignatius, David. "The bin Laden Plot to Kill President Obama." *The Washington Post,* March 16, 2012, http://www.washingtonpost.com/opinions/the-bin-laden-plot-to-kill-president-obama/2012/03/16/gIQAwN5RGS_story.html.

"Ilyas Kashmiri Killed in Drone Attack." *The Sydney Morning Herald,* June 5, 2011, http://www.smh.com.au/world/ilyas-kashmiri-killed-in-drone-attack-20110605–1fmv6.html.

"Is Osama bin Laden Killing Legal? International Law Experts Divided." *International Business Times,* May 7, 2011, http://www.ibtimes.com/articles/142448/20110507/osama-bin-laden-killing-legal-violate-international-law-experts-lawyers-divided.htm.

Isikoff, Michael. "U.S. Failure to Retaliate for USS *Cole* Attack Rankled Then—and Now." *NBCNews,* October 12, 2010, http://www.msnbc.msn.com/id/39622062/ns/us_news-security/t/us-failure-retaliate-uss-cole-attack-rankled-then-now/.

Ismayilov, Murad. "Conceptualizing Terrorist Violence." *Journal of Strategic Security* 3, no. 3 (2010): 15–26.

Jackson, Richard B. "Stick to the High Ground." *The Army Lawyer* (July 2005): 2–11, http://www.au.af.mil/au/awc/awcgate/law/high_ground.pdf.

Jackson, Richard B. "Unknown Knowns: The Subjugated Knowledge of Terrorism Studies." *Critical Studies on Terrorism* 5, no. 1 (April 2012): 11–29.

Jandora, John W. "Center of Gravity and Asymmetric Conflict: Factoring in Culture." *Joint Force Quarterly* 39 (October 2005): 78–83, http://www.au.af.mil/au/awc/awcgate/jfq/1439.pdf.

"Japanese Religion." *Patheos Library,* http://www.patheos.com/Library/Japanese-Religion.html.

Jayasena, Karunya. "Defining Suicide Terrorism." *IUP Journal of International Relations* 5, no. 3 (July 2011): 20–34, http://www.iupindia.in/1107/Interna tional%20Relations/Defining_Suicide_Terrorism.html.

Jenkins, Brian Michael. "The Land of the Fearful, or the Home of the Brave?" In *The Long Shadow of 9/11: America's Response to Terrorism,* edited by

Brian Michael Jenkins and John Paul Godges (Santa Monica, CA: RAND, August 9, 2011), 196–208, http://www.rand.org/content/dam/rand/pubs/monographs/2011/RAND_MG1107.pdf.

Johnson, David. "U.S. Says Rendition to Continue, but with More Oversight." *The New York Times,* August 24, 2009, http://www.nytimes.com/2009/08/25/us/politics/25rendition.html.

Johnson, David. "Doku Umarov Vows 'Year of Tears.'" *Johnson's Russia List,* February 7, 2011, http://www.cdi.org/russia/johnson/russia-chechnya-mili tancy-umarov-feb-308.cfm.

Joscelyn, Thomas. "Report: New Leader of al Qaeda Network in Iran Named." *The Long War Journal,* February 15, 2012, http://www.longwarjournal.org/archives/2012/02/report_new_leader_of.php.

Jost, Kenneth, and the CQ Researcher Staff. "The Obama Presidency: Can Barack Obama Deliver the Change He Promises?" *CQ Researcher Online* 19, no. 4 (January 30, 2009), http://www.sagepub.com/upm-data/31933_12.pdf.

"Kamikaze Attack, 1944." *EyeWitness to History,* 2005, http://www.eyewitnessto-history.com/kamikaze.htm.

Kaplan, Lawrence F. "To Be Sure . . .: Will We Overestimate the Importance of Osama bin Laden's Death?" *The New Republic,* May 3, 2011, http://www.tnr.com/article/crossings/87786/osama-bin-laden-barack-obama-war-terrorism.

Kapusta, Philip E., *Suicide Bombers in CONUS* (Fort Leavenworth, KS: School of Advanced Military Studies, May 7, 2007), http://www.dtic.mil/cgi-bin/GetTRDoc?AD=ADA470697&Location=U2&doc=GetTRDoc.pdf.

Karam, Zeina *AP.* "Hezbollah Rise in Lebanon Gives Syria, Iran Sway." *The Huffington Post,* June 13, 2011, http://www.huffingtonpost.com/2011/06/13/hezbollah-syria-iran-influence_n_876329.html.

Kelsay, John. "Suicide Bombers: The 'Just War' Debate, Islamic Style." *The Christian Century,* August 14–27, 2002, 22–25, http://www.religion-online.org/showarticle.asp?title=2616.

Khalezov, Dimitri. "Bio-terrorism—Anthrax Attacks Following September 11." *Veterans Today: Military and Foreign Affairs Journal,* January 9, 2011, http://mathaba.net/go/?http://www.veteranstoday.com/2011/01/09/72207/.

Kirby, Aidan. "The London Bombers as 'Self-Starters.'" *Studies in Conflict and Terrorism* 30, no. 5 (2007): 415–28.

Klingelhoefer, Mark D. *Captured Enemy Ammunition in Operation Iraqi Freedom and Its Strategic Importance in Post-Conflict Operations* (Carlisle, PA: Strategic Studies Institute, U.S. Army War College, March 18, 2005), 1–18, http://www.strategicstudiesinstitute.army.mil/pdffiles/ksil72.pdf.

Knoope, Peter, and Anno Bunnik. "Why the People of Tunisia and Egypt Confirm the Bankruptcy of Al Qaeda's Tactics." *International Institute for Counter-Ter rorism,* June 3, 2011, http://www.ict.org.il/NewsCommentaries/Commen taries/tabid/69/Articlsid/905/currentpage/2/Default.aspx.

Kramer, Mark. "The Perils of Counterinsurgency: Russia's War in Chechnya." *International Security* 29, no. 3 (Winter 2004–2005): 5–63.

Kucukcan, Talip. "Sociology of Terrorism: A Key to Understanding Social Origins?" *International Relations* 6, no. 24 (Winter 2010): 33–55.

Kukis, Mark. "With Friends Like These ... Camp Fire." *The New Republic,* February 20, 2006, http://www.tnr.com/article/friends-these.

Kurz, Robert W., and Charles K. Bartles. "Chechen Suicide Bombers." *Journal of Slavic Military Studies* 20 (2007): 529–47.

Kydd, Andrew H., and Barbara F. Walter. "The Strategies of Terrorism." *International Security* 31, no. 1 (Summer 2006): 49–79.

Lang, Chris. *A Brief History of Literary Theory VI: The Philosophy of Ludwig Wittgenstein* (Columbus, OH: Xenos Christian Fellowship, 2011), http://www.xenos.org/essays/litthry7.htm.

Lankford, Adam. "Do Past U.S. Acts Constitute Terrorism? Implications for Counterterrorism Policy." *International Criminal Justice Review* 20, no. 4 (December 2010): 417, http://icj.sagepub.com/content/20/4/417.

Laub, Karin, and Mohammed Daraghmeh. "Palestinian Fatah Looks Ill-Prepared for Election." *Yahoo News,* January 20, 2012, http://news.yahoo.com/pales tinian-fatah-looks-ill-prepared-election-064258667.html.

"Lebanon Profile." *BBC News,* January 11, 2012, http://www.bbc.co.uk/news/world-middle-east-14647308.

"Lebanon Profile: A Chronology of Key Events." *BBC News,* January 11, 2012, http://www.bbc.co.uk/news/world-middle-east-14649284.

Lecce, D.J. "International Law Regarding Pro-Democratic Intervention: A Study of the Dominican Republic and Haiti." *Naval Law Review* 45 (1998): 247–62.

Leffler, Melvyn P. "9/11 and the Past and Future of American Foreign Policy." *International Affairs* 79, no. 5 (2003): 1045–63.

Leinwand, Donna. "Colo. Man Pleads Guilty to Terror Plot." *USA Today,* February 23, 2010.

Lewis, Jason. "Now Al Qaeda Sends Women Suicide Bombers to Target West." *Mail Online,* January 24, 2010, http://www.dailymail.co.uk/news/arti cle-1245600/Now-Al-Qaeda-sends-women-suicide-bombers-target-West.html.

"Liberation Tigers of Tamil Eelam (LTTE)." *South Asia Terrorism Portal,* http://www.satp.org/satporgtp/countries/shrilanka/terroristoutfits/LTTE.HTM.

Lind, Jeremy, and Jude Howell. "Counter-terrorism and the Politics of Aid: Civil Society Responses in Kenya." *Development and Change* 41, no. 2 (2010): 335–53, http://onlinelibrary.wiley.com/doi/10.1111/j.1467-7660.2010.01637.x/abstract;jsessionid=4A7838AAB3A9F9E338376A63BCA8E328.d03t04.

Lute, Doug. Interview by John Hendren. "Military Produces Profile of Iraq Suicide Bombers." *NPR,* March 10, 2006, http://www.npr.org/templates/story/story.php?storyId=5257052.

Maass, Ekkehard. *War and History: 400 Years of Colonial Conquest—400 Years of Resistance,* translated by Kate Vanovitch (Berlin: German-Caucasian Society, 2003), http://www.d-k-g.de/downloads/Tschetschenien_Broschuere_en.pdf.

Mackey, Robert. "Suicide Attack Follow Obama's Afghanistan Visit." *The New York Times,* May 2, 2012, http://thelede.blogs.nytimes.com/2012/05/02/suicide-bomb-attacks-hours-after-president-obamas-visit-to-afghanistan/.

Madsen, Julian. "Suicide Terrorism: Rationalizing the Irrational." *Strategic Insights* 3, no. 8 (August 2004): 3, http://www.au.af.mil/au/awc/awcgate/nps/madsen_aug04.pdf.

Mariner, Joanne. "A First Look at the Military Commissions Act of 2009, Part One." *Find Law,* November 4, 2009, http://writ.news.findlaw.com/mari ner/20091104.html?pagewanted=all.

Martinez, Luis. "For First Time, More U.S. Troops in Afghanistan than Iraq." *ABC News,* May 24, 2010, http://blogs.abcnews.com/politicalpunch/2010/05/for-first-time-more-us-troops-in-afghanistan-than-iraq.html.

"Masada." *Jewish Virtual Library,* 2012, http://www.jewishvirtuallibrary.org/jsource/Judaism/masada.html.

Mazzetti, Mark. "C.I.A. Drone Is Said to Kill Al Qaeda's No. 2." *The New York Times,* August 27, 2011, http://www.nytimes.com/2011/08/28/world/asia/28qaeda.html.

McChrystal, Stanley A. "Becoming the Enemy." *Foreign Policy* 185 (2011): 10, 66–70, http:// proquest.com.

McCracken, Harrold J. *Unprivileged Belligerents: "You Can't Tell the Players without a Scorecard"* (Carlisle, PA: Strategic Studies Institute, U.S. Army War College, March 25, 2010), 1–24, www.hsdl.org/?view&did=706227.

McGeough, Paul, and Ed O'Loughlin. "Israeli Tanks Crash Border into Lebanon." *The Age,* July 23, 2006, http://www.theage.com.au/news/national/israeli-tanks-crash-border-into-lebanon/2006/07/23/1153166638729.html.

McKinley, James C., Jr., and Sarah Wheaton. "Agents Say Saudi Man Was Acting Alone in Bomb Plot." *The New York Times,* February 26, 2011, A14(L).

Merritt, Jeralyn E. "Najibullah Zazi Testifies for Government in Terrorism Trial." *Talk Left: the Politics of Crime,* April 17, 2012, http://www.talkleft.com/story/2012/4/17/172034/285.

Metz, Steven, and Raymond Millen. *Insurgency in Iraq and Afghanistan: Change and Continuity* (Carlisle, PA: Strategic Studies Institute, U.S. Army War College, August 19, 2004), http://www.au.af.mil/au/awc/awcgate/cia/nic2020/insurgency.pdf.

Michaels, Jim. "General: Taliban 'Beaten' by Surge." *USA Today,* February 11, 2011, A1.

Miglani, Sanjeev, and Hamid Shalizi. "Fear in Kabul after 20-Hour Taliban Siege." *Reuters,* September 14, 2011, http://mobile.reuters.com/article/topNews/idUSTRE78D0NC20110914.

Miller, Greg. "Counterterrorism Expert Sees Much to be Done." *The Washington Post,* May 17, 2012, http://www.washingtonpost.com/world/national-security/counterterrorism-expert-sees-much-to-be-done/2012/05/17/gIQAtPcFXU_story.html?wpisrc=nl_headlines.

Miller, Greg, and Karen DeYoung. "Al-Qaeda Airline Bomb Plot Disrupted, U.S. Says." *The Washington Post,* May 7, 2012, http://www.washingtonpost.com/world/national-security/cia-disrupts-airline-bomb-plot/2012/05/07/gIQA9qE08T_story.html.

Miyasato, Merle. "Suicide Bombers: Profiles, Methods and Techniques." *Foreign Military Studies Office,* March 16, 2007, http://fmso.leavenworth.army.mil/documents/Suicide-Bombers.pdf.

Moghadam, Assaf. "Palestinian Suicide Terrorism in the Second Intifada: Motivations and Organizational Aspects." *Studies in Conflict and Terrorism* 26 (2003): 65–92, http://werzit.com/intel/classes/amu/classes/lc514/LC514_Week_05_Motivations_and_Organizational_Aspects_of_Palestinian_Suicide_Bombers.pdf.

Moore, Christopher. "Tamils Will Present United Front/Peace Talks with Sri Lankan Government." *The Guardian,* July 31, 1985.

Moran, Lee. "Shoe Bomber in Supermax: Richard Reid Pictured for First Time Inside High Security Prison." *Mail Online,* October 10, 2011, http://www.dailymail.co.uk/news/article-2047093/Shoe-bomber-Richard-Reid-pictured-inside-US-Supermax-jail.html.

Moran, Terry, Martha Raddatz, Nick Schifrin, Brian Ross, and Jake Tapper. "Target: Bin Laden—The Death and Life of Public Enemy Number One." *ABC News The Blotter,* June 9, 2011, Chapter Six, http://abcnews.go.com/Blotter/target-bin-laden-hunt-public-enemy-number/story?id=13813681#.UDyg_8Egfox.

Mulvey, Stephen. "Russia's Suicide Bomb Nightmare." *BBC News,* February 6, 2004, http://news.bbc.co.uk/1/hi/world/europe/3020231.stm.

Murphy, Jarrett. "Beirut Barracks Attack Remembered." *CBS News World,* October 23, 2003, http://www.cbsnews.com/stories/2003/10/23/world/main579638.shtml.

Murray, Michael. "Osama Bin Laden Dead: The Navy SEALs Who Hunted and Killed Al Qaeda Leader." *ABC News,* May 2, 2011, http://abcnews.go.com/US/osama-bin-laden-dead-navy-seal-team-responsible/story?id=13509739.

Naylor, Hugh. "Palestinian Elections Delayed by Hamas-Fatah Bickering." *The National,* March 9, 2012, http://www.americantaskforce.org/daily_news_article/2012/03/09/1331269200_8.

Nettelfield, Lara J. "Terror in Chechnya: Russia and the Tragedy of Civilians in War (Review)."*Human Rights Quarterly* 33, no. 3 (August 2011): 886–90.

Noone, Gregory P., Christian P. Fleming, Robert P. Morean, John V. Danner, Jr., Philip N. Fluhr, Jr., Jonathan I. Shapiro, Sandra L. Hodgkinson, Edward J. Cook, and Dillon L. Ross, IV. "Prisoners of War in the 21st Century: Issues in Modern Warfare." *Naval Law Review* 50 (2004), http://www.dtic.mil/dtic/tr/fulltext/u2/a477125.pdf.

"Notes from A Suicide Manual." *USS Yorktown and US Navy Targets,* http://www.yorktownsailor.com/yorktown/kamikaze.htm.

Obama, Barack. "Text of President Obama's Statement to U.S. People." *Reuters,* May 2, 2011, http://www.reuters.com/article/2011/05/02/us-obama-binladen-text-idUSTRE7410ZG20110502.

Obama, Barack. "Remarks by the President in Address to the Nation on the End of Combat Operations in Iraq." *The White House,* August 31, 2010, http://www.whitehouse.gov/the-press-office/2010/08/31/remarks-president-address-nation-end-combat-operations-iraq.

Obama, Barack. "Remarks by President Obama in Address to the Nation from Afghanistan." *The White House,* May 1, 2012, http://www.whitehouse.gov/the-press-office/2012/05/01/remarks-president-obama-address-nation-afghanistan.

Oberschall, Anthony. "Theories of Social Conflict." *Annual Review of Sociology* 4 (1978): 291–315.

"Obituary: Aslan Maskhadov." *BBC News,* March 8, 2005, http://news.bbc.co.uk/2/hi/europe/459302.stm.

"Observer: A War of the Words in Washington." *Financial Times,* August 4, 2005, http://www.ft.com/intl/cms/s/0/5aceb7e8-0483-11da-a775-00000e2511c8.html#axzz24Lnu5vJ2.

O'Connel, Mary Ellen. *The Myth of Preemptive Self-Defense* (Washington, D.C.: American Society of International Law, August 2002), 1–21, http://www. asil.org/taskforce/oconnell.pdf.

O'Connor, Tom. "The Varieties of Suicide Terrorism." *Mega Links in Criminal Justice,* January 22, 2011, http://www.drtomoconnor.com/3400/3400lect05.htm.

"Officials Thought They Might Kill Awlaki on 9/11 Anniversary." *ABC News,* September 30, 2011, http://abcnews.go.com/blogs/politics/2011/09/ officials-thought-they-might-kill-awlaki-on-911-anniversary/.

Ohnuki-Tierney, Emiko. "Betrayal by Idealism and Aesthetics: Special Attack Force (Kamikaze) Pilots and Their Intellectual Trajectories (Part 1)." *Anthropology Today* 20, no. 2 (April 2004): 15–21.

O'Keefe, Ed, and Ashley Halsey, III. "Shoe Removal Requirement at Airports to Be Phased Out." *The Washington Post,* September 6, 2011, http://www. washingtonpost.com/local/shoe-removal-requirement-at-airports-to-be-phased-out/2011/09/06/gIQAknLD7J_story.html.

"Operation Desert Shield/Desert Storm Timeline." *U.S. War Dogs Association,* July 20, 2011, http://www.uswardogs.org/id105.html.

Orbell, John, and Tomonori Morikawa. "An Evolutionary Account of Suicide Attacks: The Kamikaze Case." *Political Psychology* 32, no. 2 (January 9, 2011): 297–322.

O'Rourke, Lindsey A. "What's Special about Female Suicide Terrorism?" *Security Studies* 18, no. 4 (2009): 681–718, http://dx.doi.org/10.1080/09636410903369084.

"Osama bin Laden." *Anti-Defamation League,* 2011, http://www.adl.org/terror ism_america/bin_l.asp.

Osborn, Andrew. "Moscow Bombing: Who Are the Black Widows?" *The Telegraph,* March 29, 2010, http://www.telegraph.co.uk/news/worldnews/europe/ russia/7534464/Moscow-bombing-who-are-the-Black-Widows.html.

"Pakistan Assessment 2012." *South Asian Terrorism Portal,* http://www.satp.org/ satporgtp/countries/pakistan/.

"Palestinian Parliamentary Elections 2006." *GlobalSecurity.org,* http://www.glo balsecurity.org/military/world/palestine/pa-elections2006.htm.

Pape, Robert A. "Nationalism Motivates Suicide Terrorists." In *What Motivates Suicide Bombers?* edited by Lauri S. Friedman (San Diego, CA: Greenhaven Press, 2005), 44–49.

Pape, Robert A. Interview by Kerry O'Brien. "US 'Misread Motivation' of Suicide Bombers." *The 7:30 Reports,* July 20, 2005, http://www.abc.net.au/7.30/ content/2005/s1418817.htm.

Pape, Robert A. "Introduction: What is New about Research on Terrorism." *Security Studies* 18, no. 4 (2009): 643–50, http://dx.doi.org/10.1080/ 09636410903369100.

Partlow, Joshua, and Kamran Khan. "Charity Funds Said to Provide Clues to Alleged Terrorist Plot." *The Washington Post,* August 15, 2006, http:// www.washingtonpost.com/wp-dyn/content/article/2006/08/14/ AR2006081401196.html.

Perera, Amantha. "Sri Lanka: Blood over Water." *South Asia Intelligence Review,* Weekly Assessments and Briefings 5, no. 4 (August 7, 2006), http://satp. org/satporgtp/sair/Archives/5_4.htm#assessment1.

"Photos Show Some Killed in Bin Laden Raid." *CBS News,* May 4, 2011, http:// www.cbsnews.com/8301-503543_162-20059828-503543.html.

Pillar, Paul R. "The Diffusion of Terrorism." *Mediterranean Quarterly* 21, no. 1 (Winter 2010): 1–14.

Porter, Patrick. "Review Essay: Shadow Wars: Asymmetric Warfare in the Past and Future." *Security Dialogue* 37 (2006): 551–61, http://sdi.sagepub.com/content/37/4/551.

Post, Jerrold M. *Killing in the Name of God: Osama Bin Laden and Al Qaeda,* Counterproliferation Paper No. 18 (Maxwell Air Force Base, AL: Air University, November 2002), http://cpc.au.af.mil/PDF/monograph/killinginthenameofgod.pdf.

Pratt, Nicola. "On *Suicide Terrorism* by Ami Pedahzur, Polity, 2005, 240 pp." *Democratiya* 6 (Autumn 2006): 85, http://dissentmagazine.org/democratiya/article_pdfs/d6Pratt.pdf.

Priem, Richard G., Dennis M. Hunter, and Joseph M. Polisar. "Terrorists and Suicide Tactics: Preparing for the Challenge." *Police Chief,* April 2011, http://www.policechiefmagazine.org/magazine/index.cfm?fuseaction=display_arch&article_id=1265&issue_id=92007.

"Protocol Additional to the Geneva Conventions of August 12, 1949, and Relating to the Protection of Victims of International Armed Conflicts (Protocol I), June 8, 1977." *International Humanitarian Law—Treaties & Documents,* http://www.icrc.org/ihl.nsf/WebART/470-750054?OpenDocument.

Qirko, Hector N. "Altruism in Suicide Terror Organizations." *Zygon,* 44, no. 2 (June 2009): 289–322.

Raines, Joshua. "Student Note: Osama, Augustine, and Assassination: The Just War Doctrine and Targeted Killings." *Transnational Law and Contemporary Problems* 12 (Spring 2002): 217.

Rajasingham, K. T. "Sri Lanka: The Untold Story—Rajiv Gandhi's Assassination." *Asia Times,* 1995–2005, http://www.lankalibrary.com/pol/rajiv.htm.

Ramirez, Jorge Alberto. "Iraq War: Anticipatory Self-Defense or Unlawful Unilateralism?" *California Western International Law Journal* 34 (Fall 2003): 1–27.

Raphael, Ray. "Washington's 5 Rules for Honorable War." *HistoryNet,* December 11, 2009, http://www.historynet.com/washingtons-5-rules-for-honorable-war.htm.

Rashid, Ahmed. "The Taliban: Exporting Extremism." *Foreign Affairs* (November/December 1999): 22–35.

Rashid, Ahmed. "What the Taliban Want." *New York Review Blog,* August 29, 2011, http://www.nybooks.com/blogs/nyrblog/2011/aug/29/what-taliban-wants/.

Reed, Donald J. "Beyond the War on Terror: Into the Fifth Generation War and Conflict." *Studies in Conflict and Terrorism* 31, no. 8 (2008): 664–722.

"Religion in Japan." *Wikipedia,* June 17, 2012, http://en.wikipedia.org/wiki/Religion_in_Japan.

Reuters, Thomson. "Pakistan: Female Suicide Bomber Carries out Attack Near Police Checkpost." The Guardian, August 11, 2011, http://www.guardian.co.uk/world/2011/aug/11/pakistan-female-suicide-bomber.

Reuters, Thomson. "Air Strike Kills Taliban Militants Responsible for Fatal Helicopter Crash: NATO." *National Post,* August 20, 2011, http://news.nationalpost.com/2011/08/10/air-strike-kills-taliban-leader-responsible-for-fatal-helicopter-crash-nato/#more-86515.

Reuters, Thomson. "Palestinian Leader Asks UN for Statehood." *NBCNews*, Sep
    tember 23, 2011, http://www.msnbc.msn.com/id/44638003/ns/world_
    news-mideast_n_africa/t/palestinian-leader-asks-un-statehood/.

*Review and Disposition of Individuals Detained at the Guantanamo Bay Naval Base
    and Closure of Detention Facilities.* Executive Order No. 13492, Title 3,
    § 2(b), January 22, 2009, http://edocket.access.gpo.gov/2009/pdf/E9–
    1893.pdf.

Review of Detention Policy Options. Executive Order No. 13493, Title 3, § 1(a)(e),
    January 22, 2009, http://edocket.access.gpo.gov/2009/pdf/E9–1895.pdf.

Ricolfi, Luca, and Paolo Campana. *Suicide Missions in the Palestinian Area: A New
    Database* (2004), http://www.prio.no/upload/suicide_missions.pdf.

Riechmann, Deb. "Taliban Show Resolve to Fight on after Bin Laden," *The Washing-
    ton Times,* May 13, 2011, http://www.washingtontimes.com/news/2011/
    may/13/taliban-show-resolve-fight-after-bin-laden/.

Riedel, Bruce. "Al Qaeda Strikes Back: Terrorism and al Qaeda, Afghani-
    stan." *Brookings,* May/June 2007, http://www.brookings.edu/articles/
    2007/05terrorism_riedel.aspx. This article was originally published in the
    May/June 2007 issue of *Foreign Affairs.*

Risen, James, and Eric Lichtblau. "Bush Lets U.S. Spy on Callers Without
    Courts." *The New York Times,* December 16, 2005, http://www.nytimes.
    com/2005/12/16/politics/16program.html?pagewanted=all.

Rivkin, David B., Jr., Lee A. Casey, and Mark Wendell DeLaquil. "War, Interna-
    tional Law, and Sovereignty: Reevaluating the Rules of the Game in a New
    Century: Preemption and Law in the Twenty-First Century." *Chicago Journal
    of International Law* 5, no. 2 (Winter 2005): 467–98.

Robertson, Nic, and Paul Cruickshank. "Recruits Reveal al Qaeda's Sprawling Web."
    CNN, July 30, 2009, http://articles.cnn.com/2009–07–30/justice/robertson.
    al.qaeda.full_1_al-qaeda-terror-group-intelligence-officials?_s=PM:CRIME.

Roggio, Bill. "Abu Hafs al Shahri Confirmed Killed in Predator Strike in Paki-
    stan." *The Long War Journal,* September 17, 2011, http://www.longwarjour
    nal.org/archives/2011/09/abu_hafs_al_shahri_c.php.

Roggio, Bill. "Islamic Movement of Uzbekistan Claims Panjshir Suicide Attack."
    The Long War Journal, October 17, 2011, http://www.longwarjournal.org/
    archives/2011/10/islamic_movement_of_6.php.

Rosenberger, John. "Discerning the Behavior of the Suicide Bomber." *Jour-
    nal of Religion and Health* 42, no. 1 (Spring 2003), http://www.jstor.org/
    stable/27511651.

Ross, Brian, Jake Tapper, Richard Esposito, and Nick Schifrin. "Osama Bin Laden
    Killed by Navy SEALs in Firefight." *ABC News The Blotter,* May 2, 2011, http://
    abcnews.go.com/Blotter/osama-bin-laden-killed-navy-seals-firefight/
    story?id=13505792.

Ross, Tim. "WikiLeaks: Osama bin Laden Killed after Tip-Offs from Guanta-
    namo." *The Telegraph,* May 2, 2011, http://www.telegraph.co.uk/news/
    worldnews/asia/pakistan/8488436/WikiLeaks-Osama-bin-Laden-killed-
    after-tip-offs-from-Guantanamo.html.

Rössel, Jörg, and Randall Collins. "Conflict Theory and Interaction Rituals: The
    Microfoundations of Conflict Theory." In *Handbook of Sociological Theory,* ed-
    ited by Jonathan H. Turner (New York: Kluwer Academic/Plenum, 2001),
    509–31.

Rowley, Charles K., and Jennis Taylor. "The Israel and Palestine Land Settlement Problem, 1948–2005: An Analytical History." *Public Choice* 128 (2006): 77–90.

Rozen, Laura. "Researcher: Suicide Terrorism Linked to Military Occupation." *Politico*, October 11, 2010, http://www.politico.com/blogs/laurarozen/1010/Researcher_Suicide_terrorism_linked_to_military_occupation.html.

Rozen, Laura. "Suicide Attacks Linked to Military Occupation: Report." *Huffington Post*, October 11, 2010, http://www.huffingtonpost.com/2010/10/11/suicide-attacks-military-occupation-pape_n_758759.html.

Rubin, Alissa J. "Taliban Overhaul Image to Win Allies." *The New York Times*, January 20, 2010, http://www.nytimes.com/2010/01/21/world/asia/21taliban.html?pagewanted=all.

Rubin, Alissa J. "Taliban Using Modern Means to Add to Sway." *The New York Times*, October 4, 2011, http://www.nytimes.com/2011/10/05/world/asia/taliban-using-modern-means-to-add-to-sway.html?_r=1&nl=todaysheadlines&emc=tha22.

Rudoren, Jodi, and Fares Akram. "Palestinians Sign Deal to Set Up Elections." *The New York Times*, May 20, 2012, http://www.nytimes.com/2012/05/21/world/middleeast/hamas-and-fatah-agree-in-cairo-to-begin-work-on-elections.html.

"Rumsfeld Sees Long Struggle in War on Terrorism." *Association of the United States Army (AUSA)*, October 28, 2004, http://www3.ausa.org/webpub/DeptHome.nsf/byid/CTON-6FUT4C.

"Russian Extremists Remotely Detonate Suicide Bombs." *Homeland Security News Wire*, February 8, 2011, http://homelandsecuritynewswire.com/russian-extremists-remotely-detonate-suicide-bombs.

Ryan, Michael W.S. "After Bin Laden: Al-Qaeda Strategy in Yemen." *Terrorism Monitor* 9, no. 20 (May 20, 2011), http://www.jamestown.org/programs/gta/single/?tx_ttnews%5Btt_news%5D=37949&cHash=1de1f787ecd2d22a697e3eacf3451d12.

Sageman, Marc. "Understanding Jihadi Networks." *Strategic Insights* 4, no. 4 (April 2005), http://www.au.af.mil/au/awc/awcgate/nps/sageman_apr05.pdf.

Sanburn, Josh. "A Brief History of Self-Immolation." *Time*, January 20, 2011, http://www.time.com/time/world/article/0,8599,2043123,00.html.

Sanderson, Thomas M. "Transnational Terror and Organized Crime: Blurring the Lines." *SAIS Review* 24, no. 1 (2004): 49–61.

"Sarin Gas Attack on the Tokyo Subway." *Japan-101: Information Resource*, http://www.japan-101.com/culture/sarin_gas_attack_on_the_tokyo_su.htm.

Sassòli, Marco. "Terrorism and War." *Journal of International Criminal Justice* 4, no. 5 (November 1, 2006): 959.

Savage, Charlie. "Secret U.S. Memo Made Legal Case to Kill a Citizen." *The New York Times*, October 8, 2011, http://www.nytimes.com/2011/10/09/world/middleeast/secret-us-memo-made-legal-case-to-kill-a-citizen.html?_r=1&pagewanted=all.

Scahill, Jeremy. "Washington's War in Yemen Backfires." *The Nation*, March 5–12, 2012, http://www.thenation.com/article/166265/washingtons-war-yemen-backfires.

Schifrin, Nick, Pierre Thomas, and Jake Tapper. "Al Qaeda No. 2 Atiyah Abd al-Rahman Killed in Pakistan." *ABC News*, August 27, 2011, http://abcnews.

go.com/International/al-qaeda-atiyah-abd-al-rahman-killed-pakistan/
story?id=14394690.

Schmitt, Eric, and Thom Shanker. "Washington Recasts Terror War as 'Struggle.'"
The New York Times, July 27, 2005, http://www.nytimes.com/2005/07/26/
world/americas/26iht-terror.html.

Schweitzer, Yoram. "Suicide Bombings—The Ultimate Weapon?" *International Institute for Counter-Terrorism,* July 8, 2001, http://www.ict.org.il/Articles/
tabid/66/Articlsid/68/Default.aspx. Quoted in Skaine, *Female Suicide
Bombers,* 87.

"Selected Cities in the World with 30,000 to 35,000 Inhabitants in 2005." *Mongabay.
com,* 2007, http://www.mongabay.com/igapo/2005_world_city_popula
tions/2005_city_population_24.html.

"Self-Immolation Fact Sheet." *Campaign for Tibet,* June 4, 2012, http://www.savetibet.
org/resource-center/maps-data-fact-sheets/self-immolation-fact-sheet.

"Seppuku." *Wikipedia,* June 11, 2012, http://en.wikipedia.org/wiki/Seppuku.

Sexton, Buck. "Yemen's Al Qaeda Branch Renaming Itself for Public Relations
Makeover." *The Blaze,* December 14, 2011, http://www.theblaze.com/stories/
yemens-al-qaeda-branch-renaming-itself-for-public-relations-makeover/.

Shah, Amir. "Suicide Attacks at Afghan Hotel; Hostages Taken." *Yahoo News,* June
21, 2012, http://news.yahoo.com/suicide-attacks-afghan-hotel-hostages-
taken-013108640.html.

Shah, Aqil. "Getting the Military Out of Pakistani Politics." *Foreign Affairs* 90, no.
3 (2011): 69–82.

Shane, Scott. "Wars Fought and Wars Googled." *The New York Times,* June
26, 2010, http://www.nytimes.com/2010/06/27/weekinreview/27shane.
html?_r=1.

Shane, Scott, and Charlie Savage. "Bin Laden Raid Revives Debate on Value
of Torture." *The New York Times,* May 3, 2011, http://www.nytimes.
com/2011/05/04/us/politics/04torture.html?_r=1.

Shane, Scott, Mark Mazzetti, and Robert F. Worth. "Secret Assault on Terrorism
Widens on Two Continents." *The New York Times,* August 14, 2010, http://
www.nytimes.com/2010/08/15/world/15shadowwar.html.

Shears, Richard. "Terrorist Mastermind Noordin Mohammed Top Shot Dead after
a 17-Hour Siege." *Mail Online,* August 10, 2009, http://www.dailymail.
co.uk/news/article-1205164/Terrorist-mastermind-Noordin-Mohammed-
Top-shot-dead-17-hour-seige.html.

Siddiqui, Haroon. "How Many Civilians Have Died?" *Star.com,* September 20
2007, http://www.thestar.com/columnists/article/258511.

Sindelar, Daisy. "Does Torture Work? Bin Laden's Killing Reopens Debate on 'Black-
Site' Interrogations." *Radio Free Europe/Radio Liberty,* May 4, 2011, http://
www.rferl.org/content/osama_bin_laden_does_torture_work/24091366.
html.

Singer, Peter W. "Terrorists Must Be Denied Child Recruit." *Financial Times,* January
20, 2005, http://www.brookings.edu/opinions/2005/0120humanrights_
singer.aspx.

Singh, Ajit Kumar. "Eelam War IV: Imminent End." *South Asian Outlook* 8, no. 9
(March 2009), http://www.southasianoutlook.com/issues/2009/march/
sri_lanka_eelam_war_IV_imminent_end.html.

Sitaraman, Ganesh. "Counterinsurgency, the War on Terror, and the Laws of War." *Virginia Law Review* 95, no. 7 (2009): 1745–839, http://www.virginialaw review.org/content/pdfs/95/1745.pdf.

Skaine, Rosemarie. "Neither Afghan Nor Islam." *Ethnicities* 2, no. 2 (June 2002): 142.

Sluzki, Carlos E. "Psychosocial Scenarios Following a Bioterrorist Attack." Advanced draft. Web Archive of Carlos E. Sluzki, MD, September 9–21, 2002, 102a, http://sluzki.com/?articles&id=102a.

Smith, Niel A. "Understanding Sri Lanka's Defeat of the Tamil Tigers." *Joint Force Quarterly* 59 (October 2010): 40–44, http://www.ndu.edu/press/under-standing-sri-lanka.html.

Sparago, Marta. *Terrorist Recruitment: The Crucial Case of Al Qaeda's Global Jihad Terror Network* (New York: Center for Global Affairs, New York University, Spring 2007), http://www.scps.nyu.edu/export/sites/scps/pdf/global-affairs/marta-sparago.pdf.

Spencer, Naomi. "Military Censorship of the War in Iraq." *World Socialist Web Site,* July 31, 2008, http://www.wsws.org/articles/2008/jul2008/cens-j31.shtml.

"Sri Lanka Profile." *BBC News,* May 20, 2012, http://www.bbc.co.uk/news/world-south-asia-11999611.

"Sri Lanka Warns UN Not to Release War Crimes Report." *The Guardian,* April 21, 2011, http://www.guardian.co.uk/world/2011/apr/21/sri lanka-un-war-crimes-report.

Stahn, Carsten. "Jus Post Bellum: Mapping the Discipline(s)." *American University International Law Review* 23 (2008): 311–47.

Stern, Jessica. "Mind over Martyr: How to Deradicalize Islamist Extremists." *Foreign Affairs* 89, no. 1 (January–February 2010): 95.

Stracke, Nicole. "Iraq: Suicide Bombing as Tactical Means of Asymmetric Warfare." *Insights* 5 (March 2007): 10–20.

"Suicide Pill." *NationMaster.com,* http://www.nationmaster.com/encyclopedia/Suicide-pill.

"Suicide Pill." *Wikipedia,* June 1, 2012, http://en.wikipedia.org/wiki/Suicide_pill.

Sullivan, John P. "Child Soldiers: Despair, Barbarization, and Conflict." *Air and Space Power Journal* (March 2008), http://www.airpower.au.af.mil/apjin ternational/apj-s/2008/1tri08/sullivaneng.htm.

Taarnby, Michael. Recruitment of Islamist Terrorists in Europe: Trends and Perspectives (Aarhus: Centre for Cultural Research, University of Aarhus, January 14, 2005): 16, 17, http://www.investigativeproject.org/documents/testimony/58.pdf.

Tahir, Muhammad. "Bin Laden's Death Casts a Pall over U.S.-Pakistan Relations." *Radio Free Europe/Radio Liberty,* May 5, 2011, http://www.rferl.org/con tent/in_wake_of_bin_ladens_death_relationship_between_us_pakistan_could_become_frosty/24092370.html.

Tapper, Jake. "The Terrorist Notches on Obama's Belt." *ABC News,* September 30, 2011, http://abcnews.go.com/blogs/politics/2011/09/the-terro rist-notches-on-obamas-belt/.

Tavernise, Sabrina. "U.S. Quietly Issues Estimate of Iraqi Civilian Casualties." *The New York Times,* October 30, 2005, http://www.nytimes.com/2005/10/30/international/middleeast/30civilians.html?pagewanted=1&_r=1.

Tellis, Ashley J. *Pakistan and the War on Terror: Conflicted Goals, Compromised Performance* (Washington, D.C.: Carnegie Endowment for International Peace, 2008), http://www.carnegieendowment.org/files/tellis_pakistan_final.pdf.

Terrill, W. Andrew. "The Arab Upheavals and the Future of the U.S. Military Policies and Presence in the Middle East and the Gulf." *Strategic Studies Institute*, June 27, 2011, http://www.strategicstudiesinstitute.army.mil/index.cfm/articles/Arab-Upheavals-and-the-Future-of-the-US-Military-Policies-and-Presence-in-the-Middle-East-and-the-Gulf/2011/6/27#_ednref28.

"Terrorism Law and Policy: World Anti-Terrorism Laws." *Jurist*, 2003, http://jurist.law.pitt.edu/terrorism/terrorism3a.htm.

"Terrorist Attack Cycle: Selecting the Target." *Stratfor Global Intelligence*, September 30, 2005, http://www.stratfor.com/memberships/55548/terrorist_attack_cycle_selecting_target.

"Terrorist Group Profile: The Taliban," *Terroristplanet*, July 7, 2011, http://www.terroristplanet.com/2010/02/terrorist-group-profile-the-taliban/ (accessed July 7, 2011).

"Terrorist Groups," *Terrorism Research*, http://www.terrorism-research.com/groups/.

"Terrorist Organization Profile: Hamas." *National Consortium for the Study of Terrorism and Responses to Terrorism (START)*, http://www.start.umd.edu/start/data_collections/tops/terrorist_organization_profile.asp?id=49.

"Terrorist Organizational Models." *A Military Guide to Terrorism in the Twenty-First Century*, Handbook No. 1 (Fort Leavenworth, KS: U.S. Army Training and Doctrine Command, August 15, 2007), Chapter 3, 3.1–3.14, http://www.au.af.mil/au/awc/awcgate/army/guidterr/ch03.pdf.

Terry, James P. "The President as Commander in Chief." *Ave Maria Law Review* 7, no. 2 (Spring 2009): 391–498.

Thomas, Gerald W. "Suicide Tactics: The Kamikaze during WWII." *Air Group 4 "Casablanca to Tokyo,"* 2011, http://www.airgroup4.com/kamikaze.htm.

Thomas, Timothy L. "Deciphering Asymmetry's Word Game." *Military Review* (July–August 2001): 32–37, http://www.au.af.mil/au/awc/awcgate/milreview/thomas_asym.pdf.

Tilly, Charles. "Terror as Strategy and Relational Process." *International Journal of Comparative Sociology* 46, nos. 1–2 (February–April): 11–32.

"A Timeline of Major Terror Attacks in Russia." *New Zealand Herald*, January 25, 2011.

"Timeline of the Tamil Conflict: Early Years." *BBC News*, September, 4, 2000, http://news.bbc.co.uk/2/hi/south_asia/51435.stm.

Torchia, Christopher. "The Private Worry of US Marines in Afghanistan." *Yahoo News*, September 21, 2011, http://news.yahoo.com/private-worry-us-marines-afghanistan-065944218.html.

Tosini, Domenico. "Al-Qaeda's Strategic Gamble: The Sociology of Suicide Bombings in Iraq." *Canadian Journal of Sociology* 35, no. 2 (2010): 271–308.

Tran, Mark. "CIA Admit 'Waterboarding' al-Qaida Suspects." *The Guardian*, February 5, 2008, http://www.guardian.co.uk/world/2008/feb/05/india.terrorism.

Transnational Terrorism: The Threat to Australia (Canberra: Department of Foreign Affairs and Trade, Australian Government, July 15, 2004), Chapter 1, http://www.dfat.gov.au/publications/terrorism/chapter1.html.

Trembath, Brendan. "Reports Qatar to Host Taliban Office." *ABC News,* September 13, 2011, http://www.abc.net.au/news/2011-09-13/reports-qatar-to-host-taliban-office/2897864?section=world.

"TSA Shares Tips to Streamline Summer Travel." *Transportation and Security Administration,* May 25, 2012, http://www.tsa.gov/press/releases/2012/0525.shtm.

"Umar Farouk Abdulmutallab." *The New York Times,* October 12, 2011, http://topics.nytimes.com/top/reference/timestopics/people/a/umar_farouk_abdulmutallab/index.html?inline=nyt-per.

"Underwear Bomber Gets 4 Life Sentences." *San Francisco Chronicle,* February 17, 2012, A5, http://www.sfgate.com/crime/article/Underwear-bomber-gets-4-life-sentences-3338151.php.

"United States Department of Homeland Security." *Wikipedia,* June 25, 2012, http://en.wikipedia.org/wiki/United_States_Department_of_Homeland_Security.

"U.S. Envoy: Afghanistan, Pakistan Say bin Laden's Killing Is 'Shared Achievement.'" *Voice of America,* May 3, 2011, http://www.voanews.com/english/news/asia/US-Envoy-Afghanistan-Pakistan-Say-bin-Ladens-Killing-Is-Shared-Achievement-121166614.html.

"US to Release bin Laden Home Videos, Propaganda Tapes, Officials Say." *NBC-News,* May 7, 2011, http://www.msnbc.msn.com/id/42941138/ns/world_news-death_of_bin_laden/.

Vanden Brook, Tom. "U.S. Cuts Afghan IED Toll by 37%." *USA Today,* February 17, 2011, A1, http://www.usatoday.com/printedition/news/20110217/1aied17_st.art.htm.

Veitch, James, and John Martin. *The Death of Osama bin Laden and the Future of al-Qaeda* (Dhaka: Bangladesh Institute of Peace and Security Studies, 2011), http://www.bipss.org.bd/pdf/BIPSS%20Paper.pdf.

Wade, Matt. "After Decades of Fighting, Tamils Lay Down Their Guns." *The Age,* May 18, 2009, http://www.theage.com.au/news/world/after-decades-of-fighting-tamils-lay-down-guns/2009/05/17/1242498638549.html.

Walsh, Declan. "Air Strike Kills Taliban Leader Baitullah Mehsud." *The Guardian,* August 7, 2009, http://www.guardian.co.uk/world/2009/aug/07/baitullah-mehsud-dead-taliban-pakistan.

Walt, Stephen M. "Why They Hate Us (II): How Many Muslims Has the U.S. Killed in the Past 30 Years?" *Foreign Policy,* November 30, 2009, http://walt.foreignpolicy.com/posts/2009/11/30/why_they_hate_us_ii_how_many_muslims_has_the_us_killed_in_the_past_30_years.

Waraich, Omar. "Terrorism-Linked Charity Finds New Life amid Pakistan Refugee Crisis." *Time,* May 13, 2009, http://www.time.com/time/world/article/0,8599,1898127,00.html.

"Week of 7.21.06—Timeline: Israel-Lebanon Crisis." *Now,* http://www.pbs.org/now/shows/229/middle-east-history.html.

Wehner, Peter. "The Unintended Consequences of a Retreat." *Commentary,* June 21, 2011, http://www.commentarymagazine.com/2011/06/21/the-unintended-consequences-of-a-retreat/.

Westcott, Kathryn. "Who Are Hezbollah?" *BBC News,* April, 4, 2002, http://news.bbc.co.uk/2/hi/1908671.stm.

"Who Are Hezbollah?" *BBC News,* July 4, 2010, http://news.bbc.co.uk/2/hi/middle_east/4314423.stm.

Williams, Timothy, and Duraid Adnan. "Sunnis in Iraq Allied with U.S. Re-
    join Rebels." *The New York Times,* October 16, 2010, http://www.ny
    times.com/2010/10/17/world/middleeast/17awakening.html?ref=al_
    qaeda_in_mesopotamia.

Wilson, Scott, Craig Whitlock, and William Branigin. "Osama bin Laden Killed in
    U.S. Raid, Buried at Sea." *The Washington Post,* May 2, 2011, http://www.
    washingtonpost.com/national/osama-bin-laden-killed-in-us-raid-buried-
    at-sea/2011/05/02/AFx0yAZF_story.html.

Wingfield, Thomas C. "The Convergence of Traditional Theory and Modern Re-
    ality: Just War Doctrine and Tyrannical Regimes." *Ave Maria Law Review* 2,
    no. 1 (Spring 2004): 93–122.

Wong, Kristina. "Rising Suicides Stump Military Leaders." *ABC Good Morning
    America,* September 27, 2011, http://abcnews.go.com/US/rising-suicides-
    stump-military-leaders/story?id=14578134.

Worden, William L. "Kamikaze: Aerial Banzai Charge." *Saturday Evening Post* 217,
    no. 152 (June 23, 1945): 17.

Yassin, Ahmad, ed. *The Hamas Charter (1988)* (Gelilot: Intelligence and Terror-
    ism Information Center at the Center for Special Studies, March 21, 2006),
    http://www.terrorism-info.org.il/malam_multimedia/English/eng_n/
    pdf/hamas_charter.pdf.

*"You Dress According to Their Rules" Enforcement of an Islamic Dress Code for Women
    in Chechnya.* (New York: Human Rights Watch, 2011), http://www.hrw.
    org/sites/default/files/reports/chechnya0311webwcover.pdf.

Yousafzai, Sami, and Ron Moreau. "Inside al Qaeda." *Newsweek,* September 13,
    2010, 30–37.

Yousafzai, Sami, Ron Moreau, John Barry, Faisal Enayat Khan, Babak Dehghan-
    pisheh, and Rod Nordland. "Back in Business." *Newsweek,* November 25,
    2002, 26–29.

Zajam, M. "Suicide Missions: Nothing Islamic about It." *TwoCircles.net,* February 20,
    2011, http://twocircles.net/2011feb20/suicide_missions_nothing_islamic
    _about_it.html.

Zasloff, Jonathan. "Law and the Shaping of American Foreign Policy: From the
    Gilded Age to the New Era." *New York University Law Review* 78 (April
    2003): 239–373.

Zegenhagen, Evelyn. "German Women Pilots at War, 1939 to 1945." *Air Power His-
    tory, Rockville* 56, no. 4 (Winter 2009): 11–28.

Zernike, Kate, and Michael T. Kaufman. "The Most Wanted Face of Terrorism."
    The New York Times, May 2, 2011, http://www.nytimes.com/2011/05/02/
    world/02osama-bin-laden-obituary.html?_r=1.

BOOKS

"Al Qaeda Training Manual, Part 1." *Wednesday Report,* 2004, http://www.
    mobrien.com/twr/bin_laden.htm.

Angell, Ami, and Rohan Gunaratna. *Terrorist Rehabilitation: The U.S. Experience in
    Iraq* (Boca Ratan, FL: CRC Press, 2011).

Atwan, Abdel Bari. *The Secret History of al Qaeda,* 2nd ed. (Berkeley, CA: University
    of California Press, 2008).

Axell, Albert, and Hideaki Kase. *Kamikaze: Japan's Suicide Gods* (New York: Longman, 2002).

Bercovitch, Jacob, and Richard Jackson. *Conflict Resolution in the 21st Century: Principles, Methods, and Approaches* (Ann Arbor, MI: University of Michigan Press, 2009).

Berger, Peter. *Invitation to Sociology: A Humanistic Perspective* (Garden City, NY: Doubleday, 1963).

Cambanis, Thanassis. *A Privilege to Die: Inside Hezbollah's Legions and Their Endless War against Israel* (New York: Free Press, 2010).

Charny, I. W. *Fighting Suicide Bombing: A Worldwide Campaign for Life* (Westport, CT: Praeger Security International, 2007), http://rapidlibrary.com/files/ebooksclub-org-fighting-suicide-bombing-a-worldwide-campaign-for-life-pdf_ulfq8rwrtmieon.html.

Connable, Ben, and Martin C. Libicki. *How Insurgencies End* (Santa Monica, CA: RAND Corporation, 2010), http://www.rand.org/pubs/monographs/MG965.

DeFronzo, James. *Revolutionary Movements in World History: From 1750 to Present* (Santa Barbara, CA: ABC-CLIO, 2006).

Durkheim, Emile. *Suicide: A Study in Sociology*, translated by John A. Spaulding and George Simpson, edited by George Simpson (New York: Free Press, 1951).

Eager, Paige Whaley. *From Freedom Fighters to Terrorists: Women and Political Violence* (Aldershot, England; Burlington, VT: Ashgate, 2008).

Finn, Melissa. "Terrorists, Female." In *Encyclopedia of Women in Today's World* (Thousand Oaks, CA: Sage Publications, 2011).

Gilligan, Emma. *Terror in Chechnya: Russia and the Tragedy of Civilians in War* (Princeton, NJ: Princeton University, 2010).

Hafez, Mohammed M. *Suicide Bombers in Iraq: The Strategy and Ideology of Martyrdom* (Washington, D.C.: United States Institute of Peace, 2007).

Headley, Lee A. *Suicide in Asia and the Near East* (Berkeley, CA: University of California Press, 1982).

Holmes, Ronald M., and Stephen T. Holmes. *Suicide: Theory, Practice, and Investigation* (Thousand Oaks, CA: Sage Publications, 2005).

Hughes, James. *From Nationalism to Jihad* (Philadelphia, PA: University of Pennsylvania, 2007).

Inoguchi, Rikihei, and Tadashi Nakajima. *Divine Wind: Japan's Kamikaze Force in World War II*, edited by Roger Pineau (Annapolis, MD: U.S. Naval Institute Press, 1994).

Jackson, Richard, Marie Breen Smyth, and Jeroen Gunning. *Critical Terrorism Studies: A New Research Agenda* (London: Routledge, 2009).

Jayasena, Karunya M. *Motivations of Female Suicide Bombers from a Sociological Perspective* (Northridge, CA: California State University, 2009), http://books.google.com/books/about/Motivations_of_female_suicide_bombers_fr.html?id=w4qkYgEACAAJ.

Kelsay, John. *Islam and War* (Louisville, KY: John Knox Press, 1993).

Levitt, Matthew. *Hamas: Politics, Charity, and Terrorism in the Service of Jihad* (Washington, D.C.: Washington Institute for Near East Policy, 2006).

Martin, Gus. *Understanding Terrorism: Challenges, Perspectives, and Issues*, 3rd ed. (Thousand Oaks, CA: Sage Publications, Inc., 2010).

Mills, C. Wright. *The Sociological Imagination* (New York: Oxford University Press, 1959).

Morison, Samuel Eliot. *History of United States Naval Operations in World War II*, Introduction by Dudley Wright Knox (Urbana, IL: University of Illinois Press, 2001–2002).

Ohnuki-Tierney, Emiko. *Kamikaze Diaries: Reflections of Japanese Student Soldiers* (Chicago, IL: University of Chicago Press, 2010).

Omar, Mullah. "Key Quotes from New Taliban Book." *Al Jazeera*, July 27, 2009, http://english.aljazeera.net/news/asia/2009/07/200972775236982270.html.

Pape, Robert A. *Dying to Win: The Strategic Logic of Suicide Terrorism* (New York: Random House, 2005).

Pape, Robert A., and James K. Feldman. *Cutting the Fuse: The Explosion of Global Suicide Terrorism and How to Stop It* (Chicago, IL: University of Chicago, 2010).

Polk, William R. *Neighbors and Strangers: The Fundamentals of Foreign Affairs* (Chicago, IL: University of Chicago Press, 1997).

"Q&A: The Chechen Conflict." *BBC News*, July 10, 2006, http://news.bbc.co.uk/2/hi/europe/3293441.stm.

Rabasa, Angel, Peter Chalk, Kim Cragin, Sara A. Daly, Heather S. Gregg, Theodore W. Karasik, Kevin A. O'Brien, and William Rosenau. *Beyond al-Qaeda: Part 1, The Global Jihadist Movement* (Santa Monica, CA: RAND Corporation, 2006), http://www.rand.org/pubs/monographs/MG429.html.

Rabasa, Angel, Peter Chalk, Kim Cragin, Sara A. Daly, Heather S. Gregg, Theodore W. Karasik, Kevin A. O'Brien, and William Rosenau. *Beyond al-Qaeda: Part 2, The Outer Rings of the Terrorist Universe* (Santa Monica, CA: RAND Corporation, 2006), http://www.rand.org/content/dam/rand/pubs/monographs/2006/RAND_MG430.pdf.

Rassler, Don, Gabriel Koehler-Derrick, Liam Collins, Muhammad al-Obaidi, and Nelly Lahoud. "Letters from Abbottabad: Bin Laden Sidelined?" *Combating Terrorism Center at West Point*, May 03, 2012, http://www.ctc.usma.edu/posts/letters-from-abbottabad-bin-ladin-sidelined.

Riedel, Bruce. *Search for Al Qaeda: Its Leadership, Ideology, and Future* (Washington, D.C.: Brookings Institution Press, 2008).

Ritzer, George, and Douglas J. Goodman. *Sociological Theory*. 6th ed. (Boston, MA: McGraw-Hill, 2004).

Saikia, Jaideep, and Ekaterina Stepanova, eds. *Terrorism: Patterns of Internationalization* (Thousand Oaks, CA: Sage Publications Ltd., 2009).

Schachter, Jonathan. "The End of the Second Intifada." *Canada Free Press*, November 22, 2010, http://www.canadafreepress.com/index.php/article/30258.

Skaine, Rosemarie. *Women of Afghanistan in the Post-Taliban Era: How Lives Have Changed and Where They Stand Today* (Jefferson, NC: McFarland, 2008).

Skaine, Rosemarie. *Women of Afghanistan under the Taliban* (Jefferson, NC: McFarland, 2002).

Skaine, Rosemarie. *Female Suicide Bombers* (Jefferson, NC: McFarland, 2006).

Skaine, Rosemarie. *Women in Combat: A Reference Handbook* (Santa Barbara, CA: ABC-CLIO/Greenwood, 2011).

Springer, Devin R., James L. Regens, and David N. Edger. *Islamic Radicalism and Global Jihad* (Washington, D.C.: Georgetown University Press, 2009).

Tuman, Joseph S. *Communicating Terror: The Rhetorical Dimensions of Terrorism*, 2nd ed. (Thousand Oaks, CA: Sage Publications, Inc., 2010).

Warner, Peggy, and Denis Warner. *The Sacred Warriors: Japan's Suicide Legions* (Thorold: Avon Books, 1984).

Woodward, Bob. *Obama's Wars* (New York: Simon & Schuster, 2010).

INTERVIEWS

Breen-Smyth, Marie. Chair in International Politics, Codirector, Centre for International Intervention, Director of Research, School of Politics, University of Surrey, Guildford. Interview by Rosemarie Skaine, telephone, March 18, 2012.

Gross, Max L. Former Senior Research Fellow, Islam in Southeast Asia Project, Center for Strategic Intelligence Research, Joint Military Intelligence College, Washington, D.C. and former Dean, School of Intelligence Studies, Joint Military Intelligence College. Interview by Rosemarie Skaine, telephone, February 23, 2011 and October 29, 2011.

Jackson, Richard. Department of International Politics, Aberystwyth University, Aberystwyth. Interview by Rosemarie Skaine, e-mail, June 14, 2011.

Williams, Jr., Rear Admiral (RADM) D.M., USN (Retd.). Former Commander, Naval Investigative Service (NIS) Command. Interview by Rosemarie Skaine, e-mail, July 6, 2011.

REPORTS

"1994 to 2011—Terror Attacks against Russia . . . ." *Windows to Russia,* http://windowstorussia.com/1994-to-2011-terror-attacks-against-russia.html.

Aaron, David. *In Their Own Words: Voices of Jihad—Compilation and Commentary* (Santa Monica, CA: RAND Corporation, 2008), http://www.rand.org/pubs/monographs/MG602.html.

Aboul-Enein, Youssef H., and Sherifa Zuhur. *Islamic Rulings on Warfare* (Carlisle, PA: Strategic Studies Institute, U.S. Army War College, October 2004), http://insct.syr.edu/uploadedFiles/insct/uploadedfiles/PDFs/Aboul-Enein.Zuhur.Islamic%20Rulings%20on%20Warfare(1).pdf.

"Affirmation of Armed Conflict with Al-Qaeda, the Taliban, and Associated Forces—Detention in the War on Terror," *National Defense Authorization Act of Fiscal Year 2012,* § 1034(3).

Allen, Lori. "There Are Many Reasons Why: Suicide Bombers and Martyrs in Palestine." *Middle East Report* 223 (Summer 2002): 34–37.

"America's Image in the World: Findings from the Pew Global Attitudes Project." *Pew Research Center,* March 14, 2007, http://www.pewglobal.org/2007/03/14/americas-image-in-the-world-findings-from-the-pew-global-attitudes-project.

The Arab Convention for the Suppression of Terrorism (Cairo: Council of Arab Ministers of the Interior and the Council of Arab Ministers of Justice, April 1998), http://www.al-bab.com/arab/docs/league/terrorism98.htm.

Bashi, Sari, and Kenneth Mann. *Disengaged Occupiers: The Legal Status of Gaza* (Tel-Aviv: Gisha, Legal Center for Freedom of Movement, January 2007), http://www.gisha.org/userfiles/file/report%20for%20the%20website.pdf.

Belasco, Amy. "The Cost of Iraq, Afghanistan, and Other Global War on Terror Operations since 9/11." *Congressional Research Service Report,* March 29, 2011, http://www.fas.org/sgp/crs/natsec/RL33110.pdf.

Bergen, Peter. Testimony. U.S. Senate Committee on Foreign Relations. *Al-Qaeda, the Taliban, and Other Extremist Groups in Afghanistan and Pakistan,* 111th Cong., 1st Sess., Hearing, May 24, 2011, http://foreign.senate.gov/hearings/hearing/?id=805120d6–5056-a032–5247–313a14503d33.

Bernstein, Paul I., John P. Caves, Jr., and W. Seth Carus. *Countering Weapons of Mass Destruction: Looking Back, Looking Ahead,* Occasional Paper 7 (Washington, D.C.: Center for the Study of Weapons of Mass Destruction, National Defense University Press, October 2009), http://permanent.access.gpo.gov/lps116426/op7cswmd.pdf.

Bloom, Mia. "Palestinian Suicide Bombing: Public Support, Market Share, and Outbidding." *Political Science Quarterly* 119, no. 1 (Spring 2004): 61–88.

Borja, Elizabeth C. *Brief Documentary History of the Department of Homeland Security 2001–2008* (Washington, D.C.: Homeland Security History Office, 2008), http://www.dhs.gov/xlibrary/assets/brief_documentary_history_of_dhs_2001_2008.pdf.

Bureau of South and Central Asian Affairs."Background Note: Sri Lanka," *U.S. Department of State,* April 6, 2011, http://www.state.gov/r/pa/ei/bgn/5249.htm.

Carlile, Lord of Berriew Q.C. *The Definition of Terrorism* (Norwich: Her Majesty's Stationery Office Limited, March 2007), http://www.official-documents.gov.uk/document/cm70/7052/7052.pdf.

Carney, Jay. "Press Briefing by Press Secretary Jay Carney." *The White House,* May 3, 2011, http://www.whitehouse.gov/the-press-office/2011/05/03/press-briefing-press-secretary-jay-carney-532011.

Carus, W. Seth. *Defining "Weapons of Mass Destruction,"* Occasional Paper 4 (Washington, D.C.: Center for the Study of Weapons of Mass Destruction, National Defense University Press, February 2006), 2, 3, http://www.ndu.edu/WMDCenter/docUploaded//OP4Carus.pdf.

Cavaleri, David P. *The Law of War: Can 20th-Century Standards Apply to the Global War on Terrorism?* (Fort Leavenworth, KN: Combat Studies Institute Press, 2005), http://www.dtic.mil/dtic/tr/fulltext/u2/a446304.pdf.

Chaaban, Jad, Hala Ghattas, Rima Habib, Sari Hanafi, Nadine Sahyoun, Nisreen Salti, Karin Seyfert, and Nadia Naamani. *Socio-Economic Survey of Palestinian Refugees in Lebanon* (Beirut: American University of Beirut, December 31, 2010), http://www.unrwa.org/userfiles/2011012074253.pdf.

Chesney, Robert. Testimony. U.S. Congress, House of Representatives, Committee on Armed Services. *Ten Years after the Authorization for Use of Military Force: Current Status of Legal Authorities, Detention, and Prosecution in the War on Terror,* 111th Cong., 1st Sess., Hearing, July 26, 2011, http://armedservices.house.gov/index.cfm/files/serve?File_id=dd0064b1–7416–44ab-bb0c-233d20cee4ef.

Cragin, Kim, Testimony. U.S. Congress, House Committee on Homeland Security, Subcommittee on Intelligence, Information Sharing and Terrorism Risk Assessment. *Understanding Terrorist Motivations: Hearing,* 111th Cong., 1st Sess., December 15, 2009, http://www.rand.org/content/dam/rand/pubs/testimonies/2009/RAND_CT338.pdf.

Cragin, R. Kim, and Sara A. Daly. *The Dynamic Terrorist Threat: An Assessment of Group Motivations and Capabilities in a Changing World* (Santa Monica, CA: RAND, 2003), http://www.rand.org/content/dam/rand/pubs/monograph_reports/2005/MR1782.pdf.

Cronin, Audrey Kurth. "Terrorists and Suicide Attacks." *Congressional Research Service Report*, August 28, 2003, http://www.fas.org/irp/crs/RL32058.pdf.

"Declaration of Principles—Main Points." *Israel Ministry of Foreign Affairs*, September 13, 1993, http://www.mfa.gov.il/MFA/Peace+Process/Guide+to+the+Peace+Process/Declaration+of+Principles+-+Main+Points.htm.

"Definitions [Terrorism]," *US Code*, Title 22, Ch. 38, § 2656f(d), http://www.law.cornell.edu/uscode/text/22/2656f.

"Detainee Treatment Act of 2005 [White House]." *Jurist Legal News and Research*, December 31, 2005, http://jurist.law.pitt.edu/gazette/2005/12/detainee-treatment-act-of-2005-white.php.

Dorronsoro, Gilles. *The Taliban's Winning Strategy in Afghanistan* (Washington, D.C.: Carnegie Endowment for International Peace, 2009), http://carnegieendowment.org/files/taliban_winning_strategy.pdf.

Doyle, Charles. "Terrorism: Section by Section Analysis of the USA Patriot Act." *Congressional Research Service Report*, December 10, 2001, http://www.au.af.mil/au/awc/awcgate/crs/rl31200.pdf.

Drinkwine, Brian M. *The Serpent in Our Garden: Al-Qa'ida and the Long War* (Carlisle, PA: Strategic Studies Institute, U.S. Army War College, January 2009), http://www.strategicstudiesinstitute.army.mil/pdffiles/PUB877.pdf.

Eisenhower Study Group. *The Costs of War since 2001: Iraq, Afghanistan, and Pakistan—Executive Summary* (Providence, RI: Watson Institute, Brown University, June 2011), http://costsofwar.org/sites/default/files/Costs%20of%20War%20Executive%20Summary.pdf.

Eland, Ivan. "Does U.S. Intervention Overseas Breed Terrorism? The Historical Record." *CATO Institute*, Foreign Policy Briefing No. 50, December 17, 1998, http://www.cato.org/pubs/fpbriefs/fpb-050es.html.

Engel, Steven A. Testimony. U.S. Congress, House of Representatives, Committee on Armed Services. *Ten Years after the Authorization for Use of Military Force: Current Status of Legal Authorities, Detention, and Prosecution in the War on Terror*, 111th Cong., 1st Sess., Hearing, July 26, 2011, http://armedservices.house.gov/index.cfm/files/serve?File_id=138d0ad3-4562-49af-b120-2b3d66e147eb.

Epstein, Susan B., and Alan Kronstadt. "Pakistan: U.S. Foreign Assistance." *Congressional Research Service Report*, July 28, 2011, http://www.fas.org/sgp/crs/row/R41856.pdf.

European Union. "Council Framework Decision of 13 June 2002 on Combating Terrorism." *Eur-Lex*, http://eur-lex.europa.eu/smartapi/cgi/sga_doc?smartapi!celexapi!prod!CELEXnumdoc&lg=EN&numdoc=32002F0475&model=guichett.

Exum, Andrew M., and Zachary M. Hosford. *Forging a Libya Strategy: Policy Recommendations for the Obama Administration* (Washington, D.C.: Center for a New American Security, March 2011), http://www.cnas.org/files/documents/publications/CNAS_Libya_ExumHosford.pdf.

Finel, Bernard I. "Are We Winning? Measuring Progress in the Struggle against al Qaeda and Associated Movements: 10 Report." *American Security Project*, May 1, 2010, http://americansecurityproject.org/media/AWW%202010%20Final.pdf.

"Full Statement from al Qaeda on Osama bin Laden's Death." *CNN*, May 6, 2011, http://news.blogs.cnn.com/2011/05/06/full-statement-from-al-qaeda-on-osama-bin-ladens-death/?iref=allsearch.

Gray, Colin S. *Irregular Enemies and the Essence of Strategy: Can the American Way of War Adapt?* (Carlisle, PA: Strategic Studies Institute, U.S. Army War College, March 2006), 1–64, http://www.strategicstudiesinstitute.army.mil/pdffiles/pub650.pdf.

Grier, Sam. *When Suicide Bombing Reaches the Tipping Point,* NDC Occasional Paper No. 8 (Rome: NATO Defense College, October 2005), http://www.ndc.nato.int/download/publications/op_08.pdf.

Hannah, Greg, Lindsay Clutterbuck, and Jennifer Rubin. *Understanding the Challenge of Extremist and Radicalized Prisoners* (Cambridge: RAND Europe, 2008), http://www.rand.org/content/dam/rand/pubs/technical_reports/2008/RAND_TR571.pdf.

Hassan, S. Azmat. *Countering Violent Extremism: The Fate of the Tamil Tigers* (New York: EastWest Institute, 2009), 15, http://docs.ewi.info/Tigers.pdf.

Helfstein, Scott, Nassir Abdullah, and Muhammad al-Obaidi. *Deadly Vanguards: A Study of al-Qa'ida's Violence against Muslims* (West Point, NY: Combating Terrorism Center, December 2009), http://www.ctc.usma.edu/wp-content/uploads/2010/10/deadly-vanguards_complete_l.pdf.

Hoffman, Bruce. *Lessons of 9/11: Testimony* (Arlington, VA: RAND, October 8, 2002), 11, http://www.rand.org/pubs/testimonies/2005/CT201.pdf.

Hoffman, Frank G. *Conflict in the 21st Century: The Rise of Hybrid Wars* (Arlington, VA: Potomac Institute for Policy Studies, December 2007), 1–72, http://www.potomacinstitute.org/images/stories/publications/potomac_hybridwar_0108.pdf.

The Infantry Rifle Company. Field Manual No. 3-21.10 (Washington, D.C.: U.S. Department of the Army, July 2006), Appendix G, Section 2, https://rdl.train.army.mil/soldierPortal/atia/adlsc/view/public/23168–1/FM/3–21.10/toc.htm#toc.

"Instructions for the Government of Armies of the United States in the Field (Lieber Code). 24 April 1863." *International Humanitarian Law—Treaties & Documents,* http://www.icrc.org/ihl.nsf/FULL/110?OpenDocument.

Iraq Body Count. *A Dossier of Civilian Casualties 2003–2005* (Oxford: IBC, July 2005), http://reports.iraqbodycount.org/a_dossier_of_civilian_casualties_2003-2005.pdf.

Jackson, Brian A., John C. Baker, Kim Cragin, John Parachini, Horacio R. Trujillo, and Peter Chalk. *Aptitude for Destruction*: *Case Studies of Organizational Learning in Five Terrorist Groups,* Vol. 2 (Arlington, VA: RAND, 2005), http://www.rand.org/pubs/monographs/2005/RAND_MG331.pdf.

Jackson, Brian A., Peter Chalk, R. Kim Cragin, Bruce Newsome, John V. Parachini, and William Rosenau. *Breaching the Fortress Wall: Understanding Terrorist Efforts to Overcome Defensive Technologies* (Santa Monica, CA: RAND Corporation, 2007), http://www.rand.org/pubs/monographs/2007/RAND_MG481.pdf.

Jenkins, Brian Michael. *The al Qaeda-Inspired Terrorist Threat: An Appreciation of the Current Situation,* CT-353 (Santa Monica, CA: RAND, December 6, 2010), http://www.rand.org/content/dam/rand/pubs/testimonies/2009/RAND_CT338.pdf.

Jenkins, Brian Michael. *Would-Be Warriors: Incidents of Jihadist Terrorist Radicalization in the United States since September 11, 2001* (Santa Monica, CA: RAND Corporation, 2010), http://www.rand.org/pubs/occasional_papers/OP292.

Jenkins, Brian Michael, and John Paul Godges, eds. *The Long Shadow of 9/11: America's Response to Terrorism* (Santa Monica, CA: RAND Corporation, August 9, 2011), http://www.rand.org/content/dam/rand/pubs/mono graphs/2011/RAND_MG1107.pdf.

Joint Chiefs of Staff. *Department of Defense Dictionary of Military and Associated Terms,* Joint Publication 1-02 (Washington, D.C.: U.S. Government Printing Office, June 10, 1998).

Joint Chiefs of Staff. *Irregular Warfare: Countering Irregular Threats Joint Operating Concept,* Version 2.0 (Washington, D.C.: U.S. Department of Defense, May 17, 2010), http://www.dtic.mil/futurejointwarfare/concepts/iw_joc2_0.pdf.

Joint Chiefs of Staff. *Joint Operations,* Joint Publication 3-0 (Washington, D.C.: U.S. Government Printing Office, March 22, 2010), http://www.dtic.mil/doctrine/new_pubs/jp3_0.pdf.

Kamolnick, Paul. *Delegitimizing Al-Qaeda: A Jihad-Realist Approach* (Carlisle, PA: Strategic Studies Institute, U.S. Army War College, March 2012), http://www.strategicstudiesinstitute.army.mil/pdffiles/pub1099.pdf.

Katel, Peter. "Religion; Defense and National Security." *CQ Researcher* 15, no. 36 (October 14, 2005): 857–80.

Lamont-Brown, Raymond. *Kamikaze: Japan's Suicide Samurai* (Minneapolis, MN: Booksales, 2004).

Lesser, Ian O., Bruce Hoffman, John Arquilla, David Ronfeldt, and Michele Zanini. *Countering the New Terrorism* (Santa Monica, CA: RAND, 1999), http://www.rand.org/pubs/monograph_reports/2009/MR989.pdf.

Lynch, Marc. *Rhetoric and Reality: Countering Terrorism in the Age of Obama* (Washington, D.C.: Center for a New American Security, 2010), http://www.cnas.org/files/documents/publications/CNAS_Rhetoric%20and%20Reality_Lynch.pdf.

Mandaville, Peter. *Muslim Networks and Movements in Western Europe* (Washington, D.C.: Pew Research Center, September 2010), http://www.pewforum.org/uploadedFiles/Topics/Religious_Affiliation/Muslim/Muslim-networks-full-report.pdf.

Margalit, Avishai. "The Suicide Bombers." *The New York Review of Books,* January 16, 2003, http://www.nybooks.com/articles/archives/2003/jan/16/the-suicide-bombers/.

Mark, Clyde R. "Israel's Proposal to Withdraw from Gaza." *Congressional Research Service Report,* February 2, 2005, http://fpc.state.gov/documents/organization/43994.pdf.

Meinardus, Ronald. "Terrorism as Political Ideology." *Friedrich Naumann Foundation for Liberty,* http://www.fnf.org.ph/liberallibrary/terrorism-as-political-ideology.htm.

Metz, Steven, and Phillip Cuccia. "Defining War for the 21st Century." In *2010 Strategic Studies Institute Annual Strategy Conference Report* (Carlisle, PA: Strategic Studies Institute, U.S. Army War College, February 2011), http://www.strategicstudiesinstitute.army.mil/pdffiles/PUB1036.pdf.

Military Commissions Act 2006, Public Law 109-366 [S. 3930], 109th Cong., 2nd Sess., October 17, 2006, http://www.loc.gov/rr/frd/Military_Law/pdf/PL-109-366.pdf.

Muhlhausen, David B., and Jena Baker McNeill. *Terror Trends: 40 Years' Data on International and Domestic Terrorism* (Washington, D.C.: The Heritage Foundation, May 20, 2011), http://report.heritage.org/sr0093.

Mukasey, Michael B. Testimony. U.S. Congress, House of Representatives, Committee on Armed Services, Subcommittee on Emerging Threats and Capabilities. *Ten Years On: The Evolution of the Terrorist Threat since 9/11*, 111th Cong., 1st Sess., Hearing, June 22, 2011, http://armedservices. house.gov/index.cfm/files/serve?File_id=781477e1-b064–4baf-acff-427dd9ded98d.

National Commission on Terrorist Attacks upon the United States. *The 9/11 Commission Report: Final Report of the National Commission on Terrorist Attacks upon the United States* (New York: W. W. Norton and Co., Inc., 2004), http:// govinfo.library.unt.edu/911/report/911Report_Exec.pdf.

National Counterterrorism Center. *2010 Report on Terrorism* (Washington, D.C.: U.S. Office of the Director of National Intelligence, April 30, 2011), http:// eib.edu.pl/wp-content/uploads/2012/04/2010_report_on_terrorism.pdf.

National Intelligence Council. "Global Trends 2015: A Dialogue about the Future with Nongovernment Experts." *CIA*, December 2000, https://www. cia.gov/news-information/cia-the-war-on-terrorism/terrorism-related-excerpts-from-global-trends-2015-a-dialogue-about-the-future-with-non government-experts.html.

Nichol, Jim. "Stability in Russia's Chechnya and Other Regions of the North Caucasus: Recent Developments." *Congressional Research Service Report*, December 13, 2010, http://www.fas.org/sgp/crs/row/RL34613.pdf.

Obama, Barack. "Obama's Afghan Speech: Full Text." *BBC News*, December 2, 2009, http://news.bbc.co.uk/go/pr/fr/-/2/hi/americas/8389849.stm.

Obama, Barack. "Remarks by the President at the Acceptance of the Nobel Peace Prize." *The White House*, December 10, 2009. http://www.whitehouse.gov/ the-press-office/remarks-president-acceptance-nobel-peace-prize.

Obama, Barack. "Remarks of President Barack Obama—As Prepared for Delivery on the Way Forward in Afghanistan." *Wall Street Journal*, June 22, 2011, http://blogs.wsj.com/washwire/2011/06/22/text-of-obamas-speech-on-afghanistan/.

"On Anniversary of bin Laden's Death, Little Backing of al Qaeda Survey Report." *Pew Research Center*, April 30, 2012, http://www.pewglobal.org/2012/04/ 30/on-anniversary-of-bin-ladens-death-little-backing-of-al-qaeda/.

Operations, Field Manual No. 3-0 (Washington, D.C.: U.S. Department of the Army, February 27, 2008), http://www.dtic.mil/doctrine/jel/service_pubs/fm3_ 0a.pdf.

"Osama Bin Laden's Elimination through the Prism of Al-Qaeda's Affiliates and Global Jihad Supporters—Follow-Up Report." *International Institute for Counter-Terrorism*, http://www.ict.org.il/LinkClick.aspx?fileticket=_ wciKVnJUs0%3d&tabid=428.

Perl, Raphael. "The Department of State's Patterns of Global Terrorism Report: Trends, State Sponsors, and Related Issues." *Congressional Research Service Report*, June 1, 2004, http://www.fas.org/irp/crs/RL32417.pdf.

"Press Briefing by Secretary of State Condoleezza Rice." *The White House*, July 16, 2006, http://georgewbush-whitehouse.archives.gov/news/releases/ 2006/07/20060716-2.html.

Reviewing the Decade Long Counter-Terrorism Struggle (Islamabad: Individualland, February 2011), http://www.individualland.com/index.php?option= com_rokdownloads&view=file&Itemid=160.

Rice, Earl. *Kamikazes* (San Diego, CA: Lucent Books, 1999).

Richards, Alan. *Socio-economic Roots of Radicalism? Towards Explaining the Appeal of Islamic Radicals* (Carlisle, PA: Strategic Studies Institute, U.S. Army War College, 2003), http://www.strategicstudiesinstitute.army.mil/pdffiles/pub105.pdf.

Rollins, John. "Al Qaeda and Affiliates: Historical Perspective, Global Presence, and Implications for U.S. Policy." *Congressional Research Service Report*, February 5, 2010, http://fpc.state.gov/documents/organization/137015.pdf.

Rollins, John. "Al Qaeda and Affiliates: Historical Perspective, Global Presence, and Implications for U.S. Policy." *Congressional Research Service Report*, January 25, 2011, http://fpc.state.gov/documents/organization/156542.pdf.

Roth, John, Douglas Greenburg, and Serena B. Wille. *Monograph on Terrorist Financing: Staff Report to the Commission* (Washington, D.C.: National Commission on Terrorist Attacks upon the United States, 2004), http://govinfo.library.unt.edu/911/staff_statements/911_TerrFin_Monograph.pdf.

Rumsfeld, Donald H. "Rumsfeld on Creating a 'Modular Army' for the 21st Century." *Wall Street Journal*, February 4, 2004, Op-ed.

Schlesinger, James R., *Final Report of Independent Panel to Review the Department of Defense Detention Operations* (Arlington, VA: Independent Panel to Review the DoD Detention Operations, August 24, 2004), 1–102, http://fl1.findlaw.com/news.findlaw.com/wp/docs/dod/abughraibrpt.pdf.

Schott, Paul Allan. *Reference Guide to Anti-Money Laundering and Combating the Financing of Terrorism: Second Edition and Supplement on Special Recommendation IX* (Washington, D.C.: World Bank, January 2006), http://zunia.org/uploads/media/knowledge/Reference_Guide_AMLCFT_2ndSupplement1.pdf.

Shimoshizu Air Unit in Chiba Pefecture. *Basic Instructions for To-Go Flyers* (1945), 88pp.

Simpson, Erin M., Melanie Sisson, and Donald Temple. *Breaching the Fortress Wall: Understanding Terrorist Efforts to Overcome Defensive Technologies* (Santa Monica, CA: RAND Corporation, 2007), http://www.rand.org/pubs/monographs/2007/RAND_MG481.pdf.

Söderblom, Jason D. *The Historical Pedigree and Relevance of Suicide 'Martyr' Bio-Terrorism* (Canberra: Terrorism Intelligence Centre, July 19, 2004), http://world-ice.com/Articles/Martyr.pdf.

Terror Operations: Case Studies in Terrorism, TRADOC G2 Handbook No. 1.01 (Fort Leavenworth, KS: U.S. Army Training and Doctrine Command, July 25, 2007), http://www.fas.org/irp/threat/terrorism/sup1.pdf.

"Terrorism and Illicit Finance: Executive Orders." *U.S. Department of the Treasury*, August 8, 2011, http://www.treasury.gov/resource-center/terrorist-illicit-finance/Pages/protecting-charities_exec-orders.aspx.

"Terrorist Finance Tracking Program (TFTP): Questions and Answers," *U.S. Department of the Treasury*, August 5, 2011, http://www.treasury.gov/resource-center/terrorist-illicit-finance/Terrorist-Finance-Tracking/Documents/Final%20Updated%20TFTP%20Brochure%20(8-5-11).pdf.

"Terrorist Finance Tracking Program (TFTP)." *U.S. Department of the Treasury*, site updated as of August 8, 2011, but program conceived within days post-9/11, http://www.treasury.gov/resource-center/terrorist-illicit-finance/Terrorist-Finance-Tracking/Pages/tftp.aspx.

"Terrorist Planning Cycle." *A Military Guide to Terrorism in the Twenty-First Century,*
       Handbook No. 1 (Fort Leavenworth, KS: U.S. Army Training and Doctrine
       Command, August 15, 2007), Appendix A, A-1, http://www.au.af.mil/au/
       awc/awcgate/army/guidterr/app_a.pdf.

Thiessen, Marc A., ed. *A Charge Kept: The Record of the Bush Presidency 2001–2009*
       (Washington, D.C.: Executive Office of the President, 2009), 1–128, http://
       georgewbush-whitehouse.archives.gov/infocus/bushrecord/documents/
       charge-kept.pdf.

Threat Assessment: Female Suicide Bombers. (Washington, D.C.: U.S. Customs and
       Border Protection, Office of Intelligence and Operations Coordination,
       March 2010), http://info.publicintelligence.net/femalesuicidebombers.
       pdf.

Timenes, Jr., Nicolai. *Defense against Kamikaze Attacks in World War II and Its Rele-
       vance to Anti-Ship Missile Defense; Volume I: An Analytical History of Kamikaze
       Attacks against Ships of the United States Navy during World War II* (Arlington,
       VA: Center for Naval Analyses, Operations Evaluation Group, November
       1970).

"Torture." *US Code,* Title 18, Part I, Chapter 113c.

*Typologies and Open Source Reporting on Terrorist Abuse of Charitable Operations in
       Post-Earthquake Pakistan and India.* (Washington, D.C.: U.S. Department of
       the Treasury, 2005), http://www.treasury.gov/resource-center/terrorist-il
       licit-finance/Documents/charities_post-earthquake.pdf.

U.N. Assistance Mission in Afghanistan (UNAMA). *Afghanistan Annual Report
       2011 Protection of Civilians in Armed Conflict* (Kabul: UNAMA, February
       2012), http://unama.unmissions.org/Portals/UNAMA/Documents/UN
       AMA%20POC%202011%20Report_Final_Feb%202012.pdf.

U.N. Assistance Mission in Afghanistan (UNAMA). "Suicide Attacks in Afghan-
       istan (2001–2007)." *ReliefWeb,* September 9, 2007, http://reliefweb.int/
       report/afghanistan/suicide-attacks-afghanistan-2001-2007.

U.N. General Assembly. *Follow-up to the Outcome of the Millennium Summit,*
       A/59/565, December 2, 2004, http://www.un.org/secureworld/report.pdf.

U.N. General Assembly. "International Convention for the Suppression of the Fi-
       nancing of Terrorism." Resolution 54/109, December 9, 1999, http://www.
       un.org/law/cod/finterr.htm.

U.N. General Assembly. "Measures to Eliminate International Terrorism." *84th
       Plenary Meeting,* Resolution 49/60, December 9, 1994, http://www.un.org/
       documents/ga/res/49/a49r060.htm.

U.N. General Assembly. "Resolution 2625: Declaration on Principles of Interna-
       tional Law Concerning Friendly Relations and Cooperation among States
       in Accordance with the Charter of the United Nations." *Resolutions Adopted
       by the General Assembly during Its Twenty-fifth Session,* October 24, 1970, 121–
       24, http://www.un.org/documents/ga/res/25/ares25.htm.

U.N. General Assembly. "Resolution 3314: Definition of Aggression." *Resolutions
       Adopted by the General Assembly during Its Twenty-ninth Session,* December
       14, 1974, 143, http://www.un.org/documents/ga/res/29/ares29.htm.

U.N. Office on Drugs and Crime. *Delivering Counter-Terrorism Assistance* (New
       York: United Nations, March 2009), http://www.unodc.org/documents/
       terrorism/TPB_brochure_English_final_printed_copy.pdf.

U.N. Security Council. "Threats to International Peace and Security Caused by Terrorist Acts." Resolution 1368, September 12, 2001, http://www.un.org/Docs/scres/2001/sc2001.htm.

U.N. Security Council. "Threats to International Peace and Security Caused by Terrorist Acts." Resolution 1373, September 28, 2001, http://www.un.org/Docs/scres/2001/sc2001.htm.

U.N. Security Council. "Proliferation of Nuclear, Chemical, and Biological Weapons." *4956th Meeting*, Resolution 1540, April 28, 2004, http://dac cess-dds-ny.un.org/doc/UNDOC/GEN/N04/328/43/PDF/N0432843.pdf?OpenElement.

U.N. Security Council. "Adopted by the Security Council at Its 5053rd Meeting." Resolution 1566, October 8, 2004, http://www.unrol.org/files/n0454282.pdf.

U.N. Secretary General. "International Convention for the Suppression of the Financing of Terrorism," Resolution 54/109, December 9, 1999, http://www.un.org/law/cod/finterr.htm.

U.N. Secretary General. *Report of the Secretary-General's Panel of Experts on Accountability in Sri Lanka* (Geneva: United Nations, March 31, 2011), http://www.un.org/News/dh/infocus/Sri_Lanka/POE_Report_Full.pdf.

U.S. Congress, House of Representatives, Committee on International Relations. *Afghanistan: Five Years after 9/11*, 109th Cong., 2nd Sess., Hearing, September 20, 2006, http://www.globalsecurity.org/military/library/congress/2006_hr/060920-transcript.pdf.

U.S. Constitution. Article II, § 2, cl. 1 and "Constitution of the United States: Amendments," *U.S. Senate*, http://www.senate.gov/civics/constitution_item/constitution.htm.

"U.S. Court of Appeals for the Second Circuit: American Civil Liberties Union v. Department of Justice." *FindLaw*, March 9, 2012–May 21, 2012, http://case law.findlaw.com/us-2nd-circuit/1601185.html.

U.S. Department of Defense, Deputy Chief of Staff for Intelligence (DCSINT). *Suicide Bombing in the COE (Common Operating Environment)*, Handbook No. 1.03 (Fort Leavenworth, KS: U.S. Army Training and Doctrine Command, August 10, 2006), http://www.fas.org/irp/threat/terrorism/sup3.pdf.

U.S. Department of Homeland Security, 2012, http://www.dhs.gov/index.shtm.

U.S. Department of Homeland Security. "Potential Threat to Homeland Using Heavy Transport Vehicles." *Information Bulletin*, July 30, 2004, https://www.hsdl.org/?view&did=461034.

U.S. Department of Homeland Security. *Underlying Reasons for Success and Failure of Terrorist Attacks: Selected Case Studies* (Arlington, VA: Homeland Security Institute, 2007), http://www.dtic.mil/dtic/tr/fulltext/u2/a494447.pdf.

U.S. Department of Justice. "Al Qaeda Associates Charged in Attack on USS *Cole*, Attempted Attack on Another U.S. Naval Vessel." *USDOJ*, Press Release, May 15, 2003, http://www.justice.gov/opa/pr/2003/May/03_crm_298.htm.

U.S. Department of Justice, Federal Bureau of Investigation. *Terrorism 2000–2001*, FBI Publication No. 0308 (Washington, D.C.: U.S. Government Printing Office, 2004), http://www.fbi.gov/stats-services/publications/terror/ter ror00_01.pdf.

U.S. Department of the Navy, Naval History and Heritage Command. *Anti-Suicide Action Summary*, Secret (Declassified), COMINCH P-0011, August 31, 1945, http://www.history.navy.mil/library/online/Anti_Suicide_Action_Sum mary.htm#I.

U.S. Department of State. "Background Information on Designated Foreign Terrorist Organizations," *Foreign Terrorist Organizations*, October 8, 1999, http://www.state.gov/s/ct/rls/rpt/fto/2801.htm.

U.S. Department of the Treasury. "Designated Charities and Potential Fundraising Front Organizations for Foreign Terrorist Organizations." *Foreign Terrorist Organizations*, December 1, 2010, http://www.treasury.gov/resource-cen ter/terrorist-illicit-finance/Pages/protecting-fto.aspx.

U.S. District Court, Southern District of New York. *Indictment*, SC101, 98 Cr., 1023 (LBS) vs. Usamma bin Laden et al., November 5, 1998, http://fl1.findlaw. com/news.findlaw.com/hdocs/docs/binladen/usbinladen-1a.pdf.

U.S. Federal Bureau of Investigation. "2003 Significant Events: January 30, 2003—Richard C. Reid Sentenced." *Terrorism 2002–2005*, http://www.fbi.gov/stats-services/publications/terrorism-2002–2005/terror02_05#terror_05sum.

U.S. National Counterterrorism Center. *2009 NCTC Report on Terrorism* (Washington, D.C.: National Counterterrorism Center, Office of the Director of National Intelligence, April 30, 2010), http://www.nctc.gov/witsbanner/docs/2009_report_on_terrorism.pdf.

U.S. National Counterterrorism Center. "Worldwide Incident Tracking System (WITS): 2010 Suicide Attacks by Region." *2012 Counterterrorism Calendar*, http://www.nctc.gov/site/pdfs/ct_calendar_2012_141.pdf.

U.S. Senate, Select Committee on Intelligence. *Report on the U.S. Intelligence Community's Prewar Intelligence Assessments on Iraq: Ordered Report*, 108th Cong., 2nd Sess., July 7, 2004, http://web.mit.edu/simsong/www/iraqreport2-textunder.pdf.

U.S. State Department. "Patterns of Global Terrorism 2001." *Country Reports on Terrorism*, May 2002, http://www.state.gov/j/ct/rls/crt/2001/.

U.S. State Department, Office of the Coordinator for Counterterrorism, "Chapter 1: Strategic Assessment," *Country Reports on Terrorism 2010*, August 18, 2011, http://www.state.gov/j/ct/rls/crt/2010/170253.htm.

Vaughn, Bruce. "Sri Lanka: Background and U.S. Relations." *Congressional Research Service Report*, June 16, 2011, http://www.fas.org/sgp/crs/row/RL31707. pdf.

Vidino, Lorenzo. *Radicalization, Linkage, and Diversity: Current Trends in Terrorism in Europe* (Arlington, VA.: RAND Corporation, 2011), http://www.rand. org/content/dam/rand/pubs/occasional_papers/2011/RAND_OP333. pdf.

"Washington's Farewell Address." A Century of Lawmaking for a New Nation: U.S. Congressional Documents and Debates, 1774–1875. *Annals of Congress*, 4th Cong., 2869–966, http://memory.loc.gov/cgi-bin/ampage?collId=llac& fileName=006/llac006.db&recNum=677.

"Weapons of Mass Destruction Threat." U.S. Department of State, http://www. state.gov/t/isn/wmd/.

Williams-Bridgers, Jacquelyn L. *Combating Terrorism: U.S. Government Strategies and Efforts to Deny Terrorists Safe Haven* (Washington, D.C.: GAO, June 3,

2011), http://homeland.house.gov/sites/homeland.house.gov/files/Tes timony%20Williams-Bridgers.pdf.

Wilson, Clay. "Improvised Explosive Devices in Iraq: Effects and Countermeasures." *CRS Report for Congress*, November 23, 2005, http://fpc.state.gov/ documents/organization/57512.pdf.

Yoo, John C. "The President's Constitutional Authority to Conduct Military Operations against Terrorists and Nations Supporting Them." *U.S. Department of Justice*, September 25, 2001, http://www.justice.gov/olc/warpow ers925.htm.

THESES

Jayasena, Karunya M. "Female Suicide Bombers and Sociological Analysis" (MA thesis, California State University, Northridge, 2009).

Kraner, Timothy A. "Al Qaeda in Iraq: Demobilizing the Threat" (MA thesis, Naval Postgraduate School, Monterey, CA, December 2005), http://www.nps. edu/Academics/Centers/CCC/Research/StudentTheses/kraner05.pdf.

Kruger, Lisa. "Gender and Terrorism: Motivations of Female Terrorists" (M.Sc. thesis, Joint Military Intelligence College, July 2005).

WEBSITES

Abunimah, Ali. "Full Text 'State of Palestine' UN Application and Documents." *The Electronic Intifada*, September 24, 2011, http://electronicintifada.net/ blog/ali-abunimah/full-text-state-palestine-un-application-letter-and-documents.

AEIVideos. "Peter Bergen: Pakistan Will Remain Important." *You Tube*, March 15, 2012, http://www.youtube.com/watch?v=-kWsBCtGY0w.

Afghan Mission NY. "Afghan Civilian Death Toll Jumps 31 Percent Due to Insurgent Attacks." *Permanent Mission of Afghanistan to the United States in New York*, August 10, 2010, http://www.afghanistan-un.org/2010/08/ afghan-civilian-death-toll-jumps-31-per-cent-due-to-insurgent-attacks-%E2%80%93-un/.

Al Jazeera English. Latest on al Qaeda, bin Laden, and related terrorism stories, current, http://www.aljazeera.com/.

"America and Its Profession of Arms, Is the Relationship Healthy?" Presented at U.S. Army War College's American Society and Its Profession of Arms XXII Annual Strategy Conference, Carlisle, PA, April 5–7, 2011, https://www. strategicstudiesinstitute.army.mil/.

"American President: A Reference Resource—Ronald Wilson Reagan." *Miller Center*, 2012, http://millercenter.org/president/reagan/essays/biography/ print.

"Authorization for Use of Military Force." *Find Law*, Public Law 107-40 [S.J. RES. 23], 107th Cong., September 18, 2001, http://news.findlaw.com/hdocs/ docs/terrorism/sjres23.es.html.

"Bay of Pigs." *John F. Kennedy Presidential Library and Museum*, http://www.jfkli brary.org/JFK/JFK-in-History/The-Bay-of-Pigs.aspx.

Bush, George W. In Rachel S. Taylor. "The United Nations, International Law, and the War in Iraq." *World Press Review Online*, September 17, 2002, http://www.worldpress.org/specials/iraq/.

Carpenter, John. "Conflict, War, and Terrorism." *Sociology B2: Problems of a Modern Society*, Power Point Presentation No. 15 (Bakersfield, CA: Bakersfield College, Spring 2011), www2.bakersfieldcollege.edu/jcarpenter/PowerPoint/B2/chapter15.ppt.

Center for Combating Terrorism at West Point, http://www.ctc.usma.edu/.

"Chronology of Suicide Bomb Attacks by LTTE Tamil Tiger Terrorists in Sri Lanka." *Sri Lanka News Online*, July 5, 1987–April 20, 2009, http://www.sl newsonline.net/chronology_of_suicide_bomb_attacks_by_Tamil_Tigers_in_sri_Lanka.htm.

"Combatant Status Review Tribunals/Administrative Review Boards." *U.S. Department of Defense*, http://www.defense.gov/news/Combatant_Tribu nals.html.

"Complete Inspire Al-Qaeda in the Arabian Peninsula (AQAP) Magazine." *Public Intelligence*, October 11, 2010–September 27, 2011, http://publicintelligence.net/complete-inspire-al-qaeda-in-the-arabian-peninsula-aqap-magazine/.

"Cuban Missile Crisis." *John F. Kennedy Presidential Library and Museum*, http://www.jfklibrary.org/JFK/JFK-in-History/Cuban-Missile-Crisis.aspx.

Department of Defense. *Dictionary of Military and Associated Terms*, Joint Publication 1-02, November 8, 2010 (as amended through December 31, 2010), http://www.dtic.mil/doctrine/dod_dictionary.

"Essential Military Terms You Should Know." *MilitaryDictionery.com*, 2011, http://www.militarydictionary.com/.

"Geneva Conventions of 1949 and Their Additional Protocols." *International Committee of the Red Cross*, July 7, 2011, http://www.icrc.org/eng/war-and-law/treaties-customary-law/geneva-conventions/index.jsp.

"Government Takes Policy Decision to Abrogate Failed CFA [Updated]." *Ministry of Defence and Urban Development, Democratic Socialist Republic of Sri Lanka*, December 30, 2010, http://www.defence.lk/new.asp?fname=2008 0102_12.

"Hezbollah Terrorism Incidents Database Search." *RAND Database of Worldwide Terrorism Incidents*, January 1, 1968–December 31, 2010, http://smapp.rand.org/rwtid/search_form.php.

International Committee of the Red Cross. *Customary International Humanitarian Law* (Cambridge: Cambridge University Press, 2005), http://www.icrc.org/eng/assets/files/other/customary-international-humanitarian-law-i-icrc-eng.pdf.

"Iraqi Deaths from Violence 2003–2011: Analysis and Overview." *Iraq Body Count*, January 2, 2012, http://www.iraqbodycount.org/analysis/num bers/2011/.

"Iraqi Deaths from Violence in 2010: Analysis of the Year's Civilian Death Toll from Iraq Body Count." *Iraq Body Count*, first published December 30, 2010, http://www.iraqbodycount.org/analysis/numbers/2010/.

Joint Staff, Joint Education and Doctrine Division, J-7. *DoD Dictionary of Military Terms*, December 31, 2010, http://www.dtic.mil/doctrine/dod_dictionary/.

Law-Glossary.com. 2011, http://www.law-glossary.com/.

"Legislation Related to the Attack of September 11, 2001." *The Library of Congress*, http://thomas.loc.gov/home/terrorleg.htm.

McDonald, Jim. "UN: Investigate Sri Lanka War Crimes." *Human Rights Now Blog*, April 27, 2011, http://blog.amnestyusa.org/justice/un-investigate-sri-lanka-war-crimes/.

"Measuring Systemic Peace." *Global Conflict Trends*, March 19, 2012, http://www.systemicpeace.org/conflict.htm.

"Military Policy Awareness Links (MiPAL)." *MERLN*, http://merln.ndu.edu/index.cfm?secID=149&pageID=3&type=section.

"Navy SEALs Complete bin Laden Mission." *Military Channel*, http://military.discovery.com/history/middle-east/navy-seals-bin-laden-mission.html.

"Our History: How We Began." *Transportation Security Administration*, http://www.tsa.gov/research/tribute/history.shtm.

Profiles of U.S. Presidents. (New York: Columbia University, 2011), http://www.presidentprofiles.com/.

Reuters. "Palestinian Leader Asks UN for Statehood." *NBCNews*, September 23, 2011, http://www.msnbc.msn.com/id/44638003/ns/world_news-mideast_n_africa/t/palestinian-leader-asks-un-statehood/.

Ryan, Pat. "The Growing 'Re-Insurgency' in Iraq." *Al-Sahwa Network*, October 23, 2010, http://al-sahwa.blogspot.com/2010/10/growing-re-insurgency-in-iraq.html.

"Sri Lanka Timeline—1931–2012." *South Asia Terrorism Portal*, http://www.satp.org/satporgtp/countries/shrilanka/timeline/index.html.

"Terrorist Bombing of the Marine Barracks, Beirut, Lebanon." *Arlington National Cemetery Website*, October 23, 2008, http://www.arlingtoncemetery.net/terror.htm.

Thompson, Paul. "Day of 9/11 Timeline." *Amazon S3*, http://s3.amazonaws.com/911timeline/main/dayof911.html.

"Timeline: Al-Qaeda." *BBC News*, August 7, 2008, http://news.bbc.co.uk/2/hi/in_depth/7546355.stm.

"Timeline of Hezbollah Violence." *Committee for Accuracy in Middle East Reporting in America*, July 17, 2006, http://www.camera.org/index.asp?x_context=2&x_outlet=118&x_article=1148.

"Timeline Turkey 1961–2008." *Timelines of History*, http://timelines.ws/countries/TURKEY_B.HTML.

Traboulsi, Fawwaz. Interview by Paul Jay. "Why Did Israel Attack Lebanon in 2006?" *Real News Network*, July 15, 2010, http://therealnews.com/t2/index.php?option=com_content&task=view&id=31&Itemid=74&jumival=5322.

United Nations. *Charter of the United Nations*, signed June 26, 1945, in force October 24, 1945, http://www.un.org/en/documents/charter/index.shtml.

United Nations. *Security Council Committee Pursuant to Resolutions 1267 (1999) and 1989 (2011) Concerning Al-Qaida and Associated Individuals and Entities*, http://www.un.org/sc/committees/1267/index.shtml.

United Nations. "The Question of Palestine," *UNISPAL*, 2012, http://unispal.un.org/unispal.nsf/home.htm.

United Nations. "United Nations Action against Terrorism," *UNODC*, https://www.unodc.org/tldb/en/action_sc_ga.html.

University of Chicago. *Chicago Project on Security and Terrorism (CPOST)*, October 14, 2011, http://cpost.uchicago.edu/search.php.

U.S. Air Force, Secretary of the Air Force. *Irregular Warfare*, Air Force Doctrine Document 2-3, August 1, 2007, http://www.fas.org/irp/doddir/usaf/afdd2-3.pdf.

U.S. Department of Defense. *Defend America: News about the War on Terrorism,* http://www.defendamerica.mil/backgrounders.html.

U.S. Department of State. "Types of Attacks." *National Counterterrorism Center: Annex of Statistical Information,* August 5, 2010, http://www.state.gov/j/ct/rls/crt/2009/140902.htm.

U.S. Department of State, Office of the Coordinator for Counterterrorism. "Background Information on Designated Foreign Terrorist Organizations," *Foreign Terrorist Organizations,* October 8, 1999, http://www.state.gov/s/ct/rls/rpt/fto/2801.htm.

U.S. Department of State, Office of the Coordinator for Counterterrorism. *State Sponsors of Terrorism,* 2011, http://www.state.gov/s/ct/c14151.htm.

U.S. Department of State, Office of the Coordinator for Counterterrorism. *The Terrorist Enemy,* 2010, http://www.state.gov/j/ct/enemy/index.htm.

"What Are Weapons of Mass Destruction?" *FBI,* http://www.fbi.gov/about-us/investigate/terrorism/wmd/wmd_faqs.

"The World Factbook." *CIA,* April 11, 2012, https://www.cia.gov/library/publications/the-world-factbook/index.html.

VIDEO

Bergen, Peter, and Erik Thompson. "The Last Days Osama bin Laden." *Natgeotv.com,* 23 minutes, November 6, 2011.

Cortright, David. "Killing Bin Laden." *Religion and Ethics Newsweekly,* Video, May 3, 2011, http://www.pbs.org/wnet/religionandethics/episodes/by-topic/middle-east/david-cortright-killing-bin-laden/8762/.

"Iraq: Abu Ghraib's Legacy." *CNN,* Video, December 19, 2011, http://www.cnn.com/video/#/video/world/2011/12/19/nat-abu-ghraib-legacy.cnn.

Maddow, Rachel, and Richard Engel. *Day of Destruction, Decade of War,* msnbc Documentary, September 1, 2011, http://maddowblog.msnbc.msn.com/_news/2011/08/18/7410051-day-of-destruction-decade-of-war-to-air-91-at-9-pm-et.

ngccommunitymoderator. "Remembering 9/11: New Insights 10 Years Later," *Inside NGC Blog,* July 27, 2011, http://tvblogs.nationalgeographic.com/2011/07/27/remembering-911-new-insights-10-years-later/.

"Prisoner Abuse at Abu Ghraib." *C-SPAN Video Library,* July 22, 2004, http://www.c-spanvideo.org/program/182821-1.

Sterling, John. Closing Keynote on April 7, 2011 at U.S. Army War College's American Society and Its Profession of Arms XXII Annual Strategy Conference, Carlisle, PA, April 5–7, 2011. *You Tube,* Video, http://www.youtube.com/watch?v=om1kYJHthRU&feature=mfu_in_order&list=UL.

IMMEDIATE POST BIN LADEN DOCUMENTS

"Background Briefing with Senior Defense Officials from the Pentagon and Senior Intelligence Officials by Telephone on U.S Operations Involving Osama Bin Laden." *U.S. Department of Defense,* May 2, 2011, http://www.defense.gov/transcripts/transcript.aspx?transcriptid=4818.

"Background Briefing with Senior Intelligence Official at the Pentagon on Intelligence Aspects of the U.S. Operation Involving Osama Bin Laden." *U.S. Department of Defense*, May 7, 2011, http://www.defense.gov/transcripts/transcript.aspx?transcriptid=4820.

Brady, James S. "Press Briefing by Press Secretary Jay Carney and Assistant to the President for Homeland Security and Counterterrorism John Brennan." *The White House*, May 2, 2011, http://www.whitehouse.gov/the-press-office/2011/05/02/press-briefing-press-secretary-jay-carney-and-assistant-president-homela.

Clinton, Hillary Rodham. "Remarks on the Killing of Usama bin Ladin." *U.S. Department of State*, May 2, 2011, http://www.state.gov/secretary/rm/2011/05/162339.htm.

Esanousi, Mohamed. "Death of Usama bin Ladin and the Reaction of the Muslim-American Community." *U.S. Department of State*, May 2, 2011, http://fpc.state.gov/162415.htm.

Fink, Naureen Chowdhury, and Hamed El-Said. *Transforming Terrorists: Examining International Efforts to Address Violent Extremism* (New York: International Peace Institute, May 2011), http://www.ipinst.org/media/pdf/publications/2011_05_trans_terr_final.pdf.

Foust, Joshua, ed. *"The War on Terror" One Year on: A Collection of Essays Marking One Year since the Death of Osama bin Laden* (Washington, D.C.: American Security Project, April 30, 2012), http://www.scribd.com.

Hughes, Geraint. *The Military's Role in Counterterrorism: Examples and Implications for Liberal Democracies* (Carlisle, PA: Strategic Studies Institute, U.S. Army War College, May 2011), http://www.strategicstudiesinstitute.army.mil/pdffiles/PUB1066.pdf.

Jan, Reza. "Killing bin Laden." *Critical Threats*, May 2, 2011, http://www.criticalthreats.org/al-qaeda/killing-bin-laden-may-2–2011.

Lister, Tim. "Eulogies and Fury: Jihadists Eager to Avenge bin Laden's Death." *CNN*, May 12, 2011, http://www.cnn.com/2011/WORLD/asiapcf/05/11/bin.laden.revenge/index.html.

Panetta, Leon E. "Message from the Director: Justice Done." *Central Intelligence Agency*, May 2, 2011, https://www.cia.gov/news-information/press-releases-statements/press-release-2011/justice-done.html.

Rogers, Paul. "The Current Status of Al-Qaida." *Oxford Research Group*, May 2012, http://www.oxfordresearchgroup.org.uk/sites/default/files/MayEn12_0.pdf.

Rollins, John. "Osama bin Laden's Death: Implications and Considerations." *Congressional Research Service Report*, May 5, 2011, http://www.fas.org/sgp/crs/terror/R41809.pdf.

Sayah, Reza. "Roots of Terror Untouched by bin Laden's Death." *CNN*, May 6, 2011, http://www.cnn.com/2011/WORLD/asiapcf/05/06/pakistan.terror.causes/index.html.

Starr, Barbara. "Bin Laden Was Communicating with Other Terrorists, U.S. Official Says." *CNN*, May 12, 2011, http://www.cnn.com/2011/US/05/11/bin.laden.communication/index.html?hpt=T1.

"U.S. Government Briefing Slides Abbottabad Compound 2005 and 2011." *U.S. Department of Defense*, http://www.defense.gov/DODCMSShare/briefingslide/359/110502-D-6570C-001.pdf.

Index

About the Author

ROSEMARIE SKAINE, M.A. Sociology, is an author who lives in Cedar Falls, Iowa. She has published 12 books: *Women in Combat: A Reference Handbook* (2011); *Women of Afghanistan in the Post-Taliban Era* (2008); *Women Political Leaders in Africa* (2008); *Female Suicide Bombers* (2006); *Female Genital Mutilation: Legal, Cultural and Medical Issues* (2005); *The Cuban Family: Custom and Change in an Era of Hardship* (2004); *Paternity and American Law* (2003); *The Women of Afghanistan Under the Taliban* (2002); *Women College Basketball Coaches* (2001); *A Man of the Twentieth Century: Recollections of Warren V. Keller, A Nebraskan; As Told to Rosemarie Keller Skaine and James C. Skaine* (1999); *Women at War: Gender Issues of Americans in Combat* (1999); and *Power and Gender: Issues in Sexual Dominance and Harassment* (1996). Relevant published articles/chapters include "Neither Afghan Nor Islam," Symposium on September 11, 2001: Terrorism, Islam and the West, *Ethnicities* (June 2002); "Soviet–Afghan War (1979–1989)" in Stanley Sandler (ed.), *Ground Warfare: An International Encyclopedia* (2002); and "Properly Trained Servicewomen Can Overcome Physical Shortcomings" in James Haley (ed.), *Women in the Military* (2004).

Skaine's special awards include Grand Island Senior High School Hall of Honor inductee (2009) and the Gustavus Myers Center Award for the Study of Human Rights in North America (1997) for her outstanding work on intolerance in North America for her book *Power and Gender: Issues in Sexual Dominance and Harassment* (1996). Since 2006, Skaine has been included in Marquis *Who's Who in the World, Who's Who in America,* and *Who's Who of American Women.*